Ayn Rand's Normative Ethics
The Virtuous Egoist

Ayn Rand is well known for advocating egoism, but the substance of that instruction is rarely understood. Far from representing the rejection of morality, selfishness, in Rand's view, actually demands the practice of a systematic code of ethics. This book explains the fundamental virtues that Rand considers vital for a person to achieve his objective well-being: rationality, honesty, independence, justice, integrity, productiveness, and pride. Tracing Rand's account of the harmony of human beings' rational interests, Smith examines what each of these virtues consists of, why it is a virtue, and what it demands of a person in practice. Along the way, she addresses the status of several conventional virtues within Rand's theory, considering traits such as kindness, charity, generosity, temperance, courage, forgiveness, and humility. *Ayn Rand's Normative Ethics* thus offers an in-depth exploration of several specific virtues and an illuminating integration of these with the broader theory of egoism.

Tara Smith is Professor of Philosophy at the University of Texas, Austin. She is the author of *Moral Rights and Political Freedom* and *Viable Values: A Study of Life as the Root and Reward of Morality*, and has contributed to such journals as *The Journal of Philosophy*, *American Philosophical Quarterly*, *Social Philosophy and Policy*, and *Law and Philosophy*.

Ayn Rand's Normative Ethics

The Virtuous Egoist

TARA SMITH

University of Texas

CAMBRIDGE
UNIVERSITY PRESS

CAMBRIDGE UNIVERSITY PRESS
Cambridge, New York, Melbourne, Madrid, Cape Town, Singapore,
São Paulo, Delhi, Dubai, Tokyo, Mexico City

Cambridge University Press
32 Avenue of the Americas, New York, NY 10013-2473, USA

www.cambridge.org
Information on this title: www.cambridge.org/9780521705462

First published 2006
Reprinted 2006
First paperback edition 2007
Reprinted 2007, 2008, 2009

A catalog record for this publication is available from the British Library

Library of Congress Cataloging in Publication data

Smith, Tara, 1961–
Ayn Rand's normative ethics : the virtuous egoist / Tara Smith.
p. cm.
Includes bibliographical references and index.
ISBN 0-521-86050-4 (hardback)
1. Rand, Ayn. 2. Egoism. 3. Virtues. I. Title.
B945.R234S65 2006
171'.9'092–dc22   2005018733

ISBN 978-0-521-86050-5 Hardback
ISBN 978-0-521-70546-2 Paperback

To the memory of my father, Gerald, who quietly taught me so much.

Contents

Acknowledgments

I wish to express my gratitude for the many forms of assistance I have received on this project. A fellowship from the Anthem Foundation for the Study of Objectivism and a grant from the Charles Sures Memorial Scholarship Fund of the Ayn Rand Institute have both greatly facilitated my work on this book. The University of Texas has, on several occasions, granted my requests for reduced teaching loads to enable me to make the best use of those funds. Jeff Britting helpfully steered me to materials in the Archives at the Ayn Rand Institute. My research assistants (serially: Allison Weinstein, Amy McLaughlin, Justin Tiehen, and Sherilyn Villareal) have been unfailingly diligent, allowing me the luxury of assurance that whatever I asked them to do would be done well. Marc Baer has compiled the Index.

While I was writing a first, very rough draft of the book, I met weekly with a group of graduate students – John Elia, Tom Miles, Warren von Eschenbach, and Allison Weinstein – who raised all manner of questions, objections, and alternative perspectives on my proposals (just as I had hoped – and feared). The workout they gave my initial formulations proved extremely constructive. Onkar Ghate, Robert Mayhew, Amy Peikoff, Leonard Peikoff, and Greg Salmieri all participated in a workshop on a draft of the chapter on independence; their extensive feedback greatly improved that chapter. Audiences at Bowling Green State University, the University of Colorado, and the University of Georgia offered helpful reactions to material on friendship, which is treated in the Appendix.

My understanding of the issues examined in this book has benefited, over the years, from discussions with more individuals than I can list here. Although those conversations varied a great deal in terms of their context, their frequency, their depth, and their breadth or narrowness of focus, I have gained important insights from numerous friends and colleagues – to each of whom I am sincerely grateful. I particularly wish to thank Leonard Peikoff, who, as I set to work on this book, issued an open invitation for me to raise with him whatever particular questions I encountered. On the occasions when I did so, he readily probed the issue with me at whatever length was necessary to fully clarify it. I am also extremely grateful to Allan Gotthelf who, while visiting at UT in the fall of 2002, conversed with me about several of the issues I discuss in the book. Moreover, near its completion, Allan Gotthelf and Robert Mayhew each read the entire manuscript and offered extensive comments, which have significantly strengthened the final product.

Finally, I thank Beatrice Rehl at Cambridge University Press for her support on this project, as well as the staff at the Press for their work in seeing it through to the printed page.

Some of the material in the book incorporates portions of essays (usually substantially reworked) that I have previously published elsewhere. I thank the relevant editors and publishers for their permission to do this. Those essays are: "Tolerance and Forgiveness: Virtues or Vices?" *Journal of Applied Philosophy* 14, no. 1 (1997), pp. 31–41 (Blackwell); "The Practice of Pride," *Social Philosophy & Policy* 15, no. 1 (1998), pp. 71–90 (Cambridge University Press); "Justice as a Personal Virtue," *Social Theory & Practice* 25, no. 3 (1999), pp. 361–384; "The Metaphysical Case for Honesty," *Journal of Value Inquiry* 37, no. 4 (2003), pp. 517–531 (Springer) (with kind permission of Springer Science and Business Media); "Morality Without the Wink: A Defense of Moral Perfection," *Journal of Philosophical Research* 29 (2004), pp. 315–331 (Philosophy Documentation Center); and "Egoistic Friendship," *American Philosophical Quarterly*, forthcoming (University of Illinois Press).

1

Introduction

Much recent discussion in ethics has danced around the edges of egoism, as renewed attention to virtue ethics, *eudaimonia*, and perfectionism naturally raise questions about the role of self-interest in a good
life. Although the ancient Greek conception of ethics that is currently
enjoying a revival does not fit stereotypes of egoism, it certainly does not
advocate altruism. As Rosalind Hursthouse acknowledges, much virtue
ethics portrays morality as a form of enlightened self-interest.[1] Although
authors increasingly have defended aspects of egoism (see, for instance,
David Schmidtz, Jean Hampton, Neera Badhwar),[2] the overwhelming
majority of ethicists remains averse not only to endorsing egoism but
even to seriously considering it. Those who do speak on its behalf usually
urge that we incorporate discrete elements of egoism, such as self-respect,
alongside altruistic obligations. Rather than urge that we replace altruism
with egoism, in other words, they seek to reconcile select self-beneficial
qualities with the altruism that we all already "know" morality demands.
This latter assumption remains ubiquitous. Christine Korsgaard's claim

---

[1] Rosalind Hursthouse, *On Virtue Ethics* (New York: Oxford University Press, 1999), p. 190.
Hursthouse does consider virtue ethics an "unfamiliar version of that view."
[2] David Schmidtz, "Reasons for Altruism," *Social Philosophy & Policy* 10, no. 1 (Winter
1993), pp. 52–68; Schmidtz, "Self-Interest: What's in it for Me?" *Social Philosophy &
Policy* 14, no. 1 (Winter 1997), pp. 107–121; Neera Kapur Badhwar, "Altruism versus Self-
Interest: Sometimes a False Dichotomy," *Social Philosophy & Policy* 10, no. 1 (Winter 1993),
pp. 90–117; Badhwar, "Self-Interest and Virtue," *Social Philosophy & Policy* 14, no. 1 (Winter
1997), pp. 226–263; Jean Hampton, "Selflessness and the Loss of Self," *Social Philosophy &
Policy* 10, no. 1 (Winter 1993), pp. 135–165; Jean Hampton, "The Wisdom of the Egoist:
The Moral and Political Implications of Valuing the Self," *Social Philosophy & Policy* 14,
no. 1 (Winter 1997), pp. 21–51.

that "...moral conduct by definition is not motivated by self-interest" is typical.[3]

Consequently, the questions raised by these recent developments in moral philosophy have not been adequately pursued. Is *eudaimonia* a selfish end? What does selfishness actually mean? What sorts of actions does it demand? What are the implications of pursuing *eudaimonia* for a person's relationships with others? Yet another nascent movement in ethics, perhaps spawned by virtue ethics, also points to a need to confront egoism more squarely: the advocacy of naturalism as the foundation of morality. In the past few years, Philippa Foot, Rosalind Hursthouse, and Berys Gaut have all defended the idea that the bedrock source of proper moral norms rests in needs dictated by human nature. A little earlier, James Wallace's *Virtues and Vices* (1978) advocated the same basic view.[4]

In *Natural Goodness*, Foot argues that goodness is a function of our nature. Moral evaluations reflect facts about human life, just as evaluations of sight and hearing in animals reflect facts about animals' potential and performance. Our nature dictates that we need morality: "...for human beings the teaching and following of morality is something necessary. We can't get on without it." Foot endorses Peter Geach's claim that "men need virtues as bees need stings."[5] Hursthouse follows Foot in maintaining that the "moral" does not carry distinctive authority, but is an outgrowth of our nature. We do well to start in ethics by thinking about plants, Hursthouse writes, meaning that a living thing's nature will dictate what is good for it by pointing us to its needs. What living things do is live, Hursthouse observes, and a good living thing is one that lives well. For humans, certain traits are virtuous because of facts about human needs, interests and desires, just as certain traits make for a good elephant

[3] Christine Korsgaard, *The Sources of Normativity* (New York: Cambridge University Press, 1996), p. 134. Korsgaard is attributing this view to Prichard, but she does not question it. Thomas Nagel similarly simply assumes that the source of moral requirements rests "in the claims of other persons." Nagel, *The View from Nowhere* (Oxford: Oxford University Press, 1986), p. 197. For a few other such characterizations that weave self-sacrifice into the very concept of morality, see Julia Driver, *Uneasy Virtue* (New York: Cambridge University Press, 2001), p. 105, and Laurence Thomas, *Living Morally* (Philadelphia: Temple University Press, 1989), p. vii. For a critical discussion of this conception of morality, see Kelly Rogers, "Beyond Self and Other," *Social Philosophy & Policy* 14, no. 1 (Winter 1997), pp. 1–20.
[4] Philippa Foot, *Natural Goodness* (Oxford: Clarendon Press, 2001); Hursthouse, *On Virtue Ethics*; Berys Gaut, "The Structure of Practical Reason," in Garrett Cullity and Berys Gaut, eds., *Ethics and Practical Reason* (Oxford: Clarendon Press, 1997); James D. Wallace, *Virtues and Vices* (Ithaca, NY: Cornell University Press), 1978.
[5] Foot, pp. 24, 16–17, 35, citing Peter Geach, *The Virtues* (Cambridge: Cambridge University Press, 1977), p. 17.

because of facts about elephants' needs, interests, and desires. The point relevant to egoism is that goodness is determined by what is beneficial *for the organism.*[6]

Gaut similarly sees the roots of objective values in our biological natures. Value is a teleological concept, he reasons, and for living organisms, the teleological is biological. "Trees can have *good* roots because trees have goals, specified by their nature, and good roots are those which help achieve these goals." It is human beings' physical and psychological needs that establish the nature and requirements of our flourishing.[7]

Much in these naturalistic accounts is sound, I think, such as the bridging of what are usually understood as two distinct senses of the "good life": an enjoyable life and a morally upright life. On a naturalistic account, these go hand in hand. It is only by leading a morally upright life that a person can be happy and it is for the sake of having a happy life that a person should be morally upright. I also welcome that which allows this convergence: naturalism's denial of a sharp difference in kind between the counsel of morality and the counsel of prudence. Foot sensibly regards acting morally as part of practical rationality; morality holds no further claim on us.[8] Insofar as what is good is what serves an organism's needs, it is good for that organism, such that the good makes prudential sense. In these respects, naturalism opens the way for egoism, as do versions of virtue ethics that encourage the pursuit of *eudaimonia.*

Yet this is where most philosophers draw back. Foot and Hursthouse clearly wish to distance themselves from any such implications. Foot, for instance, insists that the moral does not simply consist of doing what is good for oneself, though she concedes that a "reasonable modicum" of self-interest is permissible.[9] Reluctance to engage the potentially egoistic ramifications of their views is, I think, a serious shortcoming. Neither the virtue ethics nor naturalism movements truly challenges the altruistic prescriptions embraced in nearly all ethical theories. The charge that virtue ethics offers old wine in new bottles has definite merit, as virtue ethics has focused far more on the form of ethical guidance – virtues rather than rules or principles – than on its substance. I do not mean to minimize the value that greater attention to virtue can bring. The emphasis virtue ethicists place on an individual's context and psychology and

---

[6] Hursthouse, pp. 123, 196, 205, 230. Hursthouse's and Foot's views on this bear obvious affinities with Aristotle's.

[7] Gaut, pp. 185, 178, 184–185, 186, emphasis added.

[8] Foot, p. 9.

[9] Foot, p. 16, 17.

their more value-oriented conception of ethics (as opposed to a duty-bound, "stay out of trouble" conception) are constructive contributions. Yet the essential content of the do's and don't's being advocated has not been sufficiently questioned. Correlatively, when it comes time to explain why a particular trait is a virtue or vice, intuitions too often stand in for arguments, as possibilities that would revise received wisdom are not seriously entertained. This aversion to questioning entrenched assumptions about the substantive directions of morality is particularly surprising in naturalism, since naturalism presents observation of facts as the basis for objective judgments of value. To allow assumptions of what kinds of action are virtuous to circumscribe the account of morality's roots defeats the point of such an account. Indeed, it renders it not truly naturalistic by transforming the purported roots into mere props – drapery for normative conclusions that a theorist is already committed to and is intent on keeping. Hursthouse explicitly acknowledges this: if, early in her theorizing, it looked as if courage, honesty, justice, and charity were not to turn out as virtues, she confesses, she would abandon naturalism.[10] Such an approach obviously skews the results by preempting an open inquiry into all the possibilities, including the potentially egoistic ones.

In this book, I will present a kind of egoism that I believe escapes the concerns that usually make people loathe to even consider it. My subject, in a nutshell, is how to lead a selfish life. I will elaborate on the virtues of proper egoism – the kinds of action required for human beings to advance their interests and to flourish. More specifically, I will present the egoism of Ayn Rand. Rand's egoism is distinctive insofar as she contends that a determination of the proper way to lead our lives must begin with an analysis of the concept of value. This analysis yields a portrait of what a person's interest *is* that requires the rejection of many of the doctrines commonly associated with egoism, such as hedonism, materialism, and predation (which is based on the assumption that promotion of one's own well-being must come at the expense of others'). The pursuit of self-interest should not be driven by emotion, in Rand's view, but by reason, and reason demands the consistent practice of seven principal virtues. I will explain how to lead a selfish life primarily by elaborating on these.

If one is going to pass a judgment on egoism, it is important to know it in its strongest form. This is what I think Rand offers. It is equally important to get Rand right, as her views have been subjected to tremendous distortion over the years. (I did not recognize the Rand that Hursthouse

---

[10] Hursthouse, p. 211; see also p. 170, note 10, and p. 208.

cursorily dismisses.) [11] Whatever one's final verdict on the merits of Rand's theory, we cannot have confidence in our assessment until we give that theory a full and fair hearing.

My primary aim is to explain Rand's view of the virtues that an egoistic morality demands. In my last book, *Viable Values – A Study of Life as the Root and Reward of Morality*, I presented the case for egoism by examining the nature of morality itself, probing the fundamental nature and validation of values, from which moral prescriptions follow. [12] Here, I turn from the questions of what it is to be moral and why such prescriptions are necessary to *how* to be moral. The heart of this book fleshes out the meat of morality's practical guidance. We will consider what types of actions are virtuous, and why – how these serve a person's true interest. In essence, the book is an account of what Rand's rational egoism consists of and requires.

Because egoism is widely perceived as reckless, self-indulgent whim-worship and the selfish person as thoughtless, unprincipled, and inconsiderate of others, the suggestion that egoism can demand the disciplined adherence to a moral code will itself be surprising to many. In laying out what egoism's guidance consists in, part of what I mean to convey is that egoism does require a coherent, principled effort. In the process, I hope to indicate some of the strength of rational egoism. Yet these are secondary objectives. Although mine is a sympathetic elaboration, my aim is not to convert the reader. Much as I find Rand's egoism compelling, my paramount aim in this book is not so much to convince you, as to show you what Rand's theory is, as it has not received the attention it warrants. If we are to reach sound conclusions about the promise of virtue ethics and naturalism, we must pursue all the questions that they raise, including questions about egoism. Rand's theory offers a valuable, previously underexplored means of doing so.

A word about sources. Ayn Rand did not elaborate her moral philosophy in lengthy treatises. Her views are presented in her fiction (which includes a hero's extended philosophical speech in *Atlas Shrugged*) and in relatively brief essays. I will rely heavily on the essay "The Objectivist

---

[11] Hursthouse, pp. 253–254. Contrary to Hursthouse's description, Rand does not distinguish "the weak and the strong" and claim that they should be "evaluated differently." Nor does she hold (either implicitly or explicitly) that self-realization calls for "injustice and callousness."

[12] Tara Smith, *Viable Values – A Study of Life as the Root and Reward of Morality* (Lanham, MD: Rowman and Littlefield), 2000. Throughout this book, I will often use "egoistic" to mean rationally egoistic, unless the context clearly indicates otherwise.

Ethics," her most extended single presentation of her overall view of ethics, though I will also make use of many of her other writings. At times, I will refer to passages from her private journals and letters, published since her death, and to unpublished archival material. Whenever I do so, it is important to recognize that such passages cannot be treated as Rand's final, ready-for-publication views. I will also treat Leonard Peikoff's *Objectivism: The Philosophy of Ayn Rand*, a systematic presentation of the entirety of Rand's philosophy, from metaphysics through esthetics, as an authoritative source of her views. Peikoff studied with Rand for thirty years, and she endorsed his course on Objectivism, on which he later based this book, as fully accurate.[13] Where I venture beyond what Rand or Peikoff have themselves said about a specific question, it should be understood that I am offering my best interpretation of the position that is implied by Rand's express philosophy. Obviously, these inferences are fallible; I do not write as an official spokesman for Objectivism.

OVERVIEW

I will begin, in Chapter 2, by reviewing the defense of egoism that was presented over the course of my last book. Although necessarily abbreviated, this argument will indicate the core explanation of why we should be egoists and thus lay the foundation for exploring how to be.

On Rand's view, the phenomenon of values stands at the base of morality. Values are intelligible only in relation to a living organism's struggle for its life. Nothing is valuable to or for inanimate objects. The distinction between good and bad is an outgrowth of the nature of living things; more specifically, it reflects their survival needs. (Note the obvious similarity with the recent writings of Foot, Hursthouse, and Gaut.) Certain ends are essential if organisms are to maintain their lives. For human beings, moreover, certain types of actions are necessary if we are to achieve those ends. Accordingly, Rand argues, the standard of value is life. Value is a relational phenomenon and any particular thing's value reflects its bearing on a specific individual's life. Something can be valuable only in relation to some organism and for that end: its continued existence. This relationship obtains independently of a person's beliefs or wishes about it. Thus, on Rand's view, values are neither intrinsic (simply embedded in certain things in the external world) nor subjective (inventions projected

---

[13] Leonard Peikoff, *Objectivism: The Philosophy of Ayn Rand* (New York: Penguin, 1991), p. xiv.

by consciousness), but objective. I will also explain why, when Rand speaks of *life* as the standard of value, we must understand her to be speaking of a flourishing life rather than a minimal, bare bones subsistence. (Because happiness must also be understood by reference to such a flourishing life, in the remainder of this Introduction, I will refer to the aim of ethics and of value-pursuit interchangeably as life, flourishing, and happiness.)

Rand's account, we will see, is egoistic. Indeed, the case for ethics and the case for egoism are fundamentally one and the same. The propriety of pursuing self-interest arises from understanding that human beings need to identify and follow a particular code of action if they are to survive. Because living depends on life-sustaining action, a person must act in ways that will advance his life. Since the kind of egoism that Rand advocates is grounded in this recognition of man's need for objective values, it differs significantly from more familiar versions. Rand rejects hedonism and contends that an egoist must abide by rational principles, as these offer the only effective means of advancing his interest, long range. Principles' authority stems entirely from their egoistic practicality. Rand also rejects the dog-eat-dog image of an egoist as out to unjustly exploit others. I will explain her reasons for disputing the widely accepted premise beneath that image, the notion that individuals' interests conflict, by indicating the shallow conceptions of interest and the ignoring of context that such claims typically depend on.

The heart of the book consists in an elaboration of seven major virtues. Chapter 3 examines what Rand regards as the principal, overarching virtue, rationality. I begin by clarifying Rand's understanding of what a virtue is, given that some of her formulations may sound at odds with contemporary accounts. In the end, her conception is compatible with the prevalent characterization of virtue as a disposition to act or feel in certain ways, though Rand especially emphasizes virtues as types of action that reflect recognition of facts about the most basic demands of life.

Rationality is the acceptance of reason as one's only source of knowledge and fundamental guide to action. I will explain Rand's view of what reason is to show how a rational person is guided exclusively by the evidence of his senses and by logical inferences from that evidence. Rationality consists in a deliberate policy of grounding one's thinking in the way things are, as best as one can discern through the exercise of his perceptual and conceptual capacities. Essentially, rationality consists of fidelity to facts.

We can appreciate why rationality is a moral virtue by reminding ourselves of the reason for having morality and for considering anything a moral virtue: survival. Rationality is the fundamental means by which human beings can maintain and advance our lives. Our more specific needs can be satisfied only through what is, at root, rational action (occasional flukes aside). Because things in external reality are what they are independently of an individual's thoughts or wishes about them, because we control whether and how we use our minds, and because, as fallible beings, our beliefs are not automatically correct, human beings must exert a concerted effort to base the thinking that guides our actions on the way the world actually is. This is what rationality enables us to do.

The principal requirement of exercising this virtue is at once simple and formidable: when considering any issue, a rational person must maintain a clear focus on the relevant facts. Rationality does not demand heights of intelligence so much as a conscientious refusal to evade any thoughts, knowledge, or questions that occur to a person on the issue in question. Rationality demands seeking to know the nature of the world that a person must navigate so that he can navigate effectively; consequently, it demands trying to learn, to understand, and to integrate new information with preexisting knowledge. Although an insistence on rationality does not banish emotions from our lives, it does mean that a person must forswear emotionalism, the practice of surrendering the reins of one's judgment to one's feelings.

Chapter 4 takes up honesty, which is perhaps the most obvious virtue derivative from rationality.[14] Rand understands honesty as the refusal to fake reality. As such, honesty does not primarily concern how a person interacts with others, but how he deals with *everything* he encounters. The honest person does not pretend that things are other than they are, either to others or to himself.

The case for honesty overlaps considerably with the case for rationality. Given the independence of existents of individuals' thoughts or wishes about them, faking things is fruitless. Because misrepresenting facts does

---

[14] Although honesty and the other virtues are all derivative from rationality, Rand does not regard any particular order of these as logically mandatory. Peikoff, p. 251. I do not follow either the sequence in Rand's essay "The Objectivist Ethics," *The Virtue of Selfishness* (New York: Signet/Penguin, 1964), pp. 13–39 or in Galt's Speech in *Atlas Shrugged.* It is worth noting, however, that while life is the goal which all virtues serve, Rand identifies three "cardinal values" – reason, purpose, self-esteem – as the somewhat less abstract ends of virtue, and she links these values with the particular virtues of (respectively) rationality, productiveness, and pride. (She describes these values as, together, "the means to and the realization of one's ultimate value, one's own life." "The Objectivist Ethics," p. 27.) I am not devoting special attention to these values as a group, although I will discuss purpose and self-esteem in the chapters on productiveness and pride.

not change those facts, a person's flourishing depends on his respecting reality, which is what honesty advises. Fooling other people is not ultimately advantageous because it does not alter the facts about which one fools them. Further, faking values is no more viable than faking facts, we will see, since values are a type of facts. Pretending that something stands in a constructive relationship to one's life does not make it stand in such a constructive relationship.

Far from being the puppeteer who manipulates others, a liar makes himself subservient to other people's standards and expectations. Insofar as he tries to conceal his deception, he must coin a potentially endless stream of additional falsehoods to prop up the original lie. In doing so and then premising his actions on others' image of him rather than on the relevant facts of reality, he drifts further from a rational course, taking an increasing number of nonreality-based actions. This can only work against his objective well-being. By contrasting Rand's reasoning with the three most commonly offered rationales for honesty, we will appreciate the nonsocial roots of Rand's argument and its entirely egoistic character.

Because honesty concerns a person's basic mode of dealing with reality, the practical demands of honesty involve much more than refraining from deceiving other people. In particular, I will focus on honesty's requirements that a person renounce self-deception, develop an active mind, and act on his knowledge. I will also consider the status of honesty in two kinds of specialized circumstances: when responding to another person's use of force and when seeking to spare another person's feelings (commonly considered "white lies"), finding that misleading a person can be justified in the former cases but not in the latter.

Chapter 5 examines the virtue of independence, which concerns a person's basic method of sustaining himself, intellectually as well as materially. Independence, as Rand understands it, consists in setting one's primary orientation to reality rather than to other people. The independent person does not defer to others' beliefs or attitudes to chart his course and he does not rely on others' production to satisfy his material needs. In contrast to the parasite, the independent person accepts full responsibility for making his way in the world by forming his own judgments, adopting ends that he deems valuable, and acting to achieve those ends. He does not treat other people as his highest master, ultimate standard, or basic means of fulfilling his life's requirements.

The need for independence is implicit in the need for rationality. Because reason is human beings' basic means of survival and because the exercise of reason is inherently a do-it-yourself enterprise, independence is a precondition of rational judgment and thus vital to human life. One person cannot reason for another. Whatever the direction offered by others, a person must make up his own mind about whether to accept it. If a person were alone on a deserted island, his need to act to sustain himself and to think for himself, in order to figure out how to do that, would be plain. While our immersion in society may obscure this fact, it does not alter it. For if we imagined other people, brimming with advice, later joining the originally solitary islander, he would still have to assess their recommendations to determine whether following any of them could actually advance his life. In order to reap the substantial objective values that human beings can offer one another, in other words, individuals must exercise first-handed judgment of reality.

In elaborating on the demands of this virtue, we will see how the independent person must rely on reason (as opposed to feeling) in thinking for himself. Rand is not endorsing the value of anything that a given person thinks or desires simply because *he* thinks or desires it. Moreover, since thought and knowledge are not ends in themselves, independence further requires that a person act on his judgment and live by the work of his own mind. This does not entail that a person should be anti-social or spurn the benefits offered by other people, but it does entail that genuinely profitable relationships between individuals rely on the independence of each party. We will also see how assertions of modern man's "interdependence" typically equivocate over the meaning of dependence.

In Chapter 6, we return to a more familiar virtue: justice. Rand understands justice to consist in judging other persons objectively and treating them accordingly by giving them what they deserve (which is essentially the account that has been historically dominant: giving each person his due). Rand describes the just person's characteristic posture as that of a trader who neither seeks nor gives the unearned. It is important to appreciate, however, that the rationale for being just is, here again, thoroughly egoistic. Contrary to widespread assumptions, being just is not a sacrifice, but is in an agent's long-term interest. The reason to exercise justice is the impact that other people stand to exert on one's life. Because others can affect one's values in countless ways large and small, for good or for ill, a rational egoist has every reason to evaluate other people objectively and to treat them accordingly. Faking other individuals' actions or character neither alters their actions or character nor their potential effects on a person's life. Justice is thus a vital means of protecting and promoting one's values.

Once one fully understands the case for justice, many of its demands will be comparatively straightforward, for example, evaluating others objectively, by reason rather than emotion; judging individuals as individuals, taking into account salient features of their particular circumstances; treating others as they deserve through an array of both modest gestures and more significant rewards and punishments. It is important to recognize, however, that on Rand's account, justice demands the unfashionable practice of judging people. It forbids indefinite fence-sitting. Seeking or pretending not to notice the differences between people and the correlative effects that they can have would betray the rational pursuit of one's happiness. For similar reasons, we will also see why Rand rejects the popular doctrine of egalitarianism.

A particularly noteworthy demand of justice, in Rand's view, is that a person refuse to sanction those people and practices that he believes to be evil. While many opponents of Rand's might agree with her on this, she does not premise this demand on any intrinsic impropriety of association with evil, but on the egoistic grounds that such sanction would only assist that which is ultimately antagonistic to a person's own interest. Evil represents that which works against objective values, yet evil depends on the good for its sustenance, as we will see. Consequently, support from the good is evil's only lease on life. It is wrong to sanction evil, in short, because it is ultimately self-sabotaging.

I will also consider the practical implications of justice for two commonly praised ideals: forgiveness and mercy. Neither is a virtue, on Rand's view, though while forgiveness can be appropriate under certain conditions, mercy, which in its common meaning is undeserved leniency, cannot be. I will also clarify the relationship between justice and another principle of the Objectivist ethics, respect for individual rights. Although rights present an enormous subject unto itself, I will briefly indicate the distinct but mutually compatible kinds of guidance that the principle of rights and the virtue of justice provide.

The next virtue essential to egoism – the subject of Chapter 7 – is integrity, which Rand defines as loyalty in action to rational principles. The person of integrity permits no breach between mind and body, between his values and his actions.

The case for integrity is broadly similar to the case for honesty, with the salient point here being that a person cannot fake the contents of his consciousness any more effectively than he can fake anything else. At the foundation of the virtue of integrity stand two basic facts: life requires action according to rational principles; a person will sometimes encounter pressures that make such action difficult. As we will explain in Chapter 2, values are won through consistent, principled adherence to a rational course. To embrace certain beliefs and values but then ignore them, when it comes time for action, defeats their point. Failures of integrity, insofar as they depart from the course that a person has deemed conducive to his ends, inflict both material and spiritual damage, thwarting the achievement of the agent's material ends and weakening his self-esteem. Correspondingly, to maintain integrity is not, contrary to the usual presumptions, a sacrifice. It is a person's own well-being that stands to be served by his fidelity to his principles.

The primary practical demand of integrity is plain: acting on one's principles. To fully understand integrity's requirements, however, I will elaborate on implications concerning the formation of one's principles and the content of one's principles. The latter is a perennial question for accounts of integrity: Can devotion to seriously misguided principles (such as those of the Ku Klux Klan) constitute a virtue? Although Rand acknowledges much that is admirable in principled devotion to certain mistaken beliefs and although she clearly distinguishes errors of knowledge from breaches of morality, she also maintains that irrational principles could not be consistently practiced and could not objectively advance a person's life. We will also see how integrity requires confidence and courage (a particular form of integrity, in Rand's view) as well as the conditions in which compromise is and is not compatible with integrity. Further, I will explain that the resolve needed to maintain one's integrity is an exercise of rationality, a matter of maintaining focus on the full context to assess the values at stake in one's alternatives. Weakness of will, in effect, is a weakness of vision.

In Chapter 8, I will discuss rationality's application in another key area: productiveness. In Rand's view, productiveness is the process of creating material values. Human beings must reshape what we find in our surroundings in order to make the clothes, shelters, medicines, tools, schools, etc., that we need in order to live. Because our survival depends on goods and services that are not found, ready-made, in nature, we must create the material values that sustain us; we must give physical reality to ideas that can advance human life. And, more basically, we must make ourselves into the kinds of beings capable of creating such values by exercising this virtue. Doing so, we will see, repays spiritual as well as material rewards.

Productive work demands rationality in identifying one's ends and in devising the best means of attaining them, as well as a correlative exertion of physical effort to realize those ends. Productiveness does not demand a particularly high IQ, but it does require a person's commitment to thinking logically about his work – about how he might improve his methods, for instance, or exactly how they should be adapted in unexpected circumstances. By the same token, intellectual work must be translated into material form in order to offer objective value. Neither rational thought that is not given some material incarnation nor physical labor that is not guided by rationality can further a person's life.

Because life is not a one-time achievement but an ongoing endeavor, an egoist must adopt productive work as his central purpose. We will see why productive work should be the main activity that fills a person's days and determines the relative significance of his other values. Because a person's proper goal is his own happiness (objectively understood), there is no limit to how good – how secure, how comfortable, how enjoyable – he should strive to make his life. Correspondingly, there is no limit to how productive a person should be. To clarify the implications of this for the practical demands of productiveness, we will consider whether a productive person needs to make money as well as the application of this virtue to those who are already wealthy. We will also consider whether Rand's advocacy of egoistic productiveness commits her to an endorsement of greed, a widely denounced vice. By untangling several elements welded together in popular notions of greed, we will be able to appreciate exactly what Rand is and is not commending.

The last of rational egoism's major virtues is pride, more often considered a vice than a virtue. This is the subject of Chapter 9. Rand understands pride as moral ambitiousness, an energetic dedication to being one's best. Pride is not a disposition to boast, to impress, or to display superiority to others; nor is it simply the feeling of satisfaction with oneself that typically follows some accomplishment. In Rand's view, pride is a forward-driving commitment to achieve one's moral perfection.

So conceived, pride reflects the exercise of all the other virtues. Yet the case for recognizing pride as a virtue springs from the distinctive value of self-esteem, which pride makes possible. Because human action is volitional, it depends on motivation. A person will not have the requisite motivation to act in the ways that can achieve values and sustain his life, however, unless he has a fundamentally positive view of himself. A person must believe that he is worthy of values and that he will be able to achieve them, in order to act in the ways necessary to flourish. A person could only acquire and maintain such a positive self-appraisal, in turn, through the exercise of pride – through consistent, practiced devotion to his moral principles. Anything less than that would inject doubts that jeopardize his self-esteem and correlatively sap his motivation to act as his happiness requires.

Like all the moral virtues, the practice of pride encompasses intellectual as well as material dimensions. Pride requires that a person work to identify proper moral principles rather than simply absorb them uncritically from his surroundings, for instance, and that he strive to grasp the particular demands that these abstract principles place on *him*, in his particular circumstances. Honest introspection will be important, as a person must gauge his capacities in order to identify what it is rational to demand of himself. And, as ever, this virtue demands implementation in action, pushing oneself to unfailingly consistent adherence to one's moral principles. Pride demands doing one's best, not in the vague, insincere sense that people frequently invoke, but in the literal sense that is measured by morality's overarching standard: rationality. Pride demands that a person always act rationally.

The thorniest aspect of pride's practical demands, clearly, stems from Rand's characterization of pride as a commitment to achieving one's moral perfection, an ideal that nearly everyone considers beyond mere mortals. Yet once we explain why Rand understands perfection to consist in "unbreached rationality" and remind ourselves that all virtues' demands must be understood in context – sensitive to the particular person and situation – we will find that this initially daunting demand is completely appropriate. I will also comment on the implications of Rand's account of pride for humility, which is far more often urged as virtuous.

Although the preceding seven are the major moral virtues that Rand identifies, she does not claim that these are necessarily exhaustive. Thus, to deepen our understanding of her egoism, in Chapter 10, I consider whether certain other widely praised traits might also constitute moral virtues. Because Rand's list may seem to pay insufficient attention to a person's interactions with others, I have chosen three qualities that are social – charity, generosity, and kindness – and a fourth, temperance, whose prudential character makes it seem a likely candidate for egoism's approval.

Charity essentially consists of giving aid to people in need. On Rand's theory, charity is permissible under certain conditions and improper under others. Rational egoism recognizes no freestanding obligation to place others' welfare above one's own. Others' need *per se* does not trump the propriety of a person's pursuit of his own happiness as his highest end. When an act of charity would be a sacrifice, requiring the agent's surrender of a greater value for a lesser value, it would be antithetical to egoism. In cases in which no such sacrifice is involved, however, charity is fine. In some such cases, it can even be obligatory (when the person to be helped is a greater value to the agent than that which he offers, in lending assistance). The main point, however, is that although another person's need may provide the occasion for charity, it does not mandate it. If charity represented aid given strictly on the basis of a person's need, independent of all considerations of the recipient's value to the giver, it would never be consistent with egoism.

Rand's egoism is not opposed to good will, nor to correlative action. Strangers can sometimes be among the appropriate recipients of charity, for strangers can be a value. Egoism is opposed to self-sacrifice, however. Thus charity is not a positive virtue. The propriety of charity is determined not by the emotional tugs of empathy, natural as such empathy will often be, but by the demands of rational self-interest.

Unlike charity, generosity is not necessarily a response to need. Generosity consists in giving in excess of what custom or morality requires; it is giving another person more than he has reason or right to expect or demand. Praise of generosity often reflects the altruistic premise that others' good is valuable in itself and that a person should treat others' well-being as a more worthy end than his own. Accordingly, generosity is seen as a way of making sacrifices for others. Egoism emphatically rejects this course. A person whose primary value is his own flourishing has no reason to treat others as if they held a greater claim on his resources.

This does not mean that Rand rejects all generosity, however. Severed from altruistic motivations, an act of generosity can be perfectly compatible with rational egoism. When such an act is consistent with the seven moral virtues and with an individual's hierarchy of values, when it does not require self-sacrifice and is extended to an appropriate beneficiary, generosity is morally permitted. Indeed, we can imagine circumstances in which a failure to be generous would be hypocrisy, as when a person fails to be generous with a person he claims to value a great deal and he can easily afford to be, consistent with his other values. Generosity will sometimes be required, in other words, by the virtue of integrity. Yet in itself, I will argue, generosity is neither virtuous nor vicious. The propriety of extending generosity depends entirely on the character of the beneficiary, his relationship to the would-be benefactor, and the benefactor's resources and hierarchy of values. When generosity is appropriate, it signifies no departure from egoism, but reflects conformity with a person's selfish values. In the course of defending this view, I will also clarify the compatibility of generosity with the virtue of justice.

The next candidate, kindness, encompasses a wide range of actions that express thoughtfulness or considerateness for another person. Kind acts will sometimes also be generous or charitable, but essentially, kindness consists in acting out of consideration for another person's well-being. A benevolent attitude is not sufficient; the kind person *acts* to render his attitude of practical value to the recipient. He does something, however minor, to cheer or assist another person.

For an egoist, we will see, kindness can offer at least three kinds of value: It can further the agent's values by aiding people whom he values; it can strengthen a person's relationship with the beneficiary of his kindness; it can nurture a social climate that is more conducive to his own flourishing. Nonetheless, kindness does not constitute a moral virtue because it is not always appropriate; whether it is depends on the recipient's value to the agent. Extended toward certain individuals (e.g., an embezzler or a terrorist), kindness would be self-destructive.

The rejection of kindness as a virtue does not endorse being unkind; it simply recognizes that it is foolish to be indiscriminately kind. The standard by which to determine the propriety of kindness is not an intrinsic value that allegedly resides in all human beings. It is rational self-interest. Properly, an egoist should be kind selectively and nonsacrificially to those people who are of value to him. (This can include strangers.) When it is appropriate, as with charity and generosity, kindness will be an exercise of the virtue of integrity. Indeed, I will argue that an egoist should aspire to kindness – *toward appropriate people* – as a means of acting by his values.

The fourth purported virtue that I consider in this chapter is temperance, a more inner-directed quality than the first three. Assessment of this trait is complicated by competing interpretations of precisely what temperance is. Is it the same thing as moderation? Does it concern only physical appetites? I will take temperance to be self-restraint in the satisfaction of one's desires. (Self-restraint can take the form of either complete self-denial or moderation.) I will briefly explain the chief rationales usually given for temperance: ascetic, altruistic, and *eudaimonistic*. Since the consequences of overindulgence can be quite destructive – especially if practiced over a prolonged period – temperance may seem not merely compatible with rational egoism, but a necessary component of it. (Underindulgence also threatens to damage a person's life, although discussions of temperance typically focus on overindulgence, the greater, or at least, the more conspicuous temptation for most people.)

Under egoism, I will argue, temperance in itself is not a virtue. Although temperance often bespeaks resistance to the lure of emotionalism (which Rand would certainly applaud), what such cases reveal is not the general propriety of restraint, but the value of rationality. Appropriate as it often is to curb one's indulgence of desires, the passionate, immoderate pursuit of desires can also be appropriate in certain circumstances. To abandon or to moderate the pursuit of the most precious values in one's life sheerly for the sake of temperance would be self-sacrificial and thus immoral, by Rand's lights. The propriety of gratifying any particular desire depends entirely on the object of desire and the effects of its satisfaction on the person's overall interest. But the point is, restraint is not in all cases the route to happiness.

As with the other candidates considered in this chapter, temperance should be governed by other virtues. The proper exercise of temperance will reflect honesty about different ends' value in the agent's life and it will reflect integrity, insofar as the person pursues those ends in proportion to their value. Admittedly, invoking an ideal of temperance might sometimes supply a person with a useful caution against evading his options' true value to him. In the end, however, temperance is appropriate only when and because it serves the agent's interest. Accordingly, rational self-restraint is virtuous; self-restraint *per se* is not.

This account of seven major virtues as well as of Rand's position on a handful of commonly lauded virtues should provide a fairly full portrait of the egoism that Rand prescribes. In an Appendix, I will briefly address one additional question. How can an egoist enjoy loving relationships with others? Egoism seemingly precludes valuing another person for his own sake. If an egoist cares primarily about his own self-interest, many object, he cannot value others in the ways that make genuine love and friendship possible. This would be a decidedly un-egoistic effect of his egoism. The egoist allegedly must miss out on relationships that most people regard as among life's greatest values, and his own life will be the poorer, for it.

In response, I will explain how love itself is selfish, on Rand's view, and how loving a person for his own sake and loving a person selfishly are not mutually exclusive alternatives. Much depends on what loving a person "for his own sake" means. An egoist can love a person for his own sake not in the sense of loving him self-sacrificially, but by loving him for who he is. He can love a person for his character, that is, rather than for some narrow utilitarian purpose (such as access to a club) or for no particular reason, as some analysts of love have urged. While Rand's egoist primarily values his own well-being, it does not follow that he can value *nothing but* his own well-being. Indeed, it is only the rational egoist who can reap the value of love.

* * *

What is in store, overall, is an account of how the rational egoist should live: how he should live in order to be moral and (the same thing, on this view) how he should live in order to live – in order to continue the process of self-generated, self-sustaining actions that constitutes his life and to reap the psychological reward of such living, his happiness. Human life, long range, depends on principled action that is grounded in natural facts about life's necessary conditions. The seven virtues identify the fundamental categories of such action. In Rand's view, the popular image of the selfish person misconstrues what a person's interest consists of and how it can be achieved. The virtuous egoist who emerges from her account is, I hope to show, an ideal that cannot be dismissed so easily and an ideal that should significantly illuminate our thinking about morality.

2

Rational Egoism

A Profile of Its Foundations and Basic Character

The first question of ethics, in Ayn Rand's view, is not how to be moral, but why we should be. We cannot determine how to do anything – construct a building, teach a course, organize a campaign – until we know what it is that we are trying to accomplish. Consequently, although this book concerns how to be a rational egoist, we must first understand why one should be. The reason, in Rand's view, emerges from the reason that human beings should adhere to any moral code at all. Clearly, this is a huge subject. It occupies the entirety of my previous book, *Viable Values*, and I would particularly recommend reading Chapters 4 and 5 of that for a more complete discussion of Rand's argument.[1] What I will compress in this chapter is more an orientation to her defense of egoism than an attempted proof of it. Insofar as the present book rests on my previous one, this chapter indicates the bridge between the two by simply outlining Rand's argument for why we should be egoistic and articulating several features that distinguish her egoism from prevailing conceptions. For only with some understanding of the logic of egoism and of the kind of egoism that Rand advocates will we be able to appreciate the role of particular virtues within an egoistic moral code.

THE CASE FOR MORALITY

Morality, Rand writes, "is a code of values to guide man's choices and actions – the choices and actions that determine the purpose and the

---

[1] Smith, *Viable Values*. Also see Rand, "The Objectivist Ethics," "Causality Versus Duty," in *Philosophy: Who Needs It* (New York: Bobbs-Merrill, 1982), pp. 115–123, and Peikoff, *Objectivism*, pp. 206–249.

course of his life."[2] This captures the character of widely divergent moral
theories: theistic and atheistic, Eastern and Western, contemporary and
ancient, deontological and consequentialist, altruistic and egoistic. To
understand why we should have such a code and why value is the primary
concept in ethics, we must understand what values are.

A value is "that which one acts to gain and/or keep."[3] Water is valuable
to oak trees, bones are valuable to dogs, money, health, and friendship
are valuable to human beings insofar as oaks, dogs, and human beings
strive to secure these things. Although plants and animals do not act in
the deliberate, self-conscious sense that humans do, the point here is that
all these organisms *do* things – they exert energy, whether intentionally
or not – in order to attain certain ends. In ethics, we are concerned not
merely with what people do seek, of course, but with what they should seek
and correlatively, with how they should act. We want to know not simply
what people regard as valuable, but whether anything actually is. Rand
argues that the answer is affirmative.[4] The basis for regarding certain
ends as objectively valuable to an organism, as the kinds of things that it
should seek, Rand reasons, rests in the struggle for life. It is this struggle
that makes the concept of value possible and that makes the achievement
of certain ends – those that are objectively valuable – necessary. Let me
briefly explain each of these last two points.

Life makes values possible insofar as nothing can be valuable to nonliving things. No object or event is good or bad for a pen or a paperweight,
a car or a computer, a rock or a cave. What happens to such things might
be good or bad for some organism (e.g., the car's bad brakes are bad
for the squirrel on the road, the pen's leak is bad for the person writing
with it), but not for the objects themselves. For nonliving objects have no
interests. They have no interests because they have no needs that stand
to be satisfied or frustrated. Nothing is at stake for them.

Living things, crucially, do have something at stake: our lives. And
this is what allows us to distinguish certain things as objectively valuable.
The phenomenon of value presupposes alternatives. One thing can be
good for x only if other things would be bad for x. Alternatives can be
better or worse, in turn, only relative to some end. While human beings
pursue myriad ends relative to which we can evaluate things as good or

[2] Rand, "The Objectivist Ethics," p. 13. I will refer to "ethics" and "morality" interchangeably.
[3] Rand, "The Objectivist Ethics," p. 16.
[4] The definition of value given above is generic or neutral insofar as it encompasses things
   that people should pursue as well as things they should not. As we proceed, we will see
   Rand's account of proper values, those things that people should act to gain and/or keep.

bad, what allows any evaluations to reflect more than such circumscribed judgments and to be objective about ends as well as means is the fact that at the bottom of all of our ends rests a single alternative: life or death. This alternative is fundamental insofar as it is inescapable; every other alternative that a person faces and every action that he takes stands to affect it. However minimally or indirectly, everything that an organism does either strengthens or diminishes its fitness to survive. By studying, for instance, a person might better equip himself to earn a living. By remaining in a relationship with an abusive or a merely so-so spouse, a person may foster low self-esteem that hampers his ability to take other actions that would advance his life. By cultivating his taste for jazz or his skill at bowling, a person may make himself better able to relax after work or to keep his problems in perspective or to enjoy his life and thus have a stronger motivation to take good care of himself in other respects.

Rand's point in claiming that life makes value possible, then, is not simply that a person must be alive in order to seek value, which is true but trivial.[5] Rather, the point is that the concept of value is unintelligible in relation to nonliving things. It is only against the background of alternatives that we can meaningfully distinguish things as good or bad. And the fundamental alternative that human beings face and that allows the identification of objective values is that between life and death. As Rand writes,

The existence of inanimate matter is unconditional, the existence of life is not: it depends on a specific course of action. Matter is indestructible, it changes its forms, but it cannot cease to exist. It is only a living organism that faces a constant alternative: the issue of life or death. Life is a process of self-sustaining and self-generating action. If an organism fails in that action, it dies; its chemical elements remain, but its life goes out of existence.[6]

While a given person might declare his indifference to his life, he cannot opt out without consequences. If a person acts in ways that reflect his indifference, he will not be able to survive, long range. The greater and more consistent his life-abandoning actions, the greater the damage and the more precarious his life will become. (The person who opts out may not be moved by this, of course, but the consequences of his course are independent of his indifference, carrying significant implications for those who do wish to live.) As mortal beings, human beings' continued existence is not assured; our lives are conditional on certain needs being

---

[5] Peikoff, *Objectivism*, pp. 212–213.
[6] Rand, "The Objectivist Ethics," p. 16.

satisfied. And this leads to the second aspect of life's role as the foundation for value: life makes the achievement of values necessary. Living demands the pursuit of life-sustaining ends. If an organism is to survive, it must achieve the values that its nature requires.

Life is a process of self-generated, self-sustaining action, as Rand observes in the passage above. Because human lives are not automatically sustained, we must act to sustain them. Plants and lower animals are genetically coded to act automatically in self-sustaining ways (e.g., to absorb water, to convert sunlight into energy, to hunt). Their physiology rules; they are "deterministic value-trackers," as Irfan Khawaja puts it.[7] In the case of humans, however, although some of the requisite actions are physiologically determined (digestion and respiration, for instance), others must be deliberately performed (cooking, sewing, creating medicines). Because we choose our actions, it becomes imperative that we distinguish what will advance our lives from what will impede them and then act accordingly. That is, we must identify and pursue values – those ends that advance our lives.[8]

If life were not conditional, but assured, we would not need values. We could afford the luxury of indifference to things' effects on us. Indeed, we would have no basis for pronouncing what a person should value. Values would collapse into a matter of mere taste. In reality, however, human beings' existence depends on the achievement of life-sustaining goods. A human being must achieve the values that his existence depends on, or else he will no longer be a human being.

He must, that is, if he wishes to live. This is a crucial element of Rand's theory. Reality does not issue orders, on her view; it does not categorically command a person to prolong his life or to obey morality. As Rand explains,

If [man] chooses to live, a rational ethics will tell him what principles of action are required to implement his choice. If he does not choose to live, nature will take its course. Reality confronts a man with a great many 'must's,' but all of them are conditional: the formula of realistic necessity is: 'you must, if –' and the if stands for man's choice: 'if you want to achieve a certain goal.'[9]

---

[7] Irfan Khawaja, "Tara Smith's *Viable Values: A Study of Life as the Root and Reward of Morality*," *Reason Papers* 26 (Summer 2003), p. 74.

[8] Rand understands moral values as a subset of the wider category of values, distinguished by being fundamental and being chosen. Moral values do not arise for lower organisms. See Peikoff, *Objectivism*, p. 214.

[9] Rand, "Causality Versus Duty," p. 118–119. For more on the status of this choice, see Peikoff, *Objectivism*, pp. 244–245 and 247–248, and Smith, *Viable Values*, pp. 105–111, in which I address questions about its exact role.

Needs are always relative to ends. A need designates a necessary condition for the attainment of something else. Even the most basic, least controversial needs that people commonly speak of such as needs of food and shelter presuppose that the people in question wish to live. Rand's point here is that it is only if a person seeks to maintain his life that fulfilling life's requirements will be good and that the designation of certain ends as ones that a person *should* seek can be valid. If a person does wish to live, then morality will provide him with guidance for achieving that end. Through the analysis of value, in short, Rand argues that morality is man's means of achieving the values that his life depends on. Ethics is a code of values whose purpose is to steer human beings to the achievement of the more concrete values that fuel an individual's existence.[10]

RATIONAL EGOISM

It should not be difficult to appreciate that the moral guidance justified by this explanation of values is egoistic. Ethical egoism is the thesis that a person should act to promote his own interest. More precisely, it is the view that each person's primary moral obligation is to achieve his own well-being and he should not sacrifice his well-being for the well-being of others. This is exactly what emerges from Rand's explanation of the basis of morality. Adherence to morality is necessary to guide a person's pursuit of values. The achievement of values, in turn, is necessary in order for a person to secure his life. It is not any value attributed to life *per se* or an alleged duty to serve others' lives that creates the need for morality. Rather, it is a person's self-interest, *his* life, that

---

[10] Certain contemporary ethical naturalists strike broadly similar themes. Foot writes that "...for human beings the teaching and following of morality is something necessary. We can't get on without it." *Natural Goodness*, pp. 16–17. Further, "the way an individual *should be* is determined by what is needed for development, self-maintenance, and reproduction..." p. 33, emphasis in original. It is not merely statistical findings that underwrite norms, she holds; it is the fact that certain ways of acting matter to the life of the organism, p. 33. Peter Railton observes that "notions like good and bad have a place in the scheme of things only in virtue of facts about what matters, or could matter, to beings for whom it is possible that something matter. Good and bad would have no place within a universe consisting only of stones, for nothing matters to stones. Introduce some people, and you will have introduced the possibility of value as well. It *will* matter to people how things go in their rock-strewn world." "Facts and Values," *Philosophical Topics* 14 (Fall 1986), p. 9, emphasis in original. Also see Hursthouse, pp. 196, 230; Gaut, p. 185; Wallace, p. 18. Unlike Rand, however, none of these authors appears to challenge the altruistic content of morality's direction, and at times, some of them speak as if life is intrinsically valuable, a view that Rand rejects.

mandates adherence to a rational moral code. The reason to be moral is selfish.[11]

Rand does not offer one argument for morality and then an additional argument for egoism. Rather, in demonstrating how the alternative of life or death makes the achievement of values both possible and necessary, she is making the case for egoism.[12] If a person wishes to live, he must hold his own life as his highest value, as adherence to any alternative policy would be detrimental to and ultimately destructive of his life. To whatever extent a person elevated other ends above his life, he would be acting against the requirements of his own survival. Egoism, in other words, the paramount commitment to one's own well-being, is the necessary means of achieving one's life.

Further, if values arise only in the context of the pursuit of life, then egoism is the only moral code that can be *proper* (in the sense of appropriate or right or correct) for human beings. That is, if Rand is correct that the concept of value (as opposed to the concepts of that which is simply desired or pleasurable) is intelligible only in relation to an organism's quest for its life, then no nonegoistic ethics could be proper, since "proper" is conceptually dependent on "good." If an agent's pursuit of his own life is the only viable basis for some things being good for him and others being bad, then if one denies the propriety of egoism (i.e., that a person should work to advance his own life and that that is good for him), one has removed the basis for claiming that anything is good for him or that any course is proper. Without acknowledging the roots of the concept of good and of all its derivative concepts, we cannot coherently continue to employ these evaluations.[13]

In short, if a person does not wish to live, then nothing will be objectively valuable for him and no nonegoistic code could exert valid authority over him. Indifference to his fate renders a person comparable to an

---

[11] See Peikoff, *Objectivism*, p. 230 ff. I will henceforth use "egoism" as a shorthand for ethical egoism. Rand completely rejects psychological egoism.

[12] Strictly, Peikoff writes, egoism is "a corollary of man's life as the moral standard." *Objectivism*, p. 230. We will discuss that standard more directly, shortly.

[13] Rand regards the use of the concept "value" detached from its roots in the pursuit of life a stolen concept, her term for the fallacy of "using a higher-level concept while denying or ignoring its hierarchical roots, i.e., one or more of the earlier concepts on which it logically depends." Peikoff, *Objectivism*, p. 136; see p. 212 on this particular instance of concept stealing. Also see *Letters of Ayn Rand*, ed. Michael S. Berliner (New York: Penguin, 1995), p. 562. If a term's meaning is dependent on certain facts, when one denies those underlying facts, one no longer has a valid basis for using that term. Its continued use, at best, changes its meaning.

inanimate object; nothing could be good or bad, proper or improper, for such an entity. If a person does wish to live, however, then he must act to sustain his life. Because life's demands are ongoing and all-encompassing and because every action stands to affect a person's life, however indirectly, the pursuit of one's life cannot be a peripheral, part-time concern, an occasional endeavor juggled alongside competing ends. It must be a person's central, ruling policy.[14]

Distinctive Features

Rand's ethics is thus unequivocally egoistic. Because of her understanding of the nature of value and of what a person's interest is, however, it does not conform to the dominant conventional images of egoism. While this should become clearer as I elaborate on rational egoism's requisite virtues over the course of the book, as groundwork for that, I should immediately explain several significant aspects of Rand's egoism. With a fuller understanding of the general character of the egoism that she endorses, we will be in a better position to understand her reasoning for the specific virtues she believes it demands.

The crucial feature of Rand's theory is that value is objective. What is good for a person – what is in his interest – is not simply a subjective projection of that person's beliefs, attitudes, tastes, or desires, for those are not adequate guides to meeting his life's requirements. Although the choice to live is the condition of anything's being good for a person, the preference for a particular object does not, by itself, render that object conducive to his survival and therefore valuable. At the same time, Rand is not asserting the existence of intrinsic value. Value is not found ready-made in the external world, a freestanding feature nestled within certain things. It follows from values' grounding in life that the notion of value is empty when detached from effects on living organisms. Nothing can be good in itself. A value is always good *to* someone and *for* some end, Rand observes.[15] She explains,

The *objective* theory holds that the good is neither an attribute of "things in themselves" nor of man's emotional states, but an *evaluation* of the facts of reality by man's consciousness according to a rational standard of value. . . . The objective

---

[14] Peikoff, *Objectivism*, p. 231. This does not entail a blanket condemnation of suicide. See Peikoff, pp. 247–248, *Ayn Rand Answers*, ed. Robert Mayhew (New York: Penguin, 2005), p. 16, and Smith, *Viable Values*, pp. 143–145.

[15] Rand, "The Objectivist Ethics," p. 16.

theory holds *that the good is an aspect of reality in relation to man* – and that it must be discovered, not invented, by man.[16]

To say that values are objective, then, is to say that the things that people call good and bad stand in definite relationships to a person's life and that there is a fact of the matter as to whether those things are life-advancing or life-diminishing. An objective value is an aspect of reality that stands in a positive relation to human beings.[17] Something is objectively good for a person when it offers a net gain for his life. Notice further, however, Rand's emphasis on the good as an evaluation of facts. While values must be discovered rather than invented, they do need to be discovered. "Value requires a valuer," Peikoff observes, value "presupposes an *act of evaluation.*"[18] Although things exist independently of a person's consciousness and can carry effects on a person's life regardless of his awareness of those effects (internal chemical processes may, unbeknown to me, be aiding my health even as I write, for instance), they do not exist *as values* for a person without his identification of them as such. Values are not the equivalent of anything that is beneficial to a person.[19] The full explanation of this view depends on Rand's broader understanding of the nature of objectivity itself. In particular, it reflects her view that objectivity is methodological and pertains to the relationship between consciousness and existence rather than to either apart from the other.[20] For our purposes, it will suffice to recall that values, broadly, are those things that one acts to gain or keep. Correlatively, even when speaking exclusively of proper, objective values that a person should pursue, a person must identify a thing as carrying a potentially positive impact on his life in order to actively seek it.

Rand's egoism thus rejects subjectivism. However sophisticated or subtle any particular incarnation, all forms of subjectivism face the same fatal defect: We cannot invent values by fiat because our wills do not create things' effects on our lives. Values have a job to do: They are to advance

---

[16] Rand, "What is Capitalism?" in *Capitalism: The Unknown Ideal* (New York: Signet, 1967), p. 22, emphasis in original.

[17] Peikoff, *Objectivism*, pp. 241–243. This statement is not the entirety of his account, as my elaboration should make clear.

[18] Peikoff, *Objectivism*, p. 241, emphasis in original.

[19] See Smith, *Viable Values*, pp. 84–85.

[20] See Peikoff, *Objectivism*, on objectivity, pp. 110–151. On the objectivity of value in particular, see pp. 241–249; Rand, "Who is the Final Authority in Ethics?" *The Voice of Reason – Essays in Objectivist Thought*, ed. Peikoff (New York: New American Library, 1988), pp 17–22; Smith, *Viable Values*, pp. 97–103.

a person's life. Whether a given thing does that job is not a function of anyone's choosing.

In endorsing the objectivity of values, Rand is not asserting the universality of all values. Nothing in Rand's account entails that the entire roster of things that are objectively valuable for one person must also be valuable for every other person. Objectivity allows for a range of values that can vary (within limits) between different individuals. The limits are set by our nature. Although certain things are valuable to all human beings in virtue of our being human (e.g., food and shelter), the means through which a person pursues these basic values can vary. The need to make a living does not entail that we must all do so through the same kind of work (driving a truck or teaching grade school, for instance). The need for relaxation does not mean that we must all pursue the same hobbies or the same forms of entertainment; the need for health does not mean that the same medications will be valuable to each of us. Many values are optional or discretionary. These do not compete with more basic, universal values; rather, they are the means through which a person pursues more basic values. In pursuing such optional values, a person must respect the requirements of his life by not choosing ends that are detrimental to it. As long as he does respect those requirements, however, a great deal of variety in values is compatible with objectivity.[21]

The main point is that values' objectivity rests in the relationship between specific ends and a particular person's life. What is good must be good *for* someone in particular, but what makes a thing good is its nature and impact on the person's life independently of anyone's beliefs or wishes about what that impact is. The objectivity of values reflects a factual relationship.

Part and parcel of Rand's rejection of subjectivism is a rejection of hedonism, the doctrine that pleasure is the standard of value. Pleasure is not a reliable guide to the advancement of a human being's life, as what is pleasurable and what is in a person's interest do not always coincide. Having a confrontation with a coworker may be unpleasant but in your

---

[21] See Peikoff, *Objectivism*, pp. 323–324. In a similar vein, Railton likens goodness to nutrition, observing that while all organisms require some nutrition, they do not all require the exact same things, p. 10. A person's preferences can thus play *some* role in establishing what is in his interest. If a person chooses to set up his own law firm, for instance, the acquisition of clients will be in his interest; if a person chooses golf as a hobby, skill at putting will be in his interest. Yet Rand's point against subjectivism, that preferences cannot single-handedly dictate the content of one's interest or which things are valuable, stands.

interest; having a cocktail may be pleasant but contrary to your interest, given your medical condition or job demands. Although this distinction is not difficult to grasp in the abstract, neglect of it frequently muddles discussions of egoism, making it important to digest Rand's complete renunciation of hedonism. In fact, Rand writes, "to declare, as the ethical hedonists do, that 'the proper value is whatever gives you pleasure' is to declare that 'the proper value is whatever you happen to value.'" Far from being a policy that could nourish a person's life, this amounts to an abdication on the question of how to lead our lives.[22]

What *is* the standard of value, on Rand's view? Because it is the struggle to survive that gives rise to the phenomenon of values and that mandates the achievement of values, life is the yardstick by which to determine what is good or bad for a person. Ends and actions are to be assessed on the basis of their contribution to an individual's survival. It is not always easy to ascertain these effects, since actions and events can vary greatly in the directness, immediacy, and scope of their impact. Regardless of how readily known the effects of a given course of action, however, the basic principle is: That which aids a person's life is good; that which endangers or damages it is bad. "The standard of value of the Objectivist ethics," Rand writes, "the standard by which one judges what is good or evil – is man's life, or: that which is required for man's survival *qua* man."[23]

This does not mean a momentary or merely physical survival; the aim is not "the preservation of a physical hulk."[24] Rand explains that "'Man's survival *qua* man' means the terms, methods, conditions, and goals required for the survival of a rational being through the whole of his lifespan – in all those aspects of existence which are open to his choice."[25] The goal that anchors value, in other words, is not simply breathing, but thriving. The goal is not attainment of the barest essentials of subsistence, but a condition of flourishing – which means: living in such a manner that one is fit to continue to live, long term.[26] Correspondingly,

---

[22] Rand, "The Objectivist Ethics," p. 33.
[23] Rand, "The Objectivist Ethics," p. 25.
[24] Rand, "The Objectivist Ethics," p. 26; *Journals of Ayn Rand*, ed. David Harriman (New York: Penguin, 1997), p. 276.
[25] Rand, "The Objectivist Ethics," p. 26.
[26] This is how we normally use the term. We refer to a plant as flourishing to indicate not that it is barely clinging to life, but that it exhibits signs of hardiness, durability, the ability to withstand future adversity and to realize its potential for flowers or fruit, for instance. Similarly, we speak of a child as flourishing when we observe evidence of his robustness, his having the resources necessary to defeat illness, his developing in physical, intellectual, or emotional ways that augur further success in the future.

the standard of value is not that which is needed to maintain a pulse at any given moment, but that which is needed to flourish. For flourishing is the manner of living that will sustain a person, long range.

One might suspect that this conception of the standard of value introduces an equivocation that compromises the objectivity of value. Here, Rand may seem to be invoking a desirable quality of life as the measure of value rather than the sheer fact of life. This misunderstands her claim, however. Look again at Rand's explanation of what survival *qua* man means: "the terms, methods, conditions, and goals required" for a human being to live, long range. I believe that she writes "required" quite deliberately. Rand is not introducing independent notions of what kind of life would be enjoyable and now christening those as the standard of value, thereby departing from her original claim that it is needs of survival that explain the genesis of value. Although most people would find a flourishing life more agreeable than a day-to-day struggle to eke out subsistence, the comparative pleasure of the two conditions is not what renders flourishing the proper standard. What is good for man's survival *qua* man remains grounded in needs, not in subjective preferences. The reason that the standard of value is "that which is required for man's survival *qua* man" is that it is only by living as his nature demands that a human being can survive.

Different kinds of organisms survive through different types of actions. (The swimming that is essential for tuna, for example, is not essential for mice or men.) Any organism's default on its distinctive mode of life – its failure to live as the kind of organism that it is – correspondingly impairs its ability to function. The more severe the default, the more severe the consequences. A dog could not survive for long if it were to abandon a dog's mode of survival and adopt the methods that sustain an earthworm. A seal could not survive for long by the methods that sustain a mussel. An organism must act as its nature demands (*qua* dog, *qua* seal, etc.) in order to survive. Indeed, ordinary ways of evaluating organisms' health routinely make use of such species-specific and ideal-laden standards. A horticulturalist might tell you that a particular tree in your yard is not getting as much nutrition or shade as it needs.[27] We accept such evaluations as unproblematic because we implicitly realize that needs are correlative to the ideal of flourishing and that flourishing is relative to the kind of organism in question. The fact that the tree is alive or that it is getting as much shade as a different tree that needs less shade does

---

[27] This example is suggested by Gaut, pp. 185–186.

not refute the expert's diagnosis. Flourishing is what we are interested in when we assess an organism's health – not simply whether it is dead or alive at the time of inspection, but its broader condition and prospects for the future.[28]

The same applies to human beings. We do not regard all people as equally well simply because they are among the quick. And just as we can objectively distinguish degrees of physical health among living individuals, we can objectively distinguish degrees of broader well-being. The latter is often more complicated, given that it involves psychological dimensions and a much wider range of legitimate, life-advancing choices reflected in optional values. One person might flourish with one kind of career or romantic partner while another person's flourishing might require a quite different kind of career or partner. Yet at root, flourishing remains a function of those actions which suit a person to live.

In tying value to life *qua* man, then, Rand is not opting for a certain quality of life as opposed to life itself. Rather, she is recognizing that living requires living as man's nature requires. "Life, for any living creature, means life *as* that creature, life in accordance with its specific means of survival," Peikoff explains.[29] Correlatively, Rand holds,

The maintenance of life and the pursuit of happiness are not two separate issues. To hold one's own life as one's ultimate value, and one's own happiness as one's highest purpose are two aspects of the same achievement. Existentially, the activity of pursuing rational goals is the activity of maintaining one's life; psychologically, its result, reward and concomitant is an emotional state of happiness.[30]

Rand is not claiming that living and flourishing are indistinguishable or that flourishing is a prerequisite of being alive right now; she would hardly deny that a person can breathe without flourishing. The standard of value is life *qua* man or a flourishing life, however, because man can only survive by respecting the requirements of his distinctive nature. Living well – that is, flourishing – is one's means of living, of sustaining the process that constitutes one's life. Thus reference to life *qua* man does not represent a higher standard. The reason that life *qua* man is the appropriate standard – the reason that we want people to be well (physically or

---

[28] See James G. Lennox, "Health as an Objective Value," *Journal of Medicine and Philosophy* 20 (1995), pp. 499–511 for related discussion.

[29] Peikoff, *Objectivism*, p. 219.

[30] Rand, "The Objectivist Ethics," p. 32.

more broadly) – is that that is the surest way to *be*. Flourishing is the path to continued living.[31]

Although I have been speaking of "flourishing," Rand uses the term "happiness." She defines happiness as "that state of consciousness which proceeds from the achievement of one's values." It is a "state of non-contradictory joy . . . a joy that does not clash with any of your values."[32] Rand believes that such a state could result only from rational, virtuous living. True happiness, in the sense referred to in the passage describing happiness as the result of pursuing rational goals, implies objective flourishing, in her view. Only a person's virtue can achieve such happiness.[33] The description of a person as happy thus refers both to his psychological state and to the underlying mode of action that is responsible for that state. Henceforth, accordingly, I will refer to the standard of value as "life," "happiness," and "flourishing," interchangeably. Each term has its advantages. "Life" conjures the biological facts that stand at the base of Rand's explanation of value. Whereas "happiness," in the ears of many, denotes a state of consciousness and often connotes a passive, reactive condition, "flourishing" usefully suggests the activity that is at the heart of living. Moreover, the connotations of "flourishing" are more readily given to objective evaluation. It is easier to recognize that a person can be mistaken about whether he is flourishing than about whether he is happy, since people often use "happiness" to refer exclusively to a person's felt emotional state. Thus, "happiness" might be more easily mistaken for the subjective state that Rand rejects as the standard of value. At the same time, "happiness" has the advantage of naming the true object of people's pursuit. "Flourishing" can seem detached, impersonally clinical. People want not merely to live and flourish but to *enjoy* their lives; "happiness" better captures that.[34] Whichever term I use at any stage of the ensuing discussion, however, it is important to keep in mind that I will be using them, insofar as I refer to them as the standard of value and as the purpose of value, as fully interchangeable. The requirements

---

[31] Peikoff discusses this issue on pp. 219–220. I devote Chapter 5 of *Viable Values* to the relationship between flourishing and life. Among other things, I explore the distinctions between quality and quantity of life and between needs and wants, as well as the value of psychological well-being to physical well-being.

[32] Rand, "The Objectivist Ethics," pp. 31, 32.

[33] Rand, *Atlas Shrugged* (New York: Dutton, 1992, originally published 1957), p. 1021. Hursthouse takes a similar position, p. 176.

[34] For some useful distinctions among common meanings of "happiness," see Foot, p. 82 ff.

of one are no greater and no weaker than the requirements of the others.

I should also clarify the difference between the standard of value and the purpose.[35] The purpose in pursuing values and in following morality is an individual's own life. The standard of value is that which is required for any individual to attain that purpose. This is determined by the basic nature of man rather than by anyone's particular desires. It is also important to recognize that the purpose is not fully separable from the means prescribed by the standard. The pursuit of objective values is not simply a stepping stone to a distinct, later result. Rather, it is what the goal consists of. Life is, literally, a process. Correspondingly, the goal – a flourishing or happy life – refers to the condition of that process rather than to a detachable product. Flourishing is a manner of sustaining that process; it is itself a manner of living. Flourishing consists in living well. Thus, under any of these labels (flourishing, happiness, life), the goal is truly both end and means, since the end consists in the continued activity of living and since that activity – acting in a way that will extend one's life – is the only means to that end.[36]

Although we sometimes focus on the psychological satisfaction that results from living in a certain manner, that satisfaction is only a portion of the aim. The goal is life – complete physical and spiritual well-being. By "spiritual," Rand means "pertaining to one's consciousness."[37] Spiritual values include such things as intelligence, self-respect, art, friendship, a rewarding career. Each can make a significant contribution to a person's well-being. Rand's recognition of the importance of spiritual values also distinguishes her egoism from materialism. Although material needs are undeniable and material goods are an indispensable part of flourishing, they are not its entirety, as a person's life comprises more than his physical condition.

The immediate point, however, is that flourishing is, at core, good functioning. While a welcome effect of that is usually satisfaction, that should not be mistaken for the entire end. Because a person's psychological state is a function of particular beliefs and evaluations that may themselves be ill-founded, his feelings are not a foolproof barometer

[35] Rand addresses this in "The Objectivist Ethics," p. 27.
[36] For related comments on the relationship between values and life, see Rand, "The Objectivist Ethics," p. 27, and Allan Gotthelf, *On Ayn Rand* (Belmont, CA: Wadsworth, 2000), pp. 82–83. Also cf. Aristotle's description of *eudaimonia* as activity of the soul in accordance with virtue. *Nicomachean Ethics* 1099b 25, 1102a5.
[37] Rand, "The Objectivist Ethics," p. 35.

of his objective well-being. And because flourishing consists in a manner of living, it is also important to recognize that it must be self-authored. Flourishing is not a transferable good; a person can only achieve it through his own efforts. Others can help in a variety of concrete ways, material and spiritual, but no one can live well for another person nor supply him with the normal emotional accompaniment, happiness. If a person is to flourish, he must egoistically pursue that end for himself.[38]

The Egoist's Need for Principles

By observing Rand's position on some of the doctrines commonly associated with egoism, we should already have a sharper image of the kind of egoism that she advocates. A couple of further features are especially important to grasp its distinctive character, however.

On Rand's understanding, a person's interest is measured by the long-range, all-encompassing condition of his life. Consequently, advancing one's interest requires adherence to principles. Contrary to the prevalent image of the egoist as oblivious to all standards and moved entirely by what he wants, when he wants it, Rand sees such an erratic, emotion-driven course as a sure way to sabotage one's well-being. Serving one's interest requires action guided by the recognition of certain constant, fundamental facts. These facts are the basis of moral principles.

A principle is a "general truth on which other truths depend," Peikoff writes. Moral principles identify the relationships between the most basic kinds of choices that human beings can make and the impact of those choices on human survival.[39] The reason that human beings need principles stems from the nature of the goal – individual flourishing – and our equipment for achieving that goal. To begin to appreciate this, consider the fact that values (which constitute the stuff of flourishing) are objective. Which kinds of action advance human lives and which kinds of actions impede them is a matter of fact. Human beings' fundamental needs do not fluctuate among different individuals or days of the week. Correspondingly, effective means of serving those needs do not

---

[38] Aristotle's conception of *eudaimonia* is also self-generated, as many commentators have noted. See *Nicomachean Ethics* Book I, Chapters 7–10; Julia Annas, *The Morality of Happiness* (New York: Oxford University Press, 1993), pp. 36–37; John Cooper, *Reason and Human Good in Aristotle* (Indianapolis: Hackett, 1986), p. 124; Richard Kraut, *Aristotle on the Human Good* (Princeton: Princeton University Press, 1989), pp. 119, 253 ff, 278.

[39] Peikoff, *Objectivism*, p. 218.

fluctuate – not in essentials. Because the kinds of actions that are valuable to human beings are, at core, constant, we must be constant in respecting that, if we are to achieve values. Principles tell us what kinds of actions those are.

If values were subjective, completely the construct of an individual's beliefs or wishes, no consistent kind of action would be called for. As the aim of value-seeking action changed with individuals' assorted tastes, so would the best means of attaining such variable values. Indeed, under subjectivism, if a person thought a particular tack valuable, it would thereby be valuable. The steady guidance of principle would have no place.

Principles reflect more than the need for consistency, however. Even more important to appreciate the necessity of principles is recognition of what a complex, layered, widely encompassing phenomenon a person's flourishing is. An individual's flourishing does not consist simply in how he is faring or feeling at any given moment; it cannot be accurately measured by taking his current temperature, physical or emotional. Flourishing depends on the overall direction of a person's life; it is a function of whether a person is living in a life-furthering way. As such, a given action's impact on a person's flourishing is not the kind of thing that he can always easily decipher by superficial observation. Thousands of decisions over weeks or months or years can interact to determine whether a given action truly serves his interest. Clarity about one's goal – simply knowing, "I want to flourish" – is not enough to inform a person of the net effect of a particular action on his interest, in all its dimensions, over the long run.

Individuals typically pursue numerous ends – in their work, in recreation, in regard to health and finances, in relationships with friends and family. An ordinary person might be simultaneously trying to lower his cholesterol, win a new insurance account, train for the marathon, rebalance his portfolio, hire a new office manager, find a home for his ailing mother, improve his son's conduct at school, spend more time with his wife, read that Clinton biography – and so on. Each end requires dedicated action if it is to be achieved. The array of ends and the natural tendency for actions taken in pursuit of one end to carry effects on others create ample opportunity for a person's actions to work at cross-purposes, undercutting his ultimate well-being. In order for a person's countless daily decisions on myriad issues to work together to advance his best interest, they must be made on a coordinated, rational basis. Moral principles, by informing him of the fundamental conditions of human value-achievement, provide that basis.

Just as the complex character of the goal, flourishing, points to a need for principles, so do our capacities for achieving that goal. Human beings cannot survive by the range of the moment, merely reacting to each situation as it arises, in isolation from other circumstances. We are not programmed to survive through instinctual behavior such as building nests or burying nuts. In order to fill our needs, we must conceptually identify both what our needs are and suitable means of fulfilling them. Since we are not equipped with X-ray-like vision into any isolated action's effects on our overall flourishing, to act on a case-by-case basis and ignore knowledge available from other situations will not suffice. Because every action carries some effect on a person's broader well-being and because the here and now does not provide all the information that life-furthering action requires, total absorption in the present is a luxury that our nature does not permit. Principles offer a lens beyond a person's immediate circumstances, allowing a wider vision of contemplated actions' impact on the agent's well-being.

Moral principles are formed through the observation of numerous concrete experiences and logical inferences concerning the effects of different kinds of actions on human flourishing.[40] (A person might adopt the principle of justice, for instance, on the basis of recognizing the beneficial results of just actions in specific incidents in his personal relationships, in his workplace, in events in history or in education policy.) Principles integrate a vast quantity of data culled from a variety of circumstances into the most fully informed, rationally considered judgments we could have. It is difficult to assess the net effect of any particular action on the intricate network of values that constitutes a person's interest. Human beings lack the cognitive capacity to reliably gauge that impact accurately on the spot, as each moment unfurls. (Would it be in my interest to cheat on this exam, now that the proctor has left the room?) We have neither the memory (in volume or precision) nor the intellectual insight to penetrate to the most salient aspects of a concrete situation when it is considered in isolation from all others. Principles, however, compensate for these limitations by incorporating knowledge gleaned from many situations. Principles reflect a sober assessment of the wider and longer-range repercussions of contemplated actions. For the rational adoption of principles is based not only on recognition of a correlation between

---

[40] This is how principles are properly formed, in Rand's view; she does not believe that every person who accepts particular principles has necessarily followed this process in validating them.

certain types of actions and certain effects but also on appreciation of the reasons that explain that correlation.[41]

Acting on principle, then, means standing back from the impressions and impulses of one's immediate circumstances and proceeding on the basis of the fullest knowledge available about the effects of different actions on one's flourishing. Adherence to principles should not be blind or robotic. Principles are not a tool by which we can bypass the need for individual judgment. All principles require intelligent application to a person's particular situation. Principles are contextual, Rand holds, in that their authority and their precise prescriptions depend on the context. In order to follow a principle properly, a person must take into account all relevant particulars – for example, his and others' knowledge, abilities, goals, resources, feasible options.[42] A principle does not deliver rigid instruction of *exactly* what any person must do in a given situation. The principle of justice, for instance, in instructing a person to judge others objectively and treat them as they deserve, does not specify precisely which concretes Ed Harris should take into account when judging employee Joe Matuzak this Thursday. The person abiding by the principle of justice must thoughtfully consider all his knowledge of the other person's situation as well as his purposes in judging him to identify which factors are pertinent and how heavily to weigh them. Principles are contextual in that the details of their demands vary with the context, although the fundamental character of their direction is unwavering.[43]

On the surface, the idea that an egoist should be principled may seem puzzling. If the egoist's dominant concern is his own well-being, shouldn't he violate principles when he can get away with it? If his violations will go undetected and he can better advance his interest through periodic breaches, egoism would seem to bless such violations. This reasoning relies on assumptions about egoism that Rand's theory rejects, however.

On Rand's view, the authority of moral principles stems entirely from their practical service to self-interest, as that is judged by rational, long-range standards. (Because life is not a moment but an ongoing process, to seek one's life is to seek one's ongoing well-being.) Principles exert no

---

[41] Because moral principles represent inductive inferences about effective means of advancing human flourishing, a rational egoist must remain open to the possibility of finding errors in the principles he has adopted and needing to revise them.

[42] This is reminiscent of Aristotle's contention that the mean of virtue is relative to oneself (though Rand does not accept Aristotle's doctrine of the mean). *Nicomachean Ethics* II, 6.

[43] See Peikoff, *Objectivism*, 274–276.

autonomous claim on us. A person should follow principles because they offer effective guidance for advancing his life. Accordingly, adherence to rationally egoistic principles will not demand the sacrifice of a person's interest. If it seems to in a given case, the person has cause to reexamine the rationality of the principles he has accepted or his assessment of how his interest would best be served.

Bear in mind that actions carry consequences beyond the most conspicuous. What would a proposed action mean for a person's future options? Would it constrict them in any ways, either by its impact on his own abilities or knowledge or confidence or on others' estimates of him, for instance? What kind of choice would the action reflect? Would it fortify or weaken any virtue or vice in the agent's character? What would it do to the person's self-image? Obviously, an action could hurt a person's self-image only if he already accepted that the action is wrong. Yet people who regard certain actions as wrong still occasionally contemplate taking such actions. Thinking about an action's impact on one's character is sometimes an effective deterrent because it reminds the person of the larger repercussions of an action.[44]

The point is, contrary to the objection's implicit image of interest as defined simply by whatever prize tempts a person to violate moral principles, much more is at stake with every action than its most immediate or palpable prize. Self-interest encompasses what a person is as well as what he has.[45] Indeed, what a person is is a better indicator of his flourishing than his possessions on a given day, because *he* is his most significant means of enhancing his life, long range. If a person's principles are sound, then, what he might appear to gain through violating one of those principles would actually come at a higher cost to his interest. Cheating on rational, egoistic principles does not bring a net gain.

In maintaining that egoism requires adherence to principles, Rand is not claiming that the slightest deviation from moral principle will visit immediate and total destruction upon a person. Our alternatives are

---

[44] Edward F. McClennen observes that for many people, the realization that the means of obtaining an apparent benefit are illicit vetoes it. The fact that a person might, other things being equal, prefer an apparent payoff of free-riding does not entail that he would prefer *to* free-ride. When violating a rational moral principle is the price of obtaining that payoff, other things are not equal. McClennen, "Constrained Maximization and Resolute Choice," *Social Philosophy and Policy* 5 (1988), pp. 95–118, cited in David Schmidtz, "Reasons for Altruism," p. 64, note #20. For related discussion, see Hursthouse, pp. 176–177.

[45] Schmidtz discusses this in "Reasons for Altruism," pp. 55 ff, although he is not expounding Rand's view.

not: being alive and perfectly principled, or being dead. Indeed, Rand remarks in her *Journals* that we would be safer if we did suffer immediate retribution from error. In that case, we could not be lulled into supposing that violations of principle are harmless.[46] The damage inflicted by life-destroying actions will vary in extent and severity when violating moral principles no less than when violating medical principles. Just as a person can skip exercise or protein for short periods without suffering catastrophic consequences, a person can survive an occasional immoral action. But damage is damage, as Peikoff elaborates, and "damage, untended, is progressive." It cannot be courted or passively tolerated if one's goal is to flourish.[47] To cheat on those principles that a person recognizes as necessary for his happiness is to turn his back on that end. Since a pulse is not the goal of morality, the presence of a pulse cannot serve as the test of one's flourishing or as evidence for the egoistic value of violations of principles.[48]

No Conflicts between Rational Interests

A final distinctive feature of Rand's egoism is that it is not predatory. Rand does not view human relations as adversarial and she does not advocate unjust exploitation of other people to advance one's own good. Rational egoism is not about besting others, but about making one's own life as rewarding as possible. Indeed, egoism is not essentially a social policy, as the fundamental mandate for morality stems not from the existence of other people but from the basic requirements of living (which a person would face regardless of the presence of other people).

Altruism calls for the sacrifice of self to others. This has been the standard conception since Comte coined the term – which literally means "other-ism" – in the mid-nineteenth century.[49] E. J. Bond characterizes altruism as the policy of "always denying oneself for the sake of

---

[46] *Journals of Ayn Rand*, p. 253.

[47] Peikoff, *Objectivism*, p. 216. Peikoff offers an excellent discussion of this issue on pp. 215–216.

[48] This should become clearer in coming chapters. For further discussion of the authority of principles and the status of "goods" obtained through violation of proper principles, see Smith, *Viable Values*, pp. 164–174.

[49] Auguste Comte, *Systems in Positive Polity*, 1851. In the *Catechisme Positiviste*, Comte writes that "we are born under a load of obligations of every kind, to our predecessors, to our successors, to our contemporaries. After our birth those obligations increase..." *Catechisme Positiviste*, 1852, reprint (Rio de Janeiro: Temple du l'humanitie, 1957), quoted in Tibor Machan, *Generosity – Virtue in Civil Society* (Washington, DC: Cato Institute, 1998), p. 43.

others."⁵⁰ Burton Porter presents altruism as "the position that one should always act for the welfare of others."⁵¹ While recognizing that the term can be used more and less strictly, Lawrence Blum observes that in its most prevalent usage, altruism refers to placing the interests of others ahead of one's own.⁵² This is clearly how Rand understands altruism. She describes it as the thesis that self-sacrifice is a person's highest moral duty.⁵³ Peikoff stresses that altruism is not a synonym for kindness, generosity, or good will, but the "doctrine that man should place others above self as the fundamental rule of life."⁵⁴ A sacrifice must not be confused with an investment, in which a person foregoes a nearer reward in expectation of a greater one later. A sacrifice is the surrender of a greater value for a lesser one or for something that one does not value at all.⁵⁵

Because altruism calls for the sacrifice of self to others, people frequently assume that egoism must call for the sacrifice of others to oneself.⁵⁶ Rand explicitly rejects this view. She does so, in part, on grounds of consistency. In an oral question period, Rand said:

If [a person] decides to follow his own self-interest but to respect nobody else's, he is no longer on an objective moral base, but on a hedonistic, whim-worshiping one. If so, he has disqualified himself; he is claiming a contradiction. If he wants to maintain rationally his own self-interest, and claim he has a case for his right to self-interest, then he must concede that the ground on which he claims the right to self-interest also applies to every other human being.⁵⁷

More fundamentally, Rand rejects predation on the egoistic grounds that such a policy would not truly serve a person's interest.⁵⁸ Many of her reasons for believing this will unfold as we discuss the virtues requisite to

⁵⁰ E. J. Bond, "Theories of the Good," *Encyclopedia of Ethics*, ed. Lawrence C. Becker (New York: Garland, 1992), vol. 1, p. 410.
⁵¹ Burton F. Porter, *The Good Life* (New York: Ardley House, 1995), p. 283.
⁵² Lawrence Blum, "Altruism," *Encyclopedia of Ethics*, ed. Becker, vol. 1, p. 35. Thomas Nagel describes altruism as the "willingness to act in consideration of the interests of other persons, without the need of ulterior motives," Thomas Nagel, *The Possibility of Altruism* (Oxford: Clarendon Press, 1970), p. 79.
⁵³ See Rand, "The Objectivist Ethics," pp. 37–38, and "Faith and Force: The Destroyers of the Modern World," in *Philosophy: Who Needs It*, p. 74.
⁵⁴ Peikoff, *Objectivism*, p. 240.
⁵⁵ Rand, "The Ethics of Emergencies," in *The Virtue of Selfishness*, p. 50. Also see Peikoff, *Objectivism*, p. 232.
⁵⁶ Jan Osterberg, for instance, writes that "a person is said to act egoistically only if he ignores the interests of other people for the benefit of his own; it is possible to act egoistically only if one's interests conflict with those of other people." *Self and Others – A Study of Ethical Egoism* (Boston: Kluwer, 1988), p. 3.
⁵⁷ *Ayn Rand Answers*, p. 110.
⁵⁸ Rand, "The Objectivist Ethics," p. 30. Also see "Introduction," *The Virtue of Selfishness*, pp. ix–xi.

rational egoism. The point I wish to call to our immediate attention is the essential reason for rejecting predation, Rand's belief that individuals' interests do not conflict. More precisely, individuals' genuine, rational interests do not stand at odds. One person's enhancement of his well-being is not achieved through injury or loss to others. Human welfare is not a zero-sum game.[59]

Clearly, this is an unorthodox position whose full explanation would require a far more detailed analysis than I can offer here. Nonetheless, because it illuminates the kind of egoism that Rand embraces, I will sketch the basic reasoning behind her view.

To start, bear in mind that the egoist's end is his life, which is a process rather than a thing. A person's interest lies in his flourishing, but flourishing is a manner of living. As such, it is not the sort of thing that he could seize from others, as on the classic image of a conflict between two individuals' interests. What is valuable for a person is not an inherent component of things in the external world; it is not an intrinsic property that resides within certain things and is of interchangeable value to whomever wrests control of those things. A thing is truly valuable to a person only if his obtaining it represents a net gain. Yet whether it is a net gain depends largely on how he obtains it.

Undeniably, individuals' desires can conflict. The sheer fact that a person desires something does not mean that his having it, or his having it by any means, would be objectively good for him, however. The objects of individuals' desires often do those individuals more harm than good. Further, even when a person's desires are rational, the proper benchmark for calculating gains and losses to interest is not what a person would like but what he actually has. Realism demands that effects on a person's interest be gauged against his actual situation rather than against a wished-for situation.

To appreciate this, it may be helpful to distinguish two commonly confused situations. It is one thing for a person's advance of his interest to result in another person's suffering a loss; it is another for a person's advance of his interest to mean that another person will not obtain something that he otherwise might have.[60] The latter is what people often have

---

[59] See Rand, "The 'Conflicts' of Men's Interests," in *The Virtue of Selfishness*, pp. 57–65 for a full discussion of this issue, as well as Peikoff, *Objectivism*, pp. 234–237, and Smith, *Viable Values*, pp. 174–186. Rand also makes relevant remarks in *Journals of Ayn Rand*, p. 292.

[60] Thanks to Dan Bonevac for prodding me to clarify this. For simplicity's sake, my discussion speaks of conflicts between just two people, though more than two could be involved.

in mind when they assume that our interests can conflict – for example, two people vying for the same position, which only one of them can have, such as a job, admission to a school, or the undivided devotion of a particular lover. These cases are more accurately described as competitions rather than conflicts, however. If a conflict means that as one person's interest advances, another's must suffer, that is not what transpires in everyday cases in which individuals compete for a good that only one of them can obtain. For failing to achieve a goal cannot be equated with suffering damage to one's present position. Being turned down for a job is not the equivalent of losing your business; being passed over for another lover is not the equivalent of having your present lover die. A person's aims might be perfectly rational and their frustration, understandably disappointing (even intensely so). Yet this does not mean that aims determine what a person's interest consists in.

Consider the implications of the alternative. If a person's aims determined what was good and bad for him, could anything be ruled out as *not* in his interest? What couldn't be good or bad for him? Such a standard would render it impossible to judge any effect on a person as objectively advancing or damaging his interest. Such judgments would be hostage to the particular desires of each individual; at best, they would refer only to whether a person's desires were satisfied or frustrated. And under this scenario, to not injure a person would require, not adherence to a set of objective principles in dealing with other people, but reading each individual's mind and acquiescing to his preferences. One could only hope that (quite improbably) the actions needed to satisfy one person's desires would not frustrate anyone else's. Some aims are more rational than others, of course, yet even if we took interest to refer exclusively to individuals' rational aims, the problem remains: hopes are hopes; they reflect wishes for the future rather than a person's present reality. The disappointment of a person's hopes is not a setback to his actual condition.

A fully rational conception of interest requires that one step back from immediate desires to consider the larger context and accept the conditions necessary for the achievement of one's well-being. A person's interest is served and measured not only by what he has here and now, but by what makes possible those things that truly enhance his life. Correspondingly, a rational person should recognize that competition is itself beneficial. Rand, discussing the example of two candidates vying for a job, points out that a company could only succeed, long range, if it can choose among applicants to find the most productive people. Without the ability to evaluate many applicants and hire those it deems most likely to do well in the relevant positions, it could not ensure the quality of its personnel or its products. The business's future would be jeopardized. A condition of either candidate's obtaining the job is the existence of the company. A condition of any company's existence, however, is its ability to selectively hire suitable workers. Yet a condition of finding such workers, in turn, is the existence of competition.[61] Thus competition is beneficial not only for the "victors." Winning a specific job is not the only thing that a person stands to gain from competition. Competition enables the existence of institutions (productive businesses, quality schools, etc.) from which a person can benefit enormously and fosters an environment in which individuals are most likely to land the positions in which they can do the most good for themselves and others. Obviously, this does not always happen; the best person for the job does not always get it. Competition cannot ensure perfect information or full rationality on the part of all decision makers. A system of competition best promotes that result, however.

The insistence, "but I wanted that job! And it's a perfectly respectable desire, it would have been good for me to get it!" reflects a stubborn, subjectivist refusal to acknowledge all of the elements that enable a person's interest to be served. We cannot be cavalier in making suppositions about what would have been good for a person. Typically, we can only say that a certain outcome would have been good for a person *under certain conditions* or *if* he had been able to attain it by certain means. Absent those conditions being met, we cannot proceed as if it would have nonetheless been good for him. Attaining goals by certain means is not a net benefit for a person. Consider winning a race by using drugs that inflict crippling physical damage or turning a profit by ruining one's professional reputation and opportunities for future profits. While we naturally speak of many ends that would normally be in a person's interest, it is crucial to ensure that the necessary conditions are satisfied before concluding that an end is actually in his interest in any given case.

In short, the benefits reaped from participating in a system of competition far exceed a person's "losses" from failing to gain a particular position within that system. Indeed, one of Rand's points is that disappointed desires *per se* do not constitute a loss. My being turned down for a job I sought does not leave me worse off than I had been. (If the person

---

[61] See Rand, "The 'Conflicts' of Men's Interests," p. 64.

hired is better suited for the position, it may actually leave me better off.) Thus, the fact that two individuals sometimes seek a goal that only one of them can enjoy does not mean that their rational, all-things-considered interests are at odds. As we have seen already, a person's interest is not the sort of thing that can be accurately gauged by a snapshot of any single element of his condition in isolation from others or from the conditions required for the attainment of his well-being.[62]

The first kind of case that I distinguished from competitions, those in which one person's achievement of his interest results in another's actual loss, can sometimes arise, as when provisions on a stranded boat can sustain only one of its remaining passengers, and one person's consuming them will leave his companion worse off. Such cases are exceedingly rare, however. Indeed, they are so extraordinary as to fall beyond the province of morality's instruction, in Rand's view. Morality is designed to guide human beings in the normal course of events rather than in the once in a lifetime emergencies that never arise, in most individuals' lifetimes. For "the normal course of events" is where we live; people need guidance for navigating those circumstances that we most routinely encounter. Moreover, principled guidance is possible only for essentially predictable circumstances. Moral principles are premised on a comprehensive, long-range perspective on the types of actions conducive to human flourishing. The concept of human flourishing itself incorporates the long-range perspective. Crises such as boating accidents, eruptions of violence, or natural disasters thrust aside the propriety of following such principles, however, because the rational objective in emergencies is to escape imminent catastrophe. They thus require exclusive focus on pressing exigencies. Correspondingly, a person's interest in an emergency cannot be understood in the same way as his interest under ordinary circumstances. By their exceptional nature, emergencies are not the sorts of situations in which what are normally effective means of advancing human flourishing could work. Moral principles are both based on and intended for radically different circumstances. The actions necessary to sustain a person's life in atypical conditions cannot be used as the basis for moral principles that are to guide us in everyday living or for conclusions about the relationships among individuals' interests. (Indeed, if such crisis conditions were the norm, human life would be

---

[62] Rand offers further comments on candidates competing for a job in *Ayn Rand Answers*, pp. 111–112.

impossible.)[63] The point is, although conflicts of this type can arise, Rand denies that rational interests are at odds in the normal course of life that is the domain of morality. Conflicts do not mark human beings' characteristic condition.

Extraordinary cases aside, then, thus far, this has argued that the frequent appearance of conflicts between individuals' interests is illusory and that egoists should not seek to sacrifice others to themselves. It is instructive to recognize the deeper reason for this. As we shall see in the next chapter, the most basic means of achieving human survival is rationality. Rational thought generates the knowledge that is the basis for life-sustaining actions. Knowledge can be shared without loss, however. Indeed, its being shared often leads to greater gains, as individuals build on one another's discoveries and thereby increase the usefulness of knowledge. Unlike lower forms of life, human beings are not fated to compete for scarce resources in order to sustain ourselves. Among plants and animals, one organism's gain is typically another's loss. If this vulture devours that deer carcass, it leaves less for other animals in the region. Animals do not have the ability to increase the stock of resources that sustain them; they must make do with a static quantity of goods, fighting to obtain a portion of what they find naturally available, thereby leaving less for others and making others' lives that much more difficult. Sometimes, of course, an animal does something that benefits fellow animals as well as himself, and "cooperative" actions have been observed in certain species. But an animal cannot expand the pool of values from which he and his fellows can draw. Ultimately, animals compete over a fixed pie. Consequently, their interests do conflict. (Their situation is more akin to that of people in the lifeboat scenario.)

Human beings, by contrast, live by the mind. We do not survive simply by consuming what we find in our environment; we must create life-sustaining values (clothes, shelter, medicines, etc.) through the use of reason. Even eating requires thought, since we must distinguish the nourishing from the not so nourishing and since we do not find adequate supplies of the former readily available. We must cultivate the ingredients of a healthy diet. What is salient here is that human beings' reliance on rational production liberates us from the need to resent or resist others' gains.

---

[63] Again, "life" understood as long-range survival, not as a heartbeat today. See Rand, "The Ethics of Emergencies," pp. 49–56. Also see *Ayn Rand Answers*, pp. 113–114 for comments on situations in which morality cannot prescribe proper action. I will discuss the reason why moral principles do not rule in certain cases more fully in Chapter 4.

Because knowledge is the fundamental fuel for the productive work by which we create the values that sustain our lives and because the value of knowledge is not diminished when gained by others, our interests are not naturally inimical.[64] (As always, I am speaking of our rational, genuine interests.)

Imagine that this were not so and that knowledge could not be shared. Suppose that an idea could only be understood in one mind in the same way that a hunk of meat could only be consumed in one mouth, such that once knowledge was "consumed" by one person's mind, it could no longer be consumed by any other minds. If Bill learned that eating apples was nutritious for human beings, for instance – or how to start a fire or conduct electricity or build a bridge or tie his shoelace – no one else could acquire that knowledge. Under this scenario, individuals' interests would stand in ferocious conflict. Each person would need to work desperately to prevent others from gaining knowledge that could be useful to *him*, if only he could discover it. For once another person acquires some knowledge, that knowledge and its potential value for enhancing others' lives would be closed off.[65]

Happily, this is not the situation that we face. Because human beings produce values rather than seize them from a fixed pool and because the fundamental fuel of production is not a finite resource, one person's objective gains pose no threat to others. The same applies to the goods that human beings produce through rational thought – the material objects, services, techniques, programs, books, art, educational institutions, and so on. One person's producing such goods imposes no damage on others (as long as damage is measured rationally). In fact, others' gains offer the prospect of benefiting a person, since a producer usually finds it in his interest to trade some of his wealth in ways that others find in their interest (which is why they agree to a trade). Obviously, if one person beats me to mining a certain block of coal or farming a certain plot of land, I cannot use those very same resources. Although this

---

[64] The simultaneous rise of the earth's population and of the worldwide standard of living over the past few thousand years testifies to this.

[65] The person who discovers particular knowledge might proceed to do something with that knowledge that is valuable to others, such as making a product that they find useful. Yet if no one else can understand the knowledge that he has, then the endless array of further connections that other people might make, appreciating the usefulness of that knowledge in a range of additional contexts, would be impossible. And once that person died, so would the knowledge that informed whatever values he had created die with him. I thank Harry Binswanger for suggesting this general perspective on the issue.

might frustrate my desires, it does not injure my interest. To the extent that another person advances his rational interest by using these natural resources, he will have created objective value – thereby expanding the pool of values from which all human beings stand to benefit.

Whether we are speaking of economics or the broader realm of all life-furthering action, the point is that the kind of activity that propels human beings' survival, the creation of values, can be a boon to others rather than a loss and make their lives easier rather than harder. A policy of preying on others would fail to appreciate the profound ways in which other people can enrich one's own life, materially and spiritually. And because our rational interests are, far from being in natural conflict, often mutually advantageous, it is perfectly sensible for a rational egoist to cheer on others' virtue, believing that virtue fosters values and will thus serve the virtuous agent's interest. For others' virtue also stands to serves *his* interest.[66]

CONCLUSION

In Rand's view, the case for egoism is one with the case for morality itself. Egoism is not a response to other people so much as a response to the conditions of human existence. A person's interest depends on his needs, but needs are intelligible only in light of the alternative of life or death. This alternative is what gives rise to the phenomenon of value. It is only because an organism faces this alternative that we can distinguish certain things as good for it and other things as bad for it. A human being's existence is conditional on his achieving those ends that sustain his life. In this way, the goal of living provides the foundation for objective values.

The egoism that Rand embraces is faithful to this understanding of the roots and character of value. Rand rejects hedonistic, materialistic, and subjectivist presumptions about the content of a person's interest. It is only for a person who seeks to maintain his life that things can have value; correspondingly, the standard of value for human beings (and thus the standard of interest) is life. She explains this as life *qua* man because living as one's nature requires is necessary to sustain any organism, long range. The standard of value for human beings is thus not a minimal clinging to biological subsistence but a person's flourishing, physical and psychological. Interest, accordingly, cannot be measured by

---

[66] This will become clearer in the discussion of specific virtues.

isolated or fleeting features of a person's experience, but encompasses his long-range, all-things-considered condition.

Because interest is a more sophisticated phenomenon than dismissals of egoism typically acknowledge, a policy of promoting one's interest will require more careful thought than is usually recognized. Thus, Rand's emphasis on *rational* egoism. In particular, she contends that an egoist must be principled. Given that the effects of particular actions on the complex network of factors that constitutes a person's interest are impossible to identify in isolation from broader knowledge, principles offer the only effective epistemological tools for guiding successful egoistic action. Further, Rand argues that when self-interest is understood rationally, the conventional image of the egoist as out to hurt others in order to advance his own well-being collapses. Belief in conflicts between individuals' interests rests on simplistic, subjectivist pictures of what a person's genuine interest is. Given the enormous value that human beings can offer one another, a policy of preying on others would be self-defeating rather than self-advancing.

All of this, again, offers merely a sketch of Rand's case for rational egoism; a fuller explanation can be found in my last book. To grasp more fully the kind of egoism that Rand prescribes, however, let us now move forward by turning to the specific virtues that she believes a person's objective flourishing depends on.

3

The Master Virtue

Rationality

On Rand's view, the purpose of morality is to guide individuals to the achievement of their happiness. The selfish end of personal well-being is the reason why any person should adhere to morality's prescriptions. We turn now to the substance of those prescriptions by examining the specific virtues that she believes to be required by rational egoism. In this chapter, I begin by explaining Rand's conception of what a virtue is and then elaborate on the primary virtue, rationality. This is the central, overarching virtue from which the other major virtues are derivative. We will consider what rationality is, why it is a virtue, and what it demands of us, in practice.

THE NATURE OF VIRTUE

We saw in the previous chapter that a value is that which one acts to gain and/or keep and that an objective value is an end whose achievement would enhance an agent's life. A virtue, Rand maintains, is "the act by which one gains and/or keeps" an objective value.[1] The moral virtues thus designate the fundamental kinds of actions that will advance a person's life.[2] In Galt's speech in her novel *Atlas Shrugged*, Rand describes virtues as pertaining to the relationship between consciousness and existence

---

[1] Rand, "The Objectivist Ethics," p. 27.
[2] I am speaking of moral virtue as opposed to intellectual or any other type of virtues, and all claims about moral virtues are restricted to competent adults. Subsequent references to values will be to objective values, unless the context clearly indicates otherwise.

and she begins each paragraph introducing a virtue with the statement that that virtue is the "recognition" of a particular fact.[3]

None of these descriptions matches perfectly with conventional philosophical characterizations of virtue. Nearly all such accounts depict a virtue as a quality of a person rather than as an action or a recognition. Thinkers from Homer and Aristotle through today's moral philosophers predominantly portray virtue as a trait of character. Theorists differ, to be sure, over the exact features that distinguish moral traits from others (such as being left-handed) and about the relative significance of the disposition to feel a certain way and the disposition to act in a certain way. They are nearly unanimous, however, in considering virtue itself a disposition and thus a feature of a person.[4]

Rand's account is not as exceptional as it may initially appear, however. Its emphasis on action stems from her understanding of the entirely practical mission of morality. Irrevocable facts about human beings' nature, needs and environment demand certain actions, if we are to meet our needs. Our happiness depends on our learning about ourselves and the things around us in order to devise effective means of advancing our lives. Consciousness, in other words, must ascertain what existence demands and guide us to appropriate actions (as she indicates in the claim that virtue concerns the relationship of consciousness to existence). This is what the identification of specific virtues help us to do.[5]

Peikoff writes that virtue "consists of a man's recognizing facts and then acting accordingly."[6] Rand's descriptions of virtues as actions and as recognition of facts are not intended as alternative accounts of what virtue is; rather, she regards thought and action as two vital components of a morally proper course. One characterization of virtue highlights the intellectual and the other highlights the existential aspect of the same phenomenon. Virtue demands acting in recognition of certain facts. Virtuous action is action based on a rational moral principle. Recall from

---

[3] *Atlas Shrugged*, pp. 1018–1020.
[4] See, for instance, Hursthouse, pp. 10–11; Alasdair MacIntyre, "The Nature of the Virtues," in Roger Crisp and Michael Slote, eds., *Virtue Ethics* (Oxford: Oxford University Press, 1997), pp. 121–122; Linda Zagzebski, *Virtues of the Mind* (Cambridge University Press 1996), p. 137; Christina Sommers and Fred Sommers, eds., *Vice and Virtue in Everyday Life: Introductory Readings* (New York: Harcourt Brace Jovanovich, 1993), Introduction to Chapter 3, p. 213.
[5] James Wallace similarly conceives of particular virtues as performing functions that contribute to the human good, *Virtues and Vices*, p. 15.
[6] Peikoff, *Objectivism*, p. 250.

Chapter 2 that moral principles identify the impact on human survival of the most basic kinds of choices. Moral virtue is exercised by acting in ways that recognize those principles. Virtue, accordingly, reflects cognition. Contrary to some recent virtue ethicists, Rand does not view adherence to principles as an alternative to the cultivation of virtue. The two are complementary; it is through following rational moral principles that a person develops virtues in the conventional sense of traits of character.

Rand's characterization of virtues as recognitions of facts reflects the nature of morality's foundations. It should be clear from the last chapter that Rand rejects the widely alleged fact–value dichotomy. On Rand's theory, the pattern of reasoning that stands behind all proper moral direction is: If I recognize this fact, then I should act in this way, in order to advance my life. While a person's aim to maintain his own life is necessary for anything to be a value for that person, once that end is in place, it is recognizing an "is" that mandates an "ought." By characterizing virtue as recognition of a fact, Rand is underscoring the factual basis for morality's instruction.[7]

It is also worth noting that Aristotle's account of virtue includes the elements that Rand emphasizes. Aristotle writes "that a virtue or excellence is a characteristic involving choice, and that it consists in observing the mean relative to us, a mean which is defined by a rational principle, such as a man of practical wisdom would use to determine it."[8] Although Rand does not endorse Aristotle's doctrine of the mean, we can detect other points of agreement. A person observes the mean largely through the way he *acts*. Specifying that the mean is "defined by a rational principle" is akin to Rand's description of virtue as recognition of a fact, since the facts that Rand points to are broad, basic facts which can be stated as principles. She would agree that virtue is relative in the sense that morality's precise demands on a person depend on that person's situation. (Recall the contextual character of principles from Chapter 2.) And invoking a man of practical wisdom is consonant with Rand's view that moral principles must be applied intelligently in any particular circumstances.

While we can describe virtue as a quality of a person, then, Rand would say that this quality refers to a person's commitment, evidenced through consistent practice, to act in recognition of the relevant rational principles (honesty, justice, etc.). This is the sense in which a virtue reflects a

---

[7] For more on the fact–value relationship, see "The Objectivist Ethics," pp. 17–18, 24, and Smith, *Viable Values*, pp. 101–103.

[8] Aristotle, *Nicomachean Ethics*, 1106b35–1107a, trans. Ostwald.

disposition. The focus should be on the action, however, because action is what is required in order for a person to flourish. *You* are not the fundamental issue for moral instruction to be concerned with. Rather, the most basic concern of moral theory is to identify what a person must do in order to advance his life. A virtuous character is a consequence of proper action and is conducive to proper action, yet the purpose of a virtuous state of character is to generate the appropriate types of action. For these are what can advance a person's life.

Some might object that Rand's emphasis on action overlooks part of what is valuable about virtue. Exercising a virtue is not the equivalent of simply following a rule, as Rand's requirement of recognizing a principle might suggest. Genuine virtue involves taking the proper action with a certain spirit and inclination. Hursthouse maintains that an honest person, for instance, does the right thing "readily, eagerly, unhesitatingly, scrupulously." He will hasten to correct a false impression and will own up to having done something wrong before waiting to see whether he is likely to be found out. Paul Woodruff describes virtues as "habits of feeling" and observes that a good person "feels like doing what is right." Aristotle holds that moral virtue concerns emotions as well as actions and that "actions which conform to virtue are naturally pleasant."[9] Many would agree that virtues incorporate sympathetic inclinations alongside proper actions; without such inclinations, a person lacks true virtue.

I do not think that this objection refutes Rand's position, however. Admittedly, the person who does the right thing gladly is more appealing than the person who does the right thing grudgingly. Moreover, tangible practical benefits can result from having such virtuous inclinations. The more naturally inclined a person feels toward performing a particular proper action, the more likely he is to do it. If the action is indeed rationally egoistic, then he stands to benefit from that affective disposition. Without facing continual battles over whether to take the appropriate action, a person will more efficiently act in ways that advance his happiness. And the less of a struggle he must wage against resistant emotions, the less strain in his days and the more agreeable his experience. Nonetheless, Rand rejects the idea that a particular feeling on a given occasion is a requirement of moral virtue for the simple reason that feelings are not under a person's direct control. I cannot will myself to feel

---

9 Hursthouse, p. 11; Paul Woodruff, *Reverence – Renewing a Forgotten Virtue* (Oxford: Oxford University Press, 2001), p. 6; also see pp. 61–62; Aristotle, *Nicomachean Ethics*, trans. Ostwald, 1106b15 ff. and 1099a13.

a certain inclination right now in the way that I can will myself to take a certain action (e.g., to go to the gym or to do my taxes, even if I feel an acute aversion to doing so). We might take actions that can eventually alter some of our inclinations, such as engaging in psychological therapy, but we cannot directly and immediately manipulate our emotions and inclinations, as they are largely a product of subconscious premises. And morality cannot fairly demand what a person is incapable of delivering.[10]

Ideally, a person will readily, gladly act as morality and his flourishing demand. In her journals, Rand describes one of the heroes in her fiction, Howard Roark, as acting, when confronting difficult decisions involving his values, as if he sees only one choice open to him.[11] These are not difficult decisions for him, in other words, although they would be, for most people. Rand sees no value in struggle per se. Virtue may be more deeply engraved in the character of the person whose feelings are in sync with his beliefs about what he should do; this is both admirable and useful. It suggests a person whose conscious and subconscious beliefs and evaluations are in harmony, a person who is at peace with acting as he should and who is thus most likely to. Insofar as morality's function is to guide us toward the kinds of actions necessary for human flourishing and insofar as a person cannot control his emotions, however, emotions cannot be fairly included among morality's demands.[12] It can be in a person's interest to cultivate a certain kind of character (including certain emotional dispositions), but it is so because of the contribution that character makes to action.

The larger point to take away from all this, again, is that virtuous action is action that deliberately adheres to rational moral principles. Virtues designate the fundamental kinds of action that are necessary to sustain human life.

WHAT RATIONALITY IS

The most basic virtue, in Rand's view, and the source of all others, is rationality.[13] This virtue

means the recognition and acceptance of reason as one's only source of knowledge, one's only judge of values and one's only guide to action. It means one's

---

[10] We will see more of Rand's views on emotions later, in the discussion of rationality's demands.

[11] *Journals of Ayn Rand*, p. 171.

[12] A person's actions in the face of his emotions obviously are in his control and thus are subject to moral instruction and evaluation.

[13] Rand, "The Objectivist Ethics," p. 27.

total commitment to a state of full, conscious awareness, to the maintenance of a full mental focus in all issues, in all choices, in all of one's waking hours ... [14]

As Peikoff elaborates,

this means the application of reason to every aspect of one's life and concerns. It means choosing and validating one's opinions, one's decisions, one's work, one's love, in accordance with the normal requirements of a cognitive process, the requirements of logic, objectivity, integration. Put negatively, the virtue means never placing any consideration above one's perception of reality. This includes never attempting to get away with a contradiction, a mystic fantasy, or an indulgence in context-dropping. [15]

If human beings are to live, we must respect the nature of reality. Rationality is our means of doing so.

By "reality," Rand means "that which exists," whether a thing, an attribute, or an action. [16] Reality encompasses facts in the physical world as well as the nonphysical. I will sometimes use the term to refer to a particular fact and sometimes, to refer collectively to everything that exists. Regardless of its breadth in a given usage, "reality" refers to that which is so, to the way things are.

Reason is the capacity that enables human beings to discover the nature of the world – of entities, properties, conditions, relationships, processes, events, emotions, ideas – of everything that exists. (I will use "existents" to refer to the particular things that exist.) Although the nature and operations of reason are more epistemological and ultimately biological questions than moral ones, I should briefly indicate Rand's understanding of reason, since the virtue of rationality relies on it.

Rand understands reason to be "the faculty that identifies and integrates the material provided by man's senses." [17] Certain integrations that are instrumental to our awareness of the world are governed by physiology, such as the integration of sensations into percepts. If I close and then open my eyes, for example, I perceive the lamp before me as a single entity rather than as a flat round base, an upright black pole, a red mesh shade, and so on. And I do this automatically, without having to think particular thoughts. The kind of integration that distinguishes rationality, however, is conceptual. It is our ability to identify the relationships

---

[14] Rand, "The Objectivist Ethics," p. 28.
[15] Peikoff, *Objectivism*, p. 221. Rationality's direction thus applies equally to reasons for believing and reasons for acting.
[16] Rand, *Atlas Shrugged*, p. 1017, and *Introduction to Objectivist Epistemology*, 2nd edition, eds. Harry Binswanger and Leonard Peikoff (New York: Penguin, 1990), p. 5.
[17] Rand, "The Objectivist Ethics," p. 22.

between percepts and thereby expand our knowledge beyond what is immediately perceivable. Lower animals, lacking the power of reason, are severely limited in their awareness of the world. They can be aware of the existents immediately present to their senses and of other existents that they have perceived in the past. A given human being, by contrast, although he might have observed fewer existents of a given kind in his lifetime, can have vastly more extensive knowledge of them. As Peikoff observes, a person "can know facts pertaining to *all* trees, *every* pond and drop of water, the universal *nature* of man."[18] It is our capacity to reason that makes this possible. A person can apprehend not only the particular existents that he perceives, but what it is to be an existent of a specific type. Human beings uniquely enjoy the unit perspective, the ability to grasp particular things as *of a kind*. Human beings can grasp the *concept* of a tree or square or heat or speed or food or feeling or surviving or whatever (including the concepts of "or" and "whatever").

By selectively focusing on different existents' similarities and differences and integrating their similarities into new mental units by omitting their individual measurements, human beings form concepts that subsume an endless number of concretes. It is this power of conceptualization that enables human beings to shape our environment to suit our needs. Because we are able to command knowledge beyond the perceptual level, we are able to devise means of altering the existents we encounter in ways that achieve objective values and thereby enable us to live. Even the rudimentary knowledge of how to start a fire relies on conceptualization.

The nature of concepts and of concept formation is obviously a huge and contested subject. For a thorough presentation of Rand's views on this, one should read her *Introduction to Objectivist Epistemology*, which centers on this, as well as Peikoff's chapter elaborating on some of their crucial aspects.[19] For our purposes, this portrait of reason should suffice. As Peikoff summarizes, "[R]eason is the faculty that organizes perceptual units in conceptual terms by following the principles of logic."[20]

Although the identifications and integrations that reasoning consists of can grow quite sophisticated, reasoning is not rocket science. It is essentially a matter of grounding one's thinking in reality, of reaching

[18] Peikoff, *Objectivism*, pp. 73–74, emphasis in original.

[19] Peikoff, *Objectivism*, chapter 3, pp. 73–109. Also see Rand's condensed explanation of the essentials necessary for understanding her ethics in "The Objectivist Ethics," pp. 20–23.

[20] Peikoff, *Objectivism*, p. 152.

conclusions by observing and respecting relevant facts. Which facts are relevant will depend on a person's purpose as well as on logical inferences from past experience. Such experience provides the basis for sound conclusions about things' nature and likely behavior in the future. It teaches that different factors are more and less relevant when evaluating a person as a physician or as a singer or as a friend, for instance. However simple or complex one's project – whether it *is* rocket science or deciding what to buy a friend for Christmas – the essence of rationality consists in the effort to direct one's thinking and action by the way things are. Even where reason does not dictate a single correct answer, as in selecting a gift, rationality does demand that a person heed pertinent facts, such as the recipient's tastes and needs, previous gifts, the giver's budget. A process of reasoning begins with the recognition of reality and is governed, at every stage, by fidelity to reality. (It is governed, fundamentally, by the law of identity: A is A.)[21] The rational person accepts reality as his sovereign.

(Julia Annas has recently characterized rationality in essentially the same way. She writes, "when a life is given direction by reason, it is lived in a way that *respects reality* – it is concerned with the way things really are, both about the person herself and about the world."[22] Similar language is used throughout her essay. Annas analyzes several examples of wickedness as breakdowns in reason marked by failure to respect reality.[23])

The essential nature of rationality is seen most vividly by contrasting it with alternative modes of using one's mind: forming beliefs or making decisions on the basis of emotions, for instance, or on the basis of desires or faith or authority or consensus or tradition or prejudice or astrology or intuition. (This is hardly an exhaustive catalog.) In all such cases, whether a person proceeds by the dictates of tarot cards or big shots or his own faith or feelings, what he is not doing is identifying the relevant facts and drawing logical inferences about what those indicate. The person who simply defers to popular opinion on an issue, for instance, does not investigate the validity of that opinion, the evidence for and against it, but accepts a conclusion simply because it is widely held, ignoring the fact that popular opinion has often turned out to be mistaken. The person who uses his feelings as his basis for interacting with other people – who berates

---

[21] Peikoff, *Objectivism*, p. 153.
[22] Julia Annas, "Wickedness as Psychological Breakdown," *The Southern Journal of Philosophy* Spindel supplement XLIII (2005), p. 3, emphasis in original.
[23] Annas stresses that she does not mean this as an account of all forms of wickedness, p. 3.

or praises employees, for instance, depending on his mood – does not trouble himself to consider and logically assess their actual performance and desert. More broadly, the irrational person either does not bother to collect relevant information or he does not give it its due; he sets it aside or he minimizes or exaggerates pertinent facts' significance. In whichever of its myriad incarnations it occurs, irrationality, at bottom, distorts reality. More strictly, it distorts a person's image of reality. Various colloquial expressions testify to the reality-orientation that distinguishes rational thinking. We sometimes advise friends who are engaging in foolhardy plans or impractical dreams to "get a grip on reality." We seek to shake people out of irrational ideas by urging them to "be realistic" or to "get real." And beyond the level of casual conversation, our very category of serious mental illness – the region beyond sanity – is distinguished by whether a person has lost touch with reality. The essence of rationality, in short, in either its most impressive or most mundane manifestations, consists in grounding one's beliefs and actions in reality.[24]

WHY RATIONALITY IS A VIRTUE

With this understanding of what rationality is, we can appreciate why Rand regards it as the primary moral virtue. If a person seeks his own life and happiness, rationality is the essential means to success. Let me quote Rand at length, as she makes her reasoning plain.

Man's mind is his basic tool of survival. Life is given to him, survival is not. His body is given to him, its sustenance is not. His mind is given to him, its content is not. To remain alive, he must act, and before he can act he must know the nature and purpose of his action. He cannot obtain his food without a knowledge of food and of the way to obtain it. He cannot dig a ditch – or build a cyclotron – without a knowledge of his aim and of the means to achieve it. To remain alive, he must think.

But to think is an act of choice . . . *man is a being of volitional consciousness.* Reason does not work automatically; thinking is not a mechanical process; the connections of logic are not made by instinct. The function of your stomach, lungs or heart is automatic; the function of your mind is not. In any hour and issue of your life, you are free to think or to evade that effort. But you are not free to escape from your nature . . . [25]

---

[24] Henceforth, I will sometimes use "reason" and "rationality" interchangeably, and it should be clear from the context when I am speaking of the faculty of reason and when, of a manner of using one's mind.

[25] Rand, *Atlas Shrugged*, p. 1012, emphasis in original.

The central idea is straightforward. Human life is not maintained auto-matically or effortlessly; its constituent values are not achieved by instinct or magic or wishful thinking. Human beings must act in order to achieve our lives and happiness, but only certain actions will be effective. Unlike lower animals, we choose our actions. "Schools of fish, flocks of birds, and herds of deer respond similarly, collectively, and almost instantly to preda-tors. They don't stand (or fly or swim) around debating the matter."[26] Humans, however, not only can deliberate about what actions to take; we must. We must because we are not genetically programmed to act in survival-advancing ways. We must choose our actions on the basis of the actual conditions that we face – on the basis of reality. In other words, we must choose rationally.

Reason is man's fundamental means of survival. A human being is not equipped with claws or fangs or fur or instinct by which he can sustain his life, long range. A person must utilize his distinctive form of conscious-ness, his power to conceptualize, in order to identify his needs and to create means of satisfying them, to anticipate various eventualities and to plan and take appropriate action. Feelings of hunger might tell a person *that* he needs to eat (once he has figured out what such feelings signify), but not what can serve as nutrition, nor how to obtain it. The same goes for all of his needs.[27]

When a person fails to employ his capacity to conceptualize, he pro-ceeds as if he were a different, lesser organism. Humans' capacity to rea-son is not an optional frill that a person might utilize or not without con-sequence, however. Rationality is crucial to human existence. Moment-to-moment reactions to needs felt here and now cannot sustain beings as physically vulnerable as we are. We must outsmart other organisms (including viruses and bacteria) and alter our natural surroundings in order to maintain our existence. It is only through conceptualizing that a person can achieve the values necessary to live – the most elementary modes of shelter and clothing or the most stunning modes of medicine and communication. When a person does not reason to sustain himself, he survives to the extent that he relies on others who do use reason. If a group of people stranded on an island all behaved like beings who lacked the faculty of reason, they would die. Their survival, beyond a very short term, depends on someone's rational thinking. As Rand puts it in *Atlas*

---

[26] John Lewis Gaddis, *The Landscape of History* (New York: Oxford University Press, 2002), p. 111.

[27] Rand, "The Objectivist Ethics," p. 23. See a fuller discussion there.

Shrugged, for human beings, the question 'to be or not to be' is essentially the question 'to think or not to think.'[28]

The case for rationality is so basic that it requires little elaboration. Indeed, the belief that one should defend rationality with rational argument presupposes the propriety of rationality.[29] Nonetheless, to grasp the case fully, it is instructive to highlight three more specific conditions that necessitate rationality for anyone who seeks to live.

"Rationality is the recognition of the fact that existence exists, that nothing can alter the truth . . ."[30] Here, Rand is naming the fundamental fact to which the virtue of rationality is a response, what she calls the primacy of existence. (This is the first condition.) The primacy of existence refers to the fact that existence is independent of consciousness, that things' nature is not a product of anyone's thoughts or feelings, that wishes do not make things so. Everything that exists has a definite identity that is independent of individuals' beliefs or desires about its identity.[31]

Rand is not denying things' capacity to change or human beings' ability to alter certain things. Nor is she denying that mental phenomena can be shaped by beliefs and wishes. A person's optimism, for instance, may well be an outgrowth of his beliefs; anger typically depends on beliefs about an injustice. To understand Rand's point, we must understand her distinction between "metaphysically given" facts, such as the existence of a mountain or the chemical composition of water, and manmade facts, such as the existence of a skyscraper or the ingredients of a painkiller. The "metaphysically given" refers to "any fact inherent in existence apart from human action (whether mental or physical)," whereas the manmade refers to facts of human origin, whether physical objects, institutions, practices, musical compositions, war plans, moral codes, beliefs, and the like.[32] The primacy of existence affirms that even those things that a person can create or alter remain governed by existents' mind-independent identities. That is, the manmade is subject to the metaphysically given. I cannot ascend to the fourth floor of Waggener Hall by levitating. I can reach the fourth floor by climbing the stairs or taking the elevator, as long as those were built in ways that respect relevant materials, the weight of human beings, and the like. The point is that "the nature of nature is

---

[28] Rand, *Atlas Shrugged*, p. 1012. Also see "The Objectivist Ethics," p. 25.

[29] Rand comments on this in *Ayn Rand Answers*, pp. 159–160.

[30] Rand, *Atlas Shrugged*, p. 1018.

[31] Rand, "The Metaphysical Versus the Manmade," in *Philosophy: Who Needs It*, p. 29.

[32] Peikoff, *Objectivism*, pp. 23–24. Some of these examples are his, some mine.

outside the power of any volition."[33] Consciousness is a faculty of awareness of that which exists, not a faculty of manipulation of that which
exists. No activity of consciousness *by itself* can alter anything external to
that consciousness. Things are what they are and no amount of believing
or wishing them to be different will make them different. Rand is sec-
onding Francis Bacon's dictum that nature, to be commanded, must be
obeyed.[34]

If wishes did make things so, we would have no need for reason. Why
identify facts or integrate new information with previous knowledge, as
rationality instructs, if, instead, one could change facts at will? Why seek
to identify the cause of cancer, as part of a search for a cure, if one could
simply wish tumors into benign impotence? Why scrutinize income and
expenditures at a business, evaluating the efficiency of various aspects
of the operation, in order to increase profit margins if the relevant
facts about markets, management, and manufacturing techniques could
be altered by wish? Clearly, this is ridiculous; we know that they cannot be. The primacy of existence demands that human beings exercise
rationality.

The other two conditions that mandate rationality concern *our* nature
(which is encompassed by the primacy of existence, but is only part of
its domain). Human beings possess free will. We control our actions and,
even more basically, we control our mental processes. Even if a person
opens his eyes (which is a good start for getting to know the world),
sound conclusions will not spontaneously pour into him. He needs to
exert a deliberate effort to understand what he is observing and to tie
his thoughts to reality. Each individual decides whether to use his mind
and how to use his mind. A biologist could fudge his findings; a business
manager could cook the books; you or I could surrender to emotions or
prejudice or an array of other nonrational paths in any belief-forming
process or decision-making situation. It is only because we control how
we will proceed that the direction to be rational makes sense.

The third condition is closely related: human fallibility. With free will
comes the possibility of making better and worse choices. Our thoughts
do not necessarily reflect reality, yet they need to, for us to achieve the
values that sustain our lives. Human beings do not automatically think
rationally and even when we do exert the effort to track reality, we can

---

33 Rand, "The Metaphysical Versus the Manmade," p. 30.
34 Rand, "The Metaphysical Versus the Manmade," p. 31. See Peikoff, *Objectivism*, pp. 17–30,
   for a much fuller discussion of the primacy of existence and the metaphysically given.

make mistakes. This is why we must employ a specific method designed to keep us on track. Because our thinking is not automatically accurate, we need to take deliberate measures to achieve accuracy. We need to discipline our thinking by reason. (Reason's instruction can be specified in much greater detail through the laws of logic and epistemology, of course.)

Before leaving the rationale for rationality, consider a policy of not being rational. If rationality essentially consists in fidelity to reality, in trying to learn the relevant facts on any issue and to identify feasible means of achieving specific purposes, then irrationality is "the deliberate suspension of consciousness." It is the refusal to see or to think or to know, as Peikoff puts it.[35] It is difficult to imagine success at any enterprise from such a posture. Even in areas that might seem far removed from the rigors of rationality, such as romance or vacation or when simply "hanging out," a person must attend to the relevant facts of tastes, time, budget, and the like, if he is not to frustrate his ends. To not govern one's thinking and actions by evidence and logic, to turn away from reality, would be to jeopardize all of one's values. Knowledge cannot ensure success, but irrationality invites failure. Human beings cannot afford the luxury of indifference to reality. Since we inhabit a world of a definite nature, it behooves us to learn and respect things' nature in order for our actions to have a chance of achieving objective values and advancing our lives.

None of this recommends passive submission to the nature of things. Human beings have made staggering improvements to nature that have incalculably enriched our lives. Rand eloquently celebrates such advances. Such changes are possible, however, only by acting in recognition of things' nature and devising effective means of altering things, within the parameters set by things' nature. It is only by respecting the primacy of existence, in other words, that we can make constructive changes. It is only through rationality.

Some, no doubt, would object that although counsel to be rational is perfectly sensible, rationality is not a *moral* virtue. Rand, however, sees no authority in morality apart from its prudential necessity. Having defended a naturalistic theory in which moral prescriptions are dictated by our needs and having defended the idea that value is intelligible only in relation to an organism's quest for its life, the fact that rationality is a practical tool for advancing the values that fuel a person's life is exactly

---

[35] Peikoff, *Objectivism*, p. 222. The virtue of rationality does not require omniscience or infallibility.

what makes it moral. A naturalistic account of morality denies a sharp distinction between the moral and the prudential. Morality is prudent.[36]

The pivotal observation, again, is that reason is man's means of survival. In an ethics whose aim is life, rationality is thus critical. Rationality is our only means of learning the nature of the world we must navigate, the specific ends that can lead to our happiness, and the kinds of actions needed to achieve those ends. Thus we must be rational to succeed. Because reason is exercised by choice, we must identify the value of following reason and instruct ourselves to follow it. This is what Rand does, by naming rationality a virtue.

RATIONALITY'S PRACTICAL DEMANDS

If we now appreciate the need for rationality, we should try to understand more exactly what this virtue demands of us. As the broadest, overarching virtue, rationality requires the exercise of the six more specific virtues that I will explain in subsequent chapters. Before examining those, however, it is useful to recognize the most basic demands of rationality itself.

Focus

The core of rationality's demands is stated in a passage we have already cited: "The virtue of rationality means . . . one's total commitment to a state of full, conscious awareness, to the maintenance of a full mental focus in all issues, in all choices, in all of one's waking hours." Rand continues: "It means a commitment to the fullest perception of reality within one's power and to the constant, active expansion of one's perception, i.e., of one's knowledge."[37] The cardinal requirement of the virtue of rationality, in other words, is that a person actively strive to *know*. For knowledge is essential to a human being's ability to take the kinds of actions that will propel his life.

In some respects, this is a simple demand. Recall that Rand describes reason as the faculty by which we identify and integrate the data acquired through our senses. The importance, in a rational process, of identifying what things are is often under-appreciated. Most of us tend to regard highly abstract, complex integrations as paradigm instances of rationality.

---

[36] Foot points out that the idea of contrasting prudence and morality was alien to Plato and Aristotle, p. 68. I discuss the relationship between prudence and morality in *Viable Values*, pp. 157–158.

[37] Rand, "The Objectivist Ethics," p. 28.

Impressive as such feats can be, however, they do not exhaust the exercise of rationality. Any integration of ideas is only as valid as the identifications on which it is premised.[38] The more accurate and complete a person's identifications of facts, the better position he will be in to make fruitful integrations and thus to expand his knowledge. Accordingly, rationality demands the attempt to identify phenomena as fully and precisely as possible. Is this a case of irresponsibility on my employee's part, for instance, or an innocent mistake? Or not truly his mistake at all, but the result of some other intervening factor? Am I simply feeling down today or is there more to it? Is the real feeling bottled up anger?

The requirement to seek knowledge encompasses introspection, given that a person's own beliefs and attitudes can be pivotal to his ability to draw rational conclusions and take life-enhancing action. Acting from erroneous premises about one's own thoughts, desires, or feelings is a recipe for failure. If I suppress my misgivings about a prospective business partner, I will be more likely to make foolish, self-destructive decisions. If I fail to probe my feelings of boredom with my marriage, I will not make appropriate decisions about working to improve or to end the relationship. To be rational, a person must seek to know his own purposes and motives – indeed, all of his beliefs, desires, and feelings – as clearly as possible.[39]

However rudimentary or sophisticated the content that a person is pursuing, be it a simple identification of the fact that it is raining or a complex integration concerning improved techniques for angioplasty, what makes knowledge possible is the "full mental focus" that Rand refers to. Man's basic vice, correspondingly, "is the act of unfocusing his mind, the suspension of his consciousness, which is not blindness, but the refusal to see, not ignorance, but the refusal to know."[40] Peikoff describes focus as purposeful alertness, a readiness to think. He likens our mind's need to focus to our eyes' need to focus before they can perceive anything. To focus mentally is to raise one's level of awareness so as to use one's intelligence fully.[41] Rationality requires that a person be on

---

[38] Rand disagrees with the prevalent use of "validity" to refer exclusively to the relationship between premises and conclusion, independently of the truth of the premises. Our reason to care about such relationships is to gain knowledge, she contends, and to disregard the truth of premises obstructs that purpose. Obviously, attention to the relationship between premises and conclusion can be useful for more limited purposes.

[39] Rand, "The Objectivist Ethics," p. 28. Also see Peikoff, *Objectivism*, p. 226.

[40] Rand, "The Objectivist Ethics," pp. 27–28. Also see *Journals of Ayn Rand*, p. 626.

[41] Peikoff, *Objectivism*, pp. 56, 58.

the lookout to learn by paying attention, by exerting an active effort to gain knowledge (since knowledge is necessary for the achievement of his values).

One alternative to focus is passive drift, mentally meandering wherever one's thoughts happen to be led, releasing the reins of control and attending to ideas – or not – with no particular purpose or discipline. A more active alternative is evasion, deliberately blanking out some fact of reality. This reflects a willful disintegration of one's knowledge and thus a greater affront to rationality.[42] A person evades when he chooses not to know, not to find out, or when he pretends not to be aware of something that he knows warrants greater weight in his thinking or at least, further investigation. In forming a judgment about another person, for instance, an evader might ignore evidence contrary to the conclusion he is reaching, such as that what he had attributed to an employee's indifference is actually the result of other factors in the production process. Evasion operates again when I know that what I am doing is risky – driving this fast in this downpour – but I'd rather not think about the dangers and assess rationally whether I should proceed, so I simply charge ahead as if my misgivings never occurred to me.

When a person evades, he attempts to protect himself from certain possibilities by locking out thoughts of them, ignoring pertinent information about external facts or about his own doubts or questions. The person proceeds as if the primacy of existence did not obtain and as if not thinking about a fact could eradicate it. The result of such a practice is a diminished ability to navigate whatever circumstances the person actually does confront. Evasion cripples a person's capacity to achieve objective values and thereby advance his life. An evader might obtain some fleeting comfort from avoiding unpleasant or inconvenient thoughts. Because ignoring facts does not change them, however, evasion can only engender ill-premised, counterproductive actions.

If rationality is life's central demand and primary virtue, then evasion, the deliberate refusal to acknowledge reality, is Rand's equivalent of a mortal sin.[43] Indeed, evasion is the great enabler of more obviously immoral actions. Most people will rarely take an action in the full, conscious belief that it is wrong. Instead, typically, people ignore their awareness of the reasons not to take an action or they artfully distort those reasons by redescribing what they are doing. They step out of focus, in

---

[42] Peikoff, *Objectivism*, pp. 61, 224. Also see Rand, *Atlas Shrugged*, p. 1017.
[43] Peikoff, *Objectivism*, p. 224.

other words, to avoid identifying the true nature of the action. In this way, they can feign their own moral approval.[44]

In holding that rationality demands focus, Rand's claim is not that a person must engage in the most challenging thinking possible to him at all times, pursuing innovative integrations round the clock. Focus is not the same thing as problem solving (although focus will be needed when a person is problem solving). Focus, as the basic "set" of one's mind, is compatible with an array of more and less intellectually taxing activities; a person can be focused while relaxing, as long as he has made a rational decision to relax and he remains ready to attend to events that may warrant interrupting his relaxation.[45] Rationality does demand that a person never permit himself to drift into a complete fog, however, relinquishing control over his mind and allowing it to be pushed and pulled entirely by random stimuli.[46] While a person can focus to differing degrees, I have concentrated on the extremes in order to convey the essential idea. What is most important to grasp is the ideal: the person who maintains an active mind intent on understanding whatever it deals with, the person who "struggles to grasp facts *clearly*, with the greatest precision possible to him."[47]

Expanding One's Knowledge

In elaborating on the demands of rationality, Rand speaks of the commitment to the "constant, active expansion" of one's knowledge.[48] It is not enough for a person to rest content with the knowledge that he already possesses for the simple reason that additional information is likely to affect what his goals should be and the best means of attaining them. To take the simplest example, consider how often, in recent years, technological innovations have improved our standard of living, creating

---

[44] Rand makes a brief reference to this in her journals, remarking that rather than do what he considers evil, a man will normally suspend his rational judgment. *Journals of Ayn Rand*, p. 559.

[45] See Peikoff, *Objectivism*, p. 58. Rand refers to focus as the set of one's mind and distinguishes focus from concentration in *Ayn Rand Answers*, p. 154.

[46] Rand, "The Objectivist Ethics," p. 22. A person can mentally wander purposefully (e.g., to relax, to calm his mind, to generate potentially useful ideas), but given such a purpose, these would not be cases of allowing his mind to be tugged completely by chance. A person who is purposefully wandering will prod himself to keep wandering if he finds his thinking becoming too single-tracked, for instance.

[47] Peikoff, *Objectivism*, p. 57.

[48] Rand, "The Objectivist Ethics," p. 28.

products and services that enhance ease of communication, the efficiency of a business, or the convenience of completing everyday tasks. A person must learn of such developments, however, in order to take full advantage of them. In countless ways large and small, knowledge strengthens a person's ability to achieve values that advance his life. Everything from learning about a better route to work to learning about new treatments of an illness can significantly contribute to a person's flourishing. Knowledge is what we rely on to move our lives forward.

While I have already stressed the importance of accurate and thorough identification to rational thinking, equally crucial is the other element that Rand names in her definition of reason, integration. Integration consists of tracing the relationships between what one learns in discrete experiences so as to expand one's understanding of the world. The formation of concepts is itself one type of integration; the building of conceptual knowledge into the grasp of more sophisticated relationships is another.[49] Whether simple or complex, however, at core, integration requires that a person seek to draw logical inferences so as to widen his knowledge. He can do so largely by pursuing questions, such as, "So if this is true, what else must be true? Does this new information lend further support to any previous beliefs? Does it contradict any?" Some such questions will occur naturally to many people and might be easily answered; other questions will be less obvious or more difficult to resolve. Either way, integrating what one does know and seeking out ever more knowledge – new information as well as new relationships – are vital means of advancing one's life. A person must actively work to expand his knowledge for the simple reason that reality, and how he deals with the facts of reality, will determine whether or not he lives. The fuller a person's awareness of reality, the better able he will be to master reality to achieve his happiness.

The kind of dedication to extending knowledge that rationality calls for is not a matter of intelligence, Rand repeatedly observes.[50] It is a matter of exerting the simple effort to know more, at whatever level is possible to a person. Nor does it mean that a person must become an intellectual. The aim of rationality is not knowledge for its own sake, but

---

[49] Rand understands a concept as "a mental integration of two or more units possessing the same distinguishing characteristics with their particular measurement(s) omitted," *Introduction to Objectivist Epistemology*, p. 13.

[50] Rand explicitly distinguishes errors of knowledge from breaches of morality in *Atlas Shrugged*, p. 1059. Also see Peikoff, *Objectivism*, p. 223, and *Journals of Ayn Rand*, pp. 556, 626.

knowledge for its practical value. Indeed, this is precisely why the virtue of rationality demands integration and expansion of knowledge: These enable a person to act successfully. Knowledge equips a person to make effective decisions in every area of life: work, health, finances, recreation, politics, personal relationships, and so on.[51]

The main point, again, is that intellectual complacency and stagnation stifle a person's ability to live. Facts do not exist in isolation from one another. Developments in one area often carry effects, obvious or obscure, in others. A new kind of financial product offered on Wall Street can affect the diabetes treatments available within a couple of years; the appointment of a college dean can affect the kind of extracurricular activities encouraged in high school. Because every feature of reality stands in numerous relationships to others and because all features can carry a range of effects that bear a direct impact on a person's ability to achieve his happiness, rationality demands the integration and ongoing expansion of one's knowledge. The wider and deeper a person's knowledge, the better position he will be in to steer his life successfully.[52]

Acting by Reason

Because rationality's claim on us stems entirely from its practicality, it should be obvious that the virtue of rationality requires that a person act in accordance with rational judgments. As Aristotle observes, "someone is not intelligent simply by knowing; he must also act on his knowledge."[53] The whole point of reasoning is to guide our actions. This entails that a person adopt goals only after carefully considering his full context – goals' feasibility in light of his particular abilities, weaknesses, time, financial resources, the relative significance of his other commitments, and so on. It means making plans by heeding all relevant

---

[51] See Peikoff, *Objectivism*, p. 223. An intellectual need not pursue knowledge for its own sake, though that is a common image of intellectuals that is based on the practice of many intellectuals.

[52] Integration is actually a type of expansion, yet the two are not synonymous, since a person can expand his knowledge by acquiring completely new information that he does not or cannot yet fully integrate with his preexisting knowledge. In such a situation, a person should give himself the standing order to be on the lookout for evidence of that new information's relationship to other of his knowledge so that he can eventually integrate it. For a detailed discussion of integration, see Peikoff, *Objectivism*, pp. 121–128, especially 125–128.

[53] Aristotle, *Nicomachean Ethics* 1152a8, trans. Terence Irwin (Indianapolis: Hackett, 1985). This translation puts the point more starkly than the 1999 edition.

facts – about the propriety of his objectives, for instance, the time and energy appropriate to spend on them, the challenges he can expect to encounter in their pursuit. It means respecting his hierarchy of values and thus not acting as if a particular end is more valuable to him than it truly is (as we are often tempted to by emotions or the proximity of other people).

One of the most elementary requirements of rationality is the responsibility of respecting causality. "One must never desire effects without causes," Rand writes, and "one must never enact a cause without assuming full responsibility for its effects."[54] Whether a person is contemplating acquiring a pet or getting married, undertaking a career in plumbing or with the CIA, rationality demands identifying and accepting what will be necessary to achieve his end as well as readiness to deal with the consequences of his choices. A person "accepts" and "deals with" by taking appropriate actions. Responsibility is not discharged by merely mouthing words (as one might conclude from public officials' often hollow professions of taking responsibility). If I wish to work for the CIA, I should acquire the skills that the agency seeks; if I accept a post in foreign service, I should not continually clamor for a more stable family life stateside. Plumbing will involve dirty hands and weekend calls; a dog will have to be fed. While seemingly obvious, such requirements of rationality are frequently unappreciated.[55]

The larger point is simply that rationality requires action that is faithful to a person's rational conclusions, adherence to reality in action as well as in thought. Just as a person can evade certain thoughts when thinking about an issue, he can evade when it comes to acting by ignoring his convictions (including his knowledge of his own values or uncertainties). Such a course, by relegating reason to the plane of theory *detached* from practice, treats rationality as a game. In fact, thought divorced from action, regardless of how rational the thought, is useless, as intellectual exercises by themselves cannot sustain human lives. Rationality is a virtue because it is indispensable to the kind of action necessary to achieve human flourishing. Correspondingly, the virtue of rationality demands rationality in action.[56]

---

[54] Rand, "The Objectivist Ethics," p. 28.
[55] Rationality does not preclude a person's ever changing his mind after finding an activity different from what he had expected. It does require that he try to make informed decisions, however.
[56] See Rand, "The Objectivist Ethics," p. 58, and Peikoff, *Objectivism*, p. 226, for more on rationality's requirements of action.

Absolutism

Throughout her discussion of the virtue of rationality, Rand insists on an uncompromising adherence to reason. This virtue "means a commitment to reason, not in sporadic fits or on selected issues or in special emergencies, but as a permanent way of life." Passages already quoted include references to a "total commitment" to awareness and to "full mental focus."[57] What stands behind these strong claims is respect for the primacy of existence.

When a person misrepresents his grasp of reality, he sabotages his consciousness' role as his faculty of awareness and thereby undermines its ability to advance his life. As Rand puts it in *Atlas Shrugged*, "irrationality turns one's consciousness from the task of perceiving reality to the task of faking reality."[58] Faking cannot work, however. Any form of irrationality (deliberate irrationality, not an innocent mistake) is counterproductive, given that things' natures do not bend to accommodate the beliefs or desires of an individual's consciousness. My wish that a health irritation does not reflect a serious illness does not determine whether it does; my hope that I can pass the test without studying does not determine whether I pass.

When a person acts irrationally, he erects some consideration other than reality as his ultimate standard for drawing conclusions. He thus reveals that even on those occasions when he does proceed by reason, he does so only on the permission of that higher authority – be it his mood or intuition, his faith in the supernatural or trust in the opinion of fifty million Frenchmen or an erratically revolving series of such irrational rulers. Reason is not his sovereign.

A person's commitment to rationality must be absolute, however, because reality is absolute. The nature of reality cannot be merely an intermittent concern, flickering in and out of significance. It is a fundamental, full-time, all-encompassing master for anyone who seeks to remain in reality. Human existence does not depend on respecting facts *and* on something else that is equally, or occasionally more, important. There is no alternative, back alley route to satisfying life's requirements. Heeding reality is the only way to succeed. A person has nothing to gain from misrepresenting or trying to defy reality. The facts of reality set the terms of existence and thus of success in all activities that could fuel a person's existence. Accordingly, a person's achievement of his life

---

[57] Rand, "The Objectivist Ethics," pp. 29, 28.
[58] Rand, *Atlas Shrugged*, p. 1018.

and happiness lies in respecting those facts through uncompromising rationality.[59]

Rand's emphasis on the absolutist nature of rationality's demands is especially valuable, given the form in which we most often encounter irrationality in others and flirt with irrationality, ourselves. Few people reject reason wholesale. (It would be difficult to do so and remain alive.)[60] Rather, most people employ reason selectively, abiding by reason in some areas and not others or cutting corners on those occasions when following reason seems unpleasant or too much trouble. Given these prevalent practices, it is useful to be attuned to the importance of always, unwaveringly, guiding one's thinking by reality.

It is also worth noting that this absolutism will extend to all of the virtues, insofar as each is simply an application of rationality to specific types of issues. Rand's virtues identify the fundamental principles that human life requires. To say that rationality or honesty or justice is proper in principle is to say that it is proper in every particular case of the relevant kind. We must ascertain which cases are the relevant kind that are governed by a given principle by careful consideration of the full context, of course, but when a principle or its corresponding virtue does govern, it does so absolutely; its authority is unequivocal. Furthermore, as should become clearer over the course of the book, because all virtues reflect the master virtue of rationality, to cheat on any one of them is to abandon rationality and thus to abandon reality as the ultimate sovereign of one's action. Because all virtues concern the proper relationship of one's mind to reality (of consciousness to existence, as Rand puts it), any deliberate defiance of the proper relationship subverts the person's ability to live. Deliberate violations of valid principles are self-destructive in the same way that suicide attempts are self-destructive. Just as the person who leaps from a rooftop is subverting his life (even if he happens to be spared because of a passing, open-topped mattress truck), so the person who defies rational moral principles is subverting his ability to live. He is setting his mind on a course that is antithetical to the requirements of living.[61]

---

[59] For more on this, see Peikoff, *Objectivism*, pp. 159–163, and *Ayn Rand Answers*, pp. 168–169.

[60] Peikoff, *Objectivism*, pp. 224–225, and *Journals of Ayn Rand*, p. 558.

[61] I will discuss absolutism further in later chapters, particularly in the chapter on integrity. While discussing the suicide analogy with Onkar Ghate, Amy Peikoff, Leonard Peikoff, Robert Mayhew, and Greg Salmieri, one of them suggested the mattress scenario, but I cannot recall who.

Renouncing Emotionalism

To complete our inventory of rationality's most basic practical requirements, we should notice a negative demand, something that rationality
rules out: emotionalism. While I have noted in passing various forms of
irrationality (deference to faith, intuition, popular opinion, etc.), underlying these and posing the single greatest challenge to rationality is the
pull of emotions.[62] Thus, it is worth clarifying emotions' place vis-à-vis
rationality.

The nature of emotions is itself a subject of extensive debate at the
intersection of philosophy, psychology, and neuroscience.[63] While much
of the dispute about the nature of emotions turns on the relative roles of
cognitions, feelings, and desires, even the best characterization of competing schools of thought is a subject of disagreement.[64] Rather than
enter into these intricate debates, it should suffice for our purposes simply to indicate how Rand understands emotions.

An emotion is a state of consciousness with bodily accompaniments
and intellectual causes, Peikoff writes.[65] More specifically, an emotion
is an affective response to a subconscious evaluation of a perceived or
considered object.[66] Most basically, Rand holds, that evaluation concerns
whether the object is thought to be beneficial or harmful.[67] A sheer bodily
sensation does not depend on any such evaluations. If a person scalds his
arm, stubs his toe, has his back massaged, or immerses himself in a warm
bath, the resulting pain or pleasure is a purely physical reaction that he

---

[62] See Peikoff, *Objectivism*, pp. 160–161.

[63] See, for instance, Paul E. Griffiths, *What Emotions Really Are* (Chicago: University of
Chicago Press, 1997); Steven Pinker, *How the Mind Works* (New York: Norton, 1997);
Antonio R. Damasio, *Descartes' Error – Emotion, Reason and the Human Brain* (New York:
Avon, 1994); Robert C. Solomon, *The Passions: Emotions and the Meaning of Life* (Indianapolis: Hackett, 1993); Solomon, ed., *What Is an Emotion?: Classic and Contemporary Readings* (New York: Oxford University Press, 2003).; Solomon, ed., *Thinking About Feeling: Contemporary Philosophers on Emotions* (New York: Oxford University Press, 2004);
Martha Nussbaum, *Upheavals of Thought: The Intelligence of Emotions* (New York: Cambridge University Press, 2001); Patricia Greenspan, *Emotions and Reasons* (New York: Routledge, 1988); Ronald de Sousa, *The Rationality of Emotion* (Cambridge, MA: MIT Press,
1987); A. O. Rorty, ed., *Explaining Emotions* (Los Angeles: University of California Press,
1980).

[64] See Griffiths, chapter 1, and Paul Newberry, "Joseph Butler on Forgiveness: A Presupposed Theory of Emotion," *Journal of the History of Ideas* 62 (April 2001), pp. 233–244.

[65] Peikoff, *Objectivism*, p. 154.

[66] Harry Binswanger, "Emotions," two lectures, Objectivist Conference, Summer 2002,
Tysons Corner, VA.

[67] Rand, "The Objectivist Ethics," p. 30. See pp. 30–31 for more of Rand's explanation of
emotions.

will feel regardless of his beliefs or values. The experience of an emotion, however, depends on a person's identification of a given object and his evaluation of it. I will feel anxiety, for instance, if I come to believe that someone who I care about a great deal is in danger. I will feel elation if I come to believe that a cause that I cherish has made a substantial advance. Absent the relevant beliefs and values, I will experience no such emotions. Learning the average noontime temperature in Madagascar in March will leave me cold, as I am aware of no reason to care about that.

To observe the roots of our emotions is not to reduce emotions to those roots. An emotion remains a feeling, an affective response. With certain emotions, a person will feel a rush of adrenaline or buoyancy; with certain others, he will feel limp or lethargic. The salient point is simply that whether a person feels an emotion and what emotion he feels will depend on his beliefs about a particular object and on his evaluations of that object. This explains the familiar experience of different individuals responding to the same event with diametrically opposed emotions – for example, cheering or lamenting a Supreme Court ruling or a person's firing or a team's touchdown because they regard different outcomes as valuable. As Harry Binswanger aptly observes, emotions are the voice of values in one's consciousness.[68]

Given Rand's view of the basic nature of emotions, it should not be difficult to appreciate why the virtue of rationality forbids emotionalism. Emotionalism does not consist of feeling one's emotions, but of allowing emotions to replace thoughts as the decisive grounds for one's conclusions or actions.[69] If Alex is feeling down and therefore charges $1,000 of merchandise on eBay simply to cheer himself up – without bothering to consider whether he really needs the items in question, whether he can afford them, or has any grounds legitimizing this binge (which it is, on his income) – he is engaging in emotionalism. If Roger phones in sick simply because he doesn't feel like going to work today – without thinking through what needs to be done at work, what will happen to that work in his absence (will deadlines be missed? will deals be lost? will only heavier burdens await his return?), or what the likely effects will be on his coworkers or on his superiors' evaluation of him – he is engaging in emotionalism. When acting on emotion, a person proceeds as if his feeling is all the "reason" he needs.

[68] Binswanger, "Emotions."
[69] Peikoff, *Objectivism*, p. 162.

The problem is, it isn't. In a reasoning process, emotions cannot be substituted for facts because emotions are not tools of cognition.[70] The beliefs and values pivotal in generating a person's emotions might be invalid. A person could misinterpret the object that triggers his emotional reaction or misunderstand its impact on his values. He could also have made mistakes in originally adopting those values. Holly might consider a new directive at work a serious threat to her position and thus feel fear because she underestimates her own abilities. Megan might seek a certain candidate's election and thus feel glad at his campaign's advances, when his defeat would actually better serve her interest. Acting on the basis of emotions that are premised on faulty foundations is not an effective means of advancing one's life. Moreover, even when the beliefs and values responsible for a person's emotions are perfectly justified (suppose Roger has good reason for wanting that day off), the sheer fact that a person keenly wants something does not mean that his having it is, all things considered, in his best interest. To indulge a desire (or any emotion) at any cost, however understandable the desire or emotion, ignores an array of relevant facts. Determining the proper course of action requires attention to all of them, including the reasons for one's emotions and the effects of the various ways that one might act in the face of them. (Roger might have good reason for *wanting* a day off without having good reason, all things considered, for taking one.)

Although emotions are not tools of cognition, they can be a tip-off to certain of a person's beliefs and values. If a person examines the sources of the emotions that he feels, he can gain useful knowledge about himself. The beliefs and values underlying his emotional reactions do not necessarily accurately reflect external reality, however. "An emotion as such tells you nothing about reality, beyond the fact that something makes you feel something," Rand observes.[71]

Rationality does not forbid consulting one's emotions. In many situations, it is perfectly rational to consider one's feelings: Would I enjoy going

---

[70] Rand, *For the New Intellectual* (New York: Random House, 1961), p. 64. I am assuming that the person is not reasoning about the nature of his own experience. If he were introspecting as a means of understanding his own psychological tendencies, for instance, his emotions could be among the relevant facts.

[71] Rand, "Philosophical Detection," in *Philosophy: Who Needs It*, p. 20. Because emotions result from complex interactions of conscious and subconscious premises, it can be difficult at times to accurately diagnose the roots of one's emotions. People often attribute their feelings to superficial causes out of habit or fear of confronting deeper and potentially more disturbing roots.

to that jazz club? Do I like this person who has asked me to dinner? Do I derive satisfaction from this kind of work? For certain purposes, such feelings should be taken into account as relevant factors for making a decision. One can take feelings into account, however, without granting them the final say. Consulting one's emotions is not the same as handing emotions the sole decision-making reins. The proper weight to accord to emotions depends on the issue – on facts about the kind of issue it is that obtain independently of the person's feelings about the issue. Given that enjoyment of a night off is normally a legitimately large factor in deciding how to spend a night off, for example, considering one's likely enjoyment of a jazz club or of another person's company warrants greater weight for that decision than when contemplating taking a day off from work. The fact that I might enjoy time with Bill is a more significant factor when deciding whether to have dinner with him than whether to play hooky.

In rejecting emotionalism, then, Rand is not recommending that we ignore or suppress our emotions. The virtue of rationality does not oppose emotions per se. She recognizes that emotions are crucial to happiness.[72] As Peikoff elaborates, "Emotions play an essential role in human life, and in this role they must be felt, nourished, respected. Without such a faculty, men could not achieve happiness or even survival; they would experience no desire, no love, no fear, no motivation, no response to values."[73] The fact remains, however, that feelings are not reliable indicators of external reality. What a person feels does not directly tell him anything about the object of his feeling, but only about his estimate of it. Just as "one casts no aspersion on eating or breathing if one denies that they are means of cognition," Peikoff observes, one casts no aspersion on emotions if one insists that emotions not be treated as if they had grander powers of knowing external reality than they do.[74]

CONCLUSION

Rand understands moral virtues to encompass both cognition and action. A person's virtue reflects his demonstrated commitment, evidenced in steadfast practice, to act in recognition of a particular moral principle,

---

[72] Rand, "*Playboy*'s Interview with Ayn Rand," March 1964, reprint pamphlet published by *The Intellectual Activist*, p. 6.

[73] Peikoff, *Objectivism*, p. 161.

[74] Peikoff, *Objectivism*, pp. 161–162.

such as honesty or justice. Virtuous action is a person's means of maintaining his life. Since rationality is the fundamental requirement of human life, rationality is the fundamental moral virtue.

The virtue of rationality means the acceptance of reason as one's only source of knowledge and guidance. Essentially, rationality consists of fidelity to reality, of grounding one's beliefs and actions in the way things are (as best one can discern). Because human beings inhabit reality, we must learn and respect the nature of reality if we are to remain here. Given the primacy of existence, the volitional character of human action and human fallibility, we must discipline our thinking by rationality.

The virtue of rationality demands ongoing reality checks. More specifically, it demands an active effort to focus, to identify, to integrate, and to expand one's knowledge. Since the ultimate authority of rationality lies in its necessity for human life, rationality further demands an unwavering commitment to acting by reason and a refusal to indulge in emotionalism. Sound as this guidance is, however, it is somewhat abstract. To make rationality's instruction more concrete and more readily useable, Rand identifies six major derivative virtues. To understand better how to put rationality into practice, let us turn next to the virtue of honesty.[75]

---

[75] Peikoff reports that Rand does not necessarily regard these six as an exhaustive inventory of moral virtues. *Objectivism*, p. 251.

4

Honesty

The virtue of honesty is perhaps the most obvious outgrowth of the virtue of rationality. Indeed, in notes to herself for Galt's speech, Rand refers to honesty as "only another name for rationality, the loyalty to reality, the 'being true to truth.'"[1] Honesty often seems integral to other virtues, such as justice and integrity, and it is probably the single most widely endorsed virtue by people of divergent views on many other aspects of morality's substantive instruction. Rand's rationale for honesty is quite distinctive, however. She advocates honesty for its service to the agent's self-interest. Most people would recoil at this, assuming that egoism frequently dictates dishonesty. Although people do, often enough, maintain that honesty is the best policy prudentially, this is usually offered as an inferior, supplemental appeal to the recalcitrant who are not convinced by "purer" arguments: "If *real* moral considerations won't move you, then you ought to consider this." To understand why honesty is essential to egoism, I will proceed in the same manner as in the chapter on rationality, explaining what honesty is, why it is a virtue, and the basic kinds of practical demands that it places on us.

WHAT HONESTY IS

Honesty, in Rand's view, means that a person "must never attempt to fake reality in any manner."[2] Notice immediately the breadth of this conception. Usually, discussion of honesty revolves around intentional

[1] *Journals of Ayn Rand*, p. 648.
[2] Rand, "The Objectivist Ethics," p. 28.

deception of others, getting another person to believe something other than the truth (or other than what one believes is the truth).[3] Others' beliefs are the pivot, and arguments over the propriety of honesty largely center around the costs and benefits likely to accrue from the manipulation of others' beliefs. Even those who renounce such consequentialist considerations tend to treat honesty as a social issue, contending that such manipulation of others is wrong in itself, for instance. Rand, in contrast, understands honesty not in terms of relationships with others but in terms of reality, of facts that are independent of people's beliefs about them. Other people and their beliefs are part of reality, of course, and for certain purposes, changing others' beliefs can be objectively important (e.g., about the effectiveness of a new treatment for an illness). The point here, however, is that people's opinions in themselves do not create the external facts that are the subjects of those opinions. Thus, on Rand's view, the most basic concern of honesty is not what others believe, but the discovery and acceptance of what is so.

Correspondingly, as a policy of refusing to fake things, honesty encompasses more than refraining from telling lies. (I will nevertheless use "liar" as a convenient shorthand for a person who engages in any form of dishonesty.) "Faking" does not carry any peculiar or technical meaning, as Rand uses it. "Faking" refers to familiar forms of pretending that things are other than they are, such as deliberately omitting pertinent information about a subject, covering something up, or twisting one's account of a situation to foster misleading impressions. An actor portraying a fictional character on stage would not be faking in the relevant sense, since it is understood that he is acting and that the audience is witnessing a play. Similarly, a person who has cosmetic surgery in order to improve his appearance is not dishonest. Given that people do not live under a tacit agreement to present themselves "as is" – unshaven, uncombed, and so on – such a person is morally quite different from the person who disguises himself in order to mislead (e.g., to impersonate another person so as to perpetrate a crime).

It is important to recognize that honesty and dishonesty would be equally possible if a person lived alone, isolated from society, since a person can fake with himself as well as others. He can pretend not to have

[3] See, for instance, Sissela Bok, *Lying: Moral Choice in Public and Private Life* (New York: Random House, 1999); Richard C. Cabot, *Honesty* (New York: MacMillan, 1938), p. 8; Charles Fried, "The Evil of Lying," in Sommers and Sommers, eds., *Vice and Virtue in Everyday Life* (1989, 2nd edition), p. 373.

learned what he has, not to care about the things that he does care about, not to have the questions that he does. Self-deception can be a tempting means of avoiding confronting unwelcome facts. (We will comment further on self-deception when we consider honesty's demands.)

The heart of honesty, again, is the refusal to fake reality. The honest person accepts reality and he portrays things as he sincerely believes them to be. We can go a bit further, however. If rationality essentially consists in the commitment to reality, Peikoff explains, then honesty is the obverse: the rejection of unreality, the recognition that *only* existence exists.[4]

At first blush, this may sound strange, since few of us suppose that we are tempted to entertain unreality. Yet on reflection, it is not unusual to find cases in which people do precisely that. Dishonesty often takes the form of attempts to stretch the truth or to supplement reality with the objects of a person's desires. Consider the person who tells himself: "I know I've reached my spending limits, but surely I can afford just this one other thing..." or "I know that cheesecake isn't on the diet the doctor insisted on, but it looks so good...surely I can have that *and* the cholesterol reduction I'm after." Or consider the person who prides himself on scrupulous adherence to logic as the basis for all his beliefs and actions, except when it comes to religion. Even while he recognizes the failure of various attempts to prove the existence of god, he allows a place for a little something extra beyond what rationality tells him reality contains.[5] The point is, while the caution against entertaining unreality may initially seem odd, such commonplace attempts to enhance reality with artificial supplements amount to as much. By emphasizing the rejection of unreality as an integral component of honesty, Peikoff is observing that honesty is not merely stenography. Our needs extend beyond passively recording and relaying what we happen to learn. A steadfast refusal to fake reality reflects the value of knowing reality and correlatively, the need for a conscientious, active effort to learn about it, to find out the way things are. As we noted in our discussion of rationality in Chapter 3, knowledge is not a given for human beings. It is not standard equipment, prepackaged within a person such that the only issue that honesty poses concerns how to represent one's knowledge. Because knowledge is not innate, instruction to reject the unreal and not to fake reality also indicates the need to seek knowledge in truth-respecting ways. Human beings need to know the world; honesty is vital to learning about it.

[4] Peikoff, *Objectivism*, pp. 267–268.
[5] John Elia suggested this example to me.

(We will say more about honesty's role in the acquisition of knowledge when we discuss the demands of honesty later in the chapter.)

The basic meaning of honesty is straightforward, in Rand's view. As the refusal to fake reality, honesty consists in a deliberate, principled renunciation of any evasion, distortion, misrepresentation, or artifice. In essence, honesty means not pretending.[6]

WHY HONESTY IS A VIRTUE

The argument for recognizing honesty as a virtue overlaps considerably with the argument for rationality. In her *Journals,* Rand remarks that "The virtue of honesty is implicit in the function of the rational faculty. Man requires the greatest, most ruthless honesty of observation and reasoning in order to reach as correct a conclusion as his rational capacity will permit."[7] The basic fact mandating the virtue of honesty is "that the unreal is unreal and can have no value…"[8] What is not so is not so. Because a value is that which advances a person's objective well-being and because only that which exists can carry positive effects on a person's well-being, only that which is real can be valuable to a person.

Bear in mind that existents (specific real, existing things) can take many forms. Rand is not denying that the imagined or the planned, for instance, can have value. Yet these things must be understood for what they are: imagined or planned. Because the future is not predetermined, individuals' thoughts can affect their actions and what happens in the future. A person's plans for how he will buy the house he desires or for how he will acquire the job he seeks can be valuable in enabling him to achieve those ends. Similarly, positive imaging – picturing himself doing well at some task – can be valuable in helping a person to improve his actual performance. These are not instances of the unreal being valuable, however, for a thought (like an image or a plan) is not unreal; it is a thought. And its potential value does not arise from its defying reality. Indeed, it is only relevantly realistic thoughts that can be constructive. If a person acted as if he had already done what he merely plans to do, for instance, or if an athlete trained as if he had already attained certain conditioning or skills that he has not, these imaginings would hardly carry him to his goal. If a person's plans were based on deliberate distortions of reality, they could not be effective.

---

[6] Peikoff, *Objectivism*, p. 270.
[7] Rand, *Journals of Ayn Rand*, p. 261.
[8] Rand, *Atlas Shrugged*, p. 1019.

Rand's basic contention is that faking is futile. For it does not create an alternate universe in which a person's wishes to alter certain facts become miraculously effective, dictating what is so. Life is not a screenplay-in-progress, with each individual enjoying the powers of author, able to add, cut, and alter at will. Although an individual does control his own actions (within the parameters set by his nature), he does not possess the power to manipulate reality by sheer exertion of will. All of this is a plain implication of the primacy of existence.

The argument for honesty, as Peikoff puts it, is that "since man lives in reality, he must conform to reality."[9] Given the nature of human beings and of our environment, we must understand reality and work with reality in order to live. Success at accomplishing any life-advancing end depends on respecting the relevant aspects of reality. If a physician ignores the CT scan results, he cannot prescribe effective treatment for his patient; if an electrician ignores faulty wiring, he cannot prepare a safe building for its occupants; if a man ignores signs of his own emotional deterioration, he cannot achieve happiness.

The fatal problem with dishonesty is that misrepresenting reality does not change it. We cannot will away the laws of identity or causality; we cannot will away our needs or the consequences of our actions. A person's wanting to be thin does not eradicate his need for nutrition, as anorexics tragically discover; a person's wanting to be happy does not mean that liquor provides the path, as alcoholics bitterly discover. Pretense is metaphysically impotent.[10] Pretending that things are other than they are does not make them other than they are. Pretending might make a person feel better, temporarily – it might divert a person from dark thoughts or elevate his spirits – but it cannot alter the facts of his situation.

Some facts are changeable, of course, as we noted when discussing the primacy of existence and the distinction between the metaphysical and the manmade. A person can learn French, dye his hair, develop a better golf swing or become more self-disciplined, for instance. He cannot change an externally imposed deadline, another person's basic character, or his own current capabilities (e.g., that he does not now know how to speak French). The point is that pretense cannot change anything. What changes we can effect can be achieved only by respecting the nature of what we are dealing with.

The moral propriety of honesty is thus grounded in basic truths of metaphysics: the law of identity and the primacy of existence. A thing is

[9] Peikoff, *Objectivism*, p. 269.
[10] Peikoff, *Objectivism*, p. 267.

what it is and things' natures do not depend on a person's perception of them, opinion of them, or attitudes or desires concerning them. Like it or not, cheesecake is fattening; speeding through a school zone is dangerous; not preparing for a test is a poor strategy for scoring well on it.

All of this has argued that honesty makes sense because we cannot fake facts. Since the motivation for dishonesty is usually the attempt to gain some value, it is important to understand that we cannot fake values, either.

Because the identification of values is a more abstract enterprise than the identification of many facts, it may seem easier to fake values. If a person denies the existence of a tree directly in front of him, we know that he needs to have his eyes examined. If a person denies the existence of some objective value (i.e., that it is a value), however, we cannot as readily locate the source of his error. Because all values are relational and because different things can be valuable to different human beings in many different ways, more and less direct, the identification of something as a value can be the conclusion of numerous layers of reasoning about various things' effects and ultimate impact on an individual's life. Consider the number of steps required to demonstrate the value of food to human beings as opposed to the number of steps required to demonstrate the value of cars – or the value of a career, or of friendship, or of justice, or of art. The greater the number and range of variables that affect whether a given object is valuable, the greater the possibility of misunderstanding that object's relationship to a person's life. Knowledge of certain facts, of course, can also require highly abstract reasoning, but insofar as even the most basic values depend on their relationship to something else, the identification of values requires more sophisticated judgments than does the recognition of many facts. Because things do not wear their value on their sleeves, it can seem easier to fake values than facts.

The objectivity of values, however, means that values are facts. A thing will be objectively valuable to a person insofar as it stands in a life-advancing relationship to him. Properly understood, claims about what is valuable purport to describe the factual relation of the object in question to the goal of the person's life. The important thing to grasp in regard to honesty is that such relationships are no more subservient to a person's wishes than are any other facts.[11]

If I misrepresent facts to another person, I might succeed in getting him to do what I want and thus achieve my immediate purpose,

[11] See Peikoff, *Objectivism*, pp. 268 and 241–248.

apparently gaining some value. I might trick someone into believing that I am more cultured or more qualified, more well-read or more with-it than I actually am. I might fool a school into accepting me or an employer into hiring me by deceiving them about my grades or experience. This does not equip me to perform the relevant work, however. My lies do not change the underlying facts concerning my knowledge or lack of knowledge, experience or inexperience, abilities or inabilities. Ultimately, it is those facts that I must work with in order to sustain my life. Dishonesty can sometimes fool other people, but it cannot fool reality.

Whenever a person is dishonest with others, one prominent consequence is the need to conceal his deception. While philosophers are often cavalier in bracketing that concern ("just assume that you could be sure you won't be found out"), in real life, such assurance is rarely possible. Even aside from that concern, however (to which I shall return shortly), the deeper problem with deception of others is that invented "goods" – as invented "facts" – cannot actually advance a person's life. Pretending that something stands in a life-supporting relation to me does not make it stand in that relation.

I began this discussion by citing Rand's claim "that the unreal is unreal and can have no value..."[12] By now, it should be obvious that it is *because* the unreal is unreal that it can have no value. Real values enhance our lives; make-believe values do not. It is reality that our existence demands we negotiate, not some imagined "sister" reality of one's mind's projection. Just as Monopoly money (I am referring to the board game) would not clear a person's debts, fabricated education or experience or accomplishments on his resume will not make his education or experience or accomplishments or correlative abilities any different than they actually are. Nor will it make the job that he might dupe someone into giving him objectively valuable for him. The sheer fact that a person wants something does not mean that having it would be good for him, even if it is a respectable aim or the sort of thing that normally would be good for him. Whether something is objectively good for a person depends on its full impact on all facets of that person's long-range well-being. Is a job good for a person? Is a promotion? Money? Marriage? Under certain circumstances. And only under those circumstances. Well-being cannot be measured in isolation from the entire context. We cannot evaluate a single end as good or bad for a person without considering his means

[12] Rand, *Atlas Shrugged*, p. 1019.

of obtaining that end and the effects of those means on other of the person's values.

As we saw in Chapter 2, value is not a property inhering in certain things (such as jobs) such that whoever gets his hands on those things has thereby gained a value. Value is relational to a specific person. It is a function of a thing's playing a life-furthering role in that individual's life. Consequently, even the things that are most commonly valuable to human beings will not necessarily be valuable to anyone. A thing's value to a person depends on the role that it plays vis-à-vis his long-term flourishing. What role a thing plays, in turn, depends in part on how a person obtains it. For a person's means of obtaining one thing often carry ramifications for his ability to gain others. It would make no sense to pursue a near term "gain" by methods that sabotage one's longer-term welfare (e.g., earning a profit this year by employing means that will bankrupt the business soon thereafter, or enjoying one's retirement by spending all of one's savings on a lavish vacation as soon as one shuts the office door behind him).[13] Peikoff expresses this point more graphically: "Would anyone debate cutting off his head in order to acquire for himself a million dollars?"[14]

Consider an example involving a proposition that many would find more tempting. Suppose a philosophy graduate student has a paper accepted at a prestigious journal. The natural evaluation would be that this is very good for the student's career. If, however, the student's paper is not his own, but a lightly touched up version of a little-noted paper published a century ago by an obscure author in an obscure journal, the student's flourishing has not been genuinely enhanced, contrary to initial appearances. For starters, the publication of the piece will make his plagiarism more likely to be discovered, as the journal (naturally) has a wide and learned readership. Such discovery would trigger all sorts of obstacles to his career (including a large number of people who will want nothing to do with him). Leaving that aside, even more significantly, the acceptance of "his" paper does not reflect the skills and intellectual promise that it would for the student who had his own work accepted by that journal. The value of the paper's publication – its actually representing a gain for his objective flourishing – is dramatically altered by the student's means of securing publication.

---

[13] I assume that the person has no good reason to disregard or minimize retirement needs, such as an unexpected inheritance or a dire medical prognosis.

[14] Peikoff, *Objectivism*, p. 273. Also see my discussions of this in "The Metaphysical Case for Honesty," *Journal of Value Inquiry* 37 (2003), pp. 517–531, and *Viable Values*, pp. 167–174.

The point, again, is that attaining the object of a person's desire is valuable for that person only when it plays an all-things-considered, objectively life-advancing role in his life. Whether a given thing does play that role is not as transparent as everyday conversation often suggests. Offhand assessments of what is good or bad for people rely heavily on the assumption of other things being equal. To determine what is truly valuable for a person, however, and how he can advance his interest, we must heed all relevant aspects of reality, which requires investigating whether other things are equal in the given case.

Dependence on Others

Although the proper compass for a person's conduct of his life is reality, the person who is dishonest makes other people his lodestar. "An attempt to gain a value by deceiving the mind of others is an act of raising your victims to a position higher than reality," Rand observes.[15] Contrary to the prevalent image of the person who deceives others as enjoying a certain mastery over his victims, he actually becomes their pawn.[16] Through dishonesty, a person makes himself dependent on others – on their standards and on their ignorance.

To begin with, in the original act of dishonesty, a person elevates others' standards above his own. He misrepresents something in order to satisfy another person's criteria or expectations. He thinks that he can perform a job, for instance, but because he fears that the person hiring will not agree, he fabricates credentials. He lies to his wife about how much he has spent to cater to her standards of financial responsibility. He feigns familiarity with certain authors or musicians in order to satisfy another person's ideas of who qualifies as *au courant*. By misrepresenting his own knowledge in order to satisfy another's standards, the dishonest person proceeds as if others' judgment is more important than his own.[17]

Furthermore, once he has lied, the dishonest person is subservient to his victims' expectations. In order to avoid having his deception exposed, all of his subsequent actions must be calculated around the likely effects on their erroneous beliefs about him. He has chained himself to what they think. Even the "successful" liar is trapped, in other words, in the never-ending need to maintain the façade. He must monitor his victims'

---

[15] Rand, *Atlas Shrugged*, p. 1019.
[16] Rand, *Atlas Shrugged*, p. 1019.
[17] See *Journals of Ayn Rand*, p. 261. We will see in the next chapter that such contortions to please others are also a violation of the virtue of independence. The list of virtues in this journal passage includes some that do not make it into Rand's published work.

knowledge, acquaintances, potential knowledge – scout whether they are "getting close" – and adjust his own actions accordingly. Having sacrificed his judgment to others', for as long as the liar wishes to conceal his dishonesty, he must dance to their tune. This does not require that those he misled seek to dictate his actions. Without even knowing the power he has given them, their knowledge charts the course he must follow. Indeed, as both Rand and Peikoff point out, it is others' knowledge that he must battle and their ignorance that rules him.[18] The liar relies on his victims' gullibility and must work to keep them ignorant. Since a person actually stands to gain the most, objectively, from others' rationality and knowledge, this indicates yet a further respect in which dishonesty is self-defeating. It leads a person to encourage the very traits in others that make them least valuable to him.[19]

The more one contemplates dishonesty in practice, the more one can appreciate its destructive repercussions. A dishonest person sentences himself to the ongoing dread of being found out. This worry is exacerbated by the fact that dishonesty is impossible to contain.[20] Consider a person who misrepresents where he earned his college degree. A lie about his education will seem plausible only if bolstered by correlative lies about where the person lived during the relevant years, the jobs he held, the people he knew, how he knows other people who he met during that period, and so on. *And so on.*

A person has only one past. Once he misrepresents a single element of it, the preservation of that doctored life story will require a network of auxiliary falsehoods, indicating how the fiction could be consistent with other aspects of his actual past (and present). Because it is not, the person will need to invent additional misrepresentations in order to lend credibility to the initial lie. Every new person who the liar meets poses a threat to expose his dishonesty. Who or what might *this* person know? Where is he from? Where did he – or his sister, or best friend, or brother-in-law – go to school? The dishonest person cannot grow complacent even about the "safe" people he already knows, for you never know who they might have been talking to lately. Every new person his acquaintances meet is a further threat to reveal his deception.

The more lies a person tells to preserve the plausibility of his original lie, the more lies he must tell, to prop those up. Thus, the dishonest

---

[18] Rand, *Atlas Shrugged*, p. 1019; Peikoff, *Objectivism*, pp. 271–272.
[19] For good discussion of this, see Peikoff, *Objectivism*, pp. 268–272.
[20] Peikoff, *Objectivism*, p. 268.

person's life is comparable to that of a person on a boat that is springing leaks, frantically patching one after another. His life is set in a permanently defensive crouch, not knowing where the next leak will appear, only that he must be ready to pounce on it. And his means of covering up one falsehood – a further falsehood – creates still further holes that will need to be patched in the future.

Some, no doubt, would dismiss this as an exaggeration. The idea is not that every liar will need to mint multiple lies daily, however. The number needed will depend on individual circumstances. What is undeniable is that the dishonest person must be constantly on guard, ready to float as many fabrications as circumstances demand in order to protect his secret. As Peikoff recognizes, philosophy cannot predict how much a given liar will get away with or whether he will ever be found out. Yet although a liar may win individual battles, he cannot win the war.[21] For the liar struggles to serve two conflicting masters: reality and the false image of reality that he has circulated. This is an impossible assignment. Because each fresh deception will contradict the truth, the liar will have to juggle an ever-expanding array of fictions while the gap between his feet – one groping for reality, the other, sliding further to uphold the fiction he peddles – grows wider. Consider the effect on this person's ability to advance his objective well-being. Should he base his thinking and actions on what he knows is the case, or on the alternative scenario that he pretends is the case? To the extent that he does the latter, in order to maintain his cover, he can only make irrational decisions that will, as such, prove self-destructive.

The probable psychological fallout will also impede a person's ability to flourish. Although neither Rand nor Peikoff directly discusses this dimension of honesty, to my knowledge, I would suggest that dishonesty is likely to eat away at a person's self-esteem – at his sense of his own worthiness and ability to achieve his happiness.[22] If a person pretends to have some experience or to have obtained some end through legitimate means, it does not mean that he has. While he might fool others about that, *he* will know whether he possesses the requisite ability or character to have earned his prize. Correspondingly, if he obtains a goal such as a job through dishonesty, he cannot experience pride for having earned it.

[21] Peikoff, *Objectivism*, p. 271.
[22] This is Rand's basic understanding of what self-esteem is. Peikoff, *Objectivism*, p. 306. We will consider self-esteem further in the chapter on pride. Peikoff does make related comments when explaining the nature of evasion, observing a relationship between habitual evasion and anxiety, pp. 61–62.

Nor can the spurious achievement give him confidence concerning his future.

By employing dishonest means of securing his goal, a person creates the belief that faking things is the way to get along in life. "That is how I operate" is the implicit message that his dishonest deeds convey to him; "that is how I deal with perceived shortcomings, for instance: by covering them up." The more regularly a person employs dishonesty to attain his ends, the stronger the subconscious conclusion will grow that this is the way he *must* operate, the only way he can cope with life's challenges. Since he will simultaneously observe other people who seem to succeed without dishonesty, disquieting questions may naturally occur to him: "Why are they able to succeed honestly, while I am not? What's wrong with me? And will I be able to get what I want through my usual means again, next time? Given that honesty seems the norm, maybe I've just been lucky so far, and dishonesty is not actually a wise policy . . ." My point is not that a liar will experience guilt because he accepts the premise that honesty is morally proper. (That would clearly be question-begging.) Rather, quite apart from any moral evaluation of his actions, the damage is wrought by his awareness of his unconventional means of seeking goals. Because he will continually encounter evidence indicating that honesty does work and that faking does not, his reliance on dishonesty is likely to gradually undermine his self-confidence.[23]

Egoism

The case for honesty, like the case for morality itself, is completely egoistic. Honesty is a "profoundly selfish virtue," in Rand's view.[24] For dishonesty is self-denying and self-defeating. To willfully ignore or misrepresent reality is to subvert one's rational faculty, which most truly *is* one's self, as we will discuss in Chapter 5, on independence.[25] Dishonesty is self-defeating insofar as pretending that facts are other than they are only diverts a person from identifying and pursuing rational strategies for achieving the objective values that will advance his life. The propriety of honesty is

---

[23] The psychology of deception is no doubt an intricate matter, and deficient self-esteem may contribute to dishonesty, as well as result from it. Again, my comments concerning the impact of dishonesty on self-esteem are speculative and not part of Rand's explicit analysis of honesty.

[24] Rand, *Atlas Shrugged*, p. 1019.

[25] Aristotle similarly identifies one's self with one's rational faculty. *Nicomachean Ethics* 1168b28–1169a.

not a concession granted out of deference to some authority other than self-interest. Honesty is the only practical means of survival qua human.

To appreciate this more fully, it is worth contrasting Rand's argument for honesty with the predominant conventional rationales for honesty. One familiar line of reasoning contends that dishonesty damages social intercourse by unraveling the fragile fabric of trust and creating a climate of wariness. Burned once, or simply aware that others are sometimes dishonest, a person will be less ready to accept others' word in the future. On this view, it is not so much a single deception that is problematic, but that deception's contributing to the broader suspicion that a person might be dishonest on any given occasion.[26]

Another common argument turns on the observation that dishonesty uses other people for the liar's own gain. Typically, a person deceives another because he thinks that he could not achieve an end if he were truthful; the other person would not, if he knew the truth, act as the liar wishes. Through deception, however, a person thinks that he can manipulate his victim's choices and get what he wants. Although this may be good for the liar (according to this line), it is unfair to the victim, who is led to act under false information. Dishonesty treats the victim as if he were a tool, on hand solely to suit the liar's purposes.

Yet a third frequent argument points out the deleterious effects that dishonesty inflicts on the liar himself. Dishonesty damages a person's credibility and poisons his personal relationships. If a liar's deception is found out, he will suffer the ramifications of a tarnished reputation. People will not trust or respect him, they will be reluctant to do business with him or to befriend him. Even while a person's dishonesty goes undetected, the need to hide it will naturally make the liar fearful of discovery and thus defensive, uptight, and somewhat artificial as he tries simultaneously to cover up his lie and to affect normalcy. This will impede his ability to forge close, quality relationships.

Rand would not dispute the effects of dishonesty that each of these arguments highlights. She regards their explanations of the wrong in dishonesty as superficial, however. For their perspective is entirely social. Each erects other people as the highest concern that calls for honesty. This is obvious when one appeals to damage to society or to an individual victim, yet even the alleged negative effects on the liar himself result from

---

[26] See, for instance, G. F. Warnock, *The Object of Morality* (London: Methuen, 1974), p. 84, and Bok, p. 24. Cabot writes that dishonesty "cuts the arteries" of social life and that mutual deceit is "social murder," Cabot, p. 6.

other people's judgments of him. The artificiality injected into personal relationships stems from concern for others' knowledge of the liar. The sullied reputation and attendant harms arise from others' discovery of the liar's duplicity. Notice a striking implication of such socially-based defenses of honesty: A person could escape these harms by becoming a better liar, more adept at avoiding detection. For when others' knowledge is the obstacle to his interest, preventing that knowledge prevents the damage.

It is here that Rand's condemnation of dishonesty differs most deeply from prevailing accounts. It is not, fundamentally, relations with others that necessitate honesty, she argues; it is reality. The conventional assumption is that a person would most advance his interest if he could hoodwink other people, but honesty imposes limits on such egoism. Rand rejects this. Rather, she contends that the only effective way of achieving objective values is through refusing to fake things – regardless of how successfully a person might be able to fool others. Others' perceptions do not dictate reality any more than one's own do. Whatever anyone's beliefs about it, it is reality that a person must navigate in order to attain his objective, long-term happiness. Consequently, reality must be the rational egoist's fundamental concern.[27]

Apart from the issue of being found out, the charge that the liar mistreats those he deceives remains, and Rand would agree that a person should not treat other people as mere tools on hand for his convenience. Her reasoning here, too, is egoistic, however. Such manipulation of others would violate the virtue of justice. And the rationale for justice, as we shall see in Chapter 6, is itself egoistic.

Rand's case for honesty, in sum, is this: Because reality sets the ultimate terms of a person's survival, reality – rather than one's own or others' beliefs or wishes – must command a person's paramount allegiance. Faking reality is futile. Dishonesty only diverts a person from facing the facts that he must face, in order to act in ways that can achieve his objective flourishing.

THE PRACTICAL DEMANDS OF HONESTY

Because the basis for honesty is deeper than the facilitation of social relations, the scope of honesty's demands encompasses more than refraining

---

[27] For more on the difference between metaphysical and social arguments for honesty, see Smith, "The Metaphysical Case for Honesty." One can find elements of a realist rationale for honesty in certain other authors. See Cabot, p. 18, Fried, pp. 377–378, and Jeremy Bentham, *Theory of Legislation* (Boston: Weeks, Jordan & Co., 1840), vol. II, p. 27.

from lying to other people. Honesty demands taking cognition seriously. This requires that a person develop an active mind, seek knowledge in order to act on that knowledge, and refuse to fake any item in his mind.[28] I will elaborate first and at greatest length on the last of these, because its significance has been neglected by most philosophical discussions of honesty.

The Rejection of Self-Deception

The honest person does not fake any item in his own mind, Peikoff observes. He forswears kidding himself about what he knows and what he does not know, about the questions or doubts that occur to him, the implications of his knowledge, his abilities, his resources, his tendencies, values, priorities, and so on.[29] Self-deception is more subtle than dishonesty with others. Indeed, some have objected that self-deception is too paradoxical to be genuine: How could the same person be both deceiver and deceived? Our experience, however, makes plain that the phenomenon is quite real. The sorts of cases I have in mind are commonplace: A woman senses bad vibes with her husband, but pretends not to notice this unpleasant fact and thus does not probe either their sources or their significance. A student thinks that he should study for a test, but ignores that knowledge when opting to attend a party, instead. A man pretends not to care about something that actually means a great deal to him: "It's no big deal that they passed me over for that position." While a person cannot think "x is true" and "x is false," with each thought in clear, full focus *at the very same time,* he can choose to prevent that clear focus by pushing certain thoughts away from the spotlight of his attention. (Recall from Chapter 3 that the essence of evasion consists in deliberately pushing thoughts and knowledge aside. Self-deception is a textbook form of evasion.)

This form of dishonesty may well be more common than deception of others. Many people who would not think of misleading others seem more inclined to deceive themselves. If one regards morality as essentially concerned with social relations, such self-regarding behavior does not fall under morality's purview. Moreover, it seems easier to get away with self-deception, if "getting away with" means escaping others' detection. Others cannot know the inner reaches of a person's mind, thus self-deception seems safe from the danger of alienating others. Further, the

[28] Peikoff, *Objectivism*, p. 269.
[29] Peikoff, *Objectivism*, p. 269.

motivation for self-deception often stems from a desire to protect oneself (from pain, fear, uncertainty about how to act, etc.) rather than from a desire to hurt others, thus self-deception lacks the aura of malice that most invites moral condemnation.

Honesty demands that a person be truthful with himself, however, for the simple reason that self-deception is as counterproductive as any other type of deception. A person's kidding himself about the state of his marriage or his preparedness for an exam does not erase the relevant realities. Evading grounds for concern about his career or his health or his finances or lying to himself about how hurt he is by another's action only keeps him from doing what he can to promote his values. Faking does not work, regardless of whom a person is trying to fool. For people's beliefs are not the fundamental challenge to be met, if one is to live. A person must navigate the facts of existence in order to sustain himself rather than the contents of anyone's consciousness, others' or his own. Reality is not manipulated by a person's denials or evasions of it. And it is reality that he must ultimately master.

It is also important to appreciate the psychological repercussions wrought by self-deception. For starters, a person will have a hard time fooling himself, because he remains semi-aware of whatever he is denying, with that awareness nibbling around the perimeter of his consciousness, jostling for attention. The truth's muted but persistent nagging will take a toll on the credence of the lie. The person does not fully believe the falsehood (that his marriage is fine, that he is not sick, that he can afford the extravagant purchase that he cannot), yet he brushes his doubts aside. What does this accomplish? To the extent that he is aware of his evasion (which he must be to some extent, since it is *self*-deception), he will probably suspect that he should tend the issue that he is avoiding. Why bother to hide it, after all, if it isn't important? He may feel guilt or self-reproach for not forthrightly facing uncomfortable facts.

Accordingly, self-deception often leads to anxiety.[30] By evading threatening thoughts, the person leaves a dark cloud hovering over his days. As he goes about his activities, the fear lurks "but my marriage is about to collapse" – "I'm not going to be able to pay my bills" – "I have a serious illness." As the deflected thought periodically intrudes on his attention, all he can do is fret and fear. Whereas rational action could alleviate worry, supplying the person with the knowledge that he is doing what he can to secure his values, worry spins from being out of control. As long as the

---

[30] Recall that Peikoff notes a link between evasion and anxiety, *Objectivism*, pp. 61–62.

person does not act, he *is* out of control, at the mercy of external events that he passively waits to suffer. His self-deception paralyzes him from taking action which might actually prevent a dreaded event or minimize its damage. Action would not only make a person feel better, in other words, by providing knowledge that he is doing what he can to take good care of himself; action could also effectively combat the danger to his values. Self-deception, at best, delays the only possible action that a person could take to resist the threat.

Contrary to popular wisdom, what you don't know can and often will hurt you and will often be more damaging precisely because a person avoided facing the facts. People die of late-diagnosed diseases every day because they put off going to the doctor to investigate their symptoms; marriages collapse every day because of postponed discussions of accumulating injuries and neglects. What a person does not know may not affect his feelings in exactly the same way it would if he confronted it, but that does not mean that it will not affect *him*.[31]

Developing an Active Mind

All of this has explained why honesty demands honesty with oneself. Another of honesty's practical requirements is the effort to develop an active mind. Rand writes that intellectual honesty involves "constantly expanding one's knowledge, and *never* evading or failing to correct a contradiction. This means: the development of an *active* mind as a permanent attitude."[32]

This requirement is premised on the fact that knowledge is extremely valuable. As we saw in the discussion of rationality, it is learning about the world that enables human beings to navigate the world successfully. Information can alert a person to potential values, to effects on his existing values, and to actions he should take to secure his values. All sorts of information can carry all sorts of practical ramifications for a person's welfare: knowledge about a person, product, or therapy, knowledge about a business venture or court decision or school board policy, knowledge about friends' and colleagues' tastes and skills and experiences. If a person's highest end is his own best interest, he must be committed to learning what will be the best means to that end. To achieve the countless

---

[31] For a more extended discussion of self-deception, see Smith, "The Metaphysical Case for Honesty," pp. 526–530.

[32] Rand, "What Can One Do?" in *Philosophy: Who Needs It*, p. 247, emphasis in original.

values that contribute to his interest, he must be actively committed to the acquisition of knowledge.

The value of knowledge is so basic that few would dispute it. Still, one might wonder, how does *honesty* require the pursuit of knowledge? The answer becomes clear when we consider a thinner conception of honesty's demands: not faking anything that one does know, but not particularly trying *to* know anything. Imagine declaring a moratorium on further knowledge, adopting the stance: "I know all I need to." Such indifference would be idiotic. It would undermine the person's ability to achieve his happiness, since ignorance will not protect him from the facts he avoids learning. A posture of such passivity would mean faking reality, since human beings know, from experience every day, the value of knowledge. This is why we watch the news, check the Web, and talk to people. It is why we read reviews and go to school. It is why children – and adults – ask questions. Knowledge *is* power, as we all grasp from a very early age. Indifference to this fact is itself an evasion.

The honest person, recognizing the value of knowledge, will pursue knowledge, as Rand claims, alert to correcting any mistaken beliefs he might hold. Because knowledge is crucial to life-sustaining action and because knowledge is not acquired as effortlessly as the oxygen we breathe, human beings must cultivate active and inquisitive minds in order to obtain knowledge.

Here, as throughout Rand's account of the virtues, rational self-interest is the guiding aim. Honesty's requirement of an active mind and the expansion of one's knowledge is not the arbitrary deification of knowledge for its own sake. The active pursuit of knowledge will help a person to achieve objective values. A searching honesty is in a person's interest. This is not to say that a person must seek to become an encyclopedia.[33] A life so devoted to learning would not allow sufficient time for action, which is what the learning is for. It is to say that a person should seek knowledge as a vital means of attaining his happiness. And this feeds into the third major demand of honesty.

Acting on One's Knowledge

If part of what honesty demands is the pursuit of knowledge, another part is the application of the knowledge that a person obtains. The motivation for the acquisition of knowledge should be action. "Intellectual honesty

---

[33] See *Journals of Ayn Rand*, p. 275.

consists in taking ideas seriously," Rand writes. "To take ideas seriously means that you intend to live by, to *practice*, any idea you accept as true."[34]

Honesty demands that a person act in accordance with his beliefs. Correlatively, it demands that a person not act as if what he knows to be true were not true. When a person does not possess definite knowledge on an issue, but only opinions or tentative beliefs, honesty demands recognizing those for what they are. A person should not act as if a possibility is a certainty, for instance, or as if he does not have the questions about an issue that he does have. He should not charge ahead with penalizing a person if he has doubts about the person's culpability that he has not fully considered, for instance. Nor should he act as if grounds for a question about another person's character are the equivalent of grounds for a conclusive verdict about his character.

Every form of faking – evading, distorting, diminishing, omitting, exaggerating, rationalizing, and the rest – describes not merely a thought process confined to the intellect, but a basis for action. If I know that I have not sufficiently prepared for an important meeting, for example, but I reassure myself that I have, this exaggeration of my work leads to faking, in action. I will not do the further preparation that I should. Or if, after a prolonged search, I have finally reached a decision about which candidate to hire and then hear a disturbing report that significantly weakens my estimate of that candidate but I simply ignore this information, my dishonesty again leads to irrational action when I proceed to appoint him nonetheless.

Given that, throughout our discussion of honesty, the importance of action has never receded far from center stage, the rationale behind the demand to act on one's beliefs should need little elaboration. The entire case for honesty ultimately rests in honesty's practicality. The point of seeking knowledge and of using one's knowledge is the indispensable value of knowledge in steering rational, life-sustaining action. To believe one thing but act as if another were true would be to engage in make-believe. Given the primacy of existence, as we have seen, such games-playing is self-defeating. It only keeps a person from attaining his interest. Indeed, it defeats the point of forming beliefs in the first place.

A person's beliefs are significant, ultimately, insofar as they are the basis for his actions. Human beings are neither internally programmed nor externally manipulated to behave as we do. We choose our actions. We must seek to gain knowledge – to discover the way things are, the facts

---

[34] Rand, "Philosophical Detection," in *Philosophy: Who Needs It*, p. 19, emphasis in original.

of reality – so as to select those actions that promise to advance our values. To discard one's knowledge when the time came to act on it would be to abandon the rational pursuit of one's happiness. Whatever a person's motivation for fleeing his judgment of reality, doing so can only sabotage his happiness.

Special Cases

A. *Responding to Force*

Honesty does not demand truth-telling in absolutely all circumstances, on Rand's view. It is permissible to lie to bank robbers, burglars, kidnappers, and their ilk. A person stands under no moral obligation to divulge his knowledge to an inquiring Nazi.[35] In such cases, the person who lies is not attempting to gain a value. (If he were, it would be an ill-fated quest that rational egoism would not sanction.) Rather, he is acting rationally to protect a value under attack. Indeed, when one person demands what is not his by threatening force (the Nazi asking "Are you hiding any Jews in here?" or the gun-brandishing intruder demanding "your money or your life," for instance), to respond truthfully would implicitly accept the aggressor's insinuation that he is entitled to what he demands. In such cases, as long as he thinks he can do so safely, the victim *should* misrepresent the relevant information in order to protect the threatened values. These lies would be justified in the same way that action in self-defense is.[36]

It is important to remember the contextual character of all moral principles, on Rand's view. As we explained in Chapter 2, the purpose of moral principles is to guide a person to the achievement of the values that sustain his life. Correspondingly, a person should adhere to these principles only when doing so can serve that purpose. All moral guidance is intended for the normal course of events, since those are the conditions we ordinarily face and that allow us to identify principles that

---

[35] Peikoff discusses this sort of case, *Objectivism*, pp. 274–276.

[36] Peikoff, *Objectivism*, pp. 275–276. The proviso about a person's ability to resist safely is crucial. A victim is not endorsing the aggressor's premises when the only alternative the aggressor leaves him is his own destruction. For discussion of some other philosophers' views on honesty in this type of case, see Bok, pp. 32–46. Kant, famously, held that truthfulness "is an unconditional duty" and that "truthfulness in statements which cannot be avoided is the formal duty of an individual to everyone, however great may be the disadvantage accruing to himself or another." "On a Supposed Right to Lie from Altruistic Motives," reprinted in Bok, p. 271 and 268. Augustine took a similarly rigid stance. See pp. 250–255 in Bok.

provide effective guidance. Occasionally, the out of the ordinary strikes: A natural disaster or manmade emergency imposes an urgent threat to major values. The immediate and rational goal in such circumstances is to escape the threat and minimize the damage. There would be no point, in such cases, in adhering to principles that are designed to aid us in radically different conditions.

We observed in Chapter 2 that moral principles' concrete prescriptions will always depend on the particular context. What is important to grasp here, however, is the further point that I made when discussing the possibility of conflicts between individuals' interests in "lifeboat" scenarios, namely: Because the authority of principles stems entirely from their service to the agent's interest, whether principles govern at all in a given situation depends on whether a person is in an emergency. That is, it depends on whether adherence to those principles is in fact the means of advancing the agent's rational interest. Speaking of one person's attempt to have his way over another by use of physical force, Rand writes:

Force and mind are opposites; morality ends where a gun begins. . . . To force a man to drop his own mind and to accept your will as a substitute, with a gun in place of a syllogism, with terror in place of proof, and death as the final argument – is to attempt to exist in defiance of reality. Reality demands of man that he act for his own rational interest; your gun demands of him that he act against it. Reality threatens man with death if he does not act on his rational judgment: you threaten him with death if he does . . . [37]

The ultimatum, "Your money or your life," Rand proceeds to point out, essentially amounts to, "Your mind or your life." Yet since reason is man's means of survival, "neither is possible to man without the other."[38] Human beings cannot survive if they cannot engage in rational action. In light of this, when asked in a question period about the morality of actions taken by those who are oppressed by a dictatorship, Rand replies (in part):

In such a case, morality cannot say what to do. Under a dictatorship – under force – there is no such thing as morality. Morality ends where a gun begins . . . in such emergency situations, no one could prescribe what action is appropriate. That's my answer to all lifeboat questions. Moral rules cannot be prescribed for these situations, because only *life* is the basis on which to establish a moral code.[39]

[37] *Atlas Shrugged*, p. 1023.
[38] *Atlas Shrugged*, p. 1023.
[39] *Ayn Rand Answers*, p. 114.

Rand's point is that the authority of moral principles is premised on certain conditions, and those principles properly govern only when those conditions are in place. Reason is man's fundamental means of survival. The derivative moral virtues (honesty, justice, integrity, etc.) carry authority only when their exercise represents the application of reason. Force is the antithesis of reason, however. The force-wielding aggressor effectively alters the conditions of existence for his victim. For he makes his victim's rationality unavailable to him, rendering it a tool of self-destruction. Instead of following reason, the victim must submit to the will of his attacker. Defying the attacker's demands would cost him his life.[40]

Bear in mind that moral principles' claim on a person arises entirely from the fact that adherence to those principles is the way to advance his life. When another person uses force to try to manipulate him, however, the aggressor obliterates the relationship between moral principles and life; he cancels rational principles' ability to guide a person to that end. For the victim to nonetheless follow moral principles as usual would be to aid in his own destruction. Morality is a tool of self-preservation. It would make no sense to abide by the principles of morality when the conditions under which those principles *are* one's means of survival have been erased. The principles of morality do not, once recognized, acquire an inherent authority which is morally obligatory independently of their service to life.

A passage from the essay "The Ethics of Emergencies" might create confusion about Rand's position. There, while distinguishing "between the rules of conduct in an emergency situation and the rules of conduct in the normal conditions of human existence," Rand observes that "This does not mean a double standard of morality: the standard and the basic principles remain the same, but their application to either case" will be different.[41] This suggests that morality does govern in emergencies, but does so in different ways from the usual. The apparent discrepancy between this statement and those I quoted earlier (suggesting that morality does not govern in certain situations) is resolved, I think, by recognizing the difference between two kinds of emergencies, what we might call

---

[40] A victim's response to an aggressor's use of force (i.e., complying or resisting the attacker's demands) cannot itself be considered rational, strictly, because once physical force has been threatened, the context necessary for the rationality of action is destroyed. Only free action can be rational. Thus, a victim's response can be described as "rational" only in a circumscribed, artificial sense. I will discuss the relationship between force and reason further in the chapter on justice.

[41] Rand, "The Ethics of Emergencies," in *The Virtue of Selfishness*, p. 54.

metaphysical emergencies and *natural* emergencies, those that arise within broadly normal conditions. (The latter term is not ideal, but is preferable to "normal emergency," which sounds oxymoronic. Its meaning should become clearer momentarily.)[42]

An emergency is "an unchosen, unexpected event, limited in time, that creates conditions under which human survival is impossible..."[43] It poses a sudden, unendurable peril to a crucial value and thus requires immediate action. An emergency is metaphysical when external conditions paralyze a person's means of survival. He is plunged into physical elements in which human beings cannot survive, for instance, such as a flood, fire, or mudslide. It is no weakness or misfortune of a particular individual that he cannot walk through fire or live without oxygen. These are indelible aspects of being human. A metaphysical emergency poses a crisis, in other words, because of the very nature of man. It renders survival by man's natural means impossible. (Thus the label "metaphysical.")

In such an emergency, all a person can do is try to escape the crisis and return to metaphysically normal conditions, to conditions that are "normal in the nature of things," as Rand puts it, "and appropriate to human existence."[44] Morality is inapplicable. The long-range perspective incorporated in the principles that morality identifies as life-sustaining must be thrust aside by the urgent need to escape imminent doom. Pausing to observe the directives of morality – which, again, are premised on and intended for radically different circumstances – would only hasten a person's demise. A metaphysical emergency makes it impossible for a person to abide by morality and survive. (In terms of our immediate discussion, it is important to appreciate that one person's use of force against another creates an emergency of this kind. By paralyzing his victim's mind, the Nazi's threat of force incapacitates his means of survival.)[45]

The second type of emergency, in contrast, arises within what are broadly normal conditions. The person is on dry land, for instance, not confronting the power of a tidal wave, earthquake, bombing, or pistol. Within such normal conditions, life-threatening crises can nonetheless

---

[42] This distinction is suggested by Rand's discussion in "The Ethics of Emergencies," pp. 54–55, and was brought to my attention by Leonard Peikoff in a very helpful discussion of these issues.

[43] Rand, "The Ethics of Emergencies," p. 54.

[44] Rand, "The Ethics of Emergencies," p. 54.

[45] For a full explanation of the destructive power of physical force, see Peikoff, *Objectivism*, pp. 310–323.

erupt. A woman's husband might be injured or suddenly taken ill, for example, and need to be rushed to a hospital. Although this is obviously an emergency for these individuals, it is in the nature of human beings to die, eventually, and injury and illness are naturally occurring causes of death. In this sense, such emergencies are not metaphysical. (Rand observes that "illness and poverty are not metaphysical emergencies, they are part of the normal risks of existence.")[46] To frame the contrast from a different angle: In a natural emergency, a great value is at risk; in a metaphysical emergency, a person's very mode of survival is immobilized.

It is in these natural emergencies, I think, that the basic principles of morality remain the same, as Rand says in the passage from "The Ethics of Emergencies," but their application may deviate from the norm. In a natural emergency, a woman might be morally justified in taking a neighbor's car to rush her husband to the hospital or in breaking into a neighbor's vacant house to use his phone to call an ambulance if her own is not working.[47] Ordinarily, rational egoism would forbid such violations of others' property, but the emergency justifies it. This does not mean that morality is silenced all together and totally inapplicable, however. The person who violates the basic principles of morality is still obligated to recognize that his emergency (genuine as it is, for him) is not an emergency for everyone and does not suspend all other individuals' rights. Accordingly, he must be ready to pay compensation to those whose property he has taken. The application of morality in this type of emergency sanctions one person's taking another's property *and* demands making it up to him, after the crisis has passed. The compensation is due out of recognition of the fact that it was a crisis to one's own values, not to human life as such, that warranted the transgression of basic moral principles and out of respect for the enduring propriety of those principles.

The intricacies of the proper application of morality in all conceivable circumstances could obviously be explored in much greater depth. I raise a few of these exceptional circumstances not to exaggerate their frequency or significance (which Rand considers marginal), but only to address understandable questions that arise, in light of the absolutism of Rand's position on honesty and all the virtues. Understanding the contextual character of morality is not marginal. The main point is that, insofar as rational moral principles are premised on certain conditions, they are

---

[46] "The Ethics of Emergencies," p. 55.

[47] Various other conditions about the nonavailability of other resources would also need to be satisfied.

valid only when those conditions are in place. It is because they nearly always are that principles are tremendously useful. When the conditions do not obtain, however, moral directives premised on those conditions retain no authority.[48]

Some might worry that acknowledging the contextual character of moral principles opens the door to abuse. Mightn't context be invoked as a pretext for dishonesty when circumstances do not warrant it? Undeniably, it could be. The fact that all principles must be applied by individuals allows the possibility of misapplication. No theory can prevent that, however. Still, if a moral theory acknowledges conditions on its prescriptions, as Rand's does, does that make it especially subject to abuse? Only by those hell-bent on abusing it. If the specified conditions are rationally justified, the potential for bad faith is hardly reason to pretend otherwise. (Bear in mind also that the importance of context is not unique to moral principles. All scientific absolutes are valid only within certain conditions. Gravity does not prevent planes from sustaining flight; water boils at 212 degrees Fahrenheit *at* certain altitudes.)[49]

While we have been explaining the contextual character of all moral principles, we should close this topic by returning to the specific virtue of honesty. Peikoff offers a succinct explanation of Rand's position on lying in response to force. Lying is wrong

> when a man does it in the attempt to gain a value. But . . . lying to protect one's values from criminals is not wrong. If and when a man's honesty becomes a weapon that kidnappers or other wielders of force can use to harm him, then the normal context is reversed; his virtue would then become a means serving the ends of evil. . . . The man who tells a lie in this context is not endorsing any anti-reality principle. On the contrary, he is now the representative of the good and the true; the kidnapper is the one at war with reality (with the requirements of man's life). Morally, the con man and the lying child-protector are opposites.[50]

The thing to appreciate about Rand's position is that it is entirely of a piece with her broader explanation of the propriety of honesty. She condones particular lies not as an *ad hoc* concession to the vague cliché that every rule was meant to be broken or by claiming that some exceptions are "just obvious." Rather, the rationale for the permissibility of certain lies is a logical extension of the rationale behind honesty itself. Honesty is not intrinsically virtuous or a categorical imperative, to be

---

[48] See Rand, "The Ethics of Emergencies," especially p. 54.

[49] Peikoff, *Objectivism*, p. 275.

[50] Peikoff, *Objectivism*, pp. 275–276.

blindly obeyed regardless of circumstances. Honesty is a practical means of furthering a person's objective values and thus his life. Virtue cannot be properly demanded when it would work against that end, however. Indeed, truth-telling would not *be* virtue, in the cases in question.

B. White Lies

At the same time, Rand would reject another type of lie that people often approve of, white lies. These are told in cases where etiquette or sensitivity to another person's feelings allegedly requires misrepresentations – of how much a person likes a gift or a meal or a haircut, for instance, or of why he is declining an invitation. "The soup is *good!*" "I'm *so* sorry I can't come to dinner, but I already have a commitment that night." What might justify such lies? What principle would determine when lies are and are not white? The usual rationales offered in defense of white lies do not fare well under even modest reflection.

Some would argue that white lies are permissible simply because the stakes are minimal. Surely, it is no big deal whether I tell a friend that I like his cooking or his gift more than I do; the demands of morality do not impose obligations regarding such trivial matters. One wonders, however, about the criteria of significance being employed. Even if one agrees that many lies involve comparatively modest stakes, on what basis are some stakes too insignificant to matter, morally? Given that the object of morality is individual flourishing and that all sorts of actions carry effects on that, we cannot cavalierly dismiss any action as beyond morality's domain without clear grounds for doing so. One rarely hears such grounds articulated. In practice, the arbiter of significance is often an agent's comfort zone: whether telling the truth seems worth the teller's discomfort on a particular occasion. This is hardly a valid warrant for violating the principle of honesty. Indeed, it reflects the complete rejection of that principle *as a principle.* If the requisite level of significance for honesty to govern turns simply on the comfort or convenience of the would-be liar, all manner of lies might be acquitted. Furthermore, as we will see, the stakes of white lies are not as inconsequential as their defenders presume.[51]

A second defense of white lies contends that such deceptions are legitimated by widely accepted social conventions. We all know, allegedly, that you don't come out and say that you're not enjoying a meal that a person has prepared for you or tell a gift-giver that you think the sweater

---

[51] Full disclosure: I have told many "polite" lies, having only thought seriously about their morality in the past few years. I have recently been cleaning up my act.

he's given you is ghastly. Decency and good manners require that a person refrain from such ungracious remarks and substitute more sensitive fibs.

Here again, however, things are not so simple. The invoked social conventions are ambiguous. People often have very different understandings of exactly what these conventions permit and forbid. *How* truthful should I be? Do I need to say that I like a gift or a meal, or is a thank you and "that was nice of you" enough to fulfill my role in the charade? What types of lies are covered by the convention? A person who asks how he looks has not done something for me, like the person who has cooked me a meal or given me a gift; does that mean I should be frank? Further, how local are the conventions being appealed to? Are they conventions of a nation? of a region? Different families often have different practices governing members' level of candor with one another. And when are the conventions supposed to replace truthful communication? Is that a function of the issue or of the person? or of something else? Should I play the convention game only with friends or with strangers or newer acquaintances, too? Should truth rule at work? What about when socializing with people from work?

We could easily multiply such questions. The point is, since we find no clear, definitive answers to these questions, "convention" does not supply the ready justification of deception that some claim. It is nearly impossible to pin down precisely what this permissive convention *is*. No single convention enjoys the presumed allegiance that allows for white lies. And if individuals do not all know the rules of the game they are allegedly playing, we cannot fairly suppose that they are playing it.

Indeed, a tipoff that the convention argument will not succeed arises from the amorphousness of the very term "white lies." When asked, people offer conflicting understandings of what the concept refers to. Some believe that white lies are trivial lies while others maintain that any lie that is justified, regardless of its content or stakes, qualifies. When "white lies" is used in the latter sense, the term begs the question, which is whether any lies are ever justified and if so, on what grounds. What bleaches certain lies into moral purity? The response, "we all know, from (supposedly) entrenched conventions," assumes that some lies are justified rather than demonstrates that they are. The more immediate point, however, is simply that people's fuzzy understanding of what constitutes a white lie scuttles the idea that we are all agreeably abiding by accepted conventions when we tell such lies. In truth, we are not even sure of what "such lies" refers to.

No doubt, the motivation for white lies is frequently the intention to spare others' feelings. And this constitutes a third line of defense. White lies are permissible because the liar means well. More specifically, he means to avoid offending or hurting another person. Although it is difficult to criticize good intentions, this appeal offers too open-ended and too nonessential a criterion to justify dishonesty. (It also suggests that altruism governs the propriety of honesty: When dishonesty is intended to benefit oneself, it is wrong; when dishonesty is intended to benefit others, it is permissible.)

The most obvious problem is that truths about all sorts of issues, profound or trivial, might hurt a person's feelings. It is no fun to hear a negative evaluation of one's work, to be turned down for a job, to be denied admission to a school or a place on a team. An accountant's report or a doctor's diagnosis can provoke great distress. Nonetheless, conveying the truth in such matters is vital for a school or company to maintain its standards and for a person to learn how he can achieve his values. If the desire to soothe feelings legitimized faking, the principle of honesty would be gutted. As Rand observes in a question period, lying in order to placate another person makes emotions the standard of value.[52] Essentially, the agent is proceeding on the premise: "I want this person to experience (or not experience) certain feelings and I think I can effect that result by lying, so that's enough to license dishonesty." In fact, it is not. As we noted in Chapter 3, feelings are far from a reliable basis for determining the means of advancing our lives. It is immaterial whether the feelings in question are one's own or others'.

Benevolent intentions do not justify dishonesty because intentions, at root, are beside the point. Intentions do not create reality or bend reality, yet reality remains, inescapably, human beings' fundamental concern. The essential problem with well-intentioned dishonesty is the same as that with any dishonesty: It does not work. As Peikoff observes, a lie that attempts to protect others from certain facts is as impractical as any more blatantly sinister lies. The efficacy of faking is not improved by the identity of one's intended beneficiary. A lie becomes no stronger a means of advancing human life when the liar hopes to help a person other than himself.[53]

---

[52] *Ayn Rand Answers*, p. 130.

[53] Peikoff, *Objectivism*, p. 274. Accordingly, Rand condemns government lies to its citizens, even during wartime. In 1947 testimony before the House Un-American Activities Committee, she says: "We do not have to deceive the people at any time, in war or peace" and "I don't think the American people should ever be told any lies, publicly or privately. I don't believe that lies are practical." Quoted in Robert Mayhew, *Ayn Rand and Song of*

We can observe this impracticality quite concretely. White lies do a disservice to their "beneficiaries" by feeding them false information. By not telling a person the truth, the liar leaves the other person unaware of his actual opinion. The opportunity to put him straight about something – expectations about his job performance, one's taste in clothes, whatever – is lost. And the falsehood offers misleading cues for the future. Because the victim does not know the liar's true thoughts, he is encouraged to act on erroneous premises. Accordingly, he will not try to improve his performance on the job or he will keep buying the liar those hideous sweaters. While the deceived certainly might not agree with another's evaluation of his work or with his taste, the liar's misinformation keeps the two people from recognizing their differences, examining their merits, and changing their actions in any ways that might be appropriate. A paternalistic lie might avoid near-term unpleasantness, but to shield a person from reality does not truly help that person.[54]

Lack of candor also carries a further negative consequence: It infuses artificiality into individuals' relationships. The values that one person thinks he shares with another – similar taste in certain areas, similar standards in others, even ideas about what constitutes an enjoyable evening – are actually not shared, and the individuals' presumed closeness is fraudulent. To the extent that the victim suspects that the liar is sometimes not telling him the truth but simply being polite, he is left to engage in guesswork: When is my friend (friend?) saying what he really thinks and when is he not? Given a policy of polite deception, he has no means of knowing when, if ever, he can take the other person at his word. Indeed, the more he suspects that another person engages in white lies, the weaker that person's credibility. If a person doesn't mean what he says, how can you discover his thoughts? And what's the point of further dialogue?

Essentially, Rand holds, a person should either tell the truth about an issue or refuse to discuss it. A person cannot control how his silence might be construed, of course, but what a person may not do is pretend to tell the truth when he does not.[55] (I am leaving aside responses to force, discussed above.) None of this is to defend callousness or brutal

---

Russia – Communism and Anti-Communism in 1940s Hollywood (Lanham, MD: Scarecrow Press, 2005), pp. 146, 150.

[54] Sometimes, the "well-intentioned" liar is actually motivated by the desire to spare his own feelings. It can be acutely uncomfortable to experience another person's displeasure when one levels with him about an unwelcome truth. The desire to avoid feeling like a heel is no doubt a frequent spur to deception.

[55] In response to a question about the propriety of withholding information, Rand observes that it is especially misleading and "vicious" to "agree to discuss an issue with someone" yet "not to tell the whole truth." See her full discussion of this, *Ayn Rand Answers*, p. 129.

⸱gard for people's feelings. Any truth can be conveyed in sensitive or
⸱nsensitive ways. A person who does not like a gift can easily emphasize his
appreciation of the giver's generosity or thoughtfulness in giving it (where
those apply). One cannot legitimize well-intended lies by pretending that
the only alternative is mean-spirited truth-dumping.

Finally, beyond the impracticality of white lies, it is worth noting that
even their frequent good intentions are not very well thought through.
Falsehoods designed to protect a person's feelings can be insulting to the
intended beneficiary. The liar acts as if that person is childishly dependent
on his opinions, such that that person's fragile psyche must be protected
from the shattering truth. In fact, as Rand observes, telling a man the truth
is a form of respect.[56] It often bespeaks respect for the person's ability to
learn the truth, but more relevant here is respect for the person's ability
to handle the truth. The benevolent liar's paternalism is patronizing.

In the end, we must recognize that while indulgence in white lies may
initially seem innocuous, it actually reflects the complete rejection of the
principle of honesty. By reserving permission for occasional dishonesty
with no rationally principled grounds, a person gives himself contradic-
tory counsel: Don't fake reality (as honesty tells me); fake reality (as this
loophole urges). What decides when he should respect reality and when
it is permissible not to? Something other than the principle of honesty.
(And something other than the purpose and ground of all moral prescriptions, which governs the proper application of principles, as seen in
our earlier discussion of emergencies.) The white liar reverts to a prag-
matic, case-by-case method, proceeding as if he can tell how best to serve
his life in any situation without the aid of principles. None of the dominant rationales for white lies vindicates this tack, however, as none can
escape the fact that people's wishes and feelings do not make things so.
Even the best of intentions does not have the power to dictate reality.
Honesty demands the refusal to fake reality because facing reality is a
precondition of the achievement of human life. White lies attempt to
defy this.

CONCLUSION

Honesty is the refusal to fake reality. It is the refusal to pretend that
things are other than they are, either to others or to oneself. Whereas
most defenses of honesty focus on the social repercussions of dishonesty,

---

[56] *Letters of Ayn Rand*, p. 425.

Rand's argument stems from a prior, deeper truth: Misrepresenting facts does not change them. However successfully one might fool another person, faking is ultimately futile. For it does not alter the underlying facts. Given the primacy of existence and given that the standard of value is life *qua* man, a person must accept that reality – rather than any individuals' beliefs or wishes about reality – sets the fundamental conditions of his existence. As such, reality is the sovereign he must respect in order to achieve his flourishing. Facing reality is in a person's interest, even when certain aspects of reality are threatening, because it allows him to proceed rationally – realistically – and thus with the chance of overcoming threats and achieving happiness. The case for honesty is completely egoistic. Whatever positive effects for others may result from a person's honesty, a person should be honest because his happiness depends on it.

5

Independence

If honesty is one of the most widely praised virtues, our next virtue is one of the least commonly advocated: independence. The ideal of the self-made man has lost its luster in a world in which, we are told, we are all interdependent. When it is advocated, the value of independence is typically regarded as more prudential than moral. And those who sometimes praise independence tend to labor under conceptions of independence that have nothing in common with Rand's, hailing the "independent spirit" of an avant-garde artist who offers difference for its own sake, for example, or extolling the independence of the "leader" whose primary mission consists simply of accumulating followers. A greater number of people regard independence as a threat – to the authority of the church or the good of the community, for instance. Many religions demand submission and obedience, the antipodes of independent thought.[1] "No man

---

[1] Adam's original sin was disobedience; Galileo's, his independent thought. Anselm, who offered a proof of the existence of God, nonetheless maintained good credentials for his eventual canonization by regarding such proof as ultimately unnecessary: "No Christian ought in any way to dispute the truth of what the Catholic Church [teaches]." Quoted in W. T. Jones, *A History of Western Philosophy*, vol. II, *The Medieval Mind* (New York: Harcourt Brace & World, 1969), p. 201. Scripture has it that "rebellion is as the sin of divination, And insubordination is as iniquity and idolatry." 1 Samuel 15:23. One finds similar passages enjoining obedience in Romans 13:1–2; Hebrews 13:17; Titus 3:1; others speak specifically to the proper submission of slaves and women. Today, Canon Law posits that Christ's faithful "are bound to show Christian obedience to what the sacred Pastors, who represent Christ, declare as teachers of the faith and prescribe as rulers of the Church." (Canon 212 §1) "Bishops in communion with the head and the members of the College, while not infallible in their teaching, are the authentic instructors and teachers of the faith for Christ's faithful entrusted to their care. The faithful are bound to adhere, with a religious submission of mind, to this authentic Magisterium of their Bishops." (Canon

is an island" has become a secular truism, offering a warning to anyone thought to be driving in too independent a direction.[2]

Nearly all of Rand's treatment of independence occurs in her fiction. Independence is the central theme of *The Fountainhead*'s seven-hundred-plus pages and it figures prominently throughout *Atlas Shrugged*, as well. Having probed its roots and ramifications in depth in those works, Rand gives independence little explicit elaboration in her nonfiction. Because I cannot assume that my readers will have read Rand's fiction, I will make only brief references to episodes or characters that illustrate Rand's view. Nonetheless, she has made her understanding of the value of independence clear, thus in what follows, we will see that independence is essential to following the egoist's general directive of rationality and is thus a major virtue.[3]

WHAT INDEPENDENCE IS

Independence, according to Rand, is "one's acceptance of the responsibility of forming one's own judgments and of living by the work of one's own mind."[4] More colloquially, it is a matter of making one's own way in the world. The independent person supports himself both intellectually and materially, thinking for himself and taking productive action to sustain himself. What enables a person to make his own way is indicated in Rand's description of the hero of *The Fountainhead*, Howard Roark, as "[facing] life as if he were the first man born. Nothing stands between the evidence of his senses and the conclusions his mind draws from

753; also see Canon 752.) The term "Islam" means submission, and some Islamic sects (not all) advocate blind obedience to appropriate authorities. In the *Koran*, one reads that "It is not fitting for a Believer, man or woman, when a matter has been decided by Allah and His Messenger to have any option about their decision: if any one disobeys Allah and His Messenger, he is indeed on a clearly wrong Path" (Surah Al-Ahzab, verse 36). "By the Lord, they can have no (real) Faith, until they make thee judge in all disputes between them, and find in their souls no resistance against Thy decisions, but accept them with the fullest conviction" (Surah Nisa verse 65). Some Muslims do profess the ideal of independent thought. See Karen Armstrong, *A History of God* (New York: Ballantine Books, 1993), p. 365.

[2] One figure who did regard independence as a virtue was the abolitionist Frederick Douglass, who expressly elaborates on its benefits in his oft-delivered lecture "Self-Made Men." In John W. Blassingame and John R. McKivigan, eds., *The Frederick Douglass Papers*, Series One, Volume 5 (New Haven: Yale University Press, 1992), pp. 545–575.

[3] I discuss independence in *The Fountainhead* in "Unborrowed Vision – Independence and Egoism in *The Fountainhead*," forthcoming in *Essays on Ayn Rand's The Fountainhead*, ed. Robert Mayhew.

[4] Rand, "The Objectivist Ethics," p. 28.

them . . ."[5] Peikoff, accordingly, describes independence as a primary orientation to reality rather than to other men.[6] As the term "orientation" suggests, independence concerns a person's most basic framework for leading his life. Whether a person is independent turns on where he looks, fundamentally, for guidance in steering his course. What does he regard as his basic source of knowledge? Where does he look to discover the kind of world he lives in and, correspondingly, the kinds of values he must achieve and the kinds of actions he must take to achieve those values? What does he respect as the highest authority he must satisfy in order to gain knowledge and achieve his happiness?

The independent person, Peikoff explains, recognizes the difference between the metaphysical and the manmade and accepts the primacy of existence.[7] In every issue that human beings encounter, a person can distinguish between what people say about the issue and what reality says, what actually is so. Given the number of people who share certain views and the apparent strength of their convictions, the temptation to treat others' views as gospel is often powerful. The independent person resists it, however. He recognizes that other people's beliefs do not mold metaphysical reality any more than his own beliefs do and, consequently, that adhering to other people's standards is not the path to acquiring knowledge and achieving objective values. This is not to say that the independent person should eschew other people. As we will discuss later in this chapter, an independent person can enjoy the values of trade, education, friendship, and other personal relationships. Yet other people are "not his motor, his sustainer, or his purpose," Peikoff observes.[8] They are not what gets him going, what keeps him going, or the reason why he goes anywhere. The independent person charts his course by his own judgment of reality.[9]

---

[5] *Journals of Ayn Rand*, p. 223.

[6] Peikoff, *Objectivism*, p. 251.

[7] Peikoff, *Objectivism*, pp. 253–254.

[8] Peikoff, *Objectivism*, p. 252.

[9] Douglass's defense of independence reflects a similar respect for reality. He observes, for instance, that "Men may cheat their neighbors and may cheat themselves but they cannot cheat nature. She will only pay the wages one honestly earns," p. 560.

Rand's conception of independence should be distinguished from autonomy, which is more frequently spoken of in the philosophical literature but is used to mean different things, primarily referring to a psychological condition or a political ideal. Rand's conception of independence is essentially epistemological; accordingly, whether her conception overlaps with the psychological sense of autonomy will depend on precisely what that refers to. Also, throughout, my claims about independence apply to adults. Children are naturally existentially dependent (not necessarily intellectually dependent)

The alternative to independence is what Rand calls second-handedness. A second-hander "is one who regards the consciousness of other men as superior to his own and to the facts of reality."[10] The second-hander turns to others as his fundamental frame of reference and source of values. He treats other people as his ultimate ruler rather than his own first-hand grasp of reality. Other people *are* the ultimate reality, in his mind.

Rand's description in her journals of Peter Keating, a commonplace sort of second-hander who is another central character in *The Fountainhead*, is instructive. "[T]o Keating, all reality is second-hand – through others, by others, for others. . . . His life is an eternal concern with what others will think, what others will say, how others will react to him." Keating's "spirit is an empty space which other men have to fill. . . . His consuming ambition is to be great – in other people's eyes. Thus, at the root of his spirit, others take precedence over his own self. Others establish all his values. Others become the motive power of his will to live."[11]

Since Keating represents just one type of second-hander, we should notice a few of its other incarnations. A thief who expropriates others' property by force or a moocher who obtains property by preying on others' sympathy is clearly dependent on his victims for the goods he takes from them. Rather than work to create or otherwise earn the values he seeks, he relies on others to create them. A power-luster such as a dictator or a bully is a second-hander, as well, as he depends on bossing other people around in order to feel whole or successful. He treats others – more specifically, the manipulation of others into a subordinate position – as his lifeblood. Rand regards "the man who goes after power" as "the worst second-hander of all," dramatizing this through her portrait of Gail Wynand in *The Fountainhead*.[12] Wynand is a successful (by conventional standards) newspaper tycoon who builds an empire by pandering to the masses' tastes. When, late in the story, he attempts to *lead* public opinion by using his papers to win support for a cause that means a great deal to

---

and must be gradually weaned off that dependence as they become able to assume greater responsibility for themselves.

[10] Rand, "The Argument from Intimidation," in *The Virtue of Selfishness*, p. 165. There, she uses the term "social metaphysician." In her journals, Rand links the two when she describes social metaphysics as "the neurosis resulting from automatized second-handedness, i.e., the type of psycho-epistemology that is focused primarily on the views of others, not on reality," *Journals of Ayn Rand*, p. 678.

[11] *Journals of Ayn Rand*, pp. 225, 224. See pp. 223–230 for more on this issue.

[12] Rand, *The Fountainhead* (New York: Bobbs-Merrill, 1943), p. 660.

him, his readers desert him. For all his apparent "being in charge" and
"running things" (which he had sought), what Wynand realizes, in the
end, is that "a leash is only a rope with a noose at both ends."[13] Milton's
famous line that it is "better to reign in Hell than serve in Heaven" reflects
a false alternative, in Rand's view.[14] The choice that a person faces is "not
self-sacrifice or domination."[15]

An altruist is another type of second-hander insofar as the charter for
the altruist's actions is entirely determined by the needs of others. The
person who seeks to live for others "is a parasite in motive" who hitches his
course to theirs. His role, he believes, is simply to serve others' welfare.[16]
The person who accepts conclusions by faith rather than by reason is yet
another type of second-hander. To accept a belief on faith is to accept it
in the absence of or contrary to evidence or proof. This precludes the
possibility of independence, since a person cannot think for himself if he
refuses to *think* at all. He cannot be oriented to reality if he shuns the evidence of reality. (Although one might think that the faith-driven person
is, at least sometimes, simply indulging his *own* emotions in professing
the beliefs that he does, rule by emotions is not a hallmark of independence; rule by reality, is. I will say more on this later. The immediate
point is that the person operating by faith allows the conclusions of others
to stand in for his own, since he holds no *conclusions* (which are products of reasoning); he simply affirms certain assertions.)[17] Still another
second-hander is the person who seeks advancement through connections and favors rather than honest effort and the quality of his work.
Indeed, our varied, vivid vocabulary designating numerous species of
second-handedness – freeloader, sponge, leech, bootlicker, brown-noser,
toady, chameleon, sycophant, and so on – testifies to our recognition of
the phenomenon that Rand is highlighting.[18]

---

[13] Rand, *The Fountainhead*, p. 716.

[14] John Milton, *Paradise Lost*, Book I, line 261.

[15] Rand, *The Fountainhead*, p. 739. For more on this, see pp. 736–743.

[16] Rand, *The Fountainhead*, p. 738.

[17] In Galt's speech, Rand writes that "the alleged short-cut to knowledge, which is faith, is
only a short-circuit destroying the mind," *Atlas Shrugged*, p. 1018. For Rand's analysis of
the idea of placing faith in another person, see her letters written to her editor Archibald
Ogden, *Letters of Ayn Rand*, pp. 67–72 and 453–456. There, she makes plain that one
should base expectations of others on concrete evidence and reason, remarking that
she would consider anyone's blind trust in her insulting.

[18] *The Fountainhead* offers a rich palette of types of second-hander, including, in addition
to Keating and Wynand, Ellsworth Toohey, Lois Cook, and the Dean of the Stanton Institute's Architecture School. Roark gradually comes to understand the shared principle
that drives these characters.

It should be clear that trading with others does not relegate a person to the ranks of the second-handers. In a division of labor economy, a person who relies on his own power to create values to exchange for further values that he seeks from others does not thereby compromise his orientation around reality. Standing in a mutually advantageous relationship with another person does not require that a person surrender his judgment to theirs. An independent person may not always be able to find others willing to trade on the terms he seeks. If others do not offer what he would like, he will have to take other actions to acquire it or go without it. He is not thus reduced to the methods of a second-hander, however. The person who earns his sustenance by paying for another's goods or services and the person who obtains his sustenance by preying on others' productiveness, whether through force or flattery, duplicity or freeloading or any other second-handed means, are not moral equivalents. They cannot both be subsumed under the concept of dependents.[19]

Less conspicuous than many of the types of second-handedness I have cited but far more common, and just as parasitic, are countless people who hold jobs and pay their bills but surrender their souls by unreflectively deferring to the standards of others. Such people are quietly consumed with gaining other people's acceptance or admiration, with acquiring prestige or fame, however local or extended. They are driven by a need to fit in or to be well-thought of. This thirst for the affirmation of others can affect the jobs people take, the groups they join, the relationships they form, the goals they adopt. While the independent person will choose his career by reference to the relevant facts of reality (e.g., his enjoyment of the work, his aptitude for it, his judgment of its value, employment prospects), the second-hander will choose his career by reference to what other people think of it (e.g., becoming a physician "because everybody is impressed by doctors," joining the family business because all of his siblings have, going into a "helping" profession because society considers it noble). While the independent person adopts his political affiliations by reference to relevant reality (parties' track records, his own assessment of the causes of social problems and the most likely effects of proposed solutions, etc.), the second-hander adopts the position that is most favored among his neighbors or friends or colleagues without bothering to examine whether that position is justified. Within the realm of trade, whereas the independent person depends on his first-hand judgment to create a value and on others' first-hand judgment to recognize its value and thus

---

[19] Peikoff, *Objectivism*, pp. 257–258.

be willing to trade for it, the second-hander proceeds sheerly on the basis of others' valuations, asking only: "Do other people value x? If so, I will make it" – regardless of his own judgment of x.

These forms of second-handedness are not exhaustive, yet all of them share its essence. Whether the second-hander seeks material or spiritual values, whether he seeks property he has not earned or esteem he has not earned or direction whose validity he does not see for himself, whether, more broadly, he seeks others' approval for all he does or conformity with prevailing opinions for all he "knows," the second-hander rejects reality as his ultimate sovereign and substitutes other people in its place. As Rand puts it in *The Fountainhead*, "The [independent person's] concern is the conquest of nature. The parasite's concern is the conquest of men."[20]

In painting the alternative to independence, Rand's claim is not that all second-handers consciously decide: "I care about people more than about reality." Rather, many second-handers lose a sharp sense of the difference; extrapersonal reality fades from their conceptual inventory. The stronger a person's orientation to other people grows, the more that other people's opinions will seem all-important and the weaker that person's appreciation of the primacy of existence. The independent person, in contrast, approaches his days objectively. He does not allow the content of others' consciousness to obstruct his reliance on reality as the basis for conducting his life. Nor does he follow his own thoughts or feelings without ensuring their validity. Obviously, a person's desires are legitimately relevant to many decisions, such as choice of a career or a spouse, and a person can also learn a great deal from others. The point is that the independent person *uses* his consciousness to apprehend reality but he does not allow the contents of anyone's consciousness, simply because they are that, to substitute for reality.

Correspondingly, in commending independence, Rand is not endorsing the subjectivist view that any of a person's beliefs or desires or actions

---

[20] *The Fountainhead*, p. 738. For more on the nature and various types of second-handedness, see Rand, "The Nature of the Second-Hander," in *For The New Intellectual*, pp. 78–81, and Peikoff, *Objectivism*, pp. 253 and 258. While Peikoff, relying on the portrait Rand presents in *The Fountainhead*, lists social workers as an example of second-handers, Rand does not condemn all social workers. In a question period in 1968, she says: "I do not oppose all social workers. Both Howard Roark and Peter Keating are architects: there are good and bad men in every profession. What I am opposed to is the collectivist-altruist kind of social worker (like Katie in *The Fountainhead*). That sort is frequently encountered, but that doesn't mean all social workers are frustrated little tyrants." *Ayn Rand Answers*, p. 122.

is valid so long as it *his*. Independence is not whim worship.[21] Because independence is an orientation to reality, it requires rational judgment, since rationality is a person's means of orienting himself to reality. The call for independence is not license to indulge any urges that a person happens to experience. "One's own independent judgment is the *means* by which one must choose one's actions," Rand explains, "but it is not a moral criterion nor a moral validation..."[22] The fact that a person's conclusion is his own does not ensure that it is correct. The person pursuing his objective self-interest must be concerned with the accuracy of his judgments.

At the same time, in urging independence as a virtue, Rand is observing that a rational judgment must be a person's own judgment. (We will see why, shortly.) Rand captures the essence of independence in Roark's reference to "men of unborrowed vision."[23] An independent person looks for himself, sees for himself, and thinks and acts on that basis. Moreover, to alter the sensory metaphors, he does not listen for the echo. When he acts, he is not concerned in any fundamental way with how his action will seem to others. Reality is his guide, from start to finish.

In the end, then, independence is an issue of method – the fundamental method by which a person runs his life. To answer questions and make decisions, does he direct his focus to what other people think about reality or to reality itself? An independent person seeks neither his direction, his conclusions, nor his satisfactions from the views of others. He does not act for the sake of others in any way. Others are not his compass. Reality is.

WHY INDEPENDENCE IS A VIRTUE

As we explained in Chapter 3, reason is man's means of survival. Human beings must think and act rationally in order to create the values that sustain us. Given that the requirements of our survival are not found ready-made in nature, Rand observes, a person faces a basic choice: whether to survive by the "work of his own mind or as a parasite fed by the minds of others."[24] In identifying independence as a virtue, Rand is recognizing the strong pull that other people often exert on a person and signaling

[21] Peikoff, *Objectivism*, p. 256.
[22] Rand, "Introduction," *The Virtue of Selfishness*, p. xi, emphasis in original.
[23] Rand, *The Fountainhead*, p. 737.
[24] Rand, *The Fountainhead*, p. 738.

the kind of disciplined focus on reality that human life (including proper relations with others) requires.

"Independence is the recognition of the fact that yours is the responsibility of judgment," Rand writes, "and nothing can help you escape it – that no substitute can do your thinking, as no pinch-hitter can live your life . . ."[25] Other people's judgments are fallible, as a person's own are. More importantly, even when others' judgments are correct, they do not supersede reality. Reality remains the inexorable master that a person who wishes to live must satisfy. A person's success depends, ultimately, on his effectively navigating the world as it is, not other people's beliefs about the way the world is. Thus, it makes no sense to treat others' opinions as a higher authority than one's own grasp of facts. Independence, the orientation around reality, is imperative. (Although I will primarily refer to dependence as submission to others' beliefs and wishes, this should be understood as a shorthand for all the ways in which a person might treat other people as his lodestar, for example, seeking to stand in a certain relationship to others, such as dominating them or serving them. Also, throughout, I am not speaking of cases in which other people are themselves the *subject* of a person's thought, as when seeking to diagnose a person's illness, evaluate a job applicant, or determine whether to pursue a friendship. In such cases, facts about those people are what one needs to be most concerned with – those facts relevant to the purpose for which one is evaluating them.)

The case for independence is a direct outgrowth of the case for rationality. "Man cannot survive except through his mind," yet "the mind is an attribute of the individual. There is no such thing as a collective brain" or "a collective thought."[26] Even an agreement among several individuals is simply a convergence of the thinking performed by each individual himself. Because rational thinking is inherently self-directed, the need for independence is actually implicit in the need for rationality. Rational thought is something that a person can only engage in for himself. Reason is volitional; it works only by the reasoner's own choice; others cannot operate it on his behalf. Others might put a gun to a person's head to try to get him to think, but the decision of whether to do so remains irrevocably his. No one else can think for a person. Nor can a person reach rational conclusions or acquire knowledge without thinking for himself. Consider the familiar experience of listening to another person

[25] Rand, *Atlas Shrugged*, p. 1019.
[26] Rand, *The Fountainhead*, p. 737.

explain a difficult point and at some stage, realizing "now, I get it." Before that, although the listener might have *said* that he agreed or understood, that would not have been the case. The breakthrough occurs due to the listener's own apprehension of the relevant material. It is only through first-handed engagement with the material in question that a person can come to authentically understand that material.

While a person can learn from others, to accept another person's conclusions without thinking them through for himself – without examining the evidence for premises, for instance, or checking the logic of inferences – is to regress to the performance of a parrot. The result of such an exercise is not knowledge. The ability to recite particular words does not bespeak genuine learning (as encounters with parrots make plain). As John Locke observed,

We may as rationally hope to see with other men's eyes as to know by other men's understandings.... The floating of other men's opinions in our brains, makes us not one jot the more knowing, [even if] they happen to be true...[27]

In a similar vein, Rand writes:

No matter how vast your knowledge or how modest, it is your own mind that has to acquire it.... Your mind is your only judge of truth – and if others dissent from your verdict, reality is the court of final appeal. Nothing but a man's mind can perform that complex, delicate, crucial process of identification which is thinking. Nothing can direct the process but his own judgment.[28]

Peikoff spells out the point:

A man cannot think if he places something – anything – above his perception of reality. He cannot follow the evidence unswervingly or uphold his conclusions intransigently, while regarding compliance with other men as his moral imperative.... He cannot use his brain while surrendering his sovereignty over it, i.e., while accepting his neighbors as its owner and term-setter.[29]

Independence is a precondition of rational judgment. To the extent that any thought process is dependent, treating other people as its touchstone, it is not rational. And because independence is vital to rationality, independence is vital to life. For human beings, living depends on rational thought and action. While this is most obvious for a person alone

[27] John Locke, *An Essay Concerning Human Understanding*, Book I, Ch. III, Section 24.
[28] Rand, *Atlas Shrugged*, p. 1017.
[29] Peikoff, *The Ominous Parallels* (New York: Stein & Day, 1982), p. 334. Also see brief discussion of this in *Objectivism*, p. 255. The thesis that one cannot force a mind is powerfully dramatized in *Atlas Shrugged*.

on a desert island, regardless of whether a person exists in isolation or in society with millions, the wellspring of values – what allows a person to create those things that will genuinely advance his life – is his mind's grasp of reality. We live on independent thinking, quite literally.

Consider some things that are objective values in many people's lives – bread, aspirin, cell phones, MRI technology, eBay. What makes these things valuable? As we saw in Chapter 2, they must stand in a life-furthering relationship to the individual in question. Whether a product or service does stand in that relationship, however, depends on what it is – as opposed to: on what some people think it is. People might wish for the convenience of portable, wireless telephones, but whether a given device can provide that service depends on the materials and circuitry within it, its ability to conduct a satellite signal, and so on. People might like to have a pill that can relieve pain, but whether a given pill will do that depends on its ingredients and the chemistry of the human body.

Raindances do not coax crops from the ground. Consciousness does not dictate reality.[30] Accordingly, it does not dictate the conditions of human existence or the terms of value. This principle is equally true in those cases in which other people's attitudes can *affect* a thing's value. If eBay is a value to Eric, it is so because it allows him to trade goods at attractive prices. Obviously, the popularity of eBay can enhance its utility; the more people who use it, the better the chances of Eric's finding certain deals (though popularity may also make it harder to find certain deals, as others may outbid him). The point, however, is that people like and use eBay (at least insofar as they are independent) because of the venue it provides, not simply because other people like it. The services that eBay offers are the grounds of its popularity and of the value that people can reap from it.[31]

The same holds for any objective value. For human beings must navigate reality in order to create the values that fuel our lives, not some people's images of reality. Nothing that is not grounded on the facts of human beings' needs and on the actual means of fulfilling them can enhance a person's life. As we have seen in previous chapters, playing make-believe cannot sustain human life, however many play along.

---

[30] See Rand's discussion of this in "The Metaphysical Versus the Manmade," in *Philosophy: Who Needs It*, pp. 30 ff.

[31] Rand offers a useful distinction between a thing's market value or socially objective value and its philosophically objective value in "What is Capitalism?" in *Capitalism: The Unknown Ideal*, pp. 24–25.

Substituting other people as one's fundamental guide to action amounts to such a fruitless game.

Failing to recognize this, the second-hander inserts other people in the place of reality. While it can certainly be appropriate to consult others for guidance on occasion (about appropriate attire for an event, for example, or when buying a car), the second-hander acts solely on the basis of what others would say or do; he chooses clothes or a car or a career entirely by his projections of what others would expect or want or admire. (I will say more about consulting experts later in the chapter.) He ignores that which should guide his thoughts and actions – facts such as his own budget or abilities or enjoyment – and erects in their place a new master. Such a policy is doomed, however. By abdicating the judgment of his own mind, the second-hander relinquishes the very tool that is crucial for a human being to live. By orienting himself to other people, the second-hander leaves himself at the mercy of whomever he happens to follow. For this reason, Rand describes dependence as a course of "self-abasement and self-destruction."[32]

The independent person, by contrast, recognizes that his judgment is what counts, for him, because that is his indispensable means of achieving values. Other people may be smarter than he, but he cannot know whether their ideas are of any value to him until he assesses them for himself. Practicing the virtue of independence cannot guarantee that a person will invariably reach correct conclusions. Yet "an error made on your own is safer than ten truths accepted on faith," Rand points out, "because the first leaves you the means to correct it, but the second destroys your capacity to distinguish truth from error."[33]

In sum, because the only path to rational action is through independence and because human beings rely on rational action to survive, independence is critical to our lives.

As with any virtue, a person's failure to exercise independence will not necessarily provoke immediate catastrophe. As I discussed in Chapter 2 and at greater length in *Viable Values*, the pulse of a person who does not act virtuously does not refute the necessity of virtue for human life. Remember that life, as the standard of value, does not refer to momentary morgue-avoidance but to the condition of a person whose every aspect is operating in a life-advancing manner. All of such a person's volitional actions are directed at or, at the least, consistent with, the positive progress

[32] Rand, *Atlas Shrugged*, p. 1019. For a similar appraisal, see *Journals of Ayn Rand*, p. 401.
[33] Rand, *Atlas Shrugged*, p. 1058.

of his life. The standard of value is not simply any of a range of desired
"qualities" of life that might appeal to a given person while he remains
this side of the cemetery. The standard, rather, is a single, firm constant:
life. And because life is achieved only by life-sustaining action (an organism might endure for a time despite anti-life action, but never because
of it), this standard demands that a person act in consummately pro-life
fashion. The person who is living, in the sense that satisfies the standard
of value, is the person who is fully committed in all his thoughts and
in all his actions to achieving his survival. The person who violates the
moral principles that prescribe what is necessary to achieve such a condition, by contrast, is subverting his survival. Because all moral virtues are
demanded by rationality and because rationality is man's fundamental
means of survival, to cheat on any one moral principle is to turn one's
back on morality itself – and correlatively, to turn one's back on one's
life.

To the extent that a person remains alive while not exercising independence, he is sustained by other people's independent thought and
action. Living among other people does create the possibility of exploiting the fruits of their labor and can thus disguise the ultimate source
of the values that fuel a person's life. It does not alter the fundamental
conditions of human existence, however. A second-hander could exist
over any extended period of time only to the extent that enough other
people are first-handers who face reality as it is, who take rational, value-
producing actions, and can thus serve as his hosts. The second-hander
must be a hitchhiker of virtue, as Rand puts it, when not a direct practi-
tioner himself.[34] For if all other people were themselves second-handers,
they could not create the values that anyone's subsistence depends on. It
is only by independently heeding the relevant properties of the relevant
materials that anyone could construct a hut or a high-rise, a hammer or
a heart-pump.

While a person might be tempted to try to exploit the material and spiritual values that others have created and leave the work of independent
thought and action to them, then, to erect others as his master is an ill-
fated diversion that cannot advance his happiness. From one perspective,
it may seem that the greater the degree of dependence a person indulges
in, the more he submits blindly to others, the greater the danger to which
he exposes himself. (Consider the fate of the submissive followers of the
spiritual guru Jim Jones, who orchestrated the suicide of 912 followers

[34] Cited in Peikoff, *Objectivism*, p. 258.

who drank cyanide-laced punch in Jonestown, Guyana, in 1978.) Should a second-hander wish to minimize that risk, he would have to exert his own judgment about who are appropriate "hosts" and on which issues he should rely on them. In other words, to protect himself, he would have to violate the policy of parasitism; it is not a policy that a person could consistently adhere to.[35] This perspective does not capture the heart of the issue, however. By eschewing independence, a person abandons the chance to create the values that would advance his life and correlatively relinquishes his means of achieving his happiness, long range. In surrendering his judgment to that of others, the second-hander gambles that the people into whose hands he delivers himself will actually supply the values he needs. This is a gamble that he cannot win. The issue does not turn on a shrewd calculations of odds, but on the nature of value. Recall from Chapter 2 that nothing can be objectively valuable to a person unless he recognizes its survival-promoting relationship to his life. In rejecting both intrinsicist and subjectivist conceptions of value, Rand argues that "the good is *an evaluation* of the facts of reality by man's consciousness according to a rational standard of value."[36] Nothing can be objectively valuable to a person without that person's independent assessment of it. Things can exert certain effects independently of his awareness or evaluation, of course, but they cannot be values – things that he will, or should, act to gain or keep.

All of this has presented the central argument for independence: It is vital to all rational thought and action and thereby vital to human survival. A few further observations, however, will illuminate additional facets of its value.

The independent man is the only true egoist, Peikoff writes.[37] Because the mind is responsible for everything that distinguishes an individual – his thoughts, his actions, his character, even, to a considerable extent, the condition of his body (insofar as that depends on his actions) – it is a person's mind, more than anything else, that *is* his self.[38] By subordinating

---

[35] A person who sought to follow others' lead on absolutely all issues, 100 percent of the time – in deciding what he should eat, when he should eat, when to go to sleep, how long to sleep, when to brush his teeth, how long to brush his teeth, whether to read the newspapers this morning, which articles to read, and so on – would be paralyzed.

[36] Rand, "What is Capitalism?" p. 22, emphasis in original.

[37] Peikoff, *Objectivism*, p. 255.

[38] See Rand, "Selfishness Without a Self," in *Philosophy: Who Needs It*, p. 60, and *Atlas Shrugged*, pp. 1057, 1030. Cf. Aristotle's assertion that the understanding "above all, is what each person is," *Nicomachean Ethics*, 1169a, trans. Irwin.

his mind's grasp of reality to the judgments of others, however, a second-hander places others above himself in the deepest sense possible.

Second-handedness may not be intended as a sacrifice of oneself. On the contrary, a second-hander often believes that he is advancing his interest by pursuing a certain relationship to others. The dictators, thieves, and other second-handers we have mentioned are, by conventional standards, paradigms of selfishness. They seek to prey on others in various ways and to gratify their own desires. According to Rand, however, this interpretation is too shallow.[39] For whatever form of second-handedness a person practices, whether he seeks to serve others, to exploit others, or to erase his own thoughts and simply follow others, others dominate his landscape. The second-hander does not embrace ends based on his appraisal of reality, but as a reaction to others. He attends a party because a certain group considers it *the* place to be Saturday night; he supports a political candidate because his colleagues expect it; he attempts to dominate coworkers because success is measured by who's on top. The point is, even a person who succeeds in satisfying his desires (to rule others, to dupe others, to be admired by others, etc.), when those desires are dictated by his *relation to others*, does not genuinely advance *his* self.

Man's self is his consciousness.[40] As Peikoff explains, the self is a man's

mind or conceptual faculty, the faculty of reason. All man's spiritually distinctive attributes derive from this faculty. For instance, it is reason (man's value judgments) that leads to man's emotions. And it is reason which possesses volition, the ability to make choices.

But reason is a property of the individual. There is no such thing as a collective brain.

The term *ego* [by which Rand means the self][41] combines the above points into a single concept: it designates the mind (and its attributes) considered as an individual possession. The ego, therefore, is that which constitutes the essential identity of a human being. As one dictionary puts it, the ego is "the 'I' or self of any person; [it is] a person as thinking, feeling, and willing, and distinguishing itself from the selves of others and from the objects of its thought."[42]

---

[39] Rand considers it a "fraud" to consider such types as egoists. Rand, "The Soul of an Individualist," in *For the New Intellectual*, p. 97.

[40] Rand, *The Fountainhead*, p. 737.

[41] *Letters of Ayn Rand*, p. 351.

[42] Peikoff, "Introduction to 50th Anniversary Edition," Ayn Rand, *Anthem* (New York: Penguin, 1995), p. v.

Because he is preoccupied with other people, the second-hander's thoughts, feelings, and desires are buried. Indeed, the more regularly a person defers to others, the more inclined he will be to do so in the future and the less likely he will be even to form opinions or ends of his own *to* bury. Why bother cultivating his own convictions if they will be set aside as soon as they diverge from the thoughts of others or interfere with his occupying the "right" position in relation to others? The sense in which the second-hander's life is his is steadily eroded; his very identity, gradually extinguished. Because he is defined by his position vis-à-vis others, he forfeits a genuine self whose interest he *could* serve. The dependent person can be described more accurately as a shell, filled with the prescriptions of others. Whatever his avowed intentions, the person who allows others to chart his course abnegates himself as much as the most deliberately committed altruist. For he renounces those elements that could constitute his self and obliterates the distinction between his *self* and others. (This is eloquently depicted in the deterioration of Keating over the course of *The Fountainhead*. By the story's end, *he* is not a person; the thing that occupies his body and answers to his name is merely a conglomeration of the ideas, attitudes, and wishes of other people – all the people he sought to imitate and impress, over the years.)[43]

Egoism counsels the pursuit of self-interest. A person cannot serve himself unless he has a self, however, and it is the exercise of independence that enables a person to be a self, to be an individual possessing thoughts and ends of his own. Thus independence serves the self not only in the way that all rational virtues do, by fostering the achievement of the values that human life requires. It also helps a person to build a genuine self for whom anything could be objectively valuable.

Finally, we should note that along with the second-hander's identity is likely to go, in many cases, the flavor and enjoyment that a person could derive from his life. Second-handedness distances a person from his own experience. Because all that he does is filtered through others (his projections of others' reactions, his status in relation to them, etc.), the second-hander recedes, becoming merely a marionette of others' will. And he is likely to feel that.

A second-hander cannot obtain the satisfaction of having achieved an objective value for himself. Goods that are taken or stolen are not earned.

---

[43] See particularly the scene in which Dominique exposes this, beginning on p. 447, especially pp. 454–455, and Keating's later realization of his self-betrayal in an exchange with Catherine, p. 650.

Even with less sinister types of second-handedness, to the extent that a person pursues ends because others esteem them, he does not appreciate the rationale behind them and thus does not know whether they are truly suitable ends for him. Consequently, if he achieves such hand-me-down ends, the accomplishment will be hollow. Having fulfilled others' standards, it remains uncertain whether he has done anything good for himself. Success at implementing others' will, without the agent's first-handed endorsement of the value of that will, does not usually provide the same caliber of gratification, the same affirmation of his judgment and ability and of his broader capacity to achieve his happiness, that the successful pursuit of his own judgment could. The sense of efficacy and pride that a person can gain from accomplishments that stem from his assessment of ends and means is impossible when he simply functions as an instrument of others, mechanically executing their agenda. This applies not only to accomplishments. A person spending a Saturday night as he would like, home alone, rather than attending a party because other people expect it, is likely to enjoy himself much more than he would have at the party. Doing what a person himself rationally chooses to do is often far more enjoyable, even when the activity chosen is relatively nondescript, because charting one's own course and thereby exerting one's own identity is part of the pleasure of living.[44]

The quality of a second-hander's experience at any given moment is not the central argument for the value of independence. How satisfying a person's life feels to him will be influenced by subconscious premises that may or may not be justified. Thus we cannot issue definitive pronouncements of how any first-hander or second-hander will feel on a particular occasion. Nonetheless, a second-hander can expect to encounter diluted satisfaction from his course. Earlier, we noted that the dependent person, by not making investments in becoming the kind of person fit to achieve his happiness, does not help himself long range. Here, my point is that he is typically not helping himself short-range, either, since the satisfactions available through second-hand "achievements" tend to be stale.

The primary case for independence, again, rests in the fact that living depends on rational thought and action. In order to gain knowledge and to create the values that sustain us, human beings must proceed by reason,

---

[44] In light of this, the second-hander's course becomes especially curious. Frequently, people resist subservience to others precisely because a person made to follow others' orders has his own identity smothered; the denial of his agency leaves him unable to exert himself. The second-hander, however, imposes this position on himself. Second-handedness is a kind of self-made servitude.

accepting reality as our fundamental source of knowledge and guidance. To exercise rationality, in turn, a person must exercise independence. The second-hander's fixation with other people diverts him from that which warrants his paramount respect, reality, and abandons his means of navigating reality.

WHAT INDEPENDENCE DEMANDS

Given that independence is acceptance of the responsibility of forming one's own judgments and of living by one's own mind, the demands of independence are straightforward. I shall first clarify the intellectual demands and then the material demands. I will also address some of the implications for proper relations between individuals. While I cannot explore the full dimensions of such relations here, it will be helpful to forestall certain possible misunderstandings of Rand's position. (We will consider further aspects of social relations in the chapter on justice.)

Intellectual Requirements

At the intellectual level, independence demands that a person think for himself. In contrast to the person who passively falls into line behind others, unreflectively accepting their opinions as best, the independent person subjects beliefs and practices to his own first-hand scrutiny. He checks ideas against reality, as far as he is able. He examines evidence, questions claims, draws inferences, and adopts ends on the basis of his grasp of the relevant facts rather than by substituting the thoughts or precedents of others. Independence imposes no prohibition on consulting or learning from others, but it does rule out subjugation of one's own judgment to that of others simply because it is others'. The issue, essentially, is whether one proceeds by faith or reason.[45] An independent person does not relinquish the reins of his life to any social authority, be it religious or secular, singular or plural.[46] While others might correct his error, independence demands that a person understand that correction for himself. In working out the idea in her *Journals*, Rand puts it graphically: The independent person "must examine a theory presented to him by other men exactly as he examines any fact of physical nature,

---

[45] Peikoff, *Objectivism*, p. 256. Also see Rand's response to a question about the legitimacy of using others' ideas in *Ayn Rand Answers*, p. 145.

[46] Peikoff, *Objectivism*, p. 254.

by the same method, through the same act of independent rational judgment. He is as alone in the presence of an idea as in the presence of a
jungle."[47]

A few passages from *Atlas Shrugged* help to refine the ideal that Rand
is advocating. While the heroine, Dagny Taggart, is weighing whether to
join the strike of the rational and productive, one of the strikers, Hugh
Akston, explains: "It is not your obedience that we seek to win, but your
rational conviction. You have seen all the elements of our secret. The
conclusion is now yours to draw – we can help you to name it, but not
to accept it – the sight, the knowledge, and the acceptance, must be
yours."[48] (He refers to their way of life as a secret because they have not yet
openly declared their strike.) A little later, when Dagny is on the brink of
making her decision, Akston advises: "Consider the reasons which make
us certain that we are right, but not the fact that we are certain. If you are
not convinced, ignore our certainty. Don't be tempted to substitute our
judgment for your own." Another character, Midas Mulligan, chimes in:
"Don't rely on our knowledge of what's best for your future. We do know,
but it can't be best until *you* know it."[49]

Given the prevalence of subjectivist notions of independence, it is
important to emphasize that the basis for the independent person's conclusions is reason rather than feeling. A person's interest is not advanced
through the satisfaction of irrational desires, however genuine *his* such
desires may be. Accordingly, the virtue of independence does not consist
in indulging whatever inclinations an individual happens to experience.
The attitude appropriate to the independent person is not "me first," but
"reality first – and only I can apprehend it for myself." It is not "whatever
I want" that is most important for a rational egoist, but whatever, in fact,
will objectively serve his flourishing. Given that reality is what a person
must heed in order to flourish, all virtue demands that a person steer
himself by the compass of reality – that is, that he proceed rationally.
Indeed, because independence is a corollary of rationality, no thought
or action can be independent, in the relevant sense, unless it is rational.

Correspondingly, independence does not require that a person strive
to be different. The Emersonian ideal of nonconformity ("whoso would

---

[47] *Journals of Ayn Rand*, p. 257. Also see pp. 258 and 307, in which Rand posits that human
beings may share their knowledge, which is the result of thinking, but not their thinking
itself.

[48] Rand, *Atlas Shrugged*, p. 735.

[49] Rand, *Atlas Shrugged*, p. 802, emphasis in original. The "first rule" of the strikers' community "is that one must always see for oneself," p. 709.

be a man must be a non-conformist") corsets a person to other people, instructing him to diverge from the path of others rather than to follow it. As such, it is simply another form of second-handedness. In Rand's view, there is no shame in sometimes saying "me, too." What matters is the means by which a person reaches his conclusion rather than whether his conclusion happens to be shared by others. Remember that independence is a function of a person's method of directing his life. It consists of employing the method of objectivity.[50]

While we saw in the previous section that independence enables an individual to be a self, independence simultaneously demands a commitment to oneself. If the second-hander's own thoughts diverge from others', he shrugs off his thoughts with the observation, "well, it's good enough for them . . ." Why are others' views considered more compelling than his own? The less a person thinks of himself, the easier it is to answer this question. The person of low self-esteem will think: "What do I know? How important are my desires?" In order to resist such inclinations to defer to others and, instead, to follow through on his own judgment, a person must value himself. The exercise of independence requires a belief in one's own basic worth, a quotient of self-esteem that enables a person to view his judgment as capable and his ends as worthy. The rudiments of self-esteem and their relation to independence are more psychologically intricate than I am equipped to explore and than we need to, to discern a lesson for the requirements of independence. My point is a very basic one: Independence will be impossible for anyone who lacks a commitment to his own well-being.

We should also bear in mind that although the terms "parasite" and "second-hander" may connote the most extreme alternatives to independence such as dictators and larcenists, pirates and plagiarists, spineless yes-men and fawning sycophants, second-handedness can take many

---

[50] Several elements of Emerson's philosophy are antithetical to Rand's, such as his claims that the essence of virtue lies in "spontaneity or instinct," that a man's real self is the "universal mind," that "there is one mind common to all individual men," and his exhortations to "trust your emotions" and "rise to the sanctities of obedience and faith." Ralph Waldo Emerson, "Self-Reliance" (1841) in Charles W. Eliot, ed., *Essays and English Traits* (Danbury, CT: Grolier Enterprises, 1980), pp. 69, 66, 74, and "History," *Essays: First Series* (New York: AMS Press, 1968), vol. 2, p. 3. In a question period, Rand criticizes Emerson as a whim-worshiping enemy of reason. *Ayn Rand Answers*, pp. 162–163. Rand would also have been horrified by Emerson's praise for Napoleon as a self-made man (noted in Paul Johnson, *Napoleon* (New York: Penguin, 2002), p. 185). This mistakes a particular type of dependence (the power-luster's desire to achieve dominance over others) for independence.

more moderate forms, as well. The person who adjusts what he says to offer other people what he thinks they wish to hear, the person whose opinions are absorbed uncritically from the editorial pages or from his minister (or from Ayn Rand, for that matter), the politician who professes positions according to what polls tell him would be popular, the academic who concludes that if an author was published in *this* journal he must be a first-rate intellect, the person who is ruled by thoughts of what he is "supposed" to do ("what is expected here?" "what would others think?"), the status seeker, the name dropper, and the social climber all fail to exercise independence insofar as their thoughts and actions are essentially determined by other people.[51] Individuals can practice second-handedness in different spheres and to differing degrees. A given individual might be obsequious toward certain people but not others or he might be status-driven in regard to his professional standing but not his personal possessions. Whatever the form and whatever the degree, because these less extreme forms are more tempting to most people, it is important to realize that these, too, are inconsistent with independence. As with all the virtues, certain transgressions are more egregious and more damaging than others. My point is not to deny this, but to indicate prevalent kinds of action that the virtue of independence identifies as antithetical to individual flourishing.

Material Requirements

The material demands of independence have been implicit in much of our discussion thus far. It is important for a person to think for himself in order for him to attain knowledge. Knowledge is not an end in itself, however. Knowledge is valuable for the purpose of guiding one's actions. Correspondingly, independence is not complete unless a person follows through and acts on his first-hand judgment.

If a human being wishes to live, he must enact the causes necessary to achieve that effect. The second-hander seeks the effects of life-sustaining action without enacting the requisite cause; he intends to leave it to others to think and work, planning simply to cash in on the fruits of their labor. The independent person, in contrast, pays his own way, accepting

---

[51] Rand indirectly cautions against that "supposed to" concern in *Journals of Ayn Rand*, p. 707. She is obviously not talking about cases in which a person previously made a commitment that reasonably gives rise to expectations and does create an obligation to others.

responsibility for his own well-being and investing the appropriate effort to achieve it.[52] Essentially, the independent person lives by the work of his own mind, using his judgment and correlative action to achieve the material values necessary to sustain his life. Rather than relying on others to meet his needs (whether by begging or burgling or some subtler hybrid of such methods), the independent person exerts his own productive effort. Independence does not prescribe concretely how each individual should do this; it does not demand that every able-bodied adult hold a job, for instance, or that he spurn assistance volunteered by others. If a person's spouse is able and willing to support him, independence does not demand that the person refuse such support. One person might gain spiritual value from another person's devoting his time to un-remunerative activities (e.g., fiction writing or child-raising). Financial support that liberates a person from the need to earn a paycheck need not compromise the beneficiary's independence. As long as he conscientiously fulfills his part of the bargain, he is engaging in an honorable trade of spiritual for material goods, and both parties are the beneficiaries. (A person should refuse gifts offered on terms that would demand the sacrifice of his independence.) Indeed, a person will be able to provide genuine value to another person only to the extent that he exercises first-hand judgment in engaging in the relevant value-producing activities. If he does not rely on such judgment, he cannot generate anything that truly fosters human life and is thus objectively valuable. By the same token, one person will be able to accurately gauge another's value to him only by the yardstick of reality rather than by relying merely on still other people's opinions about that person.[53]

We will discuss morality's demands in regard to work further when we examine the virtue of productiveness in Chapter 8. The point important to grasp here is that accepting others' assistance need not mean

[52] See Peikoff, *Objectivism*, pp. 254, 258, and 257.
[53] This does not deny that a person can be valuable as a transmitter of values that another person has created. A secretary who types his boss's brilliant book or a retailer who sells goods that others have produced plays a valuable role in the dissemination of those creations. A person can play such a role reliably, however, only to the extent that he uses first-handed judgment to perform that role. When questions or unanticipated obstacles arise, for instance, he must use his own rational judgment to determine how to proceed. In any capacity, whatever genuine value a person offers stems from his first-handedness, given that heeding reality is the indispensable means of advancing human life. (Readers of *Atlas Shrugged* see this vividly illustrated in the sequence narrating the tunnel disaster. A series of individuals' shirking the responsibility of first-hand judgment leads to the catastrophe.)

reorienting one's basic method of guiding one's life; it does not entail treating a particular benefactor, or other people more generally, as the maestro who conducts one's course. The requirement of independence remains attainably intact: Underneath whatever relationships a person might enjoy with others must stand that person's first-hand assessment of reality. In a given case, he must identify and assess relevant facts about the other person and that person's potential value to him as well as the facts relevant to his own ability to offer objective value to another person.

Although I have differentiated the material and intellectual demands of independence, it is important to realize that ultimately, intellectual and material independence stand or fall together.[54] Because rationality is the root of life-sustaining action, material independence relies on intellectual independence. Human beings can only produce the material values necessary to fuel their existence through reality-focused (rather than people-focused) thought. Pleasing my neighbors or satisfying the Food and Drug Administration cannot coax coats from the clouds or medicine from the trees. Nor can it trigger the insights that inform the creation of objectively valuable products and processes. Consequently, the person who does not engage in such thought but is intellectually dependent will become materially dependent. If he is not generating value-producing ideas, he must rely on others who are for the material values that he needs in order to live.

By the same token, a person who is materially dependent on others must become intellectually dependent insofar as he will need to maintain the good graces of those on whom his material well-being depends. He will need to appease those people – family members, business associates, institutional bureaucrats, whoever – by saying what they wish to hear and acting in ways they smile upon in order to continue the stream of benefits he needs. In essence, the two facets of independence interact in a mutually reinforcing cycle: Intellectual independence allows for material independence and requires material independence, just as material independence allows for intellectual independence and requires intellectual independence.

Relations with Others

But isn't man a social animal? And aren't human beings actually interdependent more than ever before, given our increasingly global economy? People in contemporary society seem dependent on one another not

---

[54] Peikoff discusses this in *Objectivism*, p. 257.

only for material goods but for spiritual values, as well, as ease of travel and communication allow different ideas and fashions in all realms to be widely circulated and readily reinforced. Independence is an anachronism, many would contend, an ideal at best suited to a bygone era.[55]

The first thing to observe about this objection is that the claim that man is a social animal is often left ambiguous. Is the claim that a human being enjoys associating with others? That he benefits from others? That he cannot survive without others? That his character is formed by others? The truth of the claim obviously hinges on exactly what it means.

In her *Journals* and in an oral question period, Rand rejects the claim that man is a social animal, yet she also has one of the virtuous characters in *Atlas*, Akston, affirm that "man *is* a social being, but not in the way the looters preach."[56] Since she holds that human existence relies on a basic orientation to reality rather than to other people, Rand would clearly reject the contention that we are dependent on others. For all that others might offer a person, other people are not human beings' most basic source of sustenance. Reliance on the beliefs or desires or charity of others is not the route to flourishing. Nor are we social in the sense that our characters are shaped by others. This is the idea that Rand expressly rejects in her oral remarks on the question. While living in a rational society can help a man's development and living in an irrational society can make it more difficult, society cannot make or unmake a man.[57] Given Rand's understanding that reason is a volitional faculty, this makes perfect sense. As she continues, in response to the question, "Society cannot form a person. It cannot force him to accept ideas ..."[58] In support of her claim stands the obvious fact that countless individuals resist the influences of their social surroundings every day.[59] In an essay,

---

[55] This idea well predates talk of a global economy, of course, and is taken for granted in many quarters. One representative sample: "The human being is a social network, necessarily dependent and psychically interrelated, a social organism, a political animal. The self is not an 'I' but a 'we.'" Michael Novak, *The Rise of the Unmeltable Ethnics* (New York: MacMillan, 1972), p. 199. (The claim remains in his second edition of 1996, p. 235.)

[56] *Journals of Ayn Rand*, p. 280; *Ayn Rand Answers*, p. 156; *Atlas Shrugged*, p. 747, emphasis in original.

[57] *Ayn Rand Answers*, p. 156. Also see Rand's critique of B. F. Skinner's contentions that "consciousness is a social product" and that "one advantage in being a social animal is that one need not discover practices for oneself" in "The Stimulus and the Response," in *Philosophy: Who Needs It*, pp. 175, 174.

[58] *Ayn Rand Answers*, p. 156.

[59] The contention that such resistance, on the part of some, is itself a reflection of social pressures would beg the question. One could not know such a thing without taking for granted the very conclusion that is in dispute.

Rand rejects the image of man as either a "lone wolf" or a "social animal," asserting that he is, in fact, a "*contractual* animal."[60]

What Rand would readily acknowledge is that human beings, when living properly, tend both to enjoy and to benefit from one another. Indeed, this is the thrust of Akston's remark about our social nature. He is referring to the pleasant and mutually beneficial relationships among those who have fully embraced a rationally egoistic ethics and are living with one another accordingly. In terms of independence, however, even if a person is more likely to lead a flourishing life if he establishes certain relationships with others, this does not mean that his life would be enhanced by contact with *any* other person. Whatever values a person might gain from others are not to be had equally from all others, interchangeably; other people are not valuable to a person simply in virtue of being others. Whether a person is valuable to a given individual depends on the specific relationship in which he stands to that individual's life. What is critical is that in order for a person to select the others whose association would truly be valuable to him, he must exercise first-handed judgment of reality. He must weigh the qualities he observes in another person as well as his own ends, abilities, needs, tastes, and the like. Even the great value that other individuals can offer, in other words, cannot be acquired without independence.

The popular refrain that in the contemporary world, we are all interdependent rests on a confusion of beneficial relationships with dependent relationships.[61] As I observed in my comments on trade, a person can gain a great deal from interactions with others without abandoning his fundamental orientation around reality. Indeed, the independent hero of *The Fountainhead* acknowledges needing people to give him work as an architect, remarking that he is "not building mausoleums."[62]

---

[60] Rand, "A Nation's Unity – Part 2," *The Ayn Rand Letters* II, no. 2 (Oct. 23, 1972), p. 3, emphasis in original.

[61] Peikoff, *Objectivism*, pp. 257–258. Also see *Letters of Ayn Rand*, pp. 95–96.

[62] The full exchange between Howard Roark and Austen Heller:

"Then you do need other people, after all, don't you, Howard?"
"Of course. What are you laughing at?"
"I've always thought that you were the most anti-social animal I've ever had the pleasure of meeting."
"I need people to give me work. I'm not building mausoleums..."

The Fountainhead, p. 166.

Winning clients does not involve sacrificing his judgment to theirs, however.[63]

The truth that may give rise to the interdependence claim is that people have more values to offer one another today than in the past and it is generally easier to acquire those values. These facts do not alter the fundamental requirements of human survival, however. A person's failure to achieve his ends through his preferred means (as when he cannot locate others willing to trade on his terms) does not leave him less able to meet his needs or more dependent on others than he was in the past. He might be dependent on others in order to satisfy *a particular preference*, but the possibility of satisfying such a preference would not have even arisen without the relevant activities of others. I can have a chance of gratifying my preference for a car with air conditioning or for wireless Internet access, for instance, only because other people have created such things. Having a greater pool of potential values to enjoy, thanks to the efforts of others, does not weaken a person's grip on his life or weaken his ability to sustain himself. Nor would adopting the people-riveted posture of a second-hander improve his well-being, long range. Increased cooperative interactions with others do not obviate human beings' need for first-handed judgment of reality. Although many forms of cooperation can be tremendously beneficial to a person, they are so to the extent that they are governed by the participants' first-handed rather than second-handed principles.

The requirement of independence that a person make his own way, then, does not entail that a properly independent person should be indifferent or hostile toward others. It does not demand that a person refuse to listen to others' opinions, for instance, or never change his mind. If a manager implementing new policies encounters employee resistance, independence permits his taking their views into account. Indeed, to be rational, he should consider the grounds of their resistance to determine whether it has any validity and whether his plans suffer from previously unrecognized defects. If the manager does this and concludes that the policy changes should indeed be made, he should implement them in a way most likely to be effective. This, too, could involve adjusting his plans concerning the pace of implementation, for example, or the

[63] As Roark explains in a later passage, "An architect needs clients, but he does not subordinate his work to their wishes. They need him, but they do not order a house just to give him a commission." Moreover, while "an architect requires a great many men to erect his building... he does not ask them to vote on his design." *The Fountainhead*, p. 740.

explanation provided. What an independent person cannot do is abandon the changes he deems appropriate simply on the grounds that others dislike them. His assessment of all the relevant facts must be the decisive basis for his action.

In advocating independence, Rand is not denying the tremendous value that a person can gain from other people. It is rational for an egoist to take advantage of the knowledge of experts, the advice of the more experienced, the goods and services that others have created. Independence does not require that a person discover every element of knowledge or reinvent every wheel for himself. Independence, like all virtues, is not an end in itself but a means to flourishing. In order for a person to truly gain the value available from others, however, he must assess their ideas independently – by the benchmark of metaphysical reality.

It is also important to realize that an independent person may enjoy the various forms of spiritual fuel that others can provide. Love and friendship can be among the most rewarding values in a person's life. Relationships can be objectively valuable only on certain conditions, however. An independent person could enjoy the approval of others, for instance, "only when he independently approves of the approvers," as Peikoff puts it.[64] The esteem of those whose judgment he does not respect could not bring any satisfaction.

Along similar lines, one person might love another intensely and prefer not to live without that person. As long as the love is based on a first-handed appraisal of the other person's qualities and role in his life, this is not a violation of independence. If the person observes certain qualities in the other that he prizes and if he values such qualities due to his own rational conclusion about their value rather than by having absorbed those criteria uncritically from others, his independence will be intact. It is not a character flaw to regard certain things as making one's life worth living. One person can value another very highly without treating that person's mind as a replacement for his own. Independence is not a function of *what* a person values or of how much he values those things or people that he does value. Rather, again, independence turns on the method by which a person selects his values. The intense valuing of another person need not betray a person's primary orientation to reality. It can actually be an exertion of independence.[65]

---

[64] Peikoff, *Objectivism*, p. 252.

[65] On Rand's view, healthy love of another person demands independence. "To say 'I love you,'" she writes in the *The Fountainhead*, "one must first know how to say the 'I.' " p. 400. I will say more on egoistic love in the Appendix.

Finally, let me address a concern pertaining to the use of expert opinion. A reader might worry that maintaining independence in relations with others will often be impossible, since the gulf between two individuals' knowledge of a subject can be enormous. Given the scale of one person's comparative ignorance, how could a person avoid being dependent, in many circumstances, on experts such as his physician or auto mechanic?

Dependence of the sort that Rand is rejecting is not necessarily involved in these cases, however. Independence does not require special intelligence. It is a function, I have stressed, of how a person uses his mind, of where he turns most basically for guidance. When a person seeks direction from experts, he need not surrender unconditionally to whatever the expert says. He can and should remain critical, calling upon his own observations, experience, and related knowledge to assess an expert's opinions. Naturally, a layman cannot understand certain issues in nearly the depth or detail of the expert. He can ask questions, however, request clarifications, and work to understand as his level of intelligence and knowledge permits. He can inquire into the expert's education and experience, solicit a second opinion, seek the assistance of more knowledgeable friends, and assess the expert's analysis as best he can before complying with it.[66] This is not to say that the layman must come to occupy the same position in relation to the relevant knowledge that the expert occupies; that, clearly, would be impossible (at least, for all of the issues on which a person might reasonably seek others' expertise). Just as independence does not require that a person reinvent every wheel for himself, independence does not require that a person become an oncologist if he is diagnosed with cancer, become an attorney if he is sued, or become a plumber if his sink backs up. What the independent person must do is essentially twofold: He must investigate to ensure that the experts he consults are well-equipped to give him knowledge and rational recommendations on a given subject; he must strive to understand the counsel that they offer in terms that make sense to him, such that it is not merely a blur of arbitrary ideas, but has a genuine cognitive standing in his mind. Only then can he proceed rationally.

The main point, again, is that one person's advantage in knowledge does not render anyone else who consults him in order to benefit

---

[66] And as much as it is worth, relative to his hierarchy of values. In her journals, Rand remarks that "there is no moral obligation to know and solve everything, to have an independent judgment upon everything. There *is* a moral obligation that such judgments as you *do* hold *must* be your own." *Journals of Ayn Rand*, p. 275, emphasis in original.

from that knowledge a second-hander. A person *can* succumb to second-handedness when appealing to experts, but that is hardly inevitable.[67] Whether a person is dependent in the relevant sense turns on why he consults others, how he chooses whom to consult, and how he proceeds once he learns others' views. While a person often *should* engage others in order to advance his well-being, what is essential for independence – and for his ultimate flourishing – is that a person learn the reasons behind others' opinions rather than accepting them at face value, without question. When an independent person accepts others' opinions, those reasons are the foundation of his decision. What is salient for an independent person is not *that* another person holds a particular view, but the basis for the view.

Nothing in Rand's conception of virtuous independence, then, entails shunning other people. Given the tremendous value that human beings can offer one another, that would clearly be a foolish course for anyone committed to his own well-being. What independence does require, however, is that a person's thoughts and actions always be truly his own. Because human life depends on rational action and because rationality is inherently a do-it-yourself enterprise, independence is vital to human survival.

[67] Anyone able to understand the fallacy of improper appeals to authority (*ad verecundiam*) should be able to appreciate the basic difference.

6

Justice

Our next virtue is one that is much more familiar as an object of moral esteem, justice. Historically, justice has been widely regarded as a central virtue. Indeed, justice is seen as so integral to morality that people often refer to the "just" and the "moral" interchangeably.[1] *Everyone* demands justice; the charge that an action or policy is unjust tends to invite universal condemnation. And while individuals may differ over the exact demands of justice, one also finds near consensus that injustice stems from selfishness. It is the drive to advance their own interest that leads some people to treat others unjustly.

Rand disagrees. It is not egoism that stands in the way of justice, she contends, but the lack of it – the lack of thoughtful, rational egoism. Treating people as they deserve is not inherently proper, with justice a freestanding, intrinsically compelling duty. Nor does justice demand self-sacrifice. In Rand's view, the exercise of justice is a practical necessity for human life. In explaining her position, we will see that Rand correspondingly espouses other unconventional views in regard to justice, urging a readiness to judge other people, for instance, holding that forgiveness is not a virtue, and holding that egalitarianism, far from being the paradigm of justice, is actually its antithesis.

WHAT JUSTICE IS

Justice is the application of rationality to the evaluation and treatment of other individuals. The core of justice emerges from commonplace cases

---

[1] This broad sense of justice is still reflected in some of the *Oxford English Dictionary's* definitions of justice.

in which the difference between just and unjust procedures is, at least in broad outline, plain. Consider racial discrimination in hiring (when race is irrelevant to a person's ability to perform the work in question), or jurors determining a defendant's guilt by personal biases rather than evidence, testimony, and logic, or favoritism in a teacher's grading or in a police officer's ignoring a traffic violation, or framing an innocent person to take the punishment for others' wrongdoing, or stuffing ballot boxes to fix election results. In all such cases, what distinguishes the victims of injustice is that they are not treated as they deserve. The person treated unjustly is not awarded the job he is best qualified for, the evaluation of his case that he is entitled to, the grade or the penalty that his actions have earned, the absence of punishment that his innocence demands, the office that voters have elected him to. The lesson we can draw from such cases is that in its essence, as Peikoff writes, justice is the "virtue of judging men's character and conduct objectively and of acting accordingly, granting to each man that which he deserves."[2] In this, Rand's understanding of justice is consonant with the dominant conception that has been accepted for centuries. The more colloquial shorthand holds that justice is a matter of rendering each man his due.[3] Familiar as this conception of justice is, however, to digest its full meaning, it will be useful to attend to the key elements of Peikoff's formulation.

First, justice involves judging both a person's character and conduct. Justice is not concerned simply with isolated events attributable to an individual but also with the deeper messages that these incidents convey about him. The aim, in evaluating another person, is to identify his basic nature – not his nature as a human being, but as a distinct individual. For this provides the basis for projecting what a person's future conduct is likely to be. Because a person's actions are volitional, it is his conduct and character (which is the integrated product of a person's actions, over time) that best reveal what his nature is. In fact, character and conduct work hand in hand, ultimately standing in a symbiotic relationship. It is through his actions that a person forms his character and his character, in turn, influences the actions that he takes (or even contemplates taking).

[2] Peikoff, *Objectivism*, p. 276.
[3] See Brad W. Hooker, "Justice," in Robert Audi, ed., *The Cambridge Dictionary of Philosophy* (New York: Cambridge University Press, 1999), pp. 456–457, and the *Oxford English Dictionary*. One finds this account in, among others, Spinoza, *A Theologico-Political Treatise*, in *The Chief Works*, vol. 1, trans. R.H.M. Elwes (Dover Publications, 1951), p. 208; Aquinas, *Summa Theologica*, question 58, article 1; Andre Comte-Sponville, *A Small Treatise on the Great Virtues*, trans. Catherine Temerson (New York: Henry Holt, 2001), pp. 74–75.

By the same token, conduct is other people's primary means of learning about a person's character. And we care about character because we care about the conduct that it informs. Justice is a matter of evaluating other people in principle and in particular, we might say, assessing particular actions (conduct) as well as the principles that guide their actions (their character).[4]

While justice encompasses the appraisal of others' character, justice is not concerned exclusively with *moral* character or with moral judgments of others.[5] Depending on a person's purposes, he might have reason to judge numerous aspects of another person, such as his intelligence, physical attractiveness, or skill as an actor or plumber or lawyer or bridge partner or philosophy student. While a person's grades on any of these scales is not a direct marker of his moral character (there is no inconsistency in thinking that Bill is a poor actor and a good man), the pattern of proper judgment is the same when one is evaluating moral or non-moral dimensions of a person.[6] People embody many features that we can and should evaluate, in different circumstances, and rational self-interest demands the essential ingredients of justice in regard to all of them. (The case for justice, explained in the next section, should make. this clear.)

A further crucial element of justice is that evaluations of others must be objective. "Justice is the recognition of the fact that you cannot fake the character of men just as you cannot fake the character of nature," Rand writes.[7] In this sense, justice is a reflection of honesty and of rationality, and like all exercises of rationality, justice demands objectivity. The person who is rational in pursuing his ends disciplines his thinking by heeding all and only the relevant evidence and by employing logic to determine what that evidence demonstrates. This holds when it comes to the evaluation of other people as much as in the evaluation of anything else. Subjectivist departures from such a policy – e.g., evaluating political candidates on the basis of their looks, doctors on the basis of their taste in sports, or prospective nannies by one's distaste for the British – would undermine the point of justice. A person cannot learn the true nature of

---

[4] Knowing a person's character sometimes enables a person to interpret a single action of his more accurately. Taken out of the context of the person's overall character, isolated deeds can be misleading.

[5] Peikoff, *Objectivism*, pp. 278–279. Peikoff nonetheless restricts his discussion to justice in its most basic and moral form.

[6] Peikoff, *Objectivism*, p. 279.

[7] Rand, *Atlas Shrugged*, p. 1019.

other individuals by blinding himself to what the relevant evidence is or indicates.

Finally, as we will discuss much further when addressing the practical demands of this virtue, a portion of justice consists in acting on one's objective assessments and treating others as they deserve. As the *Oxford English Dictionary* testifies, desert is "the becoming worthy of recompense, i.e., of reward or punishment according to the good or ill of character or conduct." A person *does* something, in other words, in order to deserve certain responses from others. This is reflected when we think that an especially attentive waiter deserves a big tip, a hard-working staffer deserves special commendation, the corrupt politician deserves defeat, or a rapist deserves a lengthy prison sentence. Essentially, treating others as they deserve means responding to positive conduct or character with rewards and to negative conduct or character with punishments. Rand means both these terms in broad but familiar senses: A reward is a value given in recognition of a person's virtue or achievement; a punishment is a disvalue repaid for a vice or fault.[8] Rewards and punishments can thus assume many forms, material and spiritual: Bestowing friendship, money, recommendations, prerogatives, praise, or congratulations could all be rewards, for instance, while withholding such goods, or overt condemnation, ostracism, or voting against a person's promotion or election could all be forms of punishment.[9]

The heart of justice, again, lies in evaluating others objectively and treating them accordingly by giving them the good or bad that they deserve. We can now explain why doing so is an egoistic virtue.

THE CASE FOR JUSTICE

The need for justice stems from the relationship in which human beings stand to the values that sustain our lives. All values are achieved through effort. One does not become a doctor without hard work; one does not enjoy a strong marriage without giving one's partner time, honesty,

---

[8] Peikoff, *Objectivism*, p. 283. In a letter discussing legal punishment, Rand writes that retribution refers to "the imposition of painful consequences proportionate to the injury caused by the criminal act." *Letters of Ayn Rand*, p. 559. This same basic meaning can be applied to noncriminal offenses.

[9] I will clarify the difference between what a person deserves and what he has a right to in the final part of the chapter. Also, although I have spoken of justice in terms of one's relations with other people, a person can be just or unjust toward himself, as well. The primary use of this virtue, however, concerns evaluation and treatment of others.

openness, an effort to understand him. Even as primitive a value as a bowl of soup requires gathering ingredients and cooking them (or working to pay someone else to do so). However simple or sophisticated the value, whether material or spiritual, it is human action that creates values.[10]

Individuals do not single-handledly control the success of our quests for values; circumstances beyond anyone's control can influence outcomes. What is salient for our immediate purposes is the fact that other people can affect the fate of one's values, in small or large ways. We recognize this whenever we ponder whom we should avoid or befriend, believe or doubt, hire or fire. Which person should I accept a ride from? invest my money with? vote for? It makes a difference to the success of a man's business how competent a manager he hires; it makes a difference to his health which physician he sees; it makes a difference to his happiness which woman he marries. These are the sorts of facts that create the need for justice. Because other people can affect everything dear to a person, he needs to assess others' probable impact on his values and act accordingly. "You must judge all men as conscientiously as you judge inanimate objects," Rand advises.[11]

In a different context, when using justice simply as an example in a discussion of concept formation, Rand offers a very clear walk through our need for objective judgment of others:

[W]hat fact of reality gave rise to the concept "justice"? The fact that man must draw conclusions about the things, people and events around him, i.e., must judge and evaluate them. Is his judgment automatically right? No. What causes his judgment to be wrong? The lack of sufficient evidence, or his evasion of the evidence, or his inclusion of considerations other than the facts of the case. How, then, is he to arrive at the right judgment? By basing it exclusively on the factual evidence and by considering all the relevant evidence available. But isn't this a description of "objectivity"? Yes, "objective judgment" is one of the wider categories to which the concept "justice" belongs. What distinguishes "justice" from other instances of objective judgment? When one evaluates the nature or actions of inanimate objects, the criterion of judgment is determined by the particular purpose for which one evaluates them. But how does one determine a criterion for evaluating the character and actions of men, in view of the fact that men possess the faculty of volition? What science can provide an objective criterion of evaluation in regard to volitional matters? Ethics. Now, do I need a concept

---

[10] Recall the relevant discussion in Chapters 2 and 3. Even natural resources that can be put to valuable uses must have their potential value recognized and appropriate means of exploiting that value identified. See Rand, "The Objectivist Ethics," and Peikoff, *Objectivism*, pp. 193–198, 220–229, 241–249.

[11] *Atlas Shrugged*, pp. 1019–1020.

to designate the act of judging a man's character and/or actions exclusively on the basis of all the factual evidence available, and of evaluating it by means of an objective moral criterion? Yes. That concept is "justice."[12]

The basic argument for being just, then, is straightforward. Whatever ends an individual seeks, be they modest or ambitious, short-range or long – a ticket to a concert or a tenured appointment – other people can affect his success in attaining these ends, whether deliberately or inadvertently. Another person can entangle you in his irresponsibility or alcoholism or debt; he can share his enthusiasm, his knowledge (about cars, computers, cancer, cabernets) or his talents (as a tenor, tennis coach, tax attorney, technical troubleshooter). Another person could deceive you, cheat you, enlighten you, or inspire you. Human beings carry enormous potential for impact on one another. Consequently, anyone who is sincerely committed to his own happiness must be concerned with others' probable effects on him. He must evaluate other individuals objectively and treat them in ways that serve his values, supporting those who can contribute to his life and opposing, or at the least steering clear of, those likely to do damage. If a person's goal is his own happiness, he cannot escape the need to judge other individuals and to treat them as they deserve. The alternative would be treason to his values and his happiness.

Character

As we noted earlier, a person needs to evaluate others' character as well as their conduct on particular occasions. It is worth elaborating on this to fully understand why. While we often deal with others for narrow utilitarian purposes such as having the car repaired or the taxes prepared, character is the framework that governs a person's actions on particular occasions. It is thus character that ultimately determines whatever value or disvalue a person might offer to others, even within narrow bands of activity. Let me explain.

Because other people stand to affect a person's values, self-interest demands that he try to predict their likely impact on him. Because human actions are volitional, far more useful than assessing any isolated action that a person takes is learning about the source of that action, the agent's

---

[12] Rand, *Introduction to Objectivist Epistemology*, p. 51. This passage focuses on the judgment involved in justice and omits the correlative treatment of the person judged that Rand also considers vital. Also note that when a person is not judging another's moral character, his narrower purpose does come into play.

basic nature. A person's individual actions proceed from his choices and these, in turn, proceed from his *characteristic* way of using his mind and leading his life. To reach a well-grounded conclusion about another person, it is most helpful to appraise not merely scattered, discrete actions, but the character that authored those actions. Do these several episodes indicate Bill's rationality? Responsibility? Dishonesty? Does Bill display other virtues or vices, strengths or weaknesses? Answers to such questions give the appraiser a firmer basis for forecasting the person's future actions and overall relation to his own flourishing.

In one sense, then, a person's moral character is not truly a separate concern in addition to concern with his capacities in some narrower domain, such as accounting or auto mechanics. For a person's character determines the use that he makes of whatever capacities he possesses. If a mechanic is untrustworthy, for instance, it is impossible for another person to know how that might be manifested in his "strictly professional" relationship with him. (Will he be honest in investigating all possible sources of my car's trouble? Will he be honest in reporting the hours of labor to bill me for?) Although Bill may be quite skilled at filling a particular function and, other things being equal, far more valuable to Mary in that role than her alternatives, his bad character means that other things are not equal. For Bill's bad character means that his animating principles are inimical to the values that nourish human life, that his tendency is to act in ways that are antagonistic to objective values. In light of this, it would be foolhardy to continue to deal with him as if he offered genuine value. Any value one hoped to gain would be based on wishful thinking, ignoring the larger context of his fundamentally anti-life policies. When a person has concluded that another person's character is basically bad, he has warning that any actions that that person takes may well be tainted by that character and therefore value-destructive rather than value-supporting.

None of this is to suggest that reaching conclusions about another person's character is an easy or quick business. Precisely because character encompasses far more than performance in one or two limited spheres, it typically takes an extended acquaintance to warrant confident, rational conclusions about moral character. (Certain individual actions can reveal a great deal about a person's character, of course, such as acts of extraordinary heroism or brutality.) Nor can we hope to unerringly predict the *particular* actions that a person will take, however well we come to know that person. Insofar as human beings are volitional, they can act from a variety of motives in a given case and a person's character itself can change, over time. The immediate point is simply that it is important to judge others' character, as far as one is able, because character governs the use that a person will make of any more specific attributes that carry potential impact on other people. However expert my mechanic, if I know that he is dishonest, I cannot trust that he is not cheating me. (We will say more on judging character when we address the demands of justice.)

We should also recognize that it is valuable to know another person's character not only as a means of gauging his usefulness in a specific, restricted domain. For one person's value to another is not exhausted by his ability to play such narrow, functional roles. I am glad if a dramatic actor possesses the intelligence, sensitivity, discipline, and courage that drive his ability, qua actor, to captivate me on the stage. Yet in applauding his work, I sometimes applaud not only *that* performance that I cheer at the curtain's fall, but those qualities themselves. I do this because they are the kinds of qualities that typically give birth to the values that nourish my life. In principle, virtue leads to values. As we explained in Chapters 2 and 3, human beings survive by creating values rather than by finding them readymade. The essential instrument that enables a person to create values is rationality. To the extent that a person is rational, his thinking and action are guided by fidelity to reality. Such are the only kinds of thoughts and actions that could create anything objectively life-furthering. The major moral virtues identify, in broad terms, what these kinds of thoughts and actions are. Although a given action might, through fluke circumstances, fail to carry its usual effects in a particular situation, in principle, virtuous actions are the kinds that bring values into the world, and vicious actions are the kinds that destroy or impede the achievement of values. This means that others' virtue contributes to an environment from which I stand to benefit. The more virtuous other people are – the more rational and honest and productive, and so on – the more constructive companions they are to learn from and to trade with. As Craig Biddle has put it, "We can benefit enormously from *productive* people, but not from parasites. We can trust *honest* people, but not dishonest ones. We can count on people of *integrity*, but not on hypocrites. We can learn from *independent thinkers*, but not from second-handers."[13]

---

[13] Craig Biddle, *Loving Life* (Richmond, VA: Glen Allen Press, 2002), p. 95, emphasis his. Throughout this chapter, I will often use "virtue" and "vice" to designate not exclusively moral characteristics, but any life-advancing or life-impeding qualities, such as natural intelligence or practical skills. The context should make plain whether I am using these terms more widely or more strictly morally.

Virtuous individuals expand the pool of values in the world, offering not only better products or services, but role models, inspiration, encouragement, grounds for optimism and benevolence, a warmer social climate. A person can gain spiritual fuel simply from knowing of the existence of "good guys" doing good things. Because we must pay for value by creating it, in short, a person should welcome those who create values and eschew those who do not. All of this, again, indicates further reason to care about others' character.

Desert

Because justice consists not simply in evaluating other persons objectively but in treating them as they deserve, it is important to understand the rationale for this aspect of justice, as well. In the minds of many, desert is primitive. While something may seem deeply fitting about giving a person what he deserves, they have a hard time explaining the basis of this propriety. It is simply right, many believe, to give people their deserts; desert is intrinsically compelling. On Rand's view, however, desert is not an elemental starting point. Rather, desert is something that a person achieves through specific action.[14] Treating people as they deserve reflects respect for causality.

Recall from the *OED* that to deserve is to *become* worthy of reward or punishment. Accordingly, a person deserves something by earning it; He must do something in order to deserve something. Deserving is not a natural state, the kind of quality that a person could be born with. Rather, desert signifies a process: enacting a cause that warrants a certain effect.[15] In a 1961 letter, Rand writes that

The basic principle that should guide one's judgment in issues of justice is the law of causality: one should never attempt to evade or to break the connection between cause and effect – one should never attempt to deprive a man of the consequences of his actions, good or evil. (One should not deprive a man of the values or benefits *his* actions have caused, such as expropriating a man's wealth for somebody else's benefit; and one should not deflect the disaster which *his* actions have caused, such as giving relief checks to a lazy, irresponsible loafer.)[16]

---

[14] Or through deliberate omission in certain circumstances, such as by refusing to accept a bribe or to divulge confidential information.

[15] Peikoff, *Objectivism*, p. 287.

[16] *Letters of Ayn Rand*, p. 558, emphasis hers. This was a letter to the philosopher John Hospers. Peikoff elaborates on the causal nature of justice in *Objectivism*, pp. 282–288.

To treat a person as he deserves is to allow causality its natural course. In doing so, a person fosters that which is beneficial to his life and opposes that which is detrimental. For the natural consequences of virtuous actions will be values, long range, and the natural consequences of vicious actions will be disvalues. Because we all stand to gain from actions that create or nourish values and to lose from actions that destroy or damage values, we all have reason to respect this natural causal chain. Injustice disrupts it, however, by severing effects from causes. Unjust actions visit punishments upon virtuous conduct and rewards upon vicious conduct. When a person responds justly, in contrast, by rewarding or punishing as a person's actions deserve, he is recognizing the positive or negative nature of others' actions and their likely effects on *him*.

In treating another person as he deserves, one individual cannot seize control of the other's power to direct his own actions; his free will remains intact. The responder can affect whether the other's use of his will leads to success or failure, however. Through injustice, a person can deflect or mute the natural consequences of another's actions. He can make one person's virtue pay for another's vice, for instance, by retaining a worker who performs poorly and piling his ill-completed work onto more productive employees. He thereby prevents the good worker's virtue from achieving its natural reward and the poor worker from receiving his natural punishment. Similarly, the teacher who indiscriminately awards Bs to strong and weak essays alike deprives the worthy of the reward they have earned and bestows benefits on students who have not earned them.

When a person reacts to another's conduct or character, this is not a part of the "natural" causal sequence, of course. No physical, deterministic necessity governs how any individual will respond to another's actions. Others' responses can be rational or irrational, however. If a person recognizes the value-destructive nature of another person's course, he has reason to oppose that person. Correlatively, if a person recognizes the value-conducive nature of another person's course, he has reason to support and encourage that person. Because we all stand to benefit from values in the world, it is rational to repay virtue with values and vice with disvalues. And just as a person can logically expect certain consequences to follow, in nature, from his actions, so he can expect certain kinds of consequences to follow from other people, to the extent that they are rational. Indeed, when we remark of a person's success or suffering that "he deserves it," what we mean is roughly: That is the logical result of his course; it is the kind of result that one can expect from that type of conduct or character. In responding justly to another person's conduct or character, then, a person is both respecting natural causality and, in so doing, making himself a part of the volitional chain of events that the agent should expect from rational people.

Obviously, a person who treats others as they deserve cannot single-handedly manipulate all the effects of others' actions. Heath's refusal to financially assist a lazy relative will not ensure the relative's doom. Natural forces, as well as the responses of other people, can also influence the effects of a person's course. Just treatment of a person can intensify and accelerate certain effects, however. If a person rewards exemplary service generously or indifferent service indifferently, he is adding to the positive or negative effects of the relevant individuals' course and doing what he can to hasten their realization of the nature of their course. The person who refuses to help his lazy relative need make no pretense of definitively reforming him or "teaching him a lesson." By treating him as he deserves, he simply refuses to assist the other person's attempt to defy the demands of reality (in particular, the demand for productive work).[17]

In rejecting the notion that treating others as they deserve is a primitive, inherently compelling moral duty, Rand also denies that the claim to a particular desert is something that a person holds uniformly against everyone. Rather, desert is relational: what an individual deserves from one person will differ from what he deserves from another. A worker deserves different rewards from his boss and from his coworkers; a man deserves different levels of help from his best friend and from a casual acquaintance. Although people sometimes speak of desert as if it were a claim held against the universe, remarking that the criminal who was wrongly acquitted but subsequently killed in an accident "got what he deserved," for instance, this cosmic sense of desert is metaphorical. The universe can be neither just nor unjust. While naturally occurring events can benefit or harm a person, nature cannot literally reward or punish or "treat" a person as he deserves. Desert, like justice itself, is a moral concept and as such, not the sort of thing that can be attributed to nonvolitional events. What is most pertinent here is that desert is not a freestanding claim that attaches to an individual independently of his relationships

---

[17] A secondary effect of treating others as they deserve is to encourage third parties to act justly, as well (when such treatment is known to them). Seeing others exercise justice sometimes motivates individuals to exert that virtue more consistently themselves.

with specific other people. Desert can only be intelligibly asserted by specifying what one particular individual deserves from another particular individual. Desert is, in this sense, one on one.

Accordingly, the just response to a person's actions depends on who is offering the response and the relationship in which he stands to that person. For that relationship determines the kinds of effects that each carries in the other's life. What is reason for a business owner to reward his employees is not reason for him to reward other companies' employees. What is reason for a person to withdraw his association from this friend is not reason for him to withdraw association from that friend. Generally, the greater the stakes of one person's involvement with another person, the more reason he has to offer strong responses to that person's conduct. This is because the basis of one person's deserving things from another is the latter's self-interest.[18] A person deserves certain treatment not simply because of facts about him. He deserves certain treatment from certain individuals because of his impact on their well-being. The more significant the relationship between two people, the greater the impact that each stands to carry on the other and, correspondingly, the more that each person deserves from the other (be the deserts positive or negative).

It is crucial to appreciate that to govern our responses to others by anything other than objective desert would undermine the goal of individual life. It would not foster the sorts of actions that we need to foster in order to achieve values and flourish. Suppose that, instead of evaluating individuals objectively and rewarding or punishing them as they deserve, we substituted some alternative standard: treating individuals as they asked to be treated, for instance, or as they needed, or as a democratic vote prescribed. The result would be to make life more difficult for the virtuous and more easy for the vicious. Whenever rewarding the life-furthering conduct or character of other individuals would not satisfy the substituted criterion of justice, the natural effects of those persons' actions would be thwarted. When we pass over the productive worker in order to supply the needier with a job, the productive worker is denied the logical results of his good work and we are all deprived of the further benefits likely to be gained from his receiving that reward. When we promote a person on the basis of his popularity rather than his performance, we can expect the same sort of losses. Such policies would stifle the stream of values that virtue typically generates. While many would recognize this

[18] Peikoff, *Objectivism*, p. 284.

as unfair to the immediate recipients of such treatment, my point here is that it makes life harder for everyone. Failing to treat individuals as they deserve works against the demands of human survival.[19]

Given the primacy of existence, the basic kinds of actions necessary to fuel human flourishing are not a matter of our choosing. Fiddling with the standard of justice, declaring it to be something other than an objective assessment of others' deserts, does not enable us to extract value from vice. If we are to create the values that sustain our existence and if we are to safeguard these values, we need to judge individuals objectively and to treat them as positively or as negatively as they deserve.

The Egoism of Justice

By this stage, it should not be difficult to understand that the rationale for justice is entirely egoistic. The reason that a person should treat others as they deserve is ultimately grounded in the benefit of doing so to his own self-interest.

We normally think that justice benefits its recipient by ensuring that he is treated as he deserves. It does. Even if a person's vices are punished, he benefits from being alerted to the deleterious nature of his actions. (It is up to him whether to heed that message, of course.) If others failed to punish the vicious person, pretending that his course was benign, they would only be aiding his evasion.[20] This will not help him, long range. Consider a simple example. Suppose, at the end of a semester, I write glowing reports of all my teaching assistants, despite the fact that they do not all deserve such raves. Am I helping those whose performance I inflate? Short-term, their files may look better for funding in the department or for their ventures into the job market. Yet if the TAs are not in fact as spectacular as I claim they are, others will catch on to this when these TAs assist or teach for them. My unwarranted praise actually sets the recipients up for future failure, as they will disappoint unrealistic expectations – which is likely to be worse for them than candid criticism of their early teaching would have been. Furthermore, by ignoring the TAs' weaknesses, I fail to frankly address areas in which they might make changes. If a TA does need to improve in certain respects, the sooner he learns that, the better – for him, as well as for his students.

[19] See *Objectivism*, p. 283, for discussion of this.
[20] Remember that I am using "vicious" to designate any life-diminishing actions, not only those that are morally deficient.

It is even easier to see how injustice is damaging to its recipient in cases in which someone treats another person less well than he deserves. Suppose that I harshly criticize all my TAs, never recording the significant strengths that many of them display. My injustice contributes to these students' acquiring undeserved poor reputations, which is obviously harmful in limiting their prospects for advancement.

Rand would agree, then, that the recipient of justice definitely benefits. She does not agree, however, with the widespread assumption that the just person must suffer or that justice is altruistic.[21] A person should judge others objectively and treat them as they deserve so as to best promote his own well-being. It is commonly thought that justice requires self-sacrifice. This is backward. On Rand's view, it is foolish to be unjust – foolish from a self-interested point of view. If a person failed to judge other people or if he did but failed to judge people objectively – if his conclusions were merely casual impressions, compiled in a catch-as-catch-can way, hastily, sloppily, by deliberately ignoring relevant information or by including facts that he realizes are irrelevant, for instance – and if this person treated others on these bases, what could he look forward to? What would be the result? He would be surrendering his values to chance. At best, he would waste time, energy, or money on the financial adviser who manages his accounts amateurishly, on the sitter who cares for his children irresponsibly, on the physician who administers long-outdated treatments, and so on.

Justice is essential for the prudent promotion and protection of one's values. It is self-defeating to pretend that people are other than they are. As we noted earlier, faking others' conduct or character does not change that conduct or character.[22] Refusing to recognize a person's negative qualities does not make them disappear; wishful thinking does not make positive qualities come to be. It is important to judge others objectively because that provides a person with the best indication of the significance of another person's conduct and of his true character. Faking only blinds a person to others' actual characteristics. It thus disarms him from resisting their potentially harmful effects and, importantly, deprives him of the opportunity to gain from their potentially beneficial effects. The way to advance one's life is to be honest about the others one encounters – honest in accepting the need to judge them, in how one judges them, and in how one subsequently acts toward them.

---

[21] Comte-Sponville refers to justice as the virtue closest to altruism, p. 74.
[22] Peikoff observes that injustice is a form of evasion, *Objectivism*, p. 282.

Rand's insight, then, is that while those who are treated justly benefit from that treatment, so does the person exercising justice. And this is the fundamental reason to practice justice: to advance one's own life. It is right to treat others as they deserve not to fulfill an arbitrary, inherently compelling duty or as a sacrifice of one's own well-being to that of others. It is proper to judge others objectively and to treat them as they deserve because others' actions are volitional and others' use of their volitional faculty affects one's own ability to flourish. The case for justice is thoroughly egoistic.[23]

WHAT JUSTICE DEMANDS

Understanding why justice is essential to human life, we can next consider what the practice of this virtue demands. As with all virtues, justice comprises intellectual as well as existential components, and the argument for exercising justice has already indicated why both are indispensable.

Intellectual Demands

Justice emphatically demands judging people. Given the need to assess other persons' impact on one's values, justice forbids fence-sitting, pleading ignorance or retreating into agnosticism. Justice requires honesty about the facts one learns about another person and about that person's likely impact on the judger's values. Reaching such verdicts is not a matter of assuming a holier than thou posture. Nor does it require that a person become a missionary or a crusader, volunteering unsolicited appraisals to everyone he encounters.[24] Judging is a matter of evaluating evidence about other persons for the vital purpose of securing one's values and flourishing. Since justice is an application of rationality, one's verdicts must be revisable should further evidence come to light or further reflection indicate that one has drawn an erroneous conclusion. This is not justification for refraining from taking a stand on a person, however, which is itself a stand, as Peikoff observes.[25] And it is a dishonest stand,

---

[23] On the relationship between altruism and injustice, see *Objectivism*, pp. 278, 282–284; Rand, "An Untitled Letter," in *Philosophy: Who Needs It*, pp. 123–144; "The Age of Envy," in Peter Schwartz, ed., *Return of the Primitive – The Anti-Industrial Revolution* (New York: Meridian, 1999), pp. 130–158, especially pp. 139ff; and *Journals of Ayn Rand*, p. 246.

[24] Rand, "How Does One Lead a Rational Life in an Irrational Society?" in *The Virtue of Selfishness*, p. 84. Also see Peikoff, *Objectivism*, pp. 285–286.

[25] Peikoff, *Objectivism*, p. 277.

insofar as it evades the fact that individuals are different from one another and that those differences matter to one's values. Rand expresses the dishonesty involved in vivid terms: "to withhold your contempt from men's vices is an act of moral counterfeiting, and to withhold your admiration from their virtues is an act of moral embezzlement..."[26] The strong language withstands scrutiny. For in either case, the person who refrains from judgment seeks to get something for nothing. Like an embezzler, the person who withholds admiration benefits from others' virtues but offers nothing in exchange. And like a counterfeiter who peddles worthless currency, the person who refuses to condemn the vicious pretends that these persons are better than they are and that they bear objective value.

The person who withholds appropriate praise or condemnation may not mean to be dishonest or unjust; he may think that he is goodheartedly cutting a person some slack by refraining from criticism or that the deserving person "isn't really so impressive" or that "what he did was no big deal." Yet either form of agnosticism evades the fact that value is created by individual virtue and is threatened by individual vice. A person cannot prevent his impartiality from helping the vicious and harming the virtuous, even if he does not wish that to happen. Neutrality toward others' virtues and vices may blind a person to the effects of others' character on his life; it does not alter those effects. As Rand writes in *Atlas*, "your moral appraisal is the coin paying men for their virtues or vices... [and] to place any other concern higher than justice is to devaluate your moral currency and defraud the good in favor of the evil, since only the good can lose by a default of justice and only the evil can profit..."[27]

The connotations of "judging" in our society are primarily negative. The religious and nonreligious alike routinely invoke the scriptural admonition, "judge not and be not judged."[28] For many, the term conjures images of an irrationally judgmental person wagging a scolding finger. The justice that Rand advocates does not demand cynicism or

---

[26] *Atlas Shrugged*, pp. 1019–1020.

[27] *Atlas Shrugged*, pp. 1019–1020. A recent sad example of this was seen in a report on Catholic priests' abuse of children. The report cites certain bishops' looking the other way when they heard reports of such abuse, thereby leaving more children vulnerable. "Found Wanting," *The Economist*, March 6, 2003, p. 31.

[28] Matthew 7:1. Indeed, priests who diverted their suspicions or knowledge of other priests' child abuse followed this prescription. Rand refers to this as "a moral blank check" and advises that the proper policy is: "Judge, and be prepared to be judged." "How Does One Lead a Rational Life in an Irrational Society?" p. 83.

hostility toward others, however. Because the purpose of justice is the achievement of values, its impetus is actually positive. "Justice consists first not in condemning, but in admiring," Peikoff writes.[29] The just person is not poised to criticize or eager to harp on others' shortcomings. Rather, Peikoff portrays justice as "human prospecting," a search for what is good in people while, of necessity, remaining alert to what is bad. A person's flourishing demands that both the good and the bad in others be confronted for what they are. The exercise of justice, accordingly, does not entail accentuating defects or feeling superior by finding fault in others. What justice cannot abide, however, is the indefinite suspension of judgment, a permanent posture of neutrality. To refrain from judging may not smell as foul as more brazen instances of injustice such as deliberately depriving a person of his deserts, as it is often not malicious. It is every bit as destructive, however. The agnostic fails to treat others as they deserve and, in doing so, undermines his own values. "[W]hen you abstain equally from praising men's virtues and from condemning men's vices," Rand asks, "when your impartial attitude declares, in effect, that neither the good nor the evil may expect anything from you – whom do you betray and whom do you encourage?"[30]

Because justice is the application of rationality to the evaluation of other people, the judgment required must be objective. Although we noted this when discussing the basic nature of justice, it bears emphasis as we elaborate on the virtue's practical demands. A just person must base his evaluation of others on all and only the relevant facts. Which facts are relevant will depend largely on the purpose for which one person is judging another. Because we seek different qualities in a lawyer, a lover, a babysitter, or a barber, for instance, objectivity requires weighing different kinds of facts in different evaluations. When grading a calculus exam, the student's religious views are irrelevant; when ticketing parking violations, the political sympathies expressed on a bumper sticker are irrelevant.

Given that people are often emotionally invested in those whom they judge, adhering to the discipline of objectivity in this realm can be especially challenging. Even when a person is not close with the person being judged, human beings tend to value human beings, thus the sheer fact that another person is involved can trigger emotions that risk clouding judgment. Although justice places no restrictions on how much a person may feel, it does require that a person not permit emotions to replace

[29] Peikoff, *Objectivism*, p. 284.
[30] Rand, "How Does One Lead a Rational Life in an Irrational Society?" p. 82.

reason as the basis for his evaluations. The just person must deliberately dismiss the subjective and the arbitrary from his judgment; he must evaluate others as clinically as he would any less emotionally charged issue with a bearing on his values.[31]

Rational judgment demands that a person be objective not merely in applying his standards, but also in verifying that the standards he employs are themselves appropriate. The mission of morality is practical, remember. If a person held others accountable to invalid standards, he would sabotage his ability to accurately assess others' impact on his values. Rewarding a person on the basis of misguided conclusions about what sorts of behavior should be rewarded would not actually further the agent's interest.

(A rational person will also evaluate his own character and conduct in order to do the best job he can of advancing his life. And he will realize that his character and conduct need to be evaluated by others, in the rational pursuit of their interest, just as he needs to evaluate theirs. Moreover, the judgments that a person reaches about others are themselves a reflection of his character. "A judge puts himself on trial every time he pronounces a verdict," Rand observes. "A man is to be judged by the judgments he pronounces.")[32]

A few further aspects of objective evaluation of others bear special notice. Implicit in judging others objectively is judging individuals *as individuals.* Justice forbids sweeping generalizations, blanket condemnations, or benedictions on the basis of nonessential similarities among people. Insofar as human action is volitional, we must assess each individual on his merits rather than by smearing or whitewashing on the basis of conclusions about a group to which a person belongs. Although a person's membership in certain groups can reveal information relevant to certain judgments about him (his chosen political affiliations, for instance), the danger is allowing conclusions reached about others to preempt study of all the pertinent evidence about the individual in question. Given that we routinely observe salient differences between individuals who have other traits in common, it would be nonobjective to bypass these.

To evaluate a person justly, a person must be governed, at root, by what that person says and by what that person does. For this is the only objective evidence available. Third parties' reports, while often very helpful, are themselves valid to the extent that they reflect the words and deeds

---

[31] Peikoff discusses this in *Objectivism*, pp. 279–280.
[32] Rand, "How Does One Lead a Rational Life in an Irrational Society?" p. 83.

of the person under review.[33] Moreover, when a person is judging the overall moral character of another person, any fact about that person's statements and actions is potentially relevant. Even features which do not typically reflect on moral character (such as a person's preferences in restaurants or music or sports) could be based on significant features of his character, such as second-handedness or laziness or irrationality. The point is not that a just person must, KGB-style, suspiciously compile dossiers on people. The facts he should actively seek out depend on the purpose for which he is evaluating the other person and the depth and breadth of their actual or prospective relationship. (Is he considering hiring a person as a delivery boy? Evaluating him for a study group? Weighing a marriage proposal?) The point is simply that objective evaluation of a person demands attending to whatever evidence is relevant to the issue being assessed.

Along similar lines, objectivity demands that one always evaluate another person *in context*, with realistic expectations of what that person could or should have known or done. This is not a matter of inventing excuses for a person, but of weighing all relevant aspects of the circumstances the person was in in order to reach a valid conclusion about what a given action or course signified. To evaluate a person objectively, the evaluator must consider the other's knowledge, resources, abilities, and options. He must also consider the person's responsibility for being in a particular situation, as well- or ill-equipped as he was. It is not objective (or just) to hold a person accountable for things beyond his control; we should hold him accountable for that which he could control. To know the difference, though, requires evaluating the person in light of his actual circumstances.

In a related vein, objectivity demands maintaining a sense of proportionality when drawing conclusions about a person's actions, not equating the significance of major virtues with that of minor flaws, for instance. Strictly, proportionality is not a distinct "sense," but an application of rationality. The objective judge will neither exaggerate nor minimize when evaluating the facts he learns about another. Sometimes, a person will not have enough information about a person to warrant a conclusion. The only responsible course in such cases is to reserve judgment until he

---

[33] Rand warns against psychologizing: judging a person's moral character on the basis of inferences about his subconscious that are not based on his actions, statements, and conscious convictions. "The Psychology of Psychologizing," *The Objectivist* (March 1971), pp. 2–5.

acquires the necessary knowledge. This does not mean that a person must refrain from greeting passers-by until he has conducted an extensive investigation of his neighbors or refrain from shopping until he has vetted the local merchants. Justice allows granting others the benefit of the doubt (as long as one has no specific grounds for doubts about their character. "Since men are born *tabula rasa*, both cognitively and morally," Rand reasons, "a rational man regards strangers as innocent until proved guilty.")[34] The more significant the relationship a person contemplates having with another person, however – the more prolonged, the closer, the higher the stakes involved – the more reason he has to inquire into the other person's character. The ultimate reason to exercise justice, bear in mind, is self-interest. Reference to that can help us determine the degree of attention to others' character that is appropriate with different individuals.[35]

None of this, again, is to suggest that it is easy to evaluate other people. Because human action is volitional, it is difficult to forecast. Further complicating our efforts is the fact that individuals tend to combine positive and negative elements; many bad people have positive attributes and many good people have flaws. Disentangling the conflicting attributes to reach a valid conclusion about a person's overall character can be extremely difficult.[36] We must also beware of confusing another person's character with his conduct on any single occasion. To identify a person's character, one needs to learn not simply what he has done once or twice but what is typical of him. One must try to determine whether a person is *characteristically* honest or dishonest, hard-working or lazy, rational or rash. It would be a mistake to equate character with any one action because, although a person's character is a product of his actions, a person can act out of character. Not every incident is an equally reliable indicator of the dominant pattern of action that a person engages in. Obviously, a person cannot act out of character often; the more he seems to, the greater the evidence that one has misunderstood what his character is. Normally, however, no isolated action is definitive proof of an agent's character.[37] By the same token, it would be a mistake to sever a person's actions from

---

34 "The Ethics of Emergencies," p. 54. In her journals, Rand endorses "benevolent neutrality" as the proper default attitude toward others, *Journals of Ayn Rand*, p. 246.

35 Peikoff, *Objectivism*, pp. 279–280.

36 Peikoff, *Objectivism*, pp. 281–282. There are limits to *how* mixed a person's character can be, since certain extremely good or bad traits would overwhelm weaker, opposing elements in defining a person's character.

37 I say "normally" to exclude the most egregious offenses, such as rape or murder, or the most admirable displays of moral virtue, which are more telling about a person.

his character, dismissing any apparently anomalous incident as irrelevant to the person's true nature. Because character is a product of the actions that a person most routinely takes, his actions provide objective evidence of what his character is. The challenge is to steer between the errors of too readily identifying particular conduct with a person's character and too readily separating the two.[38]

Existential Demands

Because the ultimate purpose of exercising justice is the advancement of the agent's life, the objective evaluation of others would be useless if a person did not follow through on that evaluation in action. Given the practical nature of the case for justice, this should not be difficult to appreciate.

By heeding justice's intellectual requirement of judgment, a person can learn other persons' likely impact on the things that are most important to him. That knowledge is worthless unless he does something about it, however. Treating other people as they deserve is vital to actually, actively pursuing one's values. It is by treating others as his knowledge of them warrants that a person can protect and promote his ends. Such action is his means of encouraging those qualities in others that are beneficial to him and of discouraging those qualities that are detrimental. To profess devotion to certain values without taking correlative action to secure them is to reveal that devotion a fraud.

The just person, in short, must give other people the rewards and punishments that they deserve. Despite the often narrow connotations of "reward" and "punishment," which suggests the disciplining of children or the penalizing of criminals, it is important to remember the many forms that reward and punishment can assume. A person can reward another by patronizing his business, contributing money to his organization, attending his exhibitions or commending him to others, whether by a formal letter of recommendation or by informally sharing his favorable evaluation. Extending warmth, hospitality, an invitation, or a privilege can all be forms of reward, as can sharing confidences, bestowing trust, spending time with a person, listening to his problems, offering advice, or simply, in words or in writing, acknowledging a person's merit or accomplishment. Fan letters, congratulations, and "thank you's" can all be acts

---

[38] Much of my understanding of Rand's view of all of these intellectual demands has benefited from conversation with Harry Binswanger some time ago, and I now forget whether any of my specific formulations of points were originally his.

of justice.[39] Punishments, again, are the deliberate withholdings of such benefits or the delivery of disvalues such as firing, ostracizing, or sharing negative appraisals with others. Whatever the particular form of reward or punishment most appropriate on a given occasion, the virtue of justice demands that a person, in order to rationally pursue his interest, make all appropriate responses operative parts of his repertoire and employ them as others deserve.

The Rejection of Egalitarianism

The practical requirements of Rand's account of justice stand in direct opposition to a prevalent contemporary idea of justice, egalitarianism. "Egalitarianism means the belief in the equality of all men" and holds that we should treat others equally.[40] Egalitarianism advocates not simply the equal application of proper standards in a given domain to different individuals, as do many nonegalitarian theories of justice, Rand's included. (Indeed, objectivity demands the equal application of appropriate standards to all relevantly similar individuals.) Rather, egalitarianism holds that equality itself is the standard of justice. Although egalitarians may differ over the exact way in which equality should be realized (in regard to income, abilities, or opportunities, for instance), they are united in the belief that equality in some such dimension is the test and substance of justice.

John Rawls's celebrated theory of justice, insisting on the superiority of equal distributions of desirable goods and placing the burden of justification on any deviation from equality, has propelled egalitarianism's contemporary respectability.[41] The egalitarian ideal is assumed in numerous areas, such as commonplace complaints that x percent of a nation's population owns more than x percent of that nation's total wealth or complaints about big oil companies or big pharmaceutical companies or big business in general – "big" being considered bad because the big

---

[39] I have found myself writing more notes of praise and gratitude to authors and artists whose work I admire to be a pleasant consequence of my greater attention to justice, in recent years.

[40] Rand, "The Age of Envy," p. 140. John Kekes describes egalitarianism as the thesis that "all human beings should be treated with equal consideration unless there are good reasons against it," *The Illusions of Egalitarianism* (Ithaca, NY: Cornell University Press, 2003), p. 1.

[41] John Rawls, *A Theory of Justice* (Cambridge, MA: Belknap Press, 1971). While Rawls wrote a great deal after this book, it remains his most influential work, by far. Rand discusses it in "An Untitled Letter."

allegedly have more than their fair share, with a "fair" share taken to mean an equal share. Thanks largely to Rawls, differences have been put on the defensive. We see egalitarianism in education in the trend toward "social promotion" and away from failing students or leaving anyone back to repeat a grade. The operative premise is that differentiating between students' abilities or performance is wrong. At the college level, egalitarianism underlies admissions policies whereby certain state universities accept the top x percent of applicants from all high schools in that state, regardless of how bright or prepared those students are. This, it is argued, serves the goal of equal access, which trumps other goals and any other understanding of justice in student selection. Similarly, arts funding boards frequently attempt to "spread the money around" by supporting all grant applicants regardless of the quality of the applicants' proposals or track records. Granting money for some alongside denials for others would allegedly be unfair; some are "underserved" if they do not receive what others receive. In short, it has become a widespread presumption that inequalities should be eliminated or, failing that, minimized.[42]

The problem with egalitarianism, according to Rand, is that it flies in the face of a human being's need to discriminate the good from the bad in others and to treat others accordingly so as to advance his rational interest.[43] Egalitarianism is not merely inconsistent with the rational egoist's need for justice, however; it is a frontal assault on justice – and on all virtue. Egalitarianism represents a complete inversion of justice insofar as it seeks to eradicate the concepts of "deserve" and "earn" and advocates that we "punish men for their virtues and reward them for their vices" (as this is the only way to even things out and achieve the goal of equality). Rand regards such a policy as "the collapse to full depravity."[44]

The ideal of egalitarianism gains initial credibility because of areas in which equality is a legitimate principle. Human beings equally possess certain basic rights (to life, liberty, property). Citizens should be equal before the law.[45] People who are relevantly similar should be judged by the same standards. A teacher should not judge 9th grade essays by the standards suitable for college seniors, for instance, though all students in the same class should be graded by the same standards (assuming that the individuals in question are properly in that class). People should be

[42] Rand discusses further manifestations of egalitarianism in "The Age of Envy," pp. 140–141.
[43] Peikoff discusses egalitarianism in *Objectivism*, pp. 290–291.
[44] Rand, *Atlas Shrugged*, p. 1020. Also see "An Untitled Letter," p. 134.
[45] See Rand, "The Age of Envy," p. 140.

treated equally in those respects in which we are equal. Yet it is a plain fact that human beings are unequal in countless respects: intelligence, knowledge, musical talents, athletic abilities, reliability, industry, discipline, courage, creativity, trustworthiness, and so on. Insofar as egalitarianism ignores this, it is irrational. Egalitarianism replaces the standard of individual desert with the standard of sameness. It determines how an individual is to be treated not on the basis of his conduct and character, but by appeal to what people around him have or do. In this way, egalitarianism's elevation of sameness as the highest ideal comes at the expense of treating individuals as they deserve and thus at the expense of justice.

Egalitarianism is unjust, on Rand's account, for basically the same reasons that neutrality is. Thus an observation that Rand makes in discussing neutrality is also instructive here. "Indiscriminate tolerance and indiscriminate condemnation . . . are two variants of the same evasion. To declare that 'everybody is white' or 'everybody is black' or 'everybody is neither white nor black, but gray,' is not a moral judgment, but an escape from the responsibility of moral judgment."[46] Yet this is exactly the sort of evasion that egalitarianism calls for. Ignore differences, it prescribes, and make people the same in the favored respect. Such a refusal to recognize individuals' differences is no more practical when one's goal is equality than when any other goal motivates it, however. Pretending that others are better or worse than they are does not change them and does not immunize a person from others' effects on him.

Some might object that this attacks a straw man, protesting that no one advocates such unqualified egalitarianism. Notwithstanding the several examples of egalitarian policies I cited above, I would agree that most egalitarians endorse moderate incarnations or egalitarianism only in certain spheres. The reason, however, is the utter impracticality of any attempt to consistently apply an egalitarian policy. Imagine staffing a business by setting aside concern with differences among candidates for various positions: salesman, mail clerk, personnel manager, receptionist, janitor, engineer, chief executive officer. One can barely begin envisioning such a course before its natural result, the collapse of the enterprise, is obvious. What is important is not the relative merits of various gradations of egalitarianism, however. For even short of an extreme (i.e., consistent) application of the egalitarian ideal, the thesis that equality per se is what justice demands is completely antithetical to the requirements

---

[46] Rand, "How Does One Lead a Rational Life in an Irrational Society?" pp. 83–84.

of rational self-interest. Egalitarianism promotes "the greatest happiness for the least deserving," while it shackles those who are most deserving.[47] (Witness a Nobel Prize–winning economist's proposal to levy a tax on "personal capabilities," starting with a "tax on persons with high academic scores."[48] Consider, also, a federal court's finding that a successful company violated antitrust laws on the grounds that the company met demand too well, steadily and effectively seizing opportunities and expanding its capacity.)[49]

In papering over differences between individuals, egalitarianism counsels faking. This is, as ever, futile at best and self-destructive, at worst. Egalitarians may be unfazed by the self-destructive fallout of their policy, as they are typically advocates of altruism. Rational egoists, however, cannot be.

The Refusal to Sanction Evil

An important practical demand of justice, in Rand's view, is the refusal to sanction evil. "To abstain from condemning a torturer," she writes, "is to become an accessory to his crimes."[50] While the injunction to boycott evil resonates deeply with many and its propriety can seem self-evident to those who accept it, this is not an inherently compelling duty, on Rand's view; it is not intrinsically right. The case against sanctioning evil is rooted in rational self-interest as much as every other aspect of Rand's moral code.

Let me begin by clarifying the relevant sense of "evil" in this context. "Evil" is sometimes used to refer to anything that falls on the negative side of the expansive spectrum of actions and qualities that are morally good or bad. In this very broad sense, "evil" would encompass everything from stealing thousands of dollars or plotting the slaughter of millions to taking a teaspoon from a restaurant or telling a lie to spare a person's feelings. Other times, we reserve "evil" to designate those persons or actions at the extremely immoral end of the spectrum. In this sense, "evil" refers to

[47] Rand, "An Untitled Letter," pp. 135, 144.
[48] Rand, "An Untitled Letter," p. 124.
[49] *United States v. Aluminum Co. of America*, 148 F. 2d 416 (2d Cir. 1945). See the passage quoted from Learned Hand's opinion in Rand, "America's Persecuted Minority: Big Business," in *Capitalism: The Unknown Ideal*, p. 57.
[50] Rand, "How Does One Lead a Rational Life in an Irrational Society?" p. 83. The rationale for the strike in *Atlas Shrugged* is the conviction that the victims of evil should withdraw their sanction.

the most serious breaches and to those who commit them most routinely. It refers to those individuals whose deeds are most knowingly, willfully, and consistently immoral, to those who are most thoroughly vicious and whose immoral actions are of an intensity and scale that vastly exceeds everyday dimensions.[51]

We have seen already that no aspect of a person's conduct or character is, in principle, beyond the proper purview of judgment or correlative treatment that justice demands. The prohibition on sanctioning evil thus applies, strictly, to all immorality, major or minor. Nonetheless, the prohibition holds special salience in regard to extraordinary degrees of immorality because the stakes are much greater in such cases. Although all forms of wrongdoing should be recognized and treated for what they are, then, I will be using "evil" primarily in the narrower, more restrictive sense, to designate the worst offenses – the most purely *evil*. (Note that Rand refers to torture in the passage I cited rather than to more commonplace immoralities.)

The basic rationale for the refusal to sanction evil is straightforward. When a person fails to condemn evil practices or evil persons, he acts as if they are benign. This is irrational in at least three related ways. First, it may benefit evil materially, if the person is in a position to withhold material support or to materially assist others who actively oppose the evil in question. Second, it bestows on the grossly undeserving the spiritual shelter of the sanctioner's tacit approval, for that is the message that his failure to condemn conveys. Third, a person's failure to oppose evil exposes him to the damage to values that others' evil threatens.[52] The sanction of evil helps to sustain practices that work against a person's life. Ignoring others' evil does not disarm it. The greater the evil that a person indulges, the greater the potential damage to his own values. Depending on the kind and degree of evil that I sanction, I may lose my teeth (to a bully), my money (to a corrupt politician), my freedom (to a dictator). Given that what makes something evil is its adversarial relationship to objective values, whatever form of evil I sanction, by doing so, I am putting myself in a position to lose.

Evil is dangerous. But evil is parasitic on the good. It is for this reason that the withdrawal of sanction is the appropriate response to evil. For

[51] In lectures, Peikoff has distinguished more finely between the categories of "bad," "immoral," "vicious," "wicked," and "evil." October 7, 1994, lecture, Objectivist Academic Center, heard via teleconference.

[52] See Peikoff, *Objectivism*, p. 285.

it is the most effective means of resisting the dangers that evil poses. Let me spell this out in a little more detail.

Only certain actions (those broadly identified as virtuous) can actually further human life and contribute to anyone's flourishing. The evil is that which is anti-life, that which works to prevent or diminish human flourishing. The anti-life cannot fuel life, however; actions working against the requirements of human life cannot create or nourish the values that human life depends on. Because no person can survive on a diet of consistently life-diminishing actions, evil (evil persons and evil practices) can exist only to the extent that it feeds on values created by the good.[53] A slothful person must draw from the productive; a faker must draw from the honest; a second-hander must draw from the independent. If Bill does not create the material values that his existence requires, he must use the products of those who do create material values. If Bill does not face facts for what they are, he must rely on the honesty of those who do whenever he seeks to obtain values from them – be it meat from a butcher or understanding from a friend. If Bill does not think for himself in forming his beliefs, he must depend on those who do whenever he seeks to gain value from others' minds.

The point is, the support of the good is indispensable to the existence of the evil. Drained of that support, the evil would collapse; its continued existence would be only a matter of time. To sanction evil is thus to give evil the food it needs to endure. Sanction from the good is the *only* lifeline that evil has. Whether the good offer material support or spiritual support, whether the good offer crumbs or cakes, grudging concessions or hearty congratulations, such gifts supply the totality of evil's lease on life.[54]

Remember that the evil, to the extent that it is such, acts in ways that could not sustain its own existence. The refusal to sanction evil becomes imperative, therefore, because by lending support to evil, a person keeps afloat the very type of person or practice that works against his own life. He is feeding those who necessarily prey on the virtuous and seek (whether self-consciously or not) to weaken the lives of those who create objective

---

53 My references to "evil" and to "the evil" should not be taken to imply that Rand believes that evil exists as an independent force in the universe. Rather, these are simply convenient shorthands for referring to evil persons and evil practices. The parallel applies to my use of "good" and "the good."

54 A "grudging concession" is not an unavoidable compromise that is physically forced from a person. Nor is it a legitimate concession of a minor preference rather than of a moral principle. We will discuss the morality of compromises in the chapter on integrity.

values (since the evil seek to gain the values that their existence requires
without offering comparable values in exchange). In the terms of pop
psychology, those who sanction evil are quintessential "enablers."[55]

In condemning the sanction of evil, Rand is not proposing that a person must take up arms in order to battle every evil on earth. She disavows
the notion that one should "give unsolicited moral appraisals to all those
one meets" or "regard oneself as a missionary charged with the responsibility of 'saving everyone's soul.' "[56] The demand that a just person refuse
to sanction evil does not entail an obligation to make active opposition to
evil the central campaign of his life. Such an interpretation would forget
the egoistic basis of virtue. Justice is not an end in itself. Nor does justice's
prohibition of sanctioning evil demand that a person martyr himself. If a
person faces unjust punishment for speaking out on some issue, he has
no obligation to deliver himself to that. If a person *knew*, for example,
that were he to let his political views be known around the office, his manager would smear him come annual review, he need not express those
views. Morality does not demand cooperation with those who would turn
a person's virtue against him, making it a tool in his own victimization. As
Peikoff observes, "Justice cannot require that a man sacrifice himself to
someone else's evil."[57] In normal circumstances, however, where a person's silence would reasonably be taken as agreement with something he
does not support and he would not be unjustly penalized for speaking
out, he must speak.[58]

Any voicing of a dissenting opinion may well provoke some negative
repercussions, if only temporary unpleasantness between two people.
That prospect does not justify silent acquiescence to evil. The ultimate
standard for determining when a person would be sanctioning evil and
when he would not be – when he must speak up and when morality permits silence – is the same standard that is used to determine all instruction in Rand's ethics: a principled understanding of what will serve the
agent's long-range, rational interest. When speaking would be a sacrifice,
the surrender of a greater value for the sake of a lesser value, a person

---

[55] In an open letter to intellectuals in the early 1940's, Rand observes that totalitarians
do not need to corral a great deal of active support in order to advance their causes;
they merely need most people to sit at home and do nothing. *Journals of Ayn Rand*, pp.
348–349.

[56] Rand, "How Does One Lead a Rational Life in an Irrational Society?" p. 84.

[57] Peikoff, *Objectivism*, p. 286.

[58] Rand, "How Does One Lead a Rational Life in an Irrational Society?" p. 84. Also see
Peikoff, *Objectivism*, pp. 284–286.

should not speak. When *not* speaking would be a sacrifice, however, as it would be when a more fully considered perspective reveals that a person's long-range flourishing would be jeopardized by his silence, he must.[59]

The ethics of sanction, with a careful consideration of all its nuances in different situations, is easily the subject of a lengthy study in its own right. Because part of what is involved are messages that a person's inaction tacitly conveys and because that will depend largely on the exact context (on the extent of one's knowledge of another's evil, for instance), it is impossible for an abstract formula to specify particular actions that, in all circumstances, constitute sanction of others' evil. In general, the more close and sustained one person's relationship with another, the more his association lends support to that person. The endorsement one gives a person by buying newspapers at his bodega is far less than the endorsement one gives a person by hiring him to work in one's own store, for instance, which is still less than the endorsement bestowed by voting for his election to Congress or naming him the executor of one's estate. And the greater a person's evil, the less a person should associate with him at all, however casual the interactions. For the greater another person's evil, the more damage it can do.

The injunction against sanctioning evil is one reflection of Rand's broader thesis that a just person abides by a principle of trade, neither granting nor seeking the undeserved, in matter or in spirit.[60] What a just person seeks from others, he pays for, with money or work or his own good character, for instance, which makes him worthy of the car or the job or the friend that he seeks. What a just person gives to others, he expects some form of payment for; he gives in response to the values that he reaps. He respects rewards and punishments as payments given in *exchange* for virtues or vices and he treats others neither as masters nor slaves, but as independent equals.[61] Straying from the trader principle in either direction, giving or taking more than desert warrants, sabotages a person's flourishing. Prodigal giving squanders a person's resources and

---

59 Recall from chapter two that the exchange of short-term gratifications for the long-term benefits of principled action is not a sacrifice; acting by rational principles offers a net gain. Rand discusses the nature of sacrifice in "The Ethics of Emergencies," pp. 50–51, and in *Atlas Shrugged*, pp. 1028–1029. Also, while I have focused on *speaking* to express one's disapproval, the same basic account applies to all forms of action that express the refusal to sanction.

60 Rand, "The Objectivist Ethics," pp. 28, 34–35. Also see Peikoff, *Objectivism*, p. 286.

61 Rand, "The Objectivist Ethics," pp. 34–35. We will see this in the realm of friendship in the Appendix.

encourages the recipients to expect values without offering appropriate payment. Indulgent taking drains producers of the rewards and incentive that fuel their creation of values – values from which others also stand to gain. To fail to insist on value for value fakes the reality of how values come to exist, pretending that values can be had without effort. Because faking does not change things, however, such pretense is ultimately self-defeating. Facing these facts, by contrast, accepting that there is no free lunch, the just person seeks no dodges around a policy of honest trading. (Notice that people often object to a person's cheating or stealing precisely because that person attempts to get something for nothing, without offering the requisite effort or value in exchange. This suggests implicit recognition of the fact that values must be earned.)

Implications for Forgiveness and Mercy

In the face of others' wrongdoing, it is widely believed that morality calls for forgiveness and mercy.[62] Both are included in many people's lists of moral virtues. They are not on Rand's list, however, and would not qualify even as more specialized derivative virtues. Although forgiveness and mercy could each be examined at great length, here, to sharpen our understanding of the practical demands of Rand's conception of justice, I will simply sketch the implications of her account for these commonly touted "virtues."[63]

Forgiveness is a type of moral estimate, typically manifested in a reacceptance of a person who has wronged one in some way. In the light of some breach (a failure to deliver on a commitment, for instance, such as a broken confidence or marital infidelity), forgiveness involves the judgment that the person's transgression should not be treated as proof of grave moral defect or an irredeemably bad character. Forgiveness does not involve a denial of what the other person did or of his action's impropriety. Nor is it the discovery that the offender had a legitimate excuse for

---

[62] Widely, but not universally. For some at least partially dissenting views, see Joram Graf Haber, *Forgiveness* (Lanham, MD: Rowman & Littlefield, 1991); Peter A. French, *The Virtues of Vengeance* (Lawrence: University Press of Kansas, 2001); and Jeffrie Murphy's essays in Jeffrie G. Murphy and Jean Hampton, *Forgiveness and Mercy* (New York: Cambridge University Press, 1988). More recently, Murphy has developed a more forgiving view of forgiveness. See his *Getting Even – Forgiveness and its Limits* (New York: Oxford University Press, 2003).

[63] For a fuller discussion of forgiveness, see my "Tolerance and Forgiveness: Virtues or Vices?" *Journal of Applied Philosophy* 14, no. 1 (1997), pp. 31–41.

what he did. If the aggrieved learns of extenuating circumstances (e.g., the offender lacked some critical piece of knowledge about what he was doing or was physically coerced into his action) and realizes that what initially seemed an immoral action was not, then he has nothing *to* forgive. Forgiveness reflects the conclusion that, while another person did do something wrong, the victim should respond to that person's breach less harshly than would normally be appropriate.

People use the term "forgiveness" somewhat equivocally, sometimes referring to one person's judgment of another, sometimes stressing one person's feeling toward another, and still other times, referring to the way that one person acts toward another. Given that human beings cannot directly and immediately control our feelings, if forgiveness were simply a type of feeling, it would be exempt from moral evaluation. We could neither commend forgiveness, morally, nor condemn anyone for failing to forgive. If forgiveness can be morally appropriate in certain situations, therefore, the idea that forgiveness consists entirely of certain feelings must be rejected.[64]

Primarily, forgiveness concerns one person's judgment of another, although correlative action should follow from that judgment. For the reason to evaluate another person is usually (and almost always, when contemplating forgiveness) to determine how to treat him.[65] Treatment alone, however, does not constitute forgiveness. To accidentally or unintentionally treat a wrongdoer more favorably than his wrongdoing would normally warrant, without judging that this is proper, is not to forgive the person. While forgiveness typically involves a certain manner of treating a person, that treatment must be based on a certain evaluation of the person. In particular, again, forgiveness is the judgment that another person's transgression should not be understood or treated as harshly as would normally be appropriate.

In light of the need to judge others objectively and treat them accordingly, it should be clear that in Rand's view, we have no duty to forgive all those who wrong us. A standing policy of turning the other cheek is antithetical to the rational pursuit of one's happiness. It represents

---

[64] This contrasts with Bishop Butler's influential account of 1726, which depicted forgiveness as the forswearing of resentment. Joseph Butler, *Fifteen Sermons Preached at the Rolls Chapel*, especially sermons 8 and 9.

[65] When a person forgives someone who is deceased, he can obviously no longer treat that person in any particular ways. Also note that on this view, forgiving a person for the purpose of improving one's own mental health would not be genuine forgiveness, since one's actual evaluation of the offender need not change, within that therapy.

abject surrender to the injuries that others inflict and may further inflict in the future. This does not mean that justice is incompatible with forgiveness or that it would always be wrong to extend forgiveness. While forgiving means treating a person less harshly than is normally appropriate, this can be appropriate under certain conditions. Forgiveness is proper, Peikoff observes, when the offender makes restitution to his victim (if possible) and demonstrates that he understands the roots of his breach, has reformed, and will not repeat the transgression.[66] Notice that by satisfying these conditions, the wrongdoer distances himself from the offending action. Through restitution, reform, and so on, he manifests his judgment that what he did was wrong and not representative of the kind of person he wishes to be. In the absence of his meeting these conditions, however, forgiveness would sanction the wrong and leave the victim vulnerable to more of the same.

Forgiveness, then, must be earned, on Rand's view. A person should not forgive others on faith or out of blind "good will" in the absence of convincing evidence of regret and reform. The unconditional embrace of those who work against one's happiness would be a baseless disarmament that turns one's back on that goal. It is important to appreciate, however, that forgiveness *can* be earned. When the relevant conditions are satisfied, it would be wrong not to forgive the transgressor. The conditions of forgiveness are stiff. The worse the original violation, the harder it will be to fulfill them. It will also take time, of course, for a wrongdoer to meet these conditions and for others to assure themselves that he has. Although it is always difficult to appraise another person's character, it is especially challenging when, as in cases that might warrant forgiveness, one faces strongly conflicting evidence from a person's transgression and subsequent conduct. If a person does meet the conditions of forgiveness, though, what would be the grounds for denying what his character now seems to be? If, as far as one can tell, he truly has reformed, it would be dishonest to deny that.

People can change for the better. Insofar as justice demands objectivity, a just person may not freeze the evaluations he draws about another person at any one time and blot out future evidence of change. Moreover, essentially good people can do bad things on rare occasions, giving in to an uncharacteristic spell of laziness or weak will, for instance. Isolated deeds are not always accurate indicators of a person's overall character,

---

[66] Peikoff, *Objectivism*, p. 289. Murphy and Haber similarly argue that certain conditions must be satisfied to justify forgiveness, although they differ about what the conditions are.

as we noted earlier, even if those deeds can be quite hurtful to others. In this as in all evaluations of others, justice demands the honest appraisal of all relevant evidence about a person. Emotionally, a victim might remain deeply hurt by the original breach and thus reluctant to resume a close association with the transgressor. Forgiveness does not demand that a person set aside his feelings or act exactly as he would have had the offending incident never taken place. Feelings can be reason not to resume an intimate relationship, but not, in themselves, reason not to forgive. Being wronged does not license emotionalism.[67]

In short, on Rand's view of justice, sometimes a person *should* forgive because that is what the other person deserves. That desert is based on his original transgression as well as his subsequent remorse, apology, commitment to reform, etc. Forgiveness is not the unconditional good that it is often proclaimed to be, but nor is it unconditionally wrong. Like all rewards, forgiveness must be earned.[68]

Whereas forgiveness can be earned, mercy is unearned leniency. According to the *OED*, mercy consists of kind treatment of a person "who has no claim to receive kindness" and "where severity is merited or expected."[69] This is the same basic understanding employed by ethicists. Jean Hampton describes mercy as the "suspension or mitigation of a

[67] For more on this, see my "Tolerance and Forgiveness: Virtues or Vices?" p. 37.

[68] One might object that if all virtues are conditional insofar as their proper application is dependent on context and their propriety can be suspended by emergencies, then the sheer fact that forgiveness is not in all cases obligatory does not show that it is not a virtue. This objection rests on too crude an understanding of the case against regarding forgiveness as a virtue, however. While the proper *application* of a virtue does depend on the specific context, this does not mean that the virtue itself is sometimes inappropriate (short of genuine emergencies). The particular concretes that a virtue such as honesty or independence or justice demands from an individual will differ in different situations; the propriety of being honest or independent or just, however, does not. Moreover, the fact that emergencies suspend all moral virtues does not impugn Rand's position on forgiveness, since it is not conditionality *per se* that distinguishes virtues from nonvirtues. Rather, the difference turns on the *kinds* of conditions that govern the proper exercise of virtues and of nonvirtues. A virtue is something that a person ought to practice in all normal (nonemergency) circumstances. Absent an emergency, a person should always be honest, just, and independent. (Later chapters will indicate how this holds for the other virtues, as well.) The propriety of forgiveness, in contrast – of forgiving at all, and not simply of how to properly forgive – always depends on more specific facts about the wrongdoer. "Forgive, except in emergencies" is not a rationally egoistic policy. The conditions on the propriety of forgiveness are more numerous and more fine-grained, in other words, than the conditions that attach to the virtues.

[69] The full *OED* definition is: "Forbearance and compassion shown by one person to another who is in his power and who has no claim to receive kindness; kind and compassionate treatment in a case where severity is merited or expected."

punishment that would otherwise be deserved as retribution, and which is granted out of pity and compassion for the wrongdoer." It is, significantly, a gift that a wrongdoer "cannot merit."[70] Alwynne Smart understands mercy along the same lines: "When a man exercises mercy what he does is acknowledge that an offense has been committed, decide that a particular punishment would be appropriate or just, and then decide to exact a punishment of lesser severity than the appropriate or just one."[71] Essentially, as Peikoff recognizes, mercy is "the policy of identifying [a person's deserts], then *not* acting accordingly: lessening the appropriate punishment in a negative case or failing to impose any punishment."[72]

One might suppose that a person's reason for extending mercy will determine its propriety, just as one's reasons for forgiveness determine the propriety of that response. Yet in fact, nothing can justify unearned leniency. (The incompatibility between the two is precisely why the claim that God is both just and merciful has long been considered a paradox.)[73] To temper justice with mercy is to inject injustice into one's dealings. Doing so is wrong for the same basic reason that is by now familiar: Faking others' character does not change their character or its impact on one's life. Such pretense offers no protection against those aspects of others' conduct or character that jeopardize one's values. Indeed, it only exposes the merciful to further damage and leaves the unpunished in position to claim new victims.

A person's reasons for extending mercy could help to determine whether what is offered truly constitutes mercy. Taking the full context of a transgressor's actions into account, an evaluator might discover that the other's actions were justified or that he had a valid excuse for doing what he did or that he should be forgiven. In such cases, to revise one's verdicts and actions accordingly is not an expression of mercy, but a reflection of objectivity. As Murphy observes, "[T]o avoid inflicting upon persons more suffering than they deserve, or to avoid punishing the less responsible as much as the fully responsible, is a simple – indeed an obvious – demand of justice."[74]

---

[70] Jean Hampton, "The Retributive Idea," in Murphy and Hampton, pp. 158, 159, 161.
[71] Quoted in P. Twambley, "Mercy and Forgiveness," *Analysis* 36, no. 2 (January 1976), p. 84.
[72] *Objectivism*, p. 289, emphasis in original.
[73] Murphy discusses Anselm's worry about this paradox in "Mercy and Legal Justice," Murphy and Hampton, pp. 168–169.
[74] Murphy, "Mercy and Legal Justice," in Murphy and Hampton, p. 171; see also p. 166. Murphy does hold that mercy is a virtue, however, pp. 175–176.

Notice that appeals for mercy are usually appeals to compassion. "Go light on him," a person pleads, "let him slide," "cut him some slack." Or: "I know I don't deserve this, but do me this favor anyway;" "have a heart." The typical pitch urges a person to replace reason as his basis for dealing with others with emotion. Whereas forgiveness often involves a person's overcoming strong negative feelings toward another person in order to treat him as he deserves, mercy frequently involves acting in a certain way *because* of certain feelings (or because of a desire to appear to have certain feelings, e.g., to "have a heart"). We have seen already that emotions are not a reliable basis for guiding a person to objective values, however. It is as contrary to reason to indulge in this form of emotionalism as in any other.[75]

It is also important to recognize the harm that mercy imposes on the innocent, who are made to bear the burden of leniency extended to the undeserving. In *Atlas Shrugged*, Hank Rearden puts this well as he comes to appreciate his own complicity in fostering some of the unjust obstacles that he has faced:

When one acts on pity against justice, it is the good whom one punishes for the sake of the evil; when one saves the guilty from suffering, it is the innocent whom one forces to suffer. There is no escape from justice, nothing can be unearned and unpaid for in the universe, neither in matter nor in spirit – and if the guilty do not pay, then the innocent have to pay it.[76]

To briefly explain: The kinds of actions that warrant punishment are those that impede values. If life is the standard of value, what makes certain actions bad is their opposition, in some form, to objective values. When a person commits a transgression, then, *someone* must pay (as Rearden indicates) because that transgression creates losses. If we are to restore the status quo ante, something must be done to compensate for those losses. If money is stolen from me, for instance, I can get by as well as I had been before that injury only by taking from somewhere else – by working harder or by forgoing other uses of my time or money, for instance. And of course, to the extent that I must do that, I am not truly as well off as I had been; I have suffered a real loss. Cases in which third parties are harmed by mercy are also not hard to find. If I mercifully give a high grade to an undeserving student, the value of the high grades that other students earned is cheapened. They will have to work harder or do

[75] Murphy discusses the contrasting roles of emotions in mercy and forgiveness, "Forgiveness and Resentment," Murphy and Hampton, p. 34.
[76] *Atlas Shrugged*, p. 565.

still better to receive the equivalent of their previous grades in value. If I mercifully allow an inept worker to retain his job and if the business is to withstand such inefficiencies, other employees will be required to work harder to compensate for his lack of production. By their nature, bad actions create burdens and do damage. Mercy lets those who cause the damage off the hook (the hook being the need for compensation). If the guilty do not pay the compensation, as Rand observes, then the innocent must.

In the end, mercy violates the demands of justice. Treating a wrong-doer more leniently than he deserves is a form of sanctioning evil. It is understandable to wish other individuals to be better than they are and to hope that one's negative conclusions about a person are mistaken. Yet when a person has no reason to think that his conclusions are mistaken, he has no reason to act as if they are. Wishful thinking is not a sound basis for the achievement of one's rational interest.[77]

THE RELATIONSHIP BETWEEN JUSTICE AND INDIVIDUAL RIGHTS

Before concluding our examination of justice, I should attempt to fore-stall a possible misunderstanding. The rationale for justice is egoistic, we have seen. Egoism does not authorize the abuse of other individuals who a person deems not particularly beneficial to him, however. For the demands of justice do not override the obligation to respect others' rights. A full account of the nature and foundations of rights is a major subject unto itself, which I have explored in depth in *Moral Rights and Political Freedom*.[78] Because claims of rights and claims of justice are often confused, however, it is worth briefly addressing the relationship between

---

[77] Anders Floor (unpublished paper, 2003) has suggested a way in which mercy might be consistent with justice. In many cases, he argues, justice allows a range of responses to another's transgression, each of which would be equally just. If a person is merciful when he opts for one of the lighter penalties within such a range, then mercy could be deserved (and thus just) in those cases in which a lighter penalty is appropriate (e.g., for a first-time offender who seems unlikely to repeat his misdeed). The problem with Floor's proposal, however, is that this alters the ordinary meaning of mercy: a kind of treatment that is not deserved. Moreover, if a person truly deserves a light sentence, then no harsher penalties would be just – in which case the range of just responses is not as wide as Floor suggests. People might sometimes use the term "mercy" loosely to refer to what is truly a just treatment, but when they do, this reveals no error in opposing mercy as incompatible with justice. If mercy means treating people better than they deserve (as both the *OED* and philosophical discussion testify), then to engage in mercy is to betray justice.

[78] Tara Smith, *Moral Rights and Political Freedom* (Lanham, MD: Rowman & Littlefield, 1995).

the two. What follows is only a cursory sketch of Rand's position on rights rather than a full explanation or defense of her view. For a more extensive explanation, a reader should consult several works directly examining that subject.[79] This discussion will nonetheless serve, I hope, to prevent a serious misinterpretation.

The basic social principle of the Objectivist ethics is that "every living human being is an end in himself, not the means to the ends or the welfare of others..."[80] Correspondingly, Rand regards each individual as "a sovereign entity who possesses an inalienable right to his own life, a right derived from his nature as a rational being."[81] Rand understands rights in the way that they were originally conceived, as protections of an individual's freedom of action.[82] Because freedom is a prerequisite of the rationality that fuels human existence, to violate a person's rights and thereby deprive a person of freedom is to prevent him from exercising his ability to sustain himself. We have seen previously that rationality is indispensable to human survival. Human beings can meet the needs that their nature imposes only insofar as they respect reality as their sovereign. Rationality in thought and action is essential to a human being's life, yet rationality is possible only under conditions of freedom.

Freedom is the absence of other people's interference with a person's ability to govern his own actions. More specifically, freedom is the condition distinguished by the absence of other persons initiating the use or threat of physical force against a person (i.e., against his will or without his consent).[83] A person is free when, for example, no one is beating him, binding him, pointing a gun to his head and issuing demands, or threatening to lock him away unless he obeys orders. Freedom is necessary for rationality, Rand argues, because a mind cannot be forced. Rational thought cannot be beaten out of a person. When discussing the virtue of independence, we observed that thinking is by its nature a

---

[79] In addition to my book, see Rand, "Man's Rights," and "The Nature of Government," in *The Virtue of Selfishness*, pp. 108–117 and 125–134; "What is Capitalism?" in *Capitalism: The Unknown Ideal*, pp. 11–34; and Peikoff, *Objectivism*, pp. 310–323 and 351–363.

[80] Rand, "The Objectivist Ethics," p. 30.

[81] Rand, "Racism," in *The Virtue of Selfishness*, p. 150.

[82] Peikoff, *Objectivism*, p. 355; Rand, "Man's Rights," p. 110; Smith, *Moral Rights and Political Freedom*, pp. 15–29. For some other statements of this conception of rights, see John Locke, *Second Treatise on Government*; H. L. A. Hart, "Are There any Natural Rights?" in David Lyons, ed., *Rights* (Belmont, CA: Wadsworth, 1979), pp. 16, 24; Carl Wellman, *A Theory of Rights* (Totowa, NJ: Rowman & Allanheld, 1985).

[83] For a full explanation, see my *Moral Rights and Political Freedom*, pp. 123–161. Obviously, I am speaking of political freedom rather than freedom of the will.

do-it-yourself activity; no person can think for another. Similarly, no person's physical actions can coax any thoughts – let alone rational thoughts – out of another person. "A gun is not an argument," Rand observes.[84]

Physical force paralyzes a person's judgment. Rationality consists in using one's mind to identify and respect the facts of reality; force thrusts a different master before a person: the will of the aggressor. This is obvious when the application of force is direct and one person beats another into submission, shackles him, or literally drags or pushes him around, for instance. It is equally true in the case of the threat to apply physical force, however. When reality is decreed at gunpoint (or its equivalent) to be out of bounds, a rational mind is stopped in its tracks, it has no way to proceed.[85] Whatever prizes the forcer might wrest from his victim (a wallet, a ransom, obedience, professions of respect), what he cannot extract is rational thought. This is because, as Peikoff aptly expresses it, physical force cannot convert the volitional process of reasoning into a deterministic response.[86] I might be able to manipulate another person's *brain* through physical means; I cannot, through such means, manipulate his mind or gain command over his thoughts. As Peikoff explains in another work, "Force is the antonym and negation of thought. Understanding is not produced by a punch in the face; intellectual clarity does not flow from the muzzle of a gun . . ."[87]

All of this is to indicate why Rand regards freedom (the object of the protection of rights) as essential to a person's ability to live. For the immediate purpose of clarifying the relationship between rights and the virtue of justice, the principal point is that rights are a function of human nature, in Rand's view.[88] A person need not do anything to earn his basic rights. (I am speaking of general rights shared by all human beings, as opposed to more specific rights that only certain individuals hold, such as rights to a particular piece of property or to another person's performance of an agreed-upon action. These do require the satisfaction of further conditions.)[89] Our basic rights are not the sort of thing that a person can deserve in the way that he might deserve a bonus for outstanding work

[84] Rand, "What is Capitalism?" p. 17.
[85] Peikoff, *Objectivism,* p. 312.
[86] Peikoff, *Objectivism,* p. 313. Peikoff discusses the evil of the initiation of physical force on pp. 310–323.
[87] Peikoff, *The Ominous Parallels,* p. 336.
[88] Peikoff, *Objectivism,* pp. 360–361; Rand, "Man's Rights," p. 111; "The Nature of Government," p. 126; *Atlas Shrugged,* pp. 1061–1062.
[89] For a clear explanation of this distinction, see Hart, pp. 20–23.

or a rebuke for his negligence. A person might forfeit his natural rights by violating the rights of others, but he possesses rights in the first place not as a result of his having done something special to acquire them.

Bear in mind that justice governs reactions to specific qualities or actions of a given individual, such as his skill, hard work, incompetence, or carelessness. The obligation to respect rights is not contingent on such variables. A person deserves things because of what he does, as a response to his conduct and character. A person possesses rights, by contrast, simply in virtue of his nature as a human being. While a person is entitled to have his rights respected, then, strictly speaking, he does not deserve to. It is not that he deserves not to; rather, rights are not the sort of thing that a person either does or does not deserve. In everyday conversation, we sometimes speak as if they were, using claims of "rights" and "justice" interchangeably. The use of these terms in law probably encourages this. The purpose of a proper legal system is to protect individual rights and a legal system is just to the extent that it does that. In that realm, rights and justice often reflect two sides of the same issue. We must not allow the usage of these terms in the legal realm to cloud our understanding of the broader moral status of rights and justice, however.[90]

When considering the respect that is due a person's rights, what that person deserves or has or has not earned (e.g., how hard a worker he is, how inconsiderate his ways) are not appropriate considerations. An individual's rights are always held on the condition that the rightholder respects others' rights, thus throughout, I am leaving aside persons who forfeit their rights by violating the rights of others. As long as a person truly possesses rights, however, he is entitled to have them respected and his deserts are immaterial. The money I give a bum is, once given, his to spend as he likes, even if he is not a deserving recipient. A woman has a right to an inheritance (moral as well as legal) because it was bequeathed to her, even if others who were more steadfast friends to the deceased would have been more deserving beneficiaries. Desert remains relevant to other aspects of personal interactions. The question of what a person's rights entitle him to, however, is distinct from the question of how another person should treat him in order to fulfill the demands of justice.

---

[90] Even within the legal domain, rights and justice may not entirely overlap because other aspects of a legal system (the mechanisms through which a government protects its citizens' rights) might be just or unjust without directly corresponding to respect for rights. Policies for conducting elections can be just, for example, although no one's rights would be violated if Presidential elections were held on Fridays in May instead of on Tuesdays in November.

Another source of the common confusion of rights and justice rests in a tendency among many to think of a right as any valid moral claim that a person possesses, regardless of its basis. That is, some people use "rights" to refer indiscriminately to claims to freedom of action that are grounded in human nature (such as rights to life or to free speech) as well as to claims to things that a person deserves, which are grounded in distinctive facts about him and his relationships to particular others (such as his having written an excellent exam or made substantial contributions to the company). In this much wider sense, a right encompasses both what a person is entitled to and what a person deserves. Although it may sometimes be harmless to speak this way, it is important to recognize the different bases and character of these moral claims. The issue is not merely linguistic. If individuals were entitled by rights to every response that they deserved from anyone else (a standing ovation, a bonus, a congratulatory word, a reprimand, a demotion, an order to leave, etc.), we would be justified in forcibly compelling people to respond to one another's character and conduct with specific rewards and punishments. Such responses would no longer be a matter of discretion. This is not to suggest that responding to others' deserts is *morally* discretionary; it is not, as our discussion of the virtue of justice to this stage should make clear. But it should be discretionary vis-à-vis the law. If the job of the government is to protect individuals' rights (as Rand and many others believe it is), then once something is thought to belong to a person by rights, the government positively *should* coerce others to respect that right. In other words, the confusion of what a person deserves with what a person possesses by rights would mean the liquidation of individuals' freedom. For the obligations necessary to ensure that every person had "rights" to everything that he deserves respected would usher in the restrictive reign of legal moralism, under which no one would be free to do anything other than what the moral virtue of justice required. In light of this, it is crucial to respect the distinction between the moral virtue of justice, which demands that one person treat another person as he, *qua* individual, deserves, and basic rights, which demand that one person treat another as he, *qua* human being, is entitled.[91]

---

[91] Although no specific virtue in Rand's lexicon corresponds to the propriety of respecting others' rights, it is no less important a component of her normative theory. In his chapter on the moral virtues, Peikoff devotes a comparable number of pages to the evil of violating others' freedom as he gives to each of the virtues, and he returns to the subject for further analysis in a later chapter. For an explanation of why it is in an egoist's interest to respect others' rights, see my *Moral Rights and Political Freedom*, pp. 61–83, especially 70–73.

One implication of all of this is that a person can respect another person's rights while judging that person negatively and treating him accordingly. Suppose that Heath strongly disapproves of Brink's religious devotion or socialist politics or dilettantish character. Heath could punish Brink by refusing to contribute to Brink's causes or withholding his friendship or sharing his negative assessment of Brink with others, while still respecting Brink's freedom – his rights to property, to pray, to speak out on behalf on his views, and so on. Heath's position suffers from no inconsistency. He simply recognizes that what a person should do is not the same as what he should be free to do and that he (Heath) is not entitled to force others to act as he believes they ought. Insofar as Heath regards Brink as carrying negative effects on his interest, he should withdraw any sanction of Brink. Withdrawing that sanction does not license withdrawing recognition of Brink as a human being, however, who is, as such, entitled to freedom to rule his own life (again, as long as Brink's activities do not infringe on others' rights).

CONCLUSION

Because our examination of justice has led us onto a range of related topics, let me close by reiterating the core of Rand's position. Justice is the virtue of judging other people objectively and of treating them accordingly by paying them the rewards and punishments that they deserve. While this is the basic conception of justice that has prevailed for centuries, on Rand's view, the rationale for exercising justice is entirely egoistic. Because a person's values stand to be helped or harmed by the conduct and character of other people, a person needs to assess others' probable impact on his values and to treat others accordingly in order to promote his long-term flourishing. People deserve certain treatment from a person because their actions are volitional, their vices are potentially damaging to him, and their virtues are potentially valuable. Faking the character of other people is as fruitless and self-destructive as faking in regard to anything else. The failure either to judge others objectively or to treat others in ways correlative with one's judgment would be treason to one's values.

7

Integrity

The next virtue in Rand's ethics, integrity, also enjoys esteem in conventional morality. While people may differ over exactly what constitutes a breach of integrity, to impugn a person's integrity is widely seen as among the most grave sorts of censure possible. The reason why Rand considers integrity important, however, is not the reason usually given. Integrity is proper neither inherently nor because of its value to others. Rather, Rand recognizes integrity as an instrument of rational egoism. Maintaining one's integrity is essential to achieving objective values and flourishing. To see this, we shall again proceed to consider what integrity is, why it is a virtue, and the specific demands that it places on us.

WHAT INTEGRITY IS

Rand describes integrity as "loyalty to one's convictions and values; it is the policy of acting in accordance with one's values, of expressing, upholding and translating them into practical reality."[1] This virtue reflects rationality's demand that one must "never sacrifice one's convictions to the opinions or wishes of others."[2] In Peikoff's words, integrity, in essence, is "loyalty to rational principles." It "is the policy of practicing what one preaches regardless of emotional or social pressure. It is the policy of not allowing any consideration whatever to overwhelm the conclusions

[1] Rand, "The Ethics of Emergencies," pp. 52–53. Also see *Journals of Ayn Rand*, p. 260.
[2] Rand, "The Objectivist Ethics," p. 28.

of one's mind, neither one's own feelings nor those of others."[3] This portrait is consonant with prevalent images of integrity. The person of integrity is uncorrupted and true to himself; he does not merely pay lip service to ideals, but he lives by them. Gabriele Taylor observes that the person of integrity "keeps his inmost self intact," as his beliefs and deeds are of a piece.[4]

Although integrity is sometimes thought of as fidelity to *moral* principles, its scope is actually broader, on Rand's account. Integrity consists in a person's practiced devotion to his convictions and values; these include his moral principles but are not restricted to them. A person typically has convictions and values in many areas beyond morality (e.g., in regard to politics, business, sports, science, literature, movies, the media). A person's actions in regard to any of these could reflect his possession or lack of integrity. A journalist who panders to the taste of his readers against his own judgment of responsible reporting is compromising his integrity. A scholar who endorses a conclusion about global warming or cloning, for instance, not by his customary standards of evidence but because it is politically correct (or anti-politically correct) is doing the same. So is the person who fails to defend a friend from slanderous charges. In all three cases, the subject of the person's action is not morality but standards in specific fields (journalism, epistemology, friendship). Yet the breach of integrity is clear. Morals may be indirectly at stake in these cases. Failing to defend a friend betrays the moral bonds of friendship; compromising one's professional standards may violate a tacit agreement with those who depend on a person to perform a service. The point, however, is that although a person's violation of his moral standards constitutes a breach of integrity, violations of a person's other convictions and values can be a breach of integrity, as well.

---

[3] Peikoff, *Objectivism*, pp. 259–260. Throughout, I shall speak primarily of "principles," though I will often mean this to also encompass a person's values and convictions. For simplicity, I shall assume that a person's principles are rational unless the context clearly indicates otherwise. Also, given that all virtues are reflections of rationality, a reader should not be surprised if he can glimpse aspects of other virtues, such as justice or independence, infiltrating the discussion of integrity.

[4] Gabriele Taylor, "Integrity," *Proceedings of the Aristotelian Society* supp. (1981), p.143. For a generally similar portrait, see Lynne McFall, "Integrity," *Ethics* 98 (October 1987), pp. 5–20, especially 5–7. The Latin root of the word, "integritas," signifies wholeness, entireness, or completeness, giving rise to definitions of integrity as an "undivided or unbroken state" and "the condition of not being marred or violated," *Oxford English Dictionary*.

Like all virtues, on Rand's view, the need for integrity is grounded in certain basic facts. In Galt's speech, she writes:

Integrity is the recognition of the fact that you cannot fake your consciousness, just as honesty is the recognition of the fact that you cannot fake existence – that man is an indivisible entity, an integrated unit of two attributes: of matter and consciousness, and that he may permit no breach between body and mind, between action and thought, between his life and his convictions – that, like a judge impervious to public opinion, he may not sacrifice his convictions to the wishes of others, be it the whole of mankind shouting pleas or threats against him – that courage and confidence are practical necessities, that courage is the practical form of being true to existence, of being true to truth, and confidence is the practical form of being true to one's own consciousness.[5]

In our discussion of honesty, we have already seen the importance of the refusal to fake reality. Given that a person's consciousness is part of reality, honesty might be thought to include the refusal to fake one's consciousness. By identifying integrity as a distinct virtue, however, Rand is calling attention to the crucial importance of adhering to the conclusions of one's own mind. Rational judgment must drive a human being's course, if he is to live. This entails that a person cannot afford to deviate from his judgment any more than he can afford to deviate from external facts of reality.

To understand the case for integrity more fully, it is best to begin with the two facts that stand at its foundation: life requires action in accordance with rational, life-furthering principles; a person will encounter pressure against such action.

Moral principles, on Rand's view, are practical necessities. The specific function of morality is to enable human beings to live. In order for a person to live, however, he must *act* as if his values are values by identifying and abiding by rational principles. Peikoff refers to integrity as "the principle of being principled" because integrity reflects the realization that human beings need principles to guide us. We cannot steer ourselves successfully on a case-by-case basis because we cannot gauge the full impact of individual decisions on our overall happiness in isolation from other knowledge.[6] Recall our discussion of the need for principles in Chapter 2. A full appreciation of this need entails recognition that a person should not deviate from his principles, shifting, on various occasions, between

---

[5] Rand, *Atlas Shrugged*, p. 1019.
[6] See Peikoff, *Objectivism*, pp. 259–260.

what principles instruct him to do and what he feels like doing. Long-term happiness depends on a person's determining, through sober reflection, appropriate ends to embrace and rational means of attaining those ends, and then consistently relying on that knowledge in choosing his actions. The constancy of integrity is virtuous because deviation from such a rational course is self-destructive.

The second underpinning of integrity is the simple fact that abiding by one's principles is not always easy. People commonly face countervailing pressures, primarily social and emotional (which are not mutually exclusive). We are often diverted from acting on our principles by fear of others' reactions – fear of losing favor, a friend, of disrupting social tranquility. While the calculation is not always explicit, it is frequently the fear of some unwanted social repercussions that overtakes a person's commitment to his values. He does not speak at a meeting on behalf of a policy he deems important, for instance, because he thinks he will seem foolish. He fears rejection from the voters, so he tells them what he thinks they want to hear rather than his true convictions. He fears criticism from students, so he lowers his standards to offer them more palatable grades. Other times, quite apart from the anticipated reactions of others, it is a person's more self-regarding emotions that deter him from acting on his principles – his own feelings of inadequacy or fears of failure and of subsequent disappointment, for instance. "It just feels better, somehow" to stay with the familiar course rather than to venture out on the new one that he honestly thinks would be better for him. "It just feels safer" to avoid taking a risk, so he allows his feelings to prevail instead of mailing the resumes or making the phone call that his rational judgment tells him he should.

Each temptation to violate integrity offers some apparent value, which is why it is attractive. Yet its appeal rests on dropping the larger context. A fuller consideration of how the contemplated action stands to affect the agent's long-term well-being would correct the impression that it offers any genuine benefits. The virtue of integrity reflects recognition that feelings are not tools of cognition and that a person should never treat them as if they were. If a person encounters *reasons* to reconsider a previous judgment, he should; integrity is not a pretext for subjectivism. Yet the value of integrity rests in its pointing a person, in the face of pressure, to his one, fundamental source of life-sustaining action: rationality.

The lack of integrity sabotages a person's ability to live. If a person forms rational principles but then "fakes his consciousness" by ignoring them, he invites the frustration of his aims. The resulting reversals in his actions could not achieve his flourishing.

To commit to a principle is to decide in advance how one should act when confronting certain kinds of choices. The reason to do that is the realization that a person will make better decisions that way. By stepping back from the immediate pulls and pushes of a decision-making situation, a person can better grasp what kinds of actions will be, all things considered, best for him. Adopting a principle means committing to staying that predetermined course, to taking the kinds of action that the principle prescribes when the relevant occasions arise.

Integrity demands *consistent* adherence to life-promoting principles because life requires consistent adherence. Breaches of a person's principles inflict both material and spiritual damage. Materially, failures of integrity undercut a person's campaign for the values that fuel his happiness. Such violations are directly contrary to the demands of his life. Violations of the virtues we have already analyzed make this clear. A person who acts unjustly, for example, failing to judge a worker objectively and to treat him as he deserves, is ultimately hurting himself. He is encouraging harmful conduct and discouraging beneficial conduct. Likewise, the second-hander abandons his only means of achieving objective values: rational judgment, which, by its nature, must be independent. He thus consigns himself to the role of a parasite, completely dependent on others. Similarly, the dishonest person who fakes facts does not help himself to cope with those facts by pretending their nonexistence. And the harms wrought by failures of integrity do not result exclusively from violations of moral principles. A person who betrays the high value he places on a particular friend or cause or activity by not acting consistently with such valuations similarly hurts his own happiness.

Spiritually, the person who violates his principles damages his opinion of himself and thereby hinders his ability to act as he should in the future. By dismissing his principles when it comes time to act on them, he loses credibility in his own mind. The person lacking integrity will gradually come to believe that he is full of hot air, that his convictions are just talk. Failures of integrity take a toll on a person's reputation with himself, making it that much harder for him to see value in *his* ends, to commit to ends wholeheartedly, and to pursue them with the tenacity needed for success.

Failures of integrity are harmful to the agent in another way, as well. A person's dispositions are developed by the individual choices that he makes. Each virtuous action makes further virtuous action that much more likely in the future; each vicious action makes vicious action that much more likely. This is not to say that free will is diminished, but simply to observe the grooves that people often develop. Notice that when a person deliberately alters some deeply entrenched pattern of acting (involving his work habits or eating habits, for instance), the initial steps of the new regimen are typically the most difficult. The repetition of the new type of actions gradually wears down resistance to them. The point here is that failures of integrity chip away at a person's fitness to flourish. Although the impact of a single breach, in isolation, may seem insignificant, such episodes carry more lasting effects on a person's tendencies and, correlatively, on his ability to achieve his happiness.

Practicing integrity, by contrast, facilitates flourishing. The person who consistently practices his principles gradually acquires ease at it; acting in the ways that promote his life becomes second nature. Consequently, he will lead a smoother life, less strained by inner conflict and more routinely acting as he should, which is to his benefit. The person who lacks integrity, even if he does not succumb to *every* temptation to betray his principles, by repeatedly entertaining that possibility, is keeping open issues that should be closed. In this way, he sentences himself to ongoing struggles to maintain his principles and, correlatively, to the greater likelihood of his taking self-destructive actions.

In the end, a lack of integrity amounts to a lack of principles. For the erratic course of a person without integrity reveals that he might as well not have principles. Unused, or used only as his feelings permit, they are not the person's true guide. Fickle fidelity to principles is not fidelity to *principles*. And such inconstancy undercuts the benefits of those of a person's actions that *are* what they should be. The alternative to consistent adherence to one's principles, Peikoff writes, is to "dispense with cognition."[7] While this initially sounds like an exaggeration, it describes exactly what a person does when he subordinates his considered convictions to the gyrations of social or emotional tugs.

Many people, egoists and nonegoists alike, admire the person who strives to maintain a spotless character. Such a character can radiate gleaming, inspiring beauty. Good character is not an end in itself, however. Its value rests in its positioning a person to flourish. Thus purity of character is not simply an aesthetic issue, on Rand's view; it is a practical imperative. To soil one's character is to damage oneself. Rand's case for integrity is entirely egoistic. What hangs in the balance is the agent's

[7] Peikoff, *Objectivism*, pp. 260–261.

own happiness. Integrity is essential for a person to reap the benefit of rational principles: the achievement of his values. It is only by abiding by rational principles that a person can achieve the various values made possible by honest action, just action, independent action, and so on. It is only by faithful allegiance to rational principles that a person can secure his happiness.[8]

Before closing our discussion of the case for integrity, we should consider one final question. Isn't the counsel to live by one's principles implicit in each of the other virtues? Indeed, in explaining the master virtue of rationality, I emphasized its demand that a person *act* by reason. And in examining the derivative virtues, we have seen that each imposes action requirements as well as intellectual requirements. Thus the virtue of integrity may seem redundant.

Two points should be made in response. First, remember that integrity concerns fidelity to all of a person's values, not exclusively to moral principles. Consequently, practicing the other moral virtues does not exhaust the exercise of integrity. A person can exercise integrity not only by living up to the virtues of honesty or justice or independence, and so on, but also by acting in accordance with his values in other spheres. Speaking up for a candidate or policy that he values or holding his writing to exacting literary standards or taking actions to secure the kind of retirement lifestyle that he would like could all be expressions of integrity.

Second, while the instruction of integrity does partially overlap with the instruction of other virtues, integrity uniquely addresses the fact that the virtuous path is not always easy, that achieving one's values requires special effort, and that values (not only principles, but values) must be acted upon in order for a person to live. Although a human being is an integrated unit of matter and consciousness, as Rand puts it, a person can weaken that unity by acting against the conclusions of his consciousness. That way lies destruction. A person's mind must rule his actions, as a matter of regular policy, if he is to live. Integrity thus names the value of seeing oneself as integrated and of living up to one's convictions consistently. Although some of this is implicit in the other virtues, it is useful to make it explicit through a distinct virtue since a person may often be tempted to view an action apart from its effects on other

[8] Cheshire Calhoun has recently defended integrity on the squarely opposed grounds of its benefit to society. A failure of integrity lets other people down, she contends; by misleading others about one's true nature, it betrays those counting on a person. Integrity is virtuous because it renders a person more useful to the community. Calhoun, "Standing for Something," *The Journal of Philosophy* XCII, 5 (May 1995), pp. 256–260.

dimensions of his life and on *him*. The virtue of integrity reminds a person that he cannot segregate his principles or any of his actions into hermetically sealed compartments. Understanding the value of maintaining a unified, wholly rational character can help to motivate a person to care about every action he takes and thus to act rationally, at all times, to achieve his objective well-being. The virtue of integrity teaches that the stakes of each of a person's actions are real and that values are *at* stake all the time.

The distinctive value of integrity should become even clearer as we elaborate on the practical demands of integrity in the next section.

WHAT INTEGRITY DEMANDS

While the thrust of integrity's instruction highlights the need for action, the practice of this virtue, like the others, includes an intellectual component, as well. I begin with that.

Intellectual Demands

First of all, integrity requires that a person *have* principles. A person cannot be loyal to his convictions and values if he hasn't got any. Principles are not innate equipment that human beings are born with, however. Thus integrity demands a conscientious effort to identify the principles that should guide a person's life. And rationality must guide this effort. As Lynne McFall has observed, a person of integrity does not simply buy his principles wholesale from whatever is available around him. A person of integrity must "speak in the first person."[9]

Accordingly, a person's path to reaching his principles could itself reflect a failure of integrity. Suppose that a person normally exercises the virtue of independence and holds himself to rigorous, rational standards of evidence for accepting a belief. If this person has serious doubts about the validity of his family's religious beliefs but refrains from pursuing these doubts and accepts the beliefs as his own out of fear of their reactions to dissent, he betrays his values. In stifling his own thoughts to defer to theirs, he violates his usual epistemological standards. Doing so is a failure of integrity. Integrity precludes emotionalism when forming one's principles, Peikoff points out, as well as when deciding whether to abide

---

9 McFall, p. 6. In other words, a person of integrity must exercise what Rand calls the virtue of independence.

by them, once formed.[10] The motives behind a particular temptation to emotionalism (such as family peace) are irrelevant.[11]

A second demand of integrity is confidence. Self-confidence (the relevant type here, although I will henceforth refer to it simply as "confidence") is a person's positive assessment of his capacity to manage his affairs. It is the conviction of his ability to attain his goals and achieve his happiness. Properly, confidence is not naïve or groundless optimism, but a person's awareness that he is competent to solve problems, overcome obstacles, and succeed. A person acquires such an outlook through one basic source: his own rationality.[12] Since the achievement of values depends on rational action, it is by exercising rationality that a person can succeed and correlatively boost his assessment of his prospects. Rationality builds the track record that fosters a person's belief in his ability to navigate the world effectively.

In the *Atlas* passage that I quoted at the start of the chapter, Rand describes confidence as "the practical form of being true to one's consciousness." This can be understood at a few levels. First, the confident person *uses* his consciousness as his tool of survival; he relies on his capacity to think as his means of achieving values. Second, and from a slightly different angle, the confident person uses *his* convictions, the specific conclusions that he reaches, and is not deterred by others' opinions or any other pressure that challenges those conclusions. Third, the attitude of the confident person is: "I know what I know. Consequently, I don't need to alter my course when I encounter fear, others' disagreement, or for any reason other than what *my* mind directs."[13]

Although people frequently speak of *feelings* of confidence, note that I have described confidence in cognitive terms, as an assessment and correlative outlook. Obviously, different feelings normally attend different evaluations of one's abilities and prospects. Integrity's demand for confidence is not for the experience of a particular feeling, however. As we saw in Chapter 3, morality cannot properly require that a person feel any particular emotion in a given situation, on Rand's view, since feelings are not under a person's immediate volitional control. What integrity requires is a person's commitment to be true to his consciousness (something that he can control). Confidence is needed for integrity insofar as a person

---

[10] Peikoff, *Objectivism*, p. 261.
[11] Integrity does not require omniscience or infallibility. It permits a person to change his mind should he discover errors in his previous grounds for reaching a certain principle. Indeed, integrity requires self-correction in such cases. See Peikoff, *Objectivism*, p. 260.
[12] Rand, "The Age of Envy," p. 155.
[13] I thank Harry Binswanger for offering this last perspective.

would not have the strength to abide by his principles if his belief in him-self were precarious. To the extent that a person lacked a conviction of his own fundamental competence, he would find it much more difficult to stand his ground in the face of doubts or disagreements. Weak self-confidence will incline a person to surrender his values on such premises as: "I am not a good judge of these things anyway, so I might as well go along with what this other guy wants;" "Who am I to say? My opinion hasn't been that great in the past." Integrity requires confidence inas-much as confidence fortifies a person to remain faithful to his convictions. A person with confidence respects his mind as his means of achieving his happiness and thus acts on his principles even in the face of contrary pressures. (Integrity also feeds confidence. By exercising fidelity to ratio-nal principles, a person bolsters his efficacy and thereby accumulates stronger objective grounds for concluding that confidence in himself is warranted.)

Is Integrity Value-Neutral?

Accounts of integrity invariably encounter the question: If integrity demands fidelity to one's principles, is it neutral concerning the con-tents of those principles? Could a mafia boss or a knight of the Ku Klux Klan, for instance, who exhibits diligent devotion to his values, qualify as a person of integrity? Or does the virtue of integrity require that a person embrace correct principles?

We glimpsed Rand's answer when we noted Peikoff's characterization of integrity as loyalty to *rational* principles.[14] Integrity "does not mean loyalty to arbitrary notions, however strongly one feels they are true," he explains. "Adolf Hitler acting faithfully to carry out his hatred of the Jews is not an example of virtue."[15] Integrity requires correct principles because of the practical mission of morality. Virtues name the funda-mental types of action necessary for a person to live. If a person held

---

[14] Peikoff, *Objectivism*, p. 259. Also see Rand, "Doesn't Life Require Compromise?" p. 80.

[15] Peikoff, *Objectivism*, p. 261. Rand is hardly alone in thinking that the substance of a person's principles matters to moral integrity. Jody Graham has recently argued that integrity requires that the principles embraced "be those that a morally good, trustworthy person agent would stand for." Graham, "Does Integrity Require Moral Goodness?" *Ratio* XIV, 3 (2001), pp. 234–251. Gabriele Taylor argues that integrity requires rationality and that a person of integrity will not ignore relevant evidence, p. 148. Hursthouse implies a similar stand when she writes that Nazis and other "extreme racists" have no virtues at all, *On Virtue Ethics*, p. 147. We can recognize that people in different historical eras had moral blind spots, she reasons, while still distinguishing between culpable and nonculpable blind spots, p. 149. Calhoun, by contrast, holds that "to value integrity is to place value on an agent's acting from *her* reasons, whether they are good ones or not," p. 248, emphasis in original.

erroneous principles, the practice of those principles would work against his life. Indeed, a person with irrational principles could not consistently abide by them. The attempt to practice principles that are at odds with reality (which is what renders them irrational) would necessitate violations of those principles. Even the most militantly irrational mystic, for example, is compelled to defy his mystical principles and to take some rational actions in order to satisfy his most basic bodily needs. Similarly, an unjust ruler – of a country or a company – has to take some just actions in order to achieve his purposes. At a minimum, he must objectively evaluate his subordinates' suitability to carry out the tasks he demands of them. If he never judged anyone objectively or never treated anyone as they deserved, his wishes could not be effectively executed. The general point is, a person who has accepted irrational principles *must* depart from his principles. Since allegiance to irrational principles could not sustain human life, it is not what the virtue of integrity calls for.

All this notwithstanding, the truth on this issue is slightly more complicated. Even if one agrees that Hitler lacked integrity, it may seem overly restrictive to deny the integrity of all persons who lack a perfect understanding of rational principles. Indeed, we often refer to the integrity of those with whom we disagree on important issues and whose convictions we consider seriously misguided, yet whose devotion to those convictions seems unwavering. This suggests that integrity isolates a genuine phenomenon – practiced loyalty to one's values – that does not hinge on the propriety of one's values.[16]

In fact, I think Rand would agree that this is one legitimate sense of integrity. For she herself admires the integrity of certain characters in literature whose animating principles she recognizes as far from her own. She praises Cyrano de Bergerac, a character acting on altruistic premises, as a sparkling embodiment of integrity. In Victor Hugo's *Les Miserables*, she similarly praises the bishop's surrender of the candlesticks to Valjean, despite the abject self-sacrifice of his action.[17] Rand's explicit

---

[16] McFall adopts a position somewhere between the two, writing that "When we grant integrity to a person, we need not approve of his or her principles or commitments, but we must at least recognize them as ones a reasonable person might take to be of great importance," p. 11. Clearly, this renders pivotal the interpretation of "reasonable."

[17] Ayn Rand Papers, Ayn Rand Audio Collection, "The Ayn Rand Program," Series #A3, WKCR, New York, NY, 1962; and Interviews by Barbara and Nathaniel Branden, tape recording, New York, December 1960-May 1961, The Ayn Rand Archives, A Collection of the Ayn Rand Institute. Rand also refers to integrity as the theme of Hugo's *Ninety-Three* in her "Introduction," Victor Hugo, *Ninety-Three* (New York: Bantam, 1962), p. xii.

distinction between errors of knowledge and breaches of morality is instructive here.[18] That a person fails to appreciate the error of some of his principles is not a moral failing. It can be, if it results from willful evasion, but it isn't necessarily. The person who earnestly tries to adopt rational principles but does not succeed cannot be morally faulted; the person who does not try, by contrast, can be.

In discussions of integrity, two kinds of moral judgment are easily confused: the evaluation of a person for what he has done and the prescription of what a person should do. The two are obviously related and the standard of life should guide both, on Rand's view. To prescribe that the virtue of integrity requires fidelity to rational principles does not, however, render infallibility a prerequisite for a person to have a good moral character. We can recognize the innocence of a mistake while still recognizing it as a mistake. Correspondingly, we can praise the person who made such a mistake while also instructing people to practice rational principles, in order to advance their lives. The fact that a person cannot be blamed for a shortcoming does not mean that his position can be celebrated as the full moral ideal or that the rationality of a person's principles is irrelevant to principles' value. Accordingly, there is no inconsistency in holding that the ideal of integrity *prescribes* the embrace of rational principles while also praising the integrity of certain persons who have not recognized such principles but who have demonstrated unusually active devotion to their principles.

This should help us to understand the common tendency to use the term "integrity" in two senses, more and less restrictive. Strictly, a person has integrity when he both holds proper principles and he abides by them conscientiously. More liberally, a person has integrity when he displays admirable devotion to his principles, though those principles themselves are flawed. What is important, on Rand's view, is that a person strive to embrace proper principles as well as to practice his principles consistently. The virtue of integrity demands that a person be committed not merely to *his* principles, whatever they happen to be, but to getting his principles right – to identifying and then abiding by rational principles. The person who diligently practices what he preaches, even when his convictions are misguided, does seem admirable insofar as he seems to take ideas seriously. Truly taking ideas seriously involves working to grasp correct ideas, however, on the understanding that ideas direct our actions and that our lives depend on the actions that we take. The virtue of

[18] Rand, *Atlas Shrugged*, p. 1059.

integrity demands devotion to rational principles, in short, because those are the only principles on which human beings can live, long range. A neutral conception of integrity that treated integrity as independent of the propriety of a person's principles would essentially reduce integrity to sincerity or conscientiousness or "meaning well." Laudable as such qualities may be, they are not enough to constitute the virtue of integrity. For meaning well and trying hard are not adequate substitutes for being rational in one's principles and one's actions.[19]

Existential Demands

Because integrity concerns a person's integration of his mind and body, it demands that a person act according to the conclusions of his consciousness. He must unite what he thinks with what he does, making himself a seamless whole. Integrity demands that a person recognize that thoughts are for action and that particular actions will carry effects beyond the most obvious and immediate, shaping the larger fabric and course of his life. The person of integrity understands the purpose of moral principles and makes it his practice to abide by them consistently. "To be good is to be good *all* of the time," Peikoff writes, "as a matter of . . . unbreached principle."[20]

This does not mean slavish obedience to arbitrary commandments.[21] Since the authority of all moral principles stems from their practical service to individuals' flourishing and since the proper application of principles must take into account the agent's particular context, moral principles should never be reified as inherently obligatory. Integrity does require, however, the refusal to compromise one's principles. Popular accolades for compromise, often suggesting that flexibility is a good in itself and that the highest good in any dispute is to adopt a middle course, regardless of the issue and regardless of the concessions, is anathema to Rand.[22]

A compromise, according to the *OED*, is "a coming to terms, or arrangement of a dispute, by concessions on both sides; partial surrender of one's

---

[19] Rand would consider the view that they are an adequate substitute a variant of the primacy of consciousness, the alternative to the primacy of existence, which we discussed in Chapter 3.

[20] Peikoff, *Objectivism*, p. 266, emphasis in original.

[21] Peikoff, *Objectivism*, p. 276.

[22] See Rand, "Doesn't Life Require Compromise?" and Peikoff, *Objectivism*, pp. 262–267.

position, for the sake of coming to terms."[23] Rand employs the term in the same sense, referring to a compromise as "an adjustment of conflicting claims by mutual concessions."[24] Although we sometimes speak of a person compromising his principles apart from any agreement reached with another person, I will follow Rand in speaking primarily of the social sense of compromise. (The implications of her position for self-regarding compromise should be clear as the discussion unfolds.)

Rand does not condemn compromise *per se*. The validity of a compromise depends on the kind of concession that a person is making.[25] More specifically, it depends on what a person is giving up and why. Within the framework of moral principle, it can be fine to compromise on particular wishes.[26] If a buyer and seller, for instance, both accept that each must offer a value in order to obtain what he seeks from the other and eventually agree to a price different from what each would have originally preferred, that is not a vicious sellout. Neither has compromised the relevant moral principle of trade. The case is different, however, if a property owner volunteers his property to a burglar. I am not speaking of the case in which a person, confronted with coercion, surrenders something as a desperate means of self-defense. Acceding to the demands of an armed robber is perfectly permissible. To offer one's things to a burglar as if his demands for them were valid, however, would be a "total surrender," in Rand's words, "the recognition of his *right* to one's property."[27] As Peikoff explains, such a person "surrenders not only some of his property, but also the *principle* of ownership."[28]

A person does not betray his principles whenever he does something that he dislikes.[29] The conditions of mutually beneficial cooperation are such that a person's highest preferences will not always be satisfied. If a husband and wife have different preferences concerning which movie to see Friday night, for instance, the husband's acquiescing to his wife is not ordinarily a failure of integrity. If the husband repeatedly and unfailingly yields to his wife's preferences, he would be sacrificing the

---

[23] The verb "compromise" is defined as: "to come to terms by mutual concession; to come to an agreement by the partial surrender of position or principles."

[24] Rand, "Doesn't Life Require Compromise?" p. 79.

[25] Peikoff, *Objectivism*, p. 263.

[26] Rand, "Doesn't Life Require Compromise?" p. 79, 80. Rand also distinguishes improper appeasement from tactfulness and generosity, "The Age of Envy," p. 136.

[27] Rand, "Doesn't Life Require Compromise?" p. 79, emphasis in original.

[28] Peikoff, *Objectivism*, p. 263, emphasis in original.

[29] Rand, "Doesn't Life Require Compromise?" p. 80.

value of sometimes satisfying his preferences on such matters. While a healthy relationship naturally requires some give and take, all give and no take suggests self-abnegation, in which case the objective value of the relationship for that person is negated. The point, however, is that the kind of compromise that integrity forbids "is not a breach of one's comfort, but a breach of one's convictions."[30]

The reason that such compromise is wrong is not difficult to appreciate. We have already seen the crucial importance of adherence to rational principles. A compromise is simply one particular type of violation of principle: one made for the purpose of appeasing another person. As with all such violations, however, the attempt to hold a principle and also to occasionally cheat on it actually abandons that principle. For if a person subordinates his adherence to the principle to some other consideration – if he decides that he will follow the principle except when doing so would conflict with family harmony, for instance – then even in those cases in which he does abide by the principle, he does so only because his action has gained clearance from regard for family harmony. *That* is what truly rules his actions. The policy of abiding by a principle for the most part but deviating every once in a while, in order to get along with others, jettisons that principle as a principle. While people often think of violations of their principles as cheating "just a little," any cheating inevitably means abandoning those principles completely, since the cheater is enthroning something other than those principles as sovereign. (Peikoff offers the example of a judge who, to maintain the favor of party bosses, rigs his rulings only sometimes.[31] What could a person entering such a judge's courtroom expect? Even if the great majority of this judge's rulings happen to coincide with justice, they are not issued from a firm commitment to justice. A case presented before such a judge would be essentially a roll of the dice.)

The reason that abandoning a rational principle is wrong, in turn, points to the fundamental problem with compromise: It works against the

---

[30] Rand, "Doesn't Life Require Compromise?" p. 80. One should not infer that it is permissible to compromise on one's optional values, but not on nonoptional principles. For compromising one's optional values would sometimes *be* compromising on principles. Remember that optional values are an individual's means of pursuing and enjoying nonoptional values; they form the substance of his happiness, rather than an addition to it. The propriety of a compromise of optional values depends on the significance of a person's preferences for those particular optional values on a given occasion (for this movie, this restaurant, this type of work, etc.). Optional values are objective values for the person in question, and as such, important to his life. Thus, as a class, they cannot be assigned inferior status.

[31] Peikoff, *Objectivism*, p. 264.

agent's interest. Rational principles carry moral authority because adherence to such principles is what sustains a person's life. If living according to rational principles is good for a person, then a person has nothing to gain from acting on irrational bases, regardless of the frequency of the irrationalities and regardless of whether they are intended to placate another person. "In any compromise between food and poison," Rand writes, "it is only death that can win. In any compromise between good and evil, it is only evil that can profit."[32]

The rationale behind this claim should be familiar from some of our earlier discussion. As we saw when considering the sanction of evil in the chapter on justice, evil depends on good. That which is irrational and contrary to the requirements of human life can survive only as a result of sustenance obtained from that which is rational and conducive to human life. Consequently, in any compromise between good and evil – between that which represents value and that which represents disvalue – evil has everything to gain. Moreover, it has nothing (of objective value) to lose, since evil cannot generate objective values. The good, in contrast, has nothing to gain in any compromise, precisely because evil (to the extent that it is evil) does not generate objective values. ("An industrialist does not need the help of a burglar in order to succeed," Rand observes, while "a burglar needs the industrialist's achievement in order to exist at all.")[33] The good can gain only from that which is good (and among people, only from those who create values). For these reasons, Peikoff observes that "evil is not consistent and does not want to be consistent." It has no reason to be. Indeed, it couldn't be (if it is to survive). Evil is "delighted to compromise" because for evil, compromise with the good represents "total victory."[34]

The legitimacy of a compromise, I noted earlier, depends on the kind of compromise it is. It turns on the value of the thing surrendered and the person's reasons for surrendering it. A person's hierarchy of values will determine whether it is a sacrifice. What is important to appreciate is that the ultimate standard for distinguishing proper from improper compromises is the same standard that distinguishes all proper from improper action: rational self-interest, as determined by the full and long-range context of the individual's life. When a person surrenders not merely a particular preference but a basic principle, he is undermining his own flourishing. Although compromises that turn out

---

[32] Rand, *Atlas Shrugged*, p. 1054.
[33] Rand, "The Anatomy of Compromise," in *Capitalism: The Unknown Ideal*, p. 147.
[34] Peikoff, *Objectivism*, p. 266.

to be wrong usually *seem* self-interested, their typically short-range perspective, focused on alleviating some near-term irritation, brings harmful repercussions for the agent. The reputed practicality of the person ready to make compromises is a sham.[35] Through inappropriate compromise, such a person is giving up his values, the very things that fuel his happiness.[36]

In the end, integrity demands unflinching devotion to rational principles because reality demands unflinching devotion to rational principles. The basic facts that mandate independence, honesty, or any rational principle take no holidays that permit a person to deviate from those principles without paying costs. In her journals, Rand captures the spirit and the value of integrity when she warns herself against the mistake of neglecting her principles by treating any moment as if it "doesn't count." "*Every word, every action, every moment counts.*"[37]

Courage

An additional practical requirement of integrity is courage. Courage is a matter of acting on behalf of one's values in especially dangerous or fearful circumstances. Because fear is a much more subjective phenomenon than danger, I mean reasonably fearful circumstances, those that would normally induce fear in a rational person. And by "dangerous," I mean genuinely dangerous situations as well as those reasonably believed to be dangerous. We might think of courage as, as Allan Gotthelf has characterized it, "integrity under fire."[38] For courage is the form that integrity will take in conditions of significant danger. In such conditions, the courageous person remains faithful to his principles.

Courage is not the equivalent of fearlessness.[39] Fear is a feeling and as such, not within a person's direct, immediate control. The experience of fear could not, therefore, be either virtuous or vicious. What distinguishes

---

[35] Rand, "The Anatomy of Compromise," p. 144.

[36] Note that a morally legitimate compromise will be consistent with a person's highest values and is often a way of affirming one of his higher values, such as his marriage or a friendship. Although a man may reasonably value his ability to satisfy his leisure preferences, for instance, he might also value his marriage more, such that when choosing which movie to see, he does not insist on "my way or the highway." A rational person will be realistic about the conditions necessary for a marriage to offer genuine value to both partners.

[37] *Journals of Ayn Rand,* p. 282, emphasis in original.

[38] Allan Gotthelf, "Moral Heroism and Rational Selfishness in the Philosophy of Ayn Rand," address delivered at the U.S. Military Academy, West Point, March 13, 2001, p. 10.

[39] Aristotle, *Nicomachean Ethics,* Book 3, Chapter 6. Indeed, fear can often be useful in prompting a person to take sensible precautions or to reconsider a too-dangerous course of action.

the courageous person is his refusal to allow the sheer experience of fear or perception of danger to deter him from the pursuit of his values. Because rationality must be acted upon in order for a person to achieve objective values, courage is a function of a person's actions rather than of his feelings.

Integrity requires courage on appropriate occasions insofar as courage reflects realism about the path to human values. Life is won through action, yet it is natural to encounter dangers of different types and magnitudes as a person seeks to secure the values that advance his life. All action requires taking risks, if only of one's actions not being the best use of one's resources. The risks' significance depends on what the agent stands to lose. If we allowed risks to immobilize us, however, we would achieve nothing. Insofar as courage counsels acting in the face of certain dangers, it acknowledges their inevitability. Because pursuing values naturally involves dangers, we must not be deterred when we encounter the dangers that we are bound to encounter from time to time. Courage is appropriate, quite simply, because it is necessary for the successful pursuit of values. The person who allowed himself to be paralyzed when he encountered danger would not take the actions necessary to flourish. The exercise of courage enables a person to maintain fidelity to his principles and to reap the rewards of such principled action.[40]

---

[40] This does not imply that a person of integrity will act in the face of *any* dangers. While he will not allow danger *per se* to deter him, a rational evaluation of the stakes will sometimes indicate that a person should not persevere in the course he was on, running its particular risks. Courage is essentially a matter of responding rationally to dangers – sometimes carrying on regardless, sometimes making adjustments in the way that one pursues certain values, and sometimes retreating from their pursuit (or at least, retreating in those dangerous circumstances).

John Elia has pointed out to me a counterintuitive implication of this view of courage: On those occasions when the danger and values at stake indicate that a person should retreat, the person would nonetheless qualify as courageous. Although the person might be rational to retreat in such cases, many would find it odd to call him courageous. I think that this reaction stems from a common but misguided way of thinking about courage, however. People often speak of courage as if it were something within a person – a special stuff – that enables certain individuals to pursue a goal despite dangers. Such "stuff" is not in evidence when a person retreats. Yet if courage does not refer to any such "something within" but is, rather, the name for a person's characteristic tendency to take a certain kind of action, then the belief that courage does not demand action in the face of whatever danger one encountered and can be manifest in certain occasions of refraining from action is not odd at all. On Rand's view, courage reflects knowledge of what dangers are worth facing. Although we most commonly praise courage when a person bucks dangers and perseveres in pursuit of his values, courage is not exhausted by such cases.

Separately, the fact that Rand does not designate courage as one of the major virtues does not imply that it is less virtuous, but only that courage is a type of integrity (or a

Several philosophers have described courage in ways that are broadly similar to this. James Wallace classifies courage with virtues that reflect a "positive capacity for acting rationally when certain motives are apt to incline us to do otherwise" and holds that the function of courage "is to preserve practical reasoning and enable it to issue in action." Robert C. Roberts considers courage a virtue of willpower that concerns a person's capacity to manage his inclinations. Gabriele Taylor contends that the coward's life "will by her own standards not be as good as it might have been" and that "she will not achieve what she herself wants to achieve." Andre Comte-Sponville observes that without courage, other virtues would be futile.[41] A crucial difference, however, concerns the *value* of courage. Whereas Rand understands courage as serving the agent's interest, courage is more commonly portrayed as an expression of altruism. Examples intended to illustrate courage typically feature one person braving danger for the benefit of others, without selfish motivation. A man rushes into a burning building to save strangers, for instance, or he wrestles a ferocious animal to free another person from its clutches. Cowardice, correlatively, is often assumed to reflect a person's elevation of his self-interest over his obligations to others.[42]

On Rand's view, such ideas rely on an extremely shallow conception of how a person's interest is advanced. Rational principles are a man's life-preserver; adherence to such principles is his means of flourishing. Likewise, the pursuit of objective values (those he has chosen in conformity with rational principles) is his means of achieving his happiness. If the woman with whom Bill is in love were in immediate physical danger, for example, and Bill were in a position to potentially save her (perilous though the required effort might be), for him to courageously attempt the rescue and not "chicken out" would be in his interest (assuming that he values the woman's well-being more than his own life without her).[43] On Rand's view, courage calls for the strength *not* to make sacrifices.

---

requirement of integrity under the relevant circumstances) and that occasions calling for courage do not arise as frequently as those that call for integrity more broadly.

[41] Wallace, *Virtues and Vices*, pp. 61, 81; Robert C. Roberts, "Will Power and the Virtues," in Christina Sommers and Fred Sommers, eds., *Vice and Virtue in Everyday Life* (New York: Harcourt Brace Jovanovich), pp. 237–239; Gabriele Taylor, "Deadly Vices," in Roger Crisp, ed., *How Should One Live?* (Oxford: Clarendon University Press, 1996), p. 158; Comte-Sponville, p. 50, also see p. 59.

[42] For a strong statement of this view, see Comte-Sponville, pp. 46–49.

[43] Rand discusses integrity in the context of emergencies in "The Ethics of Emergencies," pp. 49–56. Other persons can be among the things that make a person's own life worth living. For brief discussion of the willingness to die for an ideal, see *Journals of Ayn Rand*, pp. 254–255.

Fidelity to one's principles requires that a person not elevate a lesser value above a higher value. Any action that did so, regardless of the danger involved, would betray one's integrity and would not be virtuous. Indeed, *that* would be cowardice: the failure, when confronted with danger, to abide by one's hierarchy of values.

Courage, then, is being "true to existence," as Rand characterizes it in *Atlas*, insofar as it demands that a person face the reality of how values are won as well as the knowledge of what one's own values are and of what their relative importance is. Courage reflects the same dedication to one's values that marks all integrity, though that dedication is more conspicuous in the especially challenging circumstances that call for courage.

Clarity of Vision

Regardless of whether or not a person is facing the special circumstances that occasion courage, integrity is a demanding virtue. In order to meet its demands and to consistently abide by his principles, a person must understand the reason why such fidelity is sensible. If he conceives of integrity as the duty to be a "good Christian soldier" or to act on behalf of ideals that are not authentically his, maintaining his integrity will seem an onerous burden and be much more difficult to motivate.

People often picture a person of integrity as acting as he should in trying situations by closing his eyes, swallowing hard, and grimly steeling himself to do the right thing. Properly, however, integrity reflects loyalty to values that a person has willingly and rationally embraced. Correspondingly, when wavering over abiding by his principles, a person must open his eyes and try to see where the alternative paths before him would lead. "The challenge of a man's life is not to struggle against immoral passions," Peikoff observes, "but to see the facts of reality clearly, in full focus."[44]

This can be difficult, given that actions' anticipated effects sometimes exert a powerful emotional appeal. Often, a person desires a certain object so intensely that he will begin to question his considered principles, eager to convince himself that they are mistaken in convenient respects or are not applicable to the present choice.[45] He might evade what he knows to be rational or try to kid himself about the relative value

---

[44] Peikoff, *Objectivism*, p. 261. Recall from chapter 3 Rand's description of *The Fountainhead*'s Howard Roark as a man who faced difficult choices easily, as if he saw only one choice open to him.

[45] I am not referring to the case in which a person is sincerely uncertain about the validity of his principles.

he places on different ends in order to rationalize a violation of his principles. Tempted to steal copyrighted material, for instance, he might disin-
genuously tell himself, "I don't really care so much about *every detail* of
respecting property." Faced with the threat of friends' disapproval of his
dissenting opinion on an important issue, he might tell himself, "I don't
really think that speaking one's mind makes a difference." When a person
is tempted to violate his principles, he will often think of those principles,
but hear another internal voice countering, "Yes, but . . ." Peikoff's point
is that what it takes to defeat such reservations is a person's deliberately
attending to all the ramifications of his decision and to the effects of his
alternatives on things that *he* cares about.

In failures of integrity, then, what passes for weakness of will is, many
times, actually weakness of vision. The person's "will" is weak because
he does not fully appreciate the stakes.[46] The person who lacks integrity
often suffers from a self-imposed nearsightedness as he puts on blinders
that shut out the larger context that would make clear to him why a
certain course is wrong – how it would be bad for him. Integrity requires
that a person focus on the big picture, actively calling to mind the full
context and identifying the relationship between his immediate alternatives and his broader values as clearly and completely as he can. Integrity
demands that a person invoke his principles and remind himself that
they are his means of living; it is only by adherence to rational principles
that a person can achieve his happiness. Understanding the mechanism
of integrity as largely a matter of vision reflects Rand's view that values
(and correlative virtues) reflect the factual relationships in which particular things stand to a person's life. Consequently, the more clearly a
person grasps these relationships, the easier it will be to act as a morality
of rational self-interest requires. Indeed, for a person committed to his
rational self-interest, seeing the facts is all the motivation he needs.[47]

Responding to Failures of Integrity
A final question about the demands of integrity: If a person has not
maintained perfect integrity but has violated his principles on a given
occasion, how should he respond?

In a word: justly. He should acknowledge his lapse, objectively evaluate
it, and dedicate himself to avoiding its recurrence. His focus should be

---

[46] This is not meant to be a complete analysis of weak will, which can result from many
factors, but only a diagnosis of one common root of it.
[47] Rand once responded to praise of her courage by remarking, "I am not brave enough
to be a coward. I see the consequences too clearly." Cited in Peikoff, *Objectivism*, p. 262.

on how to resist similar transgressions in the future. Although we frequently hear that we learn from our mistakes, lessons do not wash over a person automatically. Learning demands a person's deliberate effort to understand why he acted as he did, to identify the mental missteps that contributed to his lapse, to anticipate the kinds of attractions that are likely to exert themselves again, and to devise feasible strategies for coping with such temptations. Wallowing in guilt or condemning oneself in some final, permanent way, however, is pointless, at best, and self-destructive, at worst. For anyone who sincerely cares about morality and cares about his life, the recognition of having compromised his integrity will be a painful judgment. Pain in itself offers no value, however. An individual's happiness depends, at bottom, on one thing: his rationality. Guilt is not a virtue. It has become increasingly common to encounter self-congratulatory guilt, as people confess/boast, "I really shouldn't have done that, but at least I feel guilty about it" in a way suggesting that their guilt is an equally satisfactory alternative to proper action. While guilt may be a sign that a person retains some regard for morality (which is preferable to the alternative), feeling bad is no substitute for acting as one's life requires. Such an attitude reflects the primacy of consciousness and bespeaks the conception of morality as a game, of little real consequence. The animating force of Rand's theory is the realization that it is anything but.

CONCLUSION

Integrity is a somewhat unusual virtue. For the value of integrity, from one perspective, simply is the value of morality itself. The reason that a person should exercise integrity is the same reason that he needs to adhere to rational principles in the first place: Irrational action works against his life. Only the consistent loyalty to rational principles that integrity prescribes enables a person to reap the rewards of the other virtues and to achieve objective values. Breaches of integrity defeat a person's purpose of achieving his happiness.

8

Productiveness

The next major virtue that Rand identifies is productiveness. In certain respects, the propriety of productiveness seems quite natural, for it is difficult to dispute the value of productiveness to human life. Yet productiveness is rarely named among the moral virtues. Although people do sometimes laud "industry" and while sloth is one of the seven deadly sins of Christianity, in the eyes of many, the very usefulness of productiveness excludes it from the realm of morality; productiveness seems too prudential a concern to warrant morality's attention. Even those who recognize the utility of productiveness do not necessarily embrace it, simply for its practical payoffs. As Robert Solomon has observed, if we can believe bumper stickers, the preferred attitude in many quarters is, "I'd rather be fishin.'"[1]

Rand contends that productiveness is essential to human life. Indeed, she argues that productive work should be the central purpose of a person's life. After explaining what productiveness is, why it is a virtue, and what it demands, in practice, I will also consider whether Rand's egoistic defense of productiveness sanctions greed, which is widely considered a vice.

WHAT PRODUCTIVENESS IS

Productiveness is "the process of creating material values, whether goods or services."[2] A bit more abstractly, Peikoff characterizes productiveness

---

[1] Robert C. Solomon, "Introduction," in Solomon, ed., *Wicked Pleasures – Meditations on the Seven "Deadly" Sins* (New York: Rowman & Littlefield, 1999), p. 9.
[2] Peikoff, *Objectivism*, p. 292.

as "the adjustment of nature to man," for it is the process by which a person transforms elements of his surroundings to serve specific, life-furthering purposes.[3] A person can be productive by building a boat or a bridge, for instance, by repairing shoes or writing software, by composing music or researching biology, performing surgery, mowing lawns, selling insurance, shipping, catering, proofreading, or reporting the news.

Because productiveness turns on the creation of material values, we should clarify what these are. The term might be understood to refer to at least three different things: the material nature of the product or service in question; the means by which that good was brought into existence (physical labor), or the kind of need that the good satisfies (e.g., bodily needs for food or shelter). In arguing that life requires the creation of material values, Rand is using "material value" in the first sense. That is, a material value is physical. Rand describes productive work as "shaping matter to fit one's purpose" and "translating an idea into physical form"[4] to indicate that the product of a person's work must assume physical existence outside of the agent's mind. She sees no value in physical labor as such. Even while a person may legitimately specialize in cognition, the knowledge that he acquires must be embodied, Peikoff observes, given "some form of existence in physical reality" such as in a book or a lecture and "not merely in his consciousness."[5] A composer has not created a material value until he commits the melody he constructs in his mind to paper or a recording of some type.

In the sense in which Rand is using the term, then, and in the context of discussing productiveness, a thing's status as a material value is not a function of its contribution to a person's material well-being. Rand clearly regards the creation of art, which serves a need of man's consciousness (i.e., a spiritual need), as productive work.[6] While even spiritual values can indirectly affect a person's material well-being (the spiritual value of art or friendship, for example, can strengthen a person's capacity to tend to his physical needs), by specifying that productiveness concerns the creation of material values, Rand is highlighting the nature of what is created rather than the nature of the need that the creation serves. What

---

[3] Peikoff, *Objectivism*, p. 292.

[4] Rand, *Atlas Shrugged*, p. 1020.

[5] Peikoff, *Objectivism*, p. 293.

[6] Peikoff, *Objectivism*, p. 292. Also, in Rand's fiction, the sculptor Mallory in *The Fountainhead* and the composer Halley in *Atlas Shrugged* are engaged in productive work. For Rand's view of the value of art, see Rand, "The Psycho-Epistemology of Art," in *The Romantic Manifesto* (New York: Penguin, 1975), pp. 15–24, especially p. 17.

makes a material value material and what makes a material value valuable are two distinct attributes. A thing's value depends on the relationship in which it stands to an individual's long-term survival. We do not need to know anything about a thing's value to know whether it is material, however. The only consideration needed to establish that is whether the thing has physical existence, nonmental reality. If it does, it is material.

It is also important to recognize that not every activity that it is beneficial for a person to engage in thereby qualifies as productive. Productiveness refers to one particular type of life-advancing action: the creation of material values. Many other constructive activities, such as cultivating a friend, seeing a psychotherapist, or listening to music can be quite valuable for a given individual. Consuming values, or taking actions that will strengthen a person's longer-term ability to achieve values or to enjoy his values, is not the same as creating material values, however. Only this last constitutes productiveness. What is productive is thus a subset of all the activities that it is valuable for a person to engage in.

WHY PRODUCTIVENESS IS A VIRTUE

Material Value

The basic fact that renders productiveness a virtue is human beings' need to create the material values that sustain us. Our survival depends on material goods. These goods are not readily available, however, gushing forth from earth or sky. Human beings must create them; we must, literally, *make* our living through productive action. Productiveness is a virtue, fundamentally, because productiveness makes human survival possible. Rand presents the basic rationale as follows:

Productiveness is...your recognition of the fact that you choose to live – that productive work is the process by which man's consciousness controls his existence, a constant process of acquiring knowledge and shaping matter to fit one's purpose, of translating an idea into physical form, of remaking the earth in the image of one's values....[7]

A later statement includes a helpful addition:

The virtue of *Productiveness* is the recognition of the fact that productive work is the process by which man's mind sustains his life, the process that sets man free

[7] Rand, *Atlas Shrugged*, p. 1020.

of the necessity to adjust himself to his background, as all animals do, and gives him the power to adjust his background to himself.[8]

Note the prominence of the mind in both accounts. Productiveness is the process "by which man's consciousness controls his existence," "by which man's mind sustains his life." We have seen already that reason is man's means of survival and that reason as a purely intellectual exercise, confined to one's head, will not suffice. Our survival depends on reason's guiding our actions. While all the virtues designate distinct applications of rationality, the reason that human beings need to be guided in the particular way that productiveness prescribes is indicated in the second passage. Other animals survive by consuming ready-made values found in their environments. The values that human survival depends on, by contrast, must be conceived and created by us.[9] Human beings do not automatically absorb protein from the atmosphere; we do not spontaneously sprout sweaters on our backs. Rand observes,

. . . while animals survive by adjusting themselves to their background, man survives by adjusting his background to himself. If a drought strikes them, animals perish – man builds irrigation canals; if a flood strikes them, animals perish – man builds dams; if a carnivorous pack attacks them animals perish – man writes the Constitution of the United States. But one does not obtain food, safety or freedom – by instinct.[10]

The fundamental means of human survival, in short, are reason and production rather than impulse and appropriation. "The two essentials of the method of survival proper to a rational being are: thinking and productive work."[11] Rational productive work is essential to bringing into being the goods and services that our lives depend on. We do not create material values *ex nihilo*, of course, yet in order to alter the resources we find around us into *goods* that advance our lives, we must engage in productive work. Like the virtue of independence, productiveness concerns a person's making his own way in the world. While independence counsels a fundamental orientation to reality, however, productiveness zeroes in on a more particular need: the need to create material values.

---

[8] Rand, "The Objectivist Ethics," p. 29, emphasis in original. Throughout, I am leaving aside exceptional cases such as the terminally ill, very elderly, or severely disabled.

[9] Peikoff, *Objectivism*, p. 292.

[10] Rand, "For the New Intellectual," p. 10. Although human beings obtain certain values automatically, such as oxygen, those alone cannot sustain us.

[11] Rand, "The Objectivist Ethics," p. 25.

As with certain other virtues, if a person were alone on a desert island, the imperative to practice this virtue would be obvious. For the consequences of failing to create material values would be inescapable – and life-threatening. The creation of material values is every bit as essential in society, however, given that the most basic conditions of human existence are not altered by the company of other people.

In identifying productiveness as a virtue, Rand's thought is not that we should assign a distinct virtue to every element of human maintenance. She christens no virtues corresponding to eating your vegetables, flossing your teeth, or saving for a rainy day. Nor is she offering the trite observation that people need to put bread on the table (as we have understood for a long time, as we had to). In identifying productiveness as a virtue, rather, Rand is calling attention to the type of actions that human beings need to take in order to create the material values that our lives depend on (in effect, *how* to put bread on the table). Isolating productiveness as a virtue focuses our attention on the manner in which we can meet our needs and the nature of production for human beings. This begins with the realization that values must be created rather than appropriated, but it proceeds to identify the basic means by which we can do that. Because human beings cannot simply pluck material values from our surroundings but must create them, we must identify the conditions and types of actions necessary to enable us to create them. The virtue of productiveness directs a person to the kind of thought and action that is essential to his creation of material values.

Productiveness is a *virtue* because it is a systematic, ongoing method of meeting the challenge of survival. To haphazardly tend to scattered needs as they individually press themselves on one's awareness will not sustain a human life, long range. Human beings are not born possessing the requisite skills, knowledge, or imagination to create material values. We must acquire these by a volitional process that requires effort, purpose, and other virtues such as independence and honesty. "The ability to create material values . . . must itself be created," Peikoff observes.[12] A person must actively cultivate the capacity to create material values and thereby become self-sustaining. Productiveness, accordingly, demands not only that a person feed and clothe himself, but that he make himself into the kind of person who is able to provide all the material values that his life requires. Exercising the virtue of productiveness thus serves not only to

---

[12] Peikoff, *Objectivism*, p. 295.

satisfy a person's immediate consumption needs; it equips him to create further values and to take good care of himself in the future.

Spiritual Value

While the fundamental mandate for productiveness lies in our need to create material values, the rewards of being productive are spiritual, as well. And these are substantial.[13]

Much of the spiritual value of productiveness rests in the qualities of character called upon for a person to exercise this virtue. Rand observes that productive work requires such attributes as creativity, ambitiousness, self-assertiveness, and perseverance in the face of obstacles.[14] Consider a productive worker in any of a variety of occupations: office manager, housepainter, cab driver, deli owner, journalist, historian, ophthalmologist, police detective. The person who does not merely go through the motions of his job or mindlessly do whatever he is told but who actually creates some value (however minor his role may be in a multi-tiered enterprise) will need to employ such qualities as commitment, discipline, patience, persistence, responsibility, curiosity, ingenuity, initiative (not to mention the moral virtues, such as honesty and independence). Not all of these traits will be needed in every component of productive work, but successful work depends on the exercise of such traits in appropriate circumstances. The detective will need persistence and curiosity, for instance, when clues to a crime are not easily forthcoming; the deli owner will need discipline and ingenuity to keep his business afloat during a severe economic slump; the ophthalmologist will need patience and commitment to effectively treat a recalcitrant condition.

The most significant trait that productiveness calls upon is rationality. Because productiveness is an exercise of rationality, the productive person will be sharpening his reasoning skills. To make fruitful decisions about how best to do productive work – how to cut costs, win repeat business, devise more effective techniques of repairing or investigating or more efficient ways of distributing responsibilities, for instance – a person must be guided by observations of relevant facts and by logical inferences about their implications. In honing his rationality as well as the other qualities that productiveness calls for, the productive person is clearly helping

13 See Peikoff, *Objectivism*, p. 301.
14 Rand, "The Objectivist Ethics," p. 29.

himself in ways that will benefit him beyond the paycheck that his work may earn. For these qualities strengthen a person's ability to tackle all manner of challenges and to achieve a wide range of values (in personal relationships, emotional trials, or athletic endeavors, for instance).

As I will explain in the next section, productive work must become the central purpose of a rational egoist's life. And by occupying this role, productiveness brings with it further spiritual values. A central productive purpose will serve a person's need for coherence in his activities, providing a rational basis for choosing and weaving into an integrated, seamless fabric pursuits that might otherwise be disparate, dangling threads. A commitment to productive work, because of the dominant place it will necessarily assume, establishes what a person's life is about and thereby lends meaning to his activities, enabling them to add up to a unified, valuable whole.

In this way, productiveness will also strengthen a person's sense of his identity. If a person embraces productive work as his central purpose and devotes the requisite time and energy to it, it will become an integral part of his self-image, refining his sense of what is important to him and of who he is. The embrace of productive work as one's central purpose will naturally carry ramifications on other of a person's activities. Other things will be of interest – certain books worth reading, certain people worth meeting, certain events in the news worth following or trying to influence – because of their potential impact on that end. Not only those interests and activities most directly affecting a person's work, but the value of many of a person's ancillary ends and activities will be influenced by his central productive purpose. Thus, again, a person's overall identity and sense of identity can be more deeply and more finely engraved by his exercise of the virtue of productiveness.

Yet a further spiritual benefit of productiveness is self-esteem. A person's productive work imparts the knowledge that he is successfully taking care of himself and is competent to manage his life. Although many variables can obstruct the natural path to self-esteem, in a healthy person who has chosen his work rationally, his performance of genuinely productive work will normally tell him that he is choosing and achieving ends that bring him happiness. Even if a person does not work in his preferred field or position, as long as he does not surrender pursuit of his preferred work without a struggle and as long as he works productively in his current position, he can build self-esteem through the knowledge that he is creating material values and responsibly working to achieve his happiness. He will thereby nourish a sense of efficacy and worth that is at the heart of self-esteem. (I will discuss self-esteem further in the chapter on pride.)

What all of this demonstrates, again, is that in addition to its fundamental value in serving human beings' need to create material values, productiveness provides a host of significant spiritual values. It fosters valuable character traits, furnishes the foundation for rational coherence in a person's activities, strengthens a person's identity, and nourishes his self-esteem. By addressing our need to create material values, in short, productiveness enriches our lives spiritually as well as materially.

It is important to appreciate that Rand's defense of this virtue, like her defense of each of the others, is entirely egoistic. I noted earlier that while productiveness is rarely considered a moral virtue, sloth is sometimes considered a vice. Although the meaning of sloth has evolved over the centuries from a spiritual apathy or dereliction in fulfilling one's duties to God to a broader resistance to exerting *any* effort and, in particular, an unwillingness to work, condemnations have typically viewed the slothful person as disrespectful to god or as shirking his responsibility to his community.[15] The slothful person is seen as wasting his "gifts" or talents or failing to do "his share" and make a constructive contribution to society. Rand argues, in contrast, that a person should be productive because *he* will benefit from productive work. Indeed, his life depends on it. The sole reason to be productive is to advance one's own happiness.[16]

The heart of the case for productiveness, again, lies in human beings' need for material values. We must create the goods and services, and their necessary conditions and constituents, that our lives depend on. We must produce the food, shelter, medicines, cars, computers, books, songs, schools, legal institutions, and so on, that sustain our lives and make them worth sustaining. This does not mean that productiveness is a regrettable but inescapable burden, necessary drudgery akin to a

[15] The relevant Greek term, *akedeia,* means "without care." Neera K. Badhwar, "Self-Interest and Virtue," *Social Philosophy and Policy* 14 (Winter 1997), p. 254, note 49. Aquinas understood sloth as a laxness of faith. Solomon, "Introduction," *Wicked Pleasures,* p. 9. For observations about historical attitudes toward sloth and about sloth itself, see Thomas Pynchon, "Sloth," in Solomon, ed., *Wicked Pleasures,* pp. 81–86, and Taylor, "Deadly Vices?" pp. 157–172. Taylor's piece is particularly good on the psychological repercussions of slothful attitudes.

[16] The influence of altruism helps to explain why productiveness has not been appreciated as a virtue, Rand believes. Because the dominant ethic preaches that it is nobler to give and to serve than to produce, work has not been seen as especially praiseworthy. *Letters of Ayn Rand,* p. 82.

painful medical procedure: good for you in the long run, but agony while suffering through it. Work is not a necessary evil, like a punishment for sins in the Garden of Eden. Rather, it is entirely a good, insofar as it makes our lives and happiness possible. As the spiritual rewards of productiveness indicate, properly pursued, the very process of living productively enriches a person's life.

WHAT PRODUCTIVENESS DEMANDS

With a firmer understanding of the value of productiveness, we can now consider exactly what the exercise of this virtue requires. "Every type of productive work," Rand maintains, "involves a combination of mental and physical effort: of thought and of physical action to translate that thought into a material form." It is simply the "proportion of these two elements [that] varies in different types of work."[17] Like the other virtues we have examined, then, productiveness imposes both intellectual and existential demands.

People have little trouble understanding Francis Bacon's dictum that knowledge is power. Knowledge enables a person to take the steps necessary to achieve his ends. What is less appreciated, Peikoff points out, is the converse: Wealth (economic power) is thought.[18] Material assets stem from cognition.

A person must use reason in order to identify what he wishes to create, why it is worth creating, and how he can create it. Both the selection of ends and design of appropriate means of attaining his ends call on a person's use of his intellect. Human beings cannot mindlessly create things that will be objectively valuable to us. In carrying out even the least cerebral work to create a material value (ironing, collecting trash, filling boxes with merchandise), a person periodically encounters flaws in his plans or unexpected circumstances that necessitate adjustments in his course. Continual judgments must be made about the process he is engaged in. However basic one's goal, be it catching a fish or building a fire to cook it, a person must use reason in order to create these values. Even an activity as primitive as hunting requires that a person figure out how to make appropriate weapons and what sort of animals it would be beneficial to target.[19]

---

[17] Rand, "Patents and Copyrights," in *Capitalism: The Unknown Ideal*, p. 130.
[18] Peikoff, *Objectivism*, p. 294.
[19] *Journals of Ayn Rand*, pp. 251–252.

In the contemporary Western economy, as far fewer people devote the bulk of their working hours to physical labor to sustain themselves than did so in the past, the mind's role is especially obvious. Indeed, even the mental effort needed to perform various tasks is increasingly being reduced by "smart" technology. From the supermarket to the battlefield, individuals' decision making is being simplified by devices that "read," "interpret," and "choose" for us. Such devices must be programmed by intelligent beings' rationality, however, in order to respond to various stimuli in appropriate ways – that is, to simulate smartness and offer value to us. This particular technology aside, the larger point is simply that the mind's contribution to the creation of material values is increasingly apparent.

While productiveness imposes definite intellectual demands on us, it also requires the exertion of physical energy to bring the relevant values into reality. (In this context, by "reality" I mean extramental existence.) Because the purpose of the intellectual effort is the creation of material values, a person must take physical steps to bring his thoughts to material fruition. He must work, as Rand puts it, to translate his idea into physical form.[20] The exact form of material values can vary; productive work need not generate a physical object such as a loaf of bread or a wrench. Services can be material values, as we noted earlier. Whether the service is more physically labor-intensive, such as cleaning, cooking, delivering, or gardening, or more intellectually labor-intensive, such as educating, editing, or offering legal or financial counsel, that service must be provided through physical means and thus must alter the physical world in order to provide value. A house must be cleaner through the housekeeper's services, for instance; a package must be transported from one place to another; a teacher or broker must communicate his instruction through some physical medium. A geneticist's insight, an artist's inspiration, or any innovative idea, for that matter, must be given some physical reality in order to offer a material value. A person must document his research finding, write a play, or explain or implement a marketing plan, for example. Truly, again, a union of both intellectual and physical effort is needed for any productive work. The most intellectual work will impose at least modest physical demands, and the most physical labor will have to be guided by thought, if either is to generate genuine material values.[21]

---

[20] Rand, *Atlas Shrugged*, p. 1020.
[21] Peikoff, *Objectivism*, p. 296.

Does a productive person need to make money? Because the most basic reason that human beings should be productive is to meet our need for material values, normally, a person must seek payment for his work. He must trade his work or its product for that of others.[22] I say normally, however, because this is not always the case.

Money is not the only type of material value. Moreover, not all work that creates material values is well compensated in the market. Consequently, a person might legitimately engage in productive work beyond the work that pays his bills. He might make money at a less productive, relatively undemanding job, for instance, to enable him to do more challenging, more rewarding and more productive work (such as writing or dramatic acting) on his own time. In order to exercise the virtue of productiveness, such a person would have to engage in the latter sort of work with disciplined commitment, and he would have to find a job that allowed him adequate time and energy for that. The fact that objectively valuable work will not necessarily garner the material remuneration that a person might wish, however, places that person under no obligation to resign himself to work that is beneath his ability and to abandon more productive work. (He would be obligated to support himself through some other work, in such a case.)

An individual's moral virtue is not a hostage to others' opinions. If a person creates material values and offers them on the market but does not attract enough buyers to make his living from such work, his productiveness is intact. The fact that others do not recognize certain material values or do not reward their creator as much as he would like does not eradicate their value. Market value and objective value do not always coincide. Insofar as market value reflects people's opinions of a thing's value and objective value reflects the actual impact the thing would have on their lives, it is obvious that people frequently overvalue or undervalue things. The issue is a little more complex than this, since objective value does rely, in part, on an individual's recognition of a thing's relationship to his life, on Rand's view. Moreover, in the context of the market, she distinguishes between philosophically objective value and socially objective value. Socially objective value is "the sum of the individual judgments of all the men involved in a trade at a given time, the sum of what they valued." Philosophically objective value is "estimated from the standpoint of the best possible to man, i.e., by the criterion of

---

[22] Peikoff, *Objectivism*, p. 294.

the most rational mind possessing the greatest knowledge, in a given category, in a given period, and in a defined context." An airplane is of greater philosophically objective value to man than a bicycle, for example.[23] One could obviously explore this distinction in some depth. What is salient for our purposes is that a thing's philosophically objective value does not depend on its socially objective value. (To think that it does would be to reject the primacy of existence.) Because life requires, at root, the creation of philosophically objective material values rather than of socially objective material values, the virtue of productiveness is not contingent upon a person's ability to create the latter.

Consonant with the recognition that a person's paying job will not always involve his most productive work, Rand believes that raising children could be productive work.[24] A child requires a tremendous amount of attention. The conscientious attempt to raise a child well, giving him the education, encouragement, discipline, and overall reasoned introduction to the world that he requires if he is to grow into an independent adult, able to lead a good and happy life, is a full-time job. If a person is in a financial position to make it his full-time job, its potential rewards are on a par with those offered by more conventional species of productive work. While other careers typically create a good or service that attends to some delimited compartment of human life (manufacturing shoes, plumbing, nursing, etc.), raising a child is a more all-encompassing fostering of life, the effort to cultivate crucial abilities and transmit crucial knowledge to the child. As such, it is an equally viable candidate to serve as an individual's productive work (obviously, only for as long as the child requires that much attention).

Productive Work as One's Central Purpose

Although the virtue of productiveness does not require that a person make money from his productive work, his work does need to be his central purpose. Properly, a person's work will be the principal form that his pursuit of happiness takes. Productive work is not simply an element of a good life; it is the central element. To understand this, we need to

---

[23] Rand, "What is Capitalism?" pp. 24–25. Rand does not deny that a bicycle can be of greater value to a particular individual in his daily routine, p. 24. Philosophically objective value, however, pertains to things' value to mankind and to mankind at its best. See p. 24.

[24] "*Playboy*'s Interview with Ayn Rand," March 1964, p. 7. Peikoff also discusses this briefly in *Objectivism*, p. 302.

appreciate both why a person needs a central purpose and why productiveness should occupy this role. Let me address each, in turn.[25]

Recall that Rand regards purpose as one of the three cardinal values.[26]
"A central purpose," Peikoff explains, "is the long-range goal that constitutes the primary claimant on a man's time, energy and resources. All his
other goals, however worthwhile, are secondary and must be integrated
to this purpose. The others are to be pursued only where such pursuit
complements the primary, rather than detracting from it."[27] A person's
central purpose is the paramount end by reference to which that person can determine the importance to assign to other things in his life;
it is the anchor and standard for a rational hierarchy of values, allowing
him to prioritize various ends and, correspondingly, to be rational in his
pursuit of them. Without a central purpose, a person will not know *how*
valuable anything is to him.[28] His actions are more susceptible to being
determined by emotions, since he has no compelling reason to stay with
a particular pursuit when it becomes difficult, tedious, or mildly unpleasant. A person who lacks a clear primary objective will have no grounds
for evaluating the benefit he might derive from various activities. The
person who has embraced a central purpose, by contrast, has a reason
for doing things and a basis for deciding which things are worth doing.
Correspondingly, a central purpose can provide motivation throughout
many facets of a person's life.[29]

The chief reasons that productive work must be a person's central
purpose are three-fold. Foremost, the human need for material values is
ongoing. It is not the kind of need that can be satisfied through a single definitive action and then permanently scratched off one's "to do"
list, like a vaccination providing lifetime immunity from a disease. The
problem of survival is never solved once and for all. Throughout our
lives, we consume material values and we need still more. Consequently,

---

[25] Because the central purpose of a person's life is a large and largely psychological matter,
I can only offer some broad lines of thought about it here. For further discussion, see my
unpublished essay, "The Value of a Central Productive Purpose," and Peikoff, *Objectivism*,
pp. 297–301.

[26] Chapter 1 above, note 14; Rand, "The Objectivist Ethics," p. 27.

[27] Peikoff, *Objectivism*, p. 299.

[28] "*Playboy*'s Interview with Ayn Rand," March 1964, p. 6.

[29] Because a central purpose is not a person's only purpose, it need not crowd out all other
values. Moreover, the fact that a central purpose should receive the bulk of a person's
time, overall, does not mean that it merits any particular unit of time. That productive
work should be a person's central purpose does not mean that he should always choose
work over alternative activities, for instance.

productiveness – the creation of the requisite values – must be a continuing concern.

Second, the scale of effort required to support a human life is enormous. Bear in mind that productiveness concerns the creation of all material values, not only those that serve a person's physical needs. When you consider the array of needs of a healthy adult – the food, shelter, clothing, medicines, the education and training, the transportation and communication equipment, the basic furnishings, appliances, and utilities, the arts and entertainment, and so on, that support a modest standard of living and maintain a person's ability to *be* productive – it is clear that a person will need to devote substantial resources to securing these goods. Self-sufficiency in material values is not the sort of concern that a person can ordinarily treat as peripheral or an afterthought. Accordingly, Peikoff writes that "productiveness constitutes the main existential content of virtue, the day by day substance of the moral life..."[30]

Third, because material values are critical to human beings' existence, a person's productiveness carries a profound and far-reaching impact on all of his pursuits. A person could not effectively pursue any other ends that he might prefer to treat as central without having satisfied his need for material values. No alternative purpose – bowling, traveling, a political cause, whatever – could be successfully achieved, long term, if a person does not secure the material values that his life requires. In order to be in a position to achieve other ends, in other words, a person cannot escape the need to be productive. It is not only the tremendous demands that sustaining oneself imposes on us that explains productiveness occupying this central position, then. It is also the correlatively wide reverberations of a person's productiveness or lack of productiveness throughout every area of his life.[31]

Bear in mind that living is a process of self-generated, self-sustaining activity. This is what living literally consists of. For human beings, the fundamental self-sustaining activity is productive work. When we say that a person works in order to live, accordingly, this means that he works in order to do still further work. For productive work is the principal activity that sustains a person and normally occupies a person's days. As such, productive work ideally becomes an end as well as a means. It

---

[30] Peikoff, *Objectivism*, p. 301. Again, we are leaving aside individuals in exceptional circumstances, such as the dying. I will address the case of the extremely wealthy shortly.

[31] For further comment concerning the attempt to substitute alternatives as one's central purpose, see Rand, *Atlas Shrugged*, p. 1020, and Peikoff, *Objectivism*, p. 300.

is an indispensable means of achieving the material values that sustain a person's existence, but it should also be the activity that a person wishes to engage in further, with the time that his productive effort buys. Although I need the salary that my philosophy work provides in order to pay the mortgage and grocery bills, for example, one of the chief reasons that I am glad to be able to pay those bills is so that I can continue doing philosophical work. That work is not merely a means to other things that I value; it is itself an activity that I enjoy, that enriches my life and that I would like to pursue even if it did not pay, could I afford to do that. Obviously, many people are not in this enviable position. The point is that this is the ideal; a person should strive to do productive work that provides the greatest spiritual as well as material rewards. Indeed, it is precisely because a person typically needs to devote so much energy to the work that will sustain him that he should try to do work that provides values beyond monetary compensation. For spiritual gratification is itself vital to self-sustaining action.[32]

The larger point, again, is that productive work should be the central purpose of a rational egoist's life.

Questions about the Extent of the Demands of Productiveness

How productive should a rational egoist be? Because the standard of value is life, the answer is: as productive as he can be. No ceiling limits how rich a person should make his life nor, correspondingly, the productive course he should pursue to accomplish that. "There is no human life that is 'safe enough,' 'long enough,' 'knowledgeable enough,' 'affluent enough,' or 'enjoyable enough' . . . " Peikoff writes.[33] A little reflection bears this out. What life expectancy would suffice? Living to age seventy-five? Eighty? Ninety? Why not something much lower? As James Ogilvy asks, when have you heard enough Bach?[34] If one did declare limits, what would be their basis? By what standard would a certain quality or quantity of life be deemed enough? On Rand's theory, the point of living is the enjoyment of one's life, and the standard of value is human life. Correlatively, anything that enhances a human life is to be encouraged.

---

[32] In a 1946 letter, Rand observes that a man will not normally produce merely in order to eat. "For self-preservation to assert itself, there must be some reason for the self to wish to be preserved." *Letters of Ayn Rand*, p. 257. I discuss this at some length in *Viable Values*, pp. 136–143.

[33] Peikoff, *Objectivism*, p. 292.

[34] James Ogilvy, "Greed," in Solomon, ed., *Wicked Pleasures*, p. 104. I might prefer a few other composers, but Ogilvy's point is unimpeachable.

"We cannot fix the minimal daily requirements for the human spirit," Ogilvy observes.[35] Nor can we fix the maximal requirements, on Rand's view, by putting a cap on the kind or length of life that a person should aspire to. A person seeking his happiness should do all that that goal requires. He should seek as secure, as comfortable, and as pleasurable a life for himself as possible. The exact constituents of such a life will vary for different individuals, depending largely on their abilities and tastes. A person might, rationally, opt for a less remunerative job because he finds its work more rewarding than better-paying alternatives. Productiveness does not demand that a person maximize his income or always opt for material values over all others. A person should seek the best that he can get, however, evaluating what would truly be best for him by the full context (which includes his hierarchy of values). Accordingly, the virtue of productiveness demands that a person do all that he can to achieve that.

In holding this, Rand is not endorsing the excesses of a neurotic workaholic. Excesses are precisely that. A person should exercise productiveness in a manner that is compatible with the rational pursuit of all the values that will achieve his happiness. A person's rational self-interest – long term, in all its dimensions – remains the ultimate arbiter of the propriety of any activity. Thus it would be a mistake to treat productiveness or material wealth as ends in themselves. (We will return to this point when we discuss greed, shortly.)

At the same time, because the goal of productiveness is a person's flourishing and because (as we have observed in previous chapters) that end requires an unfaltering commitment to life-supporting action, to simply go through the motions at some job will not suffice. Productiveness does not consist in perfunctorily filling the duties of one's position while waiting for weekends. It demands doing the most and best one can, choosing a challenging field and working to expand one's knowledge and develop one's ability within that field.[36] The productive person must be alert, attentive to the value of what he is doing and actively looking for ways that it might be done more efficiently or more effectively. "'Productive work' does not mean the unfocused performance of the motions of some job," Rand writes. "It means the consciously chosen pursuit of a productive career, in any line of rational endeavor, great or modest, on any level of ability. It is not the degree of a man's ability nor the scale of his work that is ethically relevant here, but the fullest and most purposeful use of

[35] Ogilvy, p. 98.
[36] Peikoff, *Objectivism*, p. 302.

his mind."[37] The salient consideration is not the intellectual demands of
the work that a person performs but a person's attitude toward his work,
as manifested in the effort that he exerts to do it as well as possible. Is a
person content merely to keep his job or does he push himself to learn
and do more? A shop foreman who labored diligently to gain his position can exhibit far more of the virtue of productiveness than a company
president who stagnates, in Rand's view.[38]

It is also worth recognizing that human beings need to grow. Because
we encounter ever new conditions, modestly different or radically different from those we have faced in the past, we need to strengthen and
expand our abilities. Growth is necessary not only to cope with changing
circumstances but also to improve the quality of our lives. Such improvement itself carries survival value, given our need to motivate our actions. It
is the promise of "still better" that often sustains the will to live. The point
is, productiveness in the rigorous sense that Rand describes is essential
for driving life forward.

Some might object that a person can produce material values without
exhibiting the extreme commitment that I have described. In certain
jobs within a larger productive chain, for instance, as long as a person
follows orders dutifully and is sufficiently skilled at the particular tasks
he performs, he might produce a great number of widgets and be a very
productive worker, by conventional measures. If so, however, why is the
virtue that Rand describes necessary? Or why does the virtue demand any
more than this?

By now, the answer to such a question should be obvious, since the
objection is simply a variation on one that has surfaced against other
virtues. Essentially, it asks: But if a person can get away with doing less than
Rand thinks a specific virtue demands, why does she demand as much
as she does? Isn't she overstating the virtue's requirements? The answer,
here as in every case, turns on a proper understanding of the standard
of value that Rand defends: survival *qua* man, or: the life of a human
being – fit to remain a human being, long range. In this case, "getting
away with" minimal effort at a paying job does not satisfy the demands of
the virtue of productiveness because the price of vice is not the agent's
imminent destruction (as we discussed in Chapter 2). Correlatively, the
test of virtue or of being "good enough" is not a person's breath. Nor is

[37] Rand, "The Objectivist Ethics," p. 29.
[38] Rand, "From My 'Future File,'" *Ayn Rand Letter*, III, 26, p. 3, cited in Harry Binswanger,
ed., *The Ayn Rand Lexicon* (New York: New American Library, 1986), p. 63.

it a given individual's professed satisfaction with his life. A person who pleads his contentment with a low-level effort of work that pays his bills does not possess the virtue of productiveness because an individual's taste is not the yardstick of value. Emotions and preferences do not dictate the necessities of human survival. Nor do conventional economic measures (such as a manager's tally of an employee's "output") correlate with a worker's moral virtue. Rand's point is that rationality requires that we identify and respect the sources of the creation of material values, that is, the qualities from which such creation springs. Exerting less than the kind of effort that Rand claims is necessary cannot sustain a human being, long range. It is only by relying on others who do exercise productiveness in the more demanding manner that Rand calls for that a person might, as a parasite, eke out a living. A *world* of such parasites could not exist for long, however, and could not support *human* life.

(The test of isolation is helpful, here again. A person living alone, without contact with other people, could not produce the material values needed to sustain his life unless he exerted the alert, active, forward-looking thinking that distinguish a productive person. Complacent laziness and thoughtless imitation or obedience could not sustain a person if he did not find others who are productive in Rand's rigorous sense *to* imitate or obey. In principle, human life requires productiveness of the kind that Rand describes.)

Let us consider a different question about the boundaries of this virtue's demands. What if a person is wealthy? Would that preclude the need for productiveness? Or at least minimize its practical requirements? In Rand's view, a wealthy person still needs a productive career; even if he needn't make money, he must work.[39] By now, it should not be difficult to understand why.

Human beings survive, at a fundamental level, by creating material values, which is what the virtue of productiveness enjoins. This does not mean that the value of productiveness lies exclusively in the material or physical *needs* that it enables a person to fulfill, however. Remember that material values are values that have existential reality external to people's minds and that even spiritual values can only be achieved through material means. Education, art, and friendship, for example, all require physical means and manifestations.

As Bishop Butler famously observed in the eighteenth century, a person cannot attain happiness by aiming directly at it. Happiness is a result

---

[39] Peikoff, *Objectivism*, pp. 301–302.

of the achievement of more specific, substantive ends. A person will be happy when the particular things that he values fare well – his business, his children, his preferred political platform, for instance.[40] Rand agrees wholeheartedly. We observed in Chapter 2 her conception of happiness as "that state of consciousness which proceeds from the achievement of one's values."[41] Correspondingly, in a letter, she asks: "Since happiness is an emotional *response to something* (and, therefore, an effect, not a cause), how can one *pursue happiness* except by pursuing that which will make one happy?"[42]

The lesson that addresses our immediate question is that the possession of wealth does not alter the basic route to happiness; it does not extinguish a person's need to embrace definite, substantive ends. Nor does it change a person's need to organize his activities around a central purpose so that specific values *can* be achieved. (Consider the numerous "well-off" people who are actually anything but: people who treat their wealth as reason to fail to embrace a productive purpose and whose lives suffer from a restless malaise and emptiness, as a result.) A wealthy person might not need to be paid for his effort (just as the parent or the actor who moonlights as a waiter need not be paid for all of his productive work), but he must still embrace a central productive purpose. It could be volunteer work for a cause he supports; it could be the disciplined pursuit of a particular theory in rocketry or software design or playing the piano or competitive bridge. Rich or not, to drive his life materially (even if not financially) and spiritually – to attain the various spiritual values that productiveness uniquely makes possible – a person must invest in some productive activity that his life is *about.* Failing to embrace a central productive purpose chokes the primary artery of happiness. That artery is as vital to the rich as to anyone else.[43]

---

[40] Joseph Butler, *Fifteen Sermons*, in D. D. Raphael, ed., *The British Moralists – 1650–1800* (Oxford: Clarendon Press, 1969), vol. I, p. 334. See pp. 365–367 for further elaboration of Butler's reasoning.

[41] Rand, *Atlas Shrugged*, p. 1014.

[42] *Letters of Ayn Rand*, p. 538, emphasis in original.

[43] It is also worth noting that wealth does not maintain itself. Preserving wealth (selecting the best investment vehicles through continually changing economic conditions, for instance) can require intensive, ongoing effort. Moreover, a person could only be in a position to forgo making money because of his or another person's having previously made enough money to subsidize this sabbatical. In other words, the rich are not an exception to the need for productiveness. What is exceptional is the extent to which they have already satisfied some of life's material demands, not their exemption from those demands. The urgency with which they must make money may differ from that of others, but the reliance on productiveness remains.

GREED

Because the rationale for productiveness is egoistic and because I have claimed that there is no limit, in principle, to how materially rich a person should strive to make his life, it is natural to wonder whether the endorsement of productiveness as a virtue is a license for greed. To answer, we must first dissect what has become a loaded term.[44]

In conventional usage, "greed" refers to an insatiable appetite for material goods, a never-ending quest for more. The *Oxford English Dictionary* tells us that greed is "inordinate or insatiate longing, especially for wealth; avaricious or covetous desire." Avarice, in turn, is "inordinate desire of acquiring and hoarding wealth." And indeed, as people use the term, "greed" signifies overindulgence in the pursuit of material comforts, pleasures, luxuries. In a recent essay on the subject, Ogilvy claims that greed is "best understood as desire run amok."[45] The usual implication is that the greedy person is out of control – if not absolutely compulsive in his thirst to acquire, at the least, emotionally driven to excess.

Ascriptions of greed often also reflect an anti-material animus. Part of what is allegedly objectionable is that the greedy person is seeking material ends, which are taken to be, if not utterly base, decidedly inferior. Moreover, charges of greed often insinuate injustice, implying that a person's "excessive" wealth must be had by exploitation of others (by not adequately paying others or by taking more than one's "fair share," for instance). In short, greed seems pretty degenerate, to most people. It represents the irrational pursuit of a selfish desire, as the concept marries emotionalism with self-serving materialism.[46]

So understood, however, greed is an illegitimate concept. For it crudely packages reference to an activity (pursuit of material wealth) together with a nonessential evaluation of that activity (that it is emotionalist and materialist). The problem is not simply that the term "greed" has negative connotations; many terms carry such taints. The problem is that the entrenched understanding of greed treats the pursuit of material wealth as inescapably excessive, the desire for wealth as necessarily irrational. In

---

[44] I have benefited from discussion with Leonard Peikoff about this issue.

[45] Ogilvy, p. 87.

[46] The Bible offers many warnings against greed. See, for instance, Ephesians 5:3; Colossians 3:5; Luke 12:15–21; Mark 7:20–23; Matthew 19:21–24. The 12th century Jewish philosopher Maimonides urges that we repent excessive ambition and greed. Julie Salamon, *Rambam's Ladder – A Meditation on Generosity and Why it is Necessary to Give* (New York: Workman Publishing, 2003), p. 78. Islam also condemns greed. See Armstrong, *A History of God*, pp. 133, 142–143.

this way, common usage smuggles in an unwarranted evaluation. "Greed" refers at once to a rational desire and to its irrational pursuit, tarring the former in its denunciation of the latter.[47]

Suppose we stripped away the evaluative portion of greed's popular meaning and understood greed as the active, ambitious pursuit of wealth. Objectively, what might be wrong about such a pursuit? Essentially, either of two things: a person's means of pursuing wealth or his motivation for pursuing wealth (which will determine his use of wealth). Often, what provokes criticism is actually a person's unscrupulous methods of trying to attain greater wealth, such as cooking the books to defraud investors. When they slap on the label "greedy," people sloppily condemn the person's desire rather than his dishonest and unjust means of trying to satisfy that desire. Likewise, a person's reasons for seeking greater wealth might be faulty. A person might regard material goods as intrinsically valuable, for instance, or he might seek particular material goods because others are seeking them and he is second-handedly following the crowd. He might pursue material wealth in order to impress others or in order to impress himself. His mistake might rest in treating material goods as *the* highest value imaginable, regardless of the role that particular goods would actually play in his life.

While we can recognize several ways in which a given individual's pursuit of material wealth might be irrational and inappropriate, what is significant is that none of these locates the source of the difficulty in the desire for material goods itself. That desire, in fact, is unassailable. For it is necessary for human life. This is why the ambitious pursuit of material wealth is, contrary to greed's customary censure, positively good. It is perfectly proper for a person to seek the natural rewards of his productiveness. He *should* be eager for material values, for they, along with spiritual values, are the stuff of flourishing.[48]

It is important to bear in mind that material wealth is not intrinsically valuable, on Rand's view. A person should not pursue material wealth as an end in itself. The breathless, ceaseless reaching for more that precludes the enjoyment of one's life (and which is all too common)

---

[47] Rand would consider greed an "anti-concept," her term for "an unnecessary and rationally unusable term designed to replace and obliterate some legitimate concept." See her explanation of this concept in "Credibility and Polarization," *Ayn Rand Letter* I, 1, p.1, and "'Extremism,' or the Art of Smearing," in *Capitalism: The Unknown Ideal*, p. 176. Note that the common usage of "usury" is similar to that of greed.

[48] Interestingly, people are frequently unapologetic in wishing every material success for their loved ones.

defeats the point of productiveness. It is not what Rand is endorsing.[49] The point of exercising any virtue is to achieve the best life possible for oneself. Consequently, when certain material goods would, on balance, enhance the quality of an individual's life, it is right for him to pursue those goods. "[Y]our work is the process of achieving your values," Rand writes, "and to lose your ambition for values is to lose your ambition to live . . ."[50]

Because condemnations of greed often focus on the pursuit of money, it is worth noting that the reason that human beings should try to make money, on Rand's view, is the same reason that human beings should be productive, more broadly: We need material values in order to sustain our lives. The more money a person has, the more easily he can obtain those values. And the more easily he can do that, the more he can tailor his days to his liking, which in itself has life-advancing value.

We all understand the expression "time is money": Wasting time squanders the opportunity to make money (or the equivalent in material values). It is equally true that money is time, however, as Rand explains in *Atlas*.[51] Wealth represents time liberated from the task of tending one's most basic, day-to-day subsistence needs through physical labor. The greater a person's reserves of wealth, the less labor he must exert in the future to achieve the same standard of living that that wealth can buy. The more money a person has, the more easily he can meet those needs and the more time he can devote to more desirable activities. Consequently, money is valuable not only for providing a person with more material goods. It gives a person more options; it allows a greater range of choices in his activities. Money enables a person to enhance his life in whatever ways, material or spiritual, are most conducive to his overall

---

[49] Note that the heroes of her fiction do not pursue wealth in that way. In *Atlas*, for instance, Rearden refuses to sell the rights to his metal to the government despite being offered a great deal of money, pp. 180–182. Also, Rand distinguishes money makers from money appropriators, recognizing that some people (money appropriators) become rich not by creating valuable goods or services but by manipulating other people. It is the money maker, by contrast, who "does not care for money *as such*" but who creates objective values, whose path is genuinely life-advancing. "The Money-Making Personality," *Why Businessmen Need Philosophy*, ed. Richard E. Ralston (Marina Del Rey, CA: Ayn Rand Institute Press, 1999), pp. 29, 36, emphasis added. The belief that material goods are intrinsically valuable is shared by certain stingy people, as we will see in our discussion of generosity in Chapter 10.

[50] Rand, *Atlas Shrugged*, p. 1020.

[51] Rand, *Atlas Shrugged*, pp. 721–722. For a more extended discussion of the value of money, see the speech that Francisco D'Anconia delivers in *Atlas*, pp. 410–415. Also see my "Money *Can* Buy Happiness," *Reason Papers*, vol. 26 (Summer 2003), pp. 7–19.

well-being, giving him more time to cultivate friendships, for instance, or to enjoy his love of opera.

In the end, we can only answer the question of whether the virtue of productiveness sanctions greed by pinpointing precisely what the question asks. Is Rand endorsing the inordinate quest for wealth? No. The inordinate is the irrational and as such, antithetical to human life. Is Rand endorsing emotionalism? No; the master virtue of rationality rules that out. Is Rand endorsing selfishness? Yes – thoughtful, rational selfishness in regard to wealth, as to all other ends. Is Rand endorsing materialism? Not if that means the elevation of material values at the expense of spiritual values. Both material and spiritual fuel are vital to human life, thus it would be a mistake to condemn the pursuit of either, as such. Although either material or spiritual values can be pursued irrationally, neither is by nature base or unworthy of us.

On reflection, the fact that a person seeks to expand his material wealth is not, by itself, an adequate basis for determining whether he is acting irrationally or immorally. The aspects of this pursuit that are sometimes legitimately condemned, such as certain means by which a person seeks to obtain wealth, are not actions that Rand endorses, as they are not *rationally* self-interested. At the same time, it is important to recognize that Rand does endorse a person's effort to enrich his life, materially no less than in any other respect, as much as he can. If that be greed, Rand cheers it on.

CONCLUSION

Productiveness is the process of creating material values. Like the independent person, the productive person accepts responsibility for making his own way in the world, refusing to attempt to live off of others' achievements. The rationale for recognizing productiveness as a virtue, like that for each of the moral virtues, rests in the basic causal requirements of human existence. If a person seeks a particular effect – his continued existence – he must enact the requisite cause. Productiveness highlights man's need to create all of the material values that are essential to achieving that effect. Rand's point is not simply that human beings have material *needs*. Rather, it is that only productiveness – the rationally guided creation of material values – can satisfy the material as well as the spiritual needs of human existence. Productiveness demands qualities of character and delivers rewards that enable a human being to flourish.

9

Pride

If productiveness is not usually considered a moral virtue, the final of Rand's major virtues is widely considered a downright vice. The Old Testament warns that "pride goes before destruction." The New Testament agrees that "whoever exalts himself will be humbled, and whoever humbles himself will be exalted."[1] Like greed, pride ranks as one of the seven deadly sins, yet even to say this does not capture its special infamy in the Christian tradition. Pride is "the great sin," C. S. Lewis testifies, because it is "the beginning of all sin," as Ecclesiastes warns. Other sins are "mere fleabites" in comparison.[2] The antithesis of pride, humility, is what is commonly praised as virtuous.

Pride has not been universally condemned. Aristotle, famously, praised pride as the crown of the virtues. Hume ridiculed humility as a "monkish virtue" and allowed that "a due degree of pride" can afford beneficial "confidence and assurance."[3] Today, people will often support group pride proclaimed by a union or a minority, such as Hispanics or gays. Such exceptions notwithstanding, for the most part, people regard individual pride warily, typically greeting it as a fault. (One cultural illustration: the *New York Times* review of the fifth Harry Potter book, which matter-of-factly

---

[1] Proverbs 16:18; Luke 18:9–14.
[2] C. S. Lewis, *Mere Christianity* (New York: MacMillan, 1952), p. 108, 109; Lewis also refers to pride as "spiritual cancer," p. 112. Ecclesiastes 10:15. Also see Augustine, *City of God* (Garden City, NY: Doubleday, 1958), p. 308.
[3] Aristotle, *Nicomachean Ethics*, Book IV, Chapter 3; Hume, *An Enquiry Concerning the Principles of Morals*, ed. J. B. Schneewind (Indianapolis: Hackett, 1988), p. 73; *A Treatise of Human Nature*, ed. L. A. Selby-Bigge, second edition text revised by P. H. Nidditch (Oxford: Clarendon Press, 1978), pp. 596–597.

refers to the hero's need to question "his own weaknesses – anger, pride, and ambition.")[4] When it is not categorically rejected as a vice, pride tends to be only grudgingly tolerated as a necessary tool of self-defense – armor against being a doormat – rather than welcomed as a positive good.[5] To most people, even a modest quotient of pride seems a perilously small step from the abyss of narcissism. If the Christian historically saw pride as alienating a person from God,[6] the dominant contemporary view, secular as well as religious, is that the proud person is too big for his britches; he suffers from inflated self-approval and considers himself superior to others. Most people seem to agree with Spinoza that "pride is the pleasure arising from a man's thinking too highly of himself."[7]

Rand considers pride not merely tolerable, but a virtue. If a person is to flourish, the exercise of pride is indispensable. In order to appreciate this, we must begin by looking at Rand's distinctive conception of what pride is. After our usual sequence considering the basic nature of pride, its value, and its practical demands, I will comment briefly on the implications for humility.

WHAT PRIDE IS

In Rand's view, pride is "the commitment to achieve one's own moral perfection."[8] Because the essence of morality is rationality, moral perfection, in turn, consists of an "unbreached rationality."[9] More informally, Rand writes that "the virtue of pride can best be described by the term 'moral ambitiousness.'"[10]

Today, people most often think of pride as an attitude or a feeling.[11] To speak of a person's pride is to speak of his satisfaction with himself, either

---

4 Michiko Kakutani, "For Famous Young Wizard, a Darker Turn," *New York Times,* June 21, 2003.
5 Edith Sitwell praises pride as necessary for artists in the face of critics. Sitwell, "Pride," in Alexander E. Hooke, ed., *Virtuous Persons, Vicious Deeds* (Mountain View, CA: Mayfield, 1999), p. 440.
6 Jerome Neu, "Pride," in Solomon, ed., *Wicked Pleasures,* p. 54.
7 Baruch Spinoza, *The Ethics and Selected Letters,* ed. Seymour Feldman (Indianapolis: Hackett, 1982), p. 186.
8 Peikoff, *Objectivism,* p. 303; also see Rand, "The Objectivist Ethics," p. 29.
9 Rand, *Atlas Shrugged,* p. 1059.
10 Rand, "The Objectivist Ethics," p. 29.
11 I do not mean to equate attitudes with feelings, but for our purposes, I treat these together to contrast them both with Rand's conception of pride. I do mean an attitude as something less than a well-considered judgment.

with a particular trait or accomplishment or with himself more broadly.[12] The term "pride" is used most commonly to describe a person's feelings. In commending pride as a virtue, however, Rand understands pride as a policy of action and regards the feeling of pride as simply a by-product of a person's abiding by such a policy.

In the history of philosophy, Aristotle, famously, also considered pride a virtue, but it is instructive to recognize the difference between his and Rand's conceptions of pride. Aristotle describes the proud man as he "who thinks himself worthy of great things and is really worthy of them."[13] Although it is his actions that make a man worthy, one could easily understand Aristotle to be characterizing pride as a kind of self-evaluation. Indeed, it seems an application of justice, as the proud person awards himself the esteem that he deserves. By Rand's lights, this renders pride too passive. For Rand, pride is not simply an after-the-fact satisfaction (justified as such satisfaction might be), but a forward-looking ambition that drives a person to act as morality requires. It is a commitment to the course of unwaveringly rational, virtuous action. Feelings of pride and the belief that one is entitled to feel pride are the usual result of adherence to such a course, but they should not be mistaken for the virtue itself. Although Aristotle does not ignore the active element of pride (over the course of his discussion, he considers various kinds of actions that the proud man will and will not take), I emphasize the contrast between Aristotle and Rand in order to highlight the fact that the commitment to virtuous actions is the focal point throughout Rand's account. (Note that the familiar description of a person as "taking pride in himself" or in some particular realm of his life such as his appearance, his manners, or his cooking reflects the integration of the backward and forward looking dimensions of pride. Such a person's past conduct in the relevant domain provides his basis for positive self-evaluation, and the fact that he takes pride in such conduct indicates the kind of action he intends to take in the future.)

Accordingly, several popular stereotypes of the proud person are unwarranted, on Rand's account. A person can exercise the virtue of pride without being boastful, arrogant, or stubborn, for instance, and without angling to impress others or approaching life as a contest whose

---

[12] Kristjan Kristjansson, for example, depicts pride as "an emotion of self-satisfaction, arising from the belief that we have achieved something that is worth achieving." "Pridefulness," *The Journal of Value Inquiry* 35 (2001), p. 167. See also p. 169.

[13] Aristotle, *Nicomachean Ethics*, 1123b, trans. Irwin.

object is to display one's superiority to others. None of those traits is a necessary companion to taking one's moral principles seriously, which is what pride actually prescribes, according to Rand. Indeed, such traits often reflect moral or psychological deficiencies, such as a lack of independence.[14] "As a rule, a man of achievement does not flaunt his achievements," Rand observes, and "he does not evaluate himself by others – by a comparative standard. His attitude is not 'I am better than you' but 'I am good.'"[15] "Offensive boasting or self-abasing appeasement is a false alternative."[16]

Some might object that feelings of pride should not be so quickly dismissed, since a feeling of pride can sometimes influence a person's actions in salutary ways. The person who feels "worthy of great things" may correspondingly view certain actions as beneath him and therefore refuse to engage in them. "I wouldn't stoop to such methods" is a recognizable attitude among many proud people.[17] While Rand would agree that a person's self-conception can play a constructive role in guiding him to the moral course, this does not show that feelings of pride are crucial to the virtue, since it would only be proper for a person to act on such feelings if he had rationally endorsed the relevant standards – that is, if he had rationally determined that the actions in question truly are beneath appropriate standards. In such a case, the person would not be acting "on his feelings," but on his judgment. Rand has no objection to feelings of pride. Indeed, she celebrates them.[18] She recognizes, however, that feelings *per se* cannot effectively guide a person to a course of life-sustaining action and thus cannot constitute virtues. This is why she maintains that the virtue of pride (as opposed to the feeling of pride) consists in a commitment to rational action. Further, she recognizes that the genuine feeling of pride can only be sustained through the practical exercise of that commitment. A veneer of proud feeling that is not built on consistent proper action will be riddled with doubt, easily punctured,

---

[14] For some such misguided conceptions, see Robert C. Roberts, "What is Wrong with Wicked Feelings?" *American Philosophical Quarterly* 28 (Jan. 1991), pp. 15–16; C. S. Lewis, p. 109; and Hume, *Treatise*, pp. 316, 292.

[15] Rand, "The Age of Envy," p. 137.

[16] Rand, "The Age of Envy," p. 137.

[17] The *Oxford English Dictionary* recognizes this usage.

[18] In *Atlas*, she describes the statue of Nat Taggart as of a young man who "held his head as if he faced a challenge and found joy in his capacity to meet it" (p. 60), a posture I take to be symbolic of her understanding of pride. She also describes John Galt's countenance (his mouth, in particular) as exuding pride – indeed, "it was as if he took pride in being proud," p. 701.

and thus not a stable basis for virtuous action. Nor will it be very secure as a feeling.

We can further appreciate Rand's conception of pride by considering her characterization of pride as moral ambitiousness. In general, "ambition" refers to the ardent desire for a particular good or achievement.[19] We consider a person ambitious when he sets his aims above the average or commonplace or easily obtained and acts accordingly, tenaciously pursuing challenging goals. Rand understands ambition as "the systematic pursuit of achievement and of constant improvement in respect to one's goal."[20] By identifying pride with moral ambitiousness, Rand is recognizing that survival demands an ambitious commitment to moral principles. The proud person sets high standards for himself and conscientiously strives to meet them. He is dedicated not only to doing his best, but to making his best ever better. (We will say more on why, as well as on ambitiousness and moral perfection, in coming sections.)

Finally, it is worth noticing that the principal concern of pride is the self. Unlike the other virtues, the focus of pride is more inward than outward. Even integrity, which is fidelity to rational principles, is primarily concerned that a person's external actions be consistent with his convictions. The concern of pride, in contrast, is more fully on the self. Pride "means that one must earn the right to hold oneself as one's own highest value," Rand writes.[21] Peikoff observes that "a proud man struggles to achieve within himself the best possible spiritual state."[22] The virtue of pride stands on recognition of the crucial value of one's character and, consequently, of working to make one's character spotless. We will see why, as we turn to the case for pride.

WHY PRIDE IS A VIRTUE

The core of the case for pride is presented in a passage from Galt's speech:

Pride is the recognition of the fact that you are your own highest value and, like all of man's values, it has to be earned – that of any achievements open to you,

---

[19] Among the *OED*'s definitions are "the ardent desire to rise to high position, or to attain rank, influence, distinction or other preferment" and "a strong or ardent desire of anything considered advantageous, or creditable."

[20] "Tax Credits for Education," *The Ayn Rand Letter* I, 12, p. 1, quoted in Binswanger, ed., *The Ayn Rand Lexicon*, p. 12. Rand observes that in popular usage, the term "'ambition' has been perverted to mean only the pursuit of dubious or evil goals," although it is in fact a neutral term.

[21] Rand, "The Objectivist Ethics," p. 29.

[22] Peikoff, *Objectivism*, p. 303.

the one that makes all others possible is the creation of your own character – that your character, your actions, your desires, your emotions are the products of the premises held by your mind – that as man must produce the physical values he needs to sustain his life, so he must acquire the values of character that make his life worth sustaining – that as man is a being of self-made wealth, so he is a being of self-made soul – that to live requires a sense of self-value, but man, who has no automatic values, has no automatic sense of self-esteem and must earn it by shaping his soul in the image of his moral ideal, in the image of Man, the rational being he is born able to create, but must create by choice – that the first precondition of self-esteem is that radiant selfishness of soul which desires the best in all things, in values of matter and spirit, a soul that seeks above all else to achieve its own moral perfection, valuing nothing higher than itself . . .[23]

In essence, Rand's argument is that pride is necessary for self-esteem, and self-esteem is necessary for human life. "Man cannot preserve his body unless he preserves his soul."[24] A person must shape himself as well as his external surroundings into values, if he is to survive.

Self-esteem is, in Peikoff's words, "a fundamental, positive moral appraisal of oneself – of the process by which one lives and of the person one thereby creates."[25] It encapsulates the twin convictions, "I am *able* to live and I am *worthy* of living."[26] Self-esteem is a considered, deep-seated, positive assessment of one's own basic competence and value. While positive feelings will normally spring from such a self-evaluation, self-esteem is essentially cognitive. "Self-esteem is reliance on one's power to think," Rand writes.[27] Although the knowledge that one is using that power will normally bring certain positive emotions along with it, self-esteem consists not in such episodes of emotions but in the more settled and more enduring evaluation of oneself that lies beneath them. Self-esteem is, at core, a judgment.[28]

---

[23] Rand, *Atlas*, pp. 1020–1021. See a similar passage in Rand, "The Goal of My Writing," in *The Romantic Manifesto*, p. 169.

[24] *Journals of Ayn Rand*, pp. 254–255.

[25] Peikoff, *Objectivism*, p. 306.

[26] Peikoff, *Objectivism*, p. 306, emphasis his.

[27] Rand, *Atlas*, p. 1057.

[28] Pauline Chazan similarly describes self-esteem as indicating "how worthy and capable a person considers herself to be" and characterizes this as the reigning conception of self-esteem. Chazan, "Self-Esteem, Self-Respect, and Love of Self: Ways of Valuing the Self," *Philosophia* 26 (1998), p. 42. Also see Stephen L. Darwall, *Impartial Reason* (Ithaca, NY: Cornell University Press, 1983), pp. 151–156, and Kristjansson, p. 166. Contemporary philosophers often distinguish self-esteem from self-respect, though debate continues about the precise contours of this distinction. "Self-respect" is sometimes used to refer to a sense of worth that is grounded not in an individual's view of his distinctive merits (as it is with self-esteem, on Rand's and many others' accounts), but in his recognition that he

What is salient to Rand's defense of pride is that self-esteem is not a natural endowment inherited at birth.[29] Nor is it the kind of thing that can be stumbled upon through chance. Self-esteem must be acquired through a person's own choices and actions. We are what we do. Because human beings choose our actions, *what* we choose forges our individual characters. In the *Atlas* passage above, Rand claims that a person "must earn [self-esteem] by shaping his soul in the image of his moral ideal." A person will develop a positive self-evaluation, in other words, by holding himself to his considered convictions about proper principles of living. Consistently virtuous action is the path to self-esteem.

The reason to be concerned with this path, in turn, is the profound value of self-esteem. In claiming that man is a being of "self-made soul," Rand observes that just as a person needs to produce material values in order to make his way in the world, he also needs to achieve a certain spiritual condition. "As a being of volitional consciousness," a person "must know his own value in order to maintain his own life."[30] Because a person chooses his actions, he needs a fundamentally positive view of himself in order to take the kinds of actions that can effectively advance his life. The fact that man is a being of self-made soul creates the need to make one's soul *well*.[31]

Every action that a person takes, in addition to whatever changes it effects in the external world, contributes to that person's self-image. He knows that he chose that action and that he could have chosen otherwise; he knows whether he was being rational or evasive. A person also learns, over time, that his life depends on his actions, that his choices carry a

---

is a human being. Accordingly, self-respect is purportedly manifested in such things as a person's resentment of being ignored or used or having his rights violated. See David Sachs, "How to Distinguish Self-Respect from Self-Esteem," *Philosophy and Public Affairs* 10, no. 4 (1981), pp. 352–353; Chazan, p. 41. Others, however, characterize self-esteem not as different in kind from self-respect, but as a type of self-respect. See, for example, Lester H. Hunt, *Character and Culture* (Lanham, MD: Rowman & Littlefield, 1997), p. 41. Fortunately, we do not need to settle this issue. It will suffice for our purposes simply to grasp what Rand takes the essence of self-esteem to be.

[29] Peikoff, *Objectivism*, p. 306.

[30] Rand, *Atlas*, p. 1057.

[31] Recall that Rand regards self-esteem, along with reason and purpose, as the three cardinal values that together are "the means to and realization of one's ultimate value, one's own life." "The Objectivist Ethics," p. 27. For other statements of her strong view of the importance of self-esteem, see *Atlas*, pp. 1056 and 1057. Jean Hampton has also argued that morality requires that a person take a certain kind of pride in himself, though Hampton is far from a thoroughgoing egoist. "Selflessness and the Loss of Self," *Social Philosophy and Policy* 10 (Winter 1993), p. 148.

direct and potentially tremendous impact on his successes and failures, on his happiness or frustration. He learns, in short, that he must make good choices in order to achieve his values. Consequently, a person needs to develop the sense that he can rely on himself to make good choices, knowing: "I'll be rational; I *am* rational." Such knowledge is the platform for self-esteem.[32]

Awareness of the kind of person he has made himself, in turn, affects how a person will act. Pride is a virtue because a person's fundamental evaluation of himself is critical to his success in life. Aware that he controls his thoughts and actions, a person must develop a reputation with himself as a person he can trust to take good care of himself and as a person who is worth the effort. He must think well of himself in order to act well and thereby gain the values that fuel his flourishing. A person's estimate of his actions, his history, his character – of his *self* – will influence what he seeks and how hard he works to attain it; it will influence what he encourages himself to do, what he allows himself to do, and what he demands of himself. This is the manner in which, as Rand claims in the *Atlas* passage, the creation of one's character makes all other values possible.[33]

Human beings act on the basis of beliefs, however clearly articulated or dimly conceived. Most broadly, a person's actions are premised on his beliefs about what he should do and what he can do. Should I apply for the more challenging position? Why? And can I really get it? Should I ask that person out for dinner? And would she really wish to spend time with me? Should I rewrite this scene? If I did, could I make it any better? If a person thinks that he is unworthy of a particular goal or that he is incapable of attaining that goal, he will not try to achieve it. The same applies more broadly. As Peikoff observes, "A volitional being cannot accept self-preservation as his purpose unless, taking a moral inventory, he concludes that he is qualified for the task; qualified in terms of ability and value."[34]

A person's fundamental assessment of his ability and of his worthiness will inevitably color every choice that he makes. A negative verdict is debilitating. For a person will not normally waste his time on what he deems himself incapable or unworthy of.[35] Without self-esteem, a person

---

[32] See Rand, "The Age of Envy," p. 155.

[33] Rand, *Atlas*, pp. 1020–1021.

[34] Peikoff, *Objectivism*, p. 306.

[35] People do, reasonably, sometimes try to "stretch," of course. Yet such stretches – for example, setting higher targets for one's time in a race – must be based on a positive assessment of one's underlying efficacy and worth. When a person believes that a goal

will not value his own happiness sufficiently to adhere to the rational moral code that his happiness depends on. He is likely to be deterred from pursuing apparently desirable ends by the unspoken thoughts, "Why bother? I wouldn't be able to actually get that," or "I don't really deserve that kind of success." The lack of self-esteem will thus cripple a person's ability to act in the ways that his flourishing requires. With self-esteem, by contrast, a person will be more inclined to take the actions that can advance his life and disinclined to take those that will be bad for him. Self-esteem gives a person confidence in his judgment, confidence in his identification of what the proper course is, and reason to stay that course in the face of occasionally wayward inclinations.[36]

The larger point in the argument for the virtue of pride, again, is not simply that self-esteem is extremely valuable, but that pride is necessary to acquire self-esteem.[37] Remember that the source of self-esteem rests in the propriety of a person's choices and actions. More basically, it rests in a person's means of using his mind. For it is through this that a person will develop an essentially favorable or unfavorable assessment of his worth and competence. Indeed, since the self essentially is the mind, Peikoff observes that "self-esteem is mind-esteem."[38] Without a rational

is literally, utterly beyond him, he will not bother to attempt it. A person's positive assessment of his abilities in a particular field (running, engineering, public speaking, etc.) can only spur constructive action if his more basic, comprehensive evaluation of his *self* is also positive.

[36] Some recent psychological research has challenged the value of self-esteem, contending that low self-esteem is not the source of social ills that it has been widely claimed to be in recent decades. See Erica Goode, "Deflating Self-Esteem's Role in Society's Ills," *New York Times*, Oct. 1, 2002. From what this article reports, the researchers' findings seem premised on a drastically different conception of self-esteem from Rand's, however. In characterizing racists as having high self-esteem, for example, the researchers mistake what Rand would consider pseudo-self-esteem for the genuine article. See her analysis of racism as a form of collectivism in "Racism," in *The Virtue of Selfishness*, pp. 147–157. On the need to discriminate between bases of alleged self-esteem, consider Rand's statement that "Self-esteem is reliance in one's power to think. It cannot be replaced by one's power to deceive. The self-confidence of a scientist and the self-confidence of a con man are not interchangeable states, and do not come from the same psychological universe. The success of a man who deals with reality augments his self-confidence. The success of a con man augments his panic." "The Age of Envy," p. 154. Peikoff comments on the importance of the standards of measuring self-esteem, *Objectivism*, pp. 306–307. Note that Rand would dispute the conception and standards of self-esteem espoused by many of the champions of self-esteem, as well as those espoused by these more recent critics.

[37] For comment on the mutually reinforcing dynamic between pride and self-esteem, see Tara Smith, "The Practice of Pride," in Ellen Frankel Paul, Fred D. Miller, Jr., and Jeffrey Paul, eds., *Virtue and Vice* (New York: Cambridge University Press, 1998), pp. 82–83.

[38] Peikoff, *Objectivism*, p. 307.

moral code that provides a compass for navigating the world, guiding his attempts to gain values and flourish, a person will be at sea. Without the knowledge that he is doing his best to adhere to a rational moral code, the point of recognizing such a code is lost. For such a person is not using it to reap the value – the rational guidance – that it offers.[39]

Whenever a person settles for less than perfect fidelity to rational principles, he is, implicitly, rejecting either those principles or the purpose of adhering to them, namely, his own happiness. Either course sabotages his self-esteem. For the inner dialogue will be roughly: "If I'm so good, why don't I do what I think I should? If, alternatively, I don't really think I should abide by these principles, then why don't I disown them, once and for all? If these principles are an inadequate guide to my happiness, why haven't I found – or tried harder to find – better ones? Why do I pretend to accept these, if I really don't? And if my happiness isn't the appropriate goal for my actions, then what is? And why should I give a damn what I do? How good can I be, if some other aim should take precedence over my happiness?"

When a person deviates from the moral code that he accepts, he sends himself conflicting messages. "Sometimes I am worthy," he will think, "but sometimes I'm not. Many times – maybe even most of the time – I make rational decisions that advance my interest. Yet sometimes I don't." As a consequence, such a person cannot be sure of himself. And the resulting uncertainty is fatal to the calm, steady confidence that distinguishes self-esteem. The person with self-esteem is secure in his fundamental value. The person whose allegiance to his principles is erratic, by contrast, still has doubts; the verdict on his character is yet to be reached.[40]

One errant action will not normally destroy a person's self-esteem completely.[41] The problem with anything less than an unqualified dedication to moral principles, however, is that it leaves open questions – about the agent's value and about his commitment to his happiness – that should be closed. Correlatively, it jeopardizes the person's well-being. For such uncertainties can only make further violations of principle more likely and leave his self-esteem vulnerable to further erosion. Human life is achieved through life-sustaining actions, not through life-diminishing ones. Just as the fact that a person might survive a grossly irrational action

---

[39] Peikoff discusses this briefly in *Objectivism*, p. 306.

[40] In 1966 journal notes on possible themes for future articles, Rand remarks that "man *needs* a state of psychological integration – of inner unity." *Journals of Ayn Rand*, p. 689, emphasis in original. Her context there was more epistemological than ethical, but this condition also seems important to a person's ability to follow his moral code.

[41] Peikoff alludes to this, *Objectivism*, p. 308.

does not make a policy of such actions as good as any alternative, the fact that a given moral breach might leave a person's self-esteem more positive than negative does not mean that such breaches are benign. Each transgression makes further breaches, with the attendant damage to self-esteem and to other values, more likely. A commitment to one's life thus requires a commitment to nothing less than moral perfection. (I will say more on perfection in the next section.)

Before concluding our discussion of Rand's reasoning, we should distinguish it from another argument that might be confused for hers. From a quick reading of Rand, one might conclude that the case for pride simply mirrors the general case for being moral. For if pride is moral ambitiousness, then much of the value of pride stems from the value of morality itself. It is good to be morally ambitious, seemingly, for all the reasons that it is good to be moral. Because morality is our means to flourishing, it is through the conscientious exercise of all the moral virtues that a person can attain that objective. Indeed, Peikoff observes that the rewards of pride "are all the values that a proper moral character makes possible."[42]

Although all of these observations are true, they do not capture the distinctive value of pride. The pivotal fact that gives rise to the propriety of pride is our need for self-esteem and the essential role of pride in building it. Because human action is volitional, motivation is critical. (I am speaking, obviously, of intentional action.) A person will not have the requisite motivation to achieve the values that sustain his life unless he develops self-esteem – the conviction of his basic ability and worth. It is an unwavering devotion to rational principles that fosters the growth of self-esteem. A person's actions affect his character and his awareness of his character as well as his existential situation, we have seen. As Rand recognizes, a person must earn the value of his life; he must make his life the kind of life that is worth prizing. He does that by learning the rational path for attaining human happiness and then following that path with scrupulous and unswerving devotion. Because it is a person's character that makes all other values possible (insofar as one's character provides the sense of one's ability and of one's worth that is necessary to motivate life-sustaining actions), the creation of a morally proud character *is* the means to reaping all of life's values, as Peikoff observes. It is so, however, thanks to its service to self-esteem.

In identifying pride – the commitment to moral perfection – as a virtue, then, Rand is not simply underscoring her sincerity in commending the

[42] Peikoff, *Objectivism*, p. 305; also see p. 304.

other virtues, declaring, in effect, "I really mean it when I say you should practice those." More specifically, she is spotlighting the crucial spiritual value that a commitment to moral perfection makes possible. All the virtues must be embraced in this unqualified and ambitious way if a person is to achieve the confidence and joy in living that motivate the self-sustaining actions that constitute living.

Finally, we can also appreciate that pride, like all the other virtues, is completely egoistic. Rand does not urge this thoroughgoing devotion to moral principles on the grounds that it enables a person to better serve others. Nor is the point of "pushing oneself," morally, to become the best of God's soldiers, to earn a star in a cosmic grading scheme, or to attain any other objective that treats morality as an end in itself that exerts some autonomous, inherently worthy authority. Pushing oneself is good *for oneself.* The reason to ambitiously commit to moral perfection is to attain one's own happiness.

THE PRACTICAL DEMANDS OF PRIDE

With this understanding of why pride is valuable to the rational egoist, we can next consider more closely the practical demands of this demanding virtue.

Intellectual Demands

First of all, pride demands that a person exert the intellectual effort to identify proper moral principles. The proud person will not simply settle for whatever moral ideals are accepted by those around him, but will work to determine which principles are valid.[43] A person could not be morally ambitious if he passively absorbed moral principles without logically evaluating them. Indeed, it would defeat the point of abiding by principles if one's principles were themselves erroneous. A proud person cannot be casual about the content of his moral code. He must work to get it right.

Not only will a proud person seek to understand the correct moral code in the abstract; he will also work to understand what it demands of him, in particular. That is, he will engage in honest introspection about his knowledge, abilities, and values in order to grasp the proper application

---

[43] Peikoff, *Objectivism*, p. 304. I use "a proud person" in this context to refer to the person who exercises the virtue of pride, as Rand understands it, rather than to the person who simply feels pride.

of moral principles to his circumstances. He might reason to determine what justice demands in his relations with regular clients, for instance, or to determine what types of jobs productiveness rules out as beneath his abilities. Pride requires a person's ongoing monitoring of his personal situation in order to determine what he is capable of and to set his sights accordingly.

Because the essence of morality is rationality and because evasion is rationality's basic rival, an ever-present threat, the person committed to moral perfection must exert special vigilance against this vice. He must look for the particular forms of evasion that he is most prone to – particular methods of evasion, for instance, such as rushing decisions so as to avoid facing uncomfortable implications, or particular subjects on which he is most tempted to evade, such as decisions about spending or working. Perfection cannot be attained without candidly confronting all the lures that are liable to challenge one's resolve. Along similar lines, the proud person must be frank in evaluating his own moral performance. Kidding himself with flattering falsehoods will not help him to be truly virtuous or to reap virtue's rewards. Such a tack erects a competing aim – preservation of a pleasing self-image – that undercuts what is actually needed for a positive self-image, namely: honest self-assessment. Only that provides the foundation that can support self-esteem, long range. The proud person accepts that circumventing morality is not the means of advancing his life.[44]

Existential Demands

The point of establishing properly high standards is to enable a person to flourish. That will not be possible unless a person demands of himself the correlative action, however. Thus, the proud person must act according to his ideal; he cannot settle for less. He must employ the standard of moral perfection to guide his everyday choices so that practicing his principles becomes second nature.

Essentially, pride demands doing one's best. A person has done his best when he could have done no better; no available alternative would have

---

[44] Correspondingly, contrary to what some have suggested, pride poses no obstacle to seeking forgiveness on appropriate occasions. Among those who have suggested that pride is such an obstacle are Nancy Snow, "Humility," *Journal of Value Inquiry* 29 (1995), pp. 210–211, and Norvin Richards, *Humility* (Philadelphia: Temple University Press, 1992), pp. 15–17, 39–43. I discuss this in "The Practice of Pride," pp. 86–87. See that essay for further analysis of many of the issues raised in this chapter.

been morally superior. The basis for such a stringent demand is the absolutism of morality, which itself is grounded in the absolutism of reality. It is because reality is absolute that a moral code designed to guide human beings to exist in reality must be absolute. Nothing less than an unequivocal commitment to moral principles is safe, as long as a person's goal remains his life.[45]

In characterizing pride's demands in this way, I should caution against two possible misunderstandings. First, the phrase "I did my best," from frequent abuse, has acquired an aura of insincerity that has given the very concept of one's best an aura of artificiality. Often, the phrase is uttered to mean merely, "I wished this wouldn't happen" or "I did *something* to prevent it," when the person in question did not actually do his best. Moreover, "I did my best" is often said with an air of resignation, of shrugging acceptance of less than ideal outcomes. In fact, although a person can never completely control the outcomes of his actions, he does control his actions. And this is why a person's genuine best is crucial. Rand's point is that a person is fully accountable for what he chooses and that nothing less than his literal best will do, if he is to earn self-esteem.

The second possible misunderstanding is the risk of giving the impression that the other virtues are satisfied by doing less than one's best, but that *this* virtue requires more. On the contrary, in identifying pride as a necessary application of the virtue of rationality, Rand is observing that all virtues must be exercised perfectly – not selectively, not intermittently, not "to some extent" or "more often than not," but fully and consistently.[46] While pride explicitly highlights this fact, it is equally true of each of the other virtues. Correspondingly, in characterizing pride as demanding that a person do his best, I mean his "best" strictly, by a specific standard: rationality. My references to a person's best should not be mistaken for the hazy, hollow catchall claims often mouthed to cloak not doing one's best (which are all too familiar). What pride demands is one's best in a very precise sense: consistently making rational choices; the repeated refusal to evade.

To further understand the practical demands of pride, we should look more closely at the two concepts that Rand uses to explain this virtue: moral ambitiousness and perfection.

---

[45] Note that moral principles can become second nature only if a person practices them as absolutes. See Peikoff, *Objectivism*, p. 305.

[46] Cf. Peikoff, *Objectivism*, p. 305.

Moral Ambitiousness

Earlier, we observed that ambition consists in the systematic pursuit of challenging goals and of constant improvement in regard to such goals. The virtue of pride requires the adoption of this policy toward morality itself and thus toward the overall leading of one's life. The proud person seeks to make the most of himself and to get the best for himself – the best of those values that enable and enrich his happiness. A proud person has clearly identified values and principles and makes correspondingly high demands of himself. He is alert to the moral ramifications of decisions that crop up in his day, poised to act on his principles, because he realizes that such action offers the path to his happiness.

One important means of being morally ambitious is by deliberately heightening one's sensitivity to the moral dimensions of one's choices, working to become more attuned to the ways in which seemingly incidental choices can carry effects on one's values. Many people's "immoral" actions arise not so much from brazen defiance of morality as from not fully recognizing certain decisions as having moral ramifications. When this is the case, of course, a person's action is not truly immoral, since an innocent failure does not constitute immorality. Given that even honest mistakes carry negative effects on the agent's life, however, a person needs to avoid such mistakes. Inspecting one's options more thoroughly in order to recognize the significance of what one is doing, as moral ambitiousness demands, can encourage a greater number of life-advancing actions.

A further means of being morally ambitious lies in the refusal to coast or vegetate. The proud person will not resign himself to flaws in his character, but will work to spot and then overcome specific weaknesses.[47] Nor will the proud person resign himself to being "okay," or "pretty good;" his ambition impels him to be his best. In this effort, he seeks to continually strengthen his character. One means of doing this is by assigning himself specific projects of moral improvement. He might undertake a deliberate campaign to understand some aspect of morality more fully or to practice some virtue more consistently, for instance. Through introspection, a person can identify areas where his actions are not all that they could be and then adopt specific techniques for combating those weaknesses. Through such targeted campaigns, he can raise the bar of what he expects of himself and make himself a better person.

---

[47] Rand, "The Objectivist Ethics," p. 29.

It is important for a person to strengthen and expand his virtue in this way because of life's continuing basic demands. Human beings' needs to reason and to earn self-esteem are ongoing. Self-esteem is not a prize that can be acquired and then set aside, like a trophy that one can rest safely on a pedestal. Individuals continue to act every day. How a person acts establishes his character and the esteem in which he can hold it. Consequently, a person cannot afford passive drift. Allowing himself to indulge in periodic evasions or to be indifferent to whether he *is* evading would feed him negative evidence about his own commitment to his life and thereby weaken his self-esteem as well as his character. It would correlatively undermine his ability to achieve his happiness. Life *is* action; its sustenance depends on life-*advancing* action. For this reason, inertia is toxic. To the extent that a person is not taking such action and moving forward, thereby becoming better and stronger both in fact and in his rational self-appraisal, he is falling backward. Anything less than an ambitious course flirts with destruction. To put it slightly differently: Human life is an ambitious end; it can only be achieved through a correspondingly ambitious policy of rational moral action. This is what pride calls for.

Perfection

The other major concept important for understanding the practical demands of pride is perfection. Rand defines pride, recall, as a commitment to achieve one's moral perfection. Peikoff writes that "A proud man struggles to achieve . . . a state of full virtue . . . In regard to morality, nothing less than perfection will do."[48]

Perfection, according to the *OED*, is "the action, process, or fact of making perfect or bringing to completion." "Perfect," in turn, means "in the state proper to anything when completed . . . having all the essential elements, qualities or characteristics; not deficient in any particular . . . in the state of complete excellence; free from any flaw or imperfection of quality; faultless. But often used of a near approach to such a state . . ." We normally use "perfection" to designate the flawlessly complete satisfaction of a standard of value.[49] The perfect is the best possible in a given domain; it is the finest specimen or performance that it is rational to seek or expect. A perfect fit or a perfect score cannot be surpassed; perfect vision or a

[48] Peikoff, *Objectivism*, p. 303.
[49] Harry Binswanger, "The Possible Dream," *The Objectivist Forum* 2, no. 1 (Feb. 1981), p. 3.

perfect game (in bowling or baseball) represents the highest attainable level of excellence.[50]

Correspondingly, on Rand's conception, the morally perfect individual is not different in kind from "mere mortals." He is simply unusually consistent in abiding by his moral principles day in, day out. The perfect person is not infallible; his perfection is not an immunity or some sort of genetic guarantee against his ever taking an immoral action. (Nor is he a neurotic perfectionist, striving in vain to adhere to irrational standards.) Rather, a person is morally perfect when he lives up to moral principles as well as he can. He does his best, in the exact sense that I articulated earlier. The commitment to moral perfection consists in a person's conscious effort always to ascertain what he should do and then to do it.

To understand why Rand considers this ideal not only attainable but mandatory, it is critical to bear in mind the type of action that a person is to do his best *at*. She writes,

Man has a single basic choice: to think or not, and *that* is the gauge of his virtue. Moral perfection is an *unbreached rationality* – not the degree of your intelligence, but the full and relentless use of your mind, not the extent of your knowledge, but the acceptance of reason as an absolute.[51]

Because all virtues are forms of rationality, moral perfection, in its essence, consists in a single policy: the commitment to follow reason.[52] A person achieves moral perfection, Rand explains,

by never accepting any code of irrational virtues impossible to practice and by never failing to practice the virtues one knows to be rational – by never accepting an unearned guilt and never earning any, or, if one has earned it, never leaving it uncorrected – by never resigning oneself passively to any flaws in one's character . . . [53]

The thesis that morality demands perfection strikes many people as absurd. The prevalent conception of perfection presumes that it is an ideal beyond human reach; while some people might, at best, approach

[50] For a breakdown of several species of perfection such as aesthetic or obedientiary, see John Passmore, *The Perfectibility of Man* (New York: Charles Scribner's Sons, 1970), pp. 11–24.
[51] Rand, *Atlas*, p. 1059, emphasis in original.
[52] Peikoff, *Objectivism*, pp. 307–308.
[53] Rand, "The Objectivist Ethics," p. 29.

perfection, no one could actually attain it.[54] Part of the explanation of
this view lies in the widespread acceptance of altruism. An obligation of
self-denial for the sake of others *is* impossible to practice consistently,
since life depends on life-sustaining (i.e., egoistic) action. If a person
believes that sacrifice to others is what morality requires, therefore, he
will naturally conclude that perfection is a pipe dream.[55] Another part of
the explanation for this skepticism toward perfection lies in a distorted
conception of what perfection is. This is what I will focus on here.

The key to appreciating how perfection is possible is context. That
is, as with all the virtues, we must understand the requirements of perfection realistically. Typically, people's idea of perfection stems from the
image of a god for whom it is, by nature, impossible to act wrongly. In
popular imagination, this being never strays because he could not possibly stray. And this model is used as the benchmark for human perfection.
Such a paradigm is completely invalid, however. A standard of perfection
premised on imagined capacities attributed to fictional beings serves no
practical purpose. Indeed, it can actually inflict great damage, as I will
explain a bit later. The fact that we might dream up beings for whom
moral action is automatic and assured regardless of circumstances does
not render that the proper yardstick against which to measure actual
human beings. (If moral action were assured, it would not be truly moral
since it would not be volitional.) Reality, rather than fantasy, must guide
the construction of moral principles if those principles are to serve their
purpose.

On Rand's view, a person is perfect when he does his best. A person's best must be understood relative to his particular circumstances,
however. It cannot be identified apart from the individual's knowledge,
experience, abilities, resources, or options. Notice that many everyday

54 See, for instance, T. H. Green, *Prolegomena to Ethics* (Oxford: Clarendon Press, 1899),
    pp. 433–434; Henry Sidgwick, *Methods of Ethics* (Indianapolis: Hackett, 1981, 7th edition),
    p. 10, note 4, and p. 78; Immanuel Kant, *The Metaphysics of Morals*, in *Ethical Philosophy*,
    ed. Warner Wick (Indianapolis: Hackett, 1983), pp. 110–111; Marcia Baron, "On de-
    Kantianizing the Perfectly Moral Person," *Journal of Value Inquiry* 17 (1983), p. 283;
    Bertrand Russell, "A Free Man's Worship," *Why I am Not a Christian* (George Allen &
    Unwin, 1957), p. 109; Alan Gewirth, *Self-Fulfillment* (Princeton: Princeton University
    Press, 1998), pp. 59, 133, 182–183.
55 Peikoff observes that people will "need to find a loophole or breathing space" from
    certain moral doctrines. They will "need to smuggle into their days some self-preserving
    behavior. If one upholds an ethics of life, however, he does not need to smuggle in any
    speck of its opposite. One does not need breathing space – from breathing." *Objectivism*,
    pp. 309–310.

references to perfection recognize the importance of context. We do not dispute a test score as perfect simply because the test was not more diffi- cult (being pitched to 4th graders, for instance, rather than 12th graders). We do not deny that a person has perfect vision because other animals or machines can see something that he cannot. The perfect is construed as the best possible to a certain type of being in a certain situation, on a reality-governed conception of the possible.[56]

In order for perfection to be a proper ideal that can constructively guide a person's actions, it must be a goal that a person could actually achieve. Most of us readily understand that it would be unjust to hold a person to unattainable standards. Because individuals cannot completely control the outcomes of their actions, for instance, outcomes *per se* are not treated as the test of moral virtue. A person is not condemned as dishonest if he passes along false information that he responsibly believes to be true, just as a person is not faulted as lazy if physical illness prevents him from producing a great deal.[57] By the same logic, when considering the demands of pride, it is important to recognize that unattainable standards of perfection do not provide practical guidance. Thus, they are not what Rand is endorsing. She is explicit in rejecting such impossible ideals:

If, in a complex moral issue, a man struggles to determine what is right, and fails or makes an honest error, he cannot be regarded as "gray"; morally, he is "white." Errors of knowledge are not breaches of morality; no proper moral code can demand infallibility or omniscience.[58]

Morality can and should demand doing one's best, however. And the only rational interpretation of a person's "best" must account for such realities as who that person is, what he is doing, and the time he has in which to act. To know what pride demands, we must answer such questions as: How experienced is the agent? How knowledgeable and skilled in the relevant areas? How important is the task in question and how difficult is

---

[56] The ancient Greeks, to a considerable extent, shared a reality-bounded concept of per- fection. The ideal was understood in terms relative to human capacities. Men were not to pattern themselves after the gods, but to cultivate the excellences available to *their* natures. Georgios Anagostopoulos, "Ancient Perfectionism and its Modern Critics," *Social Philosophy and Policy* 16 (Winter 1999), pp. 200–201; Passmore, pp. 28ff.

[57] Note that a person who creates few goods could exercise the *virtue* of productiveness to an equal or greater degree than another person who creates more. Differences in their abilities and circumstances would explain the discrepancy in their moral characters.

[58] Rand, "The Cult of Moral Grayness," in *The Virtue of Selfishness*, p. 88. In a question period, Rand observes that "sainthood," in a secular sense, is "open to each man according to his ability." *Ayn Rand Answers*, ed. Mayhew, p. 131.

it? Is the person acting in an emergency? Under a deadline? Do other tasks warrant more time or care? Different answers will call for adjustments in the precise requirements of perfection in a given case. Yet the standard remains constant: unbreached rationality.[59]

The thesis that perfection is contextual may prompt concern that Rand makes perfection seem an appropriate demand only by diluting it. If moral perfection can be widely achieved, some might argue, she is actually weakening morality's rigor. This objection does not withstand scrutiny, however. To think that acknowledging the relevance of context slackens moral standards is to retain a fantasy-based standard of perfection. That is, if understanding moral perfection as achievable by heeding the realities of an individual's situation represents a lowering of moral standards, the implication is that the morally proper is that which lies beyond man's reach. It reflects the premise that an imaginary universe inhabited by morally infallible beings we concoct and call "perfect" is a more suitable basis for our moral standards than reality is. That makes no sense.

In fact, the contextual character of perfection is a reflection of the objectivity of moral principles. Values reflect relationships, as we explained in Chapter 2. Values are not intrinsic givens that issue categorical commands, blind to an individual's circumstances. Something is valuable (and correlatively, a particular action is virtuous) only when it plays an essentially life-furthering role in an individual's life. The recognition that perfection is contextual simply mirrors the fact that all moral principles are to be applied with reference to the realities of a given person's actual situation. Acknowledging the relevance of context does not weaken the demands of morality. On the contrary, it renders them truly attainable and thus preserves the goal of perfection as truly useful.

It is crucial to appreciate that a normative standard that is beyond our reach is not a genuine standard. For it fails to serve the function of a moral standard, which is to provide practicable instruction. Human beings need

---

[59] Montaigne commented on the folly of trying to achieve a perfection that is beyond us. Montaigne, *Essays* III.9, quoted in J. B. Schneewind, *The Invention of Autonomy – A History of Modern Moral Philosophy* (New York: Cambridge University Press, 1998), p. 48, note 17. Pelagius, the fourth-century British monk who was dismissed as a heretic, argued that God would only command perfection, as he does in Matthew's gospel, if perfection were possible for man. See Passmore, pp. 68–69. Benjamin Franklin intended to write a book showing that anyone who tried could achieve moral perfection. Edmund S. Morgan, "Poor Richard's New Year," *New York Times*, Dec. 31, 2002. Franklin himself deliberately set out to achieve perfection, we know from his *Autobiography* (New York: Collier Books, 1962), p. 82.

moral guidance designed for *us*, as our nature and circumstances allow us to be. Rejecting an unattainable standard such as noncontextual perfection does not mean the loss of something better or "higher" than contextualized perfection. It means replacing pseudo-guidance with authentic guidance. The need to take into account certain contextual variations reflects the practicality of morality – the fact that moral principles are to be implemented in action, *lived*. It is sensitivity to the facts of individuals' differing capabilities, knowledge, and so on, that allows morality to be followed and that means: It really should be. This is what Rand is insisting on. Peikoff has succinctly captured the ideal: The perfect person "does not demand of himself the impossible, but he does demand every ounce of the possible."[60]

The initially daunting proposal that pride demands perfection, then, will seem *too* demanding only if one employs an unrealistic conception of what perfection is. It is crucial to remember Rand's understanding of perfection: unbreached rationality. This reflects the fact that rationality is the essence of all moral action. And if perfection does consist in unbreached rationality, we can pose to those who object to this standard a simple question: What is to breach it? No one is doomed to act irrationally. Irrationality is not like an invasive virus that seizes control of a person's mind. The rationality of a person's thought and action is wholly within his hands. The demand for unbreached rationality means that whenever a person acts, based on everything he knows and on the best of his reasoning capacities at that stage in his development, he must do what is rational. He must act as his firsthand observation of reality and logical tracing of relationships among the relevant facts dictate. That is eminently doable. The basis for the objection that perfection is too demanding, therefore, collapses.

The larger point, again, is that perfection is not merely possible, but required. And this, again, rests on the absolutism of all moral principles. Since the facts that give rise to morality are absolute, morality's prescriptions are absolute. The same rationale for acting morally in the first place prescribes acting consistently morally, unfailingly morally. Because an individual's flourishing depends on fidelity to rational moral principles, any breach of such principles is self-defeating. "If man's life is the standard by reference to which virtue is defined," Peikoff writes, "then vice is not a temptation or a tolerable option, but a mortal threat. Moral

---

[60] Peikoff, *Objectivism*, p. 304.

imperfection, in any area, means movement toward destruction."[61] The
mandate for perfection is a natural implication of the factual and practical foundations of all moral prescriptions.

While this is the fundamental rationale for perfection, it is also important to recognize the damage wrought by the failure to treat perfection as
the proper ideal. The dismissal of perfection as impossible undermines
people's respect for morality. By supplying the readymade excuse, "you
can't really abide by morality's demands, since imperfection is inevitable,"
it contradicts the belief that one should abide by moral principles. After
all, no one can demand the impossible. The rejection of perfection as an
unattainable goal thus grants permission for immorality and contributes
to many people's sense that morality is a farce, a lot of talk amounting to
little of substance. The unseriousness about morality that is conveyed by
cavalierly instructing people both that they should be moral and that they
shouldn't be (because they allegedly can't be) is what actually weakens
moral standards.[62]

Finally, it should be clear that the case for perfection, like the case for
pride itself, is completely egoistic. A person has no reason to be morally
perfect other than to serve his own well-being. Rand alludes to this at
the end of her long description of pride, when she speaks of the "radiant
selfishness of soul which desires the best in all things, in values of matter and spirit, a soul that seeks above all else to achieve its own moral
perfection, valuing nothing higher than itself."[63] It is because a rational
person is committed to his own happiness that he will not sabotage his
interest by indulging in imperfection, that is, by violating the very principles that further his interest. By cheating morality, a person would only
cheat himself.

In a letter written in 1944, Rand remarks on the popular notion that
"idealism is not practical." In truth, she observes, "nothing is practical,
except idealism."[64] If one's ideals are valid, practicing those ideals is the
only way to achieve their ultimate objective. Reminding ourselves of the

[61] Peikoff, *Objectivism*, p. 304.
[62] Peikoff discusses related ideas in *Objectivism*, pp. 308–309. For more on the danger of
rejecting the ideal of perfection as well as further consideration of specific objections to
the possibility of perfection and of sources of hostility toward that thesis, see my "Morality
Without the Wink: A Defense of Moral Perfection," *Journal of Philosophical Research* 29
(2004), pp. 315–331.
[63] Rand, *Atlas*, pp. 1020–1021.
[64] *Letters of Ayn Rand*, p. 140.

practicality of morality, then, should help us to remember that moral perfection is not about genuflecting to a deity, to society, or to morality as an end in itself. Being perfectly moral is the essential path to living a human life. It is a person's path to values and happiness.

HUMILITY

Given this overall portrait of pride, we should briefly address an implication of Rand's view for another commonly touted virtue. Rand rejects the widely held doctrine that humility is a virtue.

According to the *OED*, humility is "the quality of being humble or having a lowly opinion of oneself." "Humble," in turn, means "having a low estimate of one's importance, worthiness, or merits; marked by the absence of self-assertion or self-exaltation; lowly; the opposite of proud." Historically, this has been the prevailing conception of humility and precisely what many urge as a virtue. Aquinas, for example, praised humility as a type of self-abasement that expels pride, suppresses confidence in oneself, and makes man submissive to divine grace.[65] Anselm saw humility as a person's recognition of his contemptible nature and as the knowledge and desire of his own abasement.[66] Ignatius Loyola held that humility reflects understanding oneself as a "wound and ulcer."[67] Today, Comte-Sponville praises humility for teaching us that even one's virtue "is nothing to be proud of."[68] The consistent theme is that a person should take no joy in himself.

In her journals, Rand describes humility as "the acceptance of one's moral imperfection, the willingness to be imperfect, which means: the indifference to moral values and to yourself, i.e., self-abnegation."[69] She

---

[65] Thomas Aquinas, *Summa Theologica* (London: Burns, Oates & Washbourne, 1932), pp. 216, 220, 226.

[66] Cited in Aquinas, pp. 228, 231.

[67] *The Spiritual Exercises of St. Ignatius Loyola*, trans. "A Benedictine of Stanbrook," ed. the Rev. E. Lattey, S. J. (St. Louis: B. Herder, 1928), p. 30.

[68] Comte-Sponville, p. 140. In a similar vein, Comte-Sponville applauds a person not taking himself too seriously, though he categorizes this as a manifestation of the virtue of simplicity, p. 151. Henry Sidgwick characterizes humility (which he is not endorsing as a virtue) as prescribing a low opinion of one's merits. *The Methods of Ethics*, 1874, 7th edition (Chicago: University of Chicago Press, 1962), p. 334. C. S. Lewis, in a discussion of pride and humility, claims that "the real test of being in the presence of God is that you either forget about yourself altogether or see yourself as a small, dirty object," *Mere Christianity*, p. 111.

[69] *Journals of Ayn Rand*, p. 649.

regards "self-abasement" as "the antithesis of morality."[70] Thus the opposition between humility and Rand's conception of pride – between humility and her entire moral theory, for that matter – is plain. It requires little comment. It *is* worth noting, however, that some who defend the virtue of humility today make it seem palatable by distorting what humility is. Norvin Richards, for instance, describes humility as "an inclination to keep one's accomplishments, traits, and so on in unexaggerated perspective."[71] Nancy Snow defines humility as "the disposition to allow the awareness of and concern about your limitations to have a realistic influence on your attitudes and behavior."[72] Such dispositions are unobjectionable, from Rand's perspective. So described, humility would simply be a form of honesty. Yet one cannot accurately label these dispositions as humility. The salient feature of the concept, reflected both in dictionary definitions and in longstanding usage, is not honesty, accuracy, realism, or self-knowledge, but the belief in or projection of oneself as base or unworthy. The fact that certain figures might have thought that a realistic self-estimate would be a low one does not, contrary to Richards, render realism the pivotal concern of humility.[73] The word's root, "humus," means ground or earth and is linked with the idea of baseness rather than with honesty.[74] And, true to its traditional spirit, Snow's ensuing arguments for cultivating humility reveal a less innocuous ideal, as she avers that "humility is occasioned by a recognition of the insignificance of your concerns."[75] Richards, likewise, proceeds to claim that "humility provides an understanding that one is not special, from the point of view of the universe . . ." (without explaining why the elusive "point of view of the universe" is the proper perspective from which to judge such matters).[76]

One might object that Rand is unjustified in characterizing humility as a *willingness* to be imperfect. Surely, one might suppose, those who have preached humility have stressed people's failings in order to urge a fiercer commitment to self-improvement. Yet the very concept of humility

---

[70] Rand, "Moral Inflation," in Gary Hull and Leonard Peikoff, eds., *The Ayn Rand Reader* (New York: Penguin, 1999), p. 103.

[71] Richards, *Humility*, p. 8.

[72] Snow, "Humility," p. 210.

[73] Richards makes that claim on p. 20.

[74] This root is given in the *OED* entry for "humble." Note that when Hume disparages humility as a monkish virtue, he is not knocking honesty in self-evaluation.

[75] Snow, p. 206.

[76] Richards, p. 189. He also maintains that his weakened notion of humility is not incompatible with feeling satisfaction or with "proper pride," p. 8 and 201 ff.

prevents such a logical inference. Rand's comment is borne out by the way in which the virtue of humility is typically advocated: emphasizing a person's defects to insist that defects are inescapable and are the truest indication of a person's basic nature. Both ideas are inimical to the achievement of self-esteem and, thus, to a commitment to self-improvement. For self-improvement requires self-esteem.

In advocating the rational pursuit of self-interest – in particular, in advocating moral ambitiousness – Rand hardly sanctions complacency about one's shortcomings. A person should never leave his transgressions uncorrected, we have seen her saying, nor resign himself to flaws in his character.[77] The claim that it is proper always to find faults and to emphasize faults is dishonest, however, and ultimately disabling. It is dishonest insofar as, by any rational measure, many individuals will not always be able to find fault in their performance. Given that a person's actions are not fated, we have no reason to assume a person's inevitable irrationality. Humility will thus sometimes require fabricating flaws rather than finding them.[78] Accepting the propriety of humility is disabling insofar as the conviction that one is doomed to deficiency will undermine a person's motivation to try to act as he should. Why bother, when failure is assured? This, I think, is the reasoning beneath Rand's claim that humility engenders indifference to moral values and acceptance of one's imperfection. If a person believes that, regardless of how earnestly he tries to follow morality's prescriptions, he will necessarily fall short, he will conclude, at the least, that perfection is beyond his reach. Resignation to his imperfection, in other words, is his only option.

(It is also worth noticing that humility is a natural handmaiden to altruism. For if a person thinks little of himself, as humility encourages, he will more readily deny his own desires and acquiesce to altruism's call to place others first. In the words of C. S. Lewis, "a really humble man . . . will not be thinking about himself at all."[79])

Finally, a quick clarification may be helpful. It is important not to confuse humility with modesty. Although the two terms are sometimes used interchangeably in casual conversation, modesty concerns the comparatively stylistic issue of how a person presents his accomplishments to others. In rejecting the ideal of humility, Rand is not applauding showoffs

---

[77] Recall the passage cited earlier from "The Objectivist Ethics," p. 29.

[78] As a child, I participated in the practice adopted by many Catholics of inventing sins to confess to a priest.

[79] Lewis, p. 114. See Rand, "Moral Inflation," pp. 103–104, for discussion of the relationship between humility and altruism.

or counseling immodesty. The self-esteem that pride makes possible is *self*-esteem and cannot be supplied by the esteem of others. Indeed, the person impelled to boast is often driven by a second-hander's lack of self and hopes of gaining a sense of self by impressing others. Although one could obviously explore the relationships among pride, humility, and modesty in great detail, the immediate point is simply that the ideal of humility, insofar as it urges self-abnegation, is antithetical to the pursuit of rational self-interest. Pride, in contrast, is vital to it.[80]

---

[80] For more on humility, see Smith, "The Practice of Pride," pp. 78–79 and 86–88. Peikoff discusses humility briefly in *Objectivism*, pp. 309–310.

Implications for Certain Conventional Virtues

Charity, Generosity, Kindness, Temperance

We have now examined the major virtues that Rand considers crucial to the life of a human being. These, together, shed considerable light on the kind of conduct and character that will distinguish the rational egoist. Nonetheless, because Rand's moral ideal is so at odds with long and widely entrenched views, it is natural to wonder about other kinds of actions traditionally regarded as virtues. Although I have commented on the implications of Rand's theory for a few of these (courage, forgiveness, mercy, humility), many others remain. Particularly because Rand does not claim that the moral virtues she identifies are exhaustive,[1] it will strengthen our understanding of her view to consider how certain additional kinds of action conventionally praised as virtues stand vis-à-vis Rand's theory. Space permits us to consider only a handful and one could explore even these in far greater depth than I will here. My aim is simply to indicate, based on what we have learned about Rand's reasoning, the implications for certain conventional virtues. Looking at these few, I hope, will provide insight into how she would evaluate others, as well. Because Rand's ideal person often strikes people as excessively self-absorbed, three of the traits I have chosen concern a person's relation with others: charity, generosity, and kindness. (Rand believes that the acceptance of altruism has created many confusions about proper human relationships.)[2] We will also consider a fourth, temperance, whose prudential character makes it seem a strong candidate to win egoism's blessing. I should note at the outset that

---

[1] Peikoff, *Objectivism*, p. 251.
[2] Rand, "The Question of Scholarships," in *The Voice of Reason*, p. 40, and "The Ethics of Emergencies," in *The Virtue of Selfishness*, p. 50.

Rand and Peikoff have said very little about this quartet in print. I will begin with charity because Rand says the most on this and we can glean some guidance from her discussion for the other candidates. Yet even charity receives only a fraction of the attention given to the major virtues in Galt's speech, "The Objectivist Ethics," and Peikoff's book. The reader should thus bear in mind that my analysis of these topics benefits from less explicit textual guidance than the discussion in previous chapters.

CHARITY

Charity, most broadly, means love – the Christian ideal of brotherly love in attitude and action toward one's fellow human beings. Comte-Sponville describes charity as love that has "become permanent and chronic, extended to the universality of men."[3] More narrowly and more commonly, these days, charity refers to almsgiving. It has come to refer primarily to giving aid to people in need. Loren Lomasky characterizes charity as "the disposition to be moved by and respond to distress"; a charitable act "intends the melioration of another person's misfortune."[4] The *Oxford English Dictionary* defines charity as "the Christian love of our fellow man"; "benevolence to one's neighbors, especially to the poor; the practical beneficences in which this manifests itself"; "that which is given in charity; alms."

Veneration of charity is longstanding and all but universal. (The ancient Greeks are a notable exception.) One finds commandments of charity in nearly all the world's religions.[5] The Jewish philosopher Maimonides held that once a stranger announces his need, one should give immediately.[6] The Dalai Lama preaches giving as one of the six "perfections" of Buddhism.[7] Almsgiving is one of the five pillars of Islam, as important as prayer or fasting.[8] In the gospel of Matthew, Christ implores his followers to sell their possessions and give to the poor.[9] Charity is often understood as the very heart of morality, the single most telling indicator

[3] Comte-Sponville, p. 285, quoting Vladimir Jankelevitch, *Traite des vertus* (Champs-Flammarion, 1986), vol. 2, p. 171.

[4] Loren Lomasky, "Justice to Charity," *Social Philosophy and Policy* 12 (Summer 1995), pp. 32, 34.

[5] A. Campbell Garnett, "Charity and Natural Law," *Ethics* 66, no. 2 (Jan. 1956), p. 117.

[6] Salamon, *Rambam's Ladder*, p. 77.

[7] Dalai Lama, "On Pride, Courage, and Self," in Hooke, ed., *Virtuous Persons, Vicious Deeds*, p. 436.

[8] Armstrong, *A History of God*, p. 143; *The Economist*, July 31, 2004, p. 58.

[9] Matthew 19: 21–24. *New American Standard Bible* (Carol Stream, IL: Creation House, 1973).

of a person's character. Aquinas wrote that "All the moral virtues are infused together with charity."[10]

While we do not invoke the term "charity" as much as in times past, that may well be because the message that a person should assist others in need has been so deeply absorbed. Mother Teresa is widely touted as the epitome of virtue precisely on the grounds of her charitable labors.[11] When the exhortations of the ethicist Peter Singer do not increase charitable contributions, they do increase guilt for many people because they accept the premise that they should be giving more to others. Volunteer work on behalf of the less fortunate is sufficiently esteemed to be increasingly required in American schools; "give something back" has become an unchallengeable mantra.

The propriety of charity is so widely taken for granted that it seems churlish to question it. Charity toward others is a large part of what being moral *means*, in many people's minds; its status as a virtue is regarded as self-evident. Correspondingly, one encounters few arguments for charity. Scripture and the examples provided by various gods and prophets are all the argument deemed necessary. As one ethicist has observed, "Christian thinkers did not feel it incumbent upon them to prove, on rational grounds, that there is a duty of universal brotherly love. That affirmation was based on revelation."[12] Christians have hardly been alone in this. To the extent that more specific arguments are sometimes offered, they seem patched-together afterthoughts rather than serious attempts to substantiate a controversial conclusion. We occasionally hear such rationales for charity as "what goes around comes around" – if I help others in their distress, others will help me, when I need it. Or: "There but for the grace of God go I." It is merely a matter of luck that some individuals are better off than others. Consequently, a person should not treat his prosperity as if it is rightfully *his*; everyone should share. "We're all God's children" and "We're all in this together" are similar attempts to prop up the assertion that charity is obligatory.

None of these rationales fares well under critical scrutiny; their vagueness, their sweep, and their invocations of divine will can all be easily punctured. Such rationales are not typically subjected to much scrutiny, however, as they are designed more to lend the appearance of logic than to furnish its reality. In most quarters, the contention that charity is

---

[10] Quoted in Garnett, p. 119.
[11] The order of nuns that she founded is called the Missionaries of Charity.
[12] Garnett, p. 119.

obligatory is not truly open for debate. Occasionally, one hears a more hard-nosed argument for charity: Those who are able should assist the poor so as to keep the unruly masses quiescent and thereby better preserve their own security and comfort. Rewards in a hereafter or from the Internal Revenue Service are also used to goad charitable giving. Such appeals are widely denounced, however, as entirely too self-interested to reflect the proper spirit of charity. Even if appeals to self-interest may help to motivate charitable giving, these are usually seen as external to the *morality* of charity. What is noteworthy is that for the most part, the ground invoked for charity is not the recipient's value to the giver. Most people would agree with Aquinas in insisting that virtuous charity demands action without expectation of reciprocity or any other type of repayment, on earth or elsewhere.[13]

Perhaps in recognition of the poor quality of the traditional arguments for charity, in recent decades, calls for charity have gravitated into the territory of justice. Appeals increasingly contend that charitable deeds are necessary to fulfill the demands of that virtue. This is not an entirely novel development; Augustine, Aquinas, Saint Ambrose, Saint Basil, Saint Gregory, Blaise Pascal, and John Locke, among others, have also linked the two.[14] The Hebrew word for charity, *tzedakeh*, is derived from the Hebrew word for justice.[15] Yet a shift in the very language in which we discuss charity testifies to the sharp inroads that this perspective has made in recent years. We rarely speak of "a charity case," for instance, as it is deemed demeaning to refer so baldly to a person's need as the basis for assistance. We speak, much more commonly, of giving something back, which suggests that a person took something and justice demands repayment. "Doing your fair share" similarly implies that justice governs helping others. People are encouraged to "give youth a second chance" by buying magazine subscriptions or raffle tickets they do not particularly desire on the grounds that everyone deserves a second chance and failing to offer one would be an injustice. Even the dominant mode of referring

[13] Stephen Pope, "Aquinas on Almsgiving, Justice and Charity: An Interpretation and Reassessment," *The Heythrop Journal* 32 (April 1991), p. 168. Tertullian was candid in describing the appeal to heavenly rewards as an incentive to charity: "How can you love, unless you are afraid not to love?" Quoted in Garnett, p. 119, from Tertullian, *Contra Marcion*, i. 27.

[14] Douglas Den Uyl, "The Right to Welfare and the Virtue of Charity," *Social Philosophy and Policy* 10 (Winter 1993), pp. 209 and Pope, p. 176. For differing interpretations of Aquinas's view of the relationship between justice and charity, see Den Uyl, pp. 206–207, and Pope, p. 170.

[15] Salamon, p. 34.

to the poor as the "less fortunate" implies that a person's prosperity is a matter of chance and it would be unfair of those who are "more fortunate" to be possessive about what mere fortune has happened to bestow on them. Doing so would unjustly punish a person for his bad luck.[16]

This backdoor defense of charity fails for the simple reason that charity and justice are distinct phenomena. I am not being charitable when I give a person something that is his (e.g., when I repay a loan). Justice concerns respect for a person's desert, whereas charity is a response to a person's need. Although desert and need can coincide (such that a person both deserves x and needs x), a person can also deserve something that he does not need (having earned it through hard work, despite being independently wealthy) and a person can need something that he does not deserve (having exerted no effort to earn it). (Moreover, note that any assimilation of charity with justice undermines many ethicists' conception of charity as an "imperfect duty" – morally virtuous, but a duty the performance of which is not on all relevant occasions obligatory and to which no correlative rights of others attach. The familiar claim is that the failure to make a charitable contribution on a specific occasion is not a failure of virtue, as long as the refuser does sometimes make such contributions. Indeed, charity is frequently cited as the paradigm of an imperfect duty. Although the entire concept of imperfect duties is problematic [an issue for another day], the point here is simply that if charity is required to fulfill the virtue of justice, it can no longer be considered an imperfect duty, since the demands of justice are not to be filled simply at the individual's discretion.)

One could obviously explore the arguments for charity and the nature and extent of its demands in much greater depth. For our purposes, the principal question is whether charity is compatible with rational egoism. And the answer to that is straightforward.

In the moral theory that Rand defends, a person's own flourishing is, properly, his highest end. Indeed, as I sketched in Chapter 2 and as I explain in much greater detail in *Viable Values*, it is only if a person embraces that end that the phenomenon of value arises for him and that a code of moral virtues assumes authority over him. Because values are the means and the substance of a person's flourishing, to surrender one's

---

[16] In her journals, Rand comments on the related phenomenon of people increasingly demanding not only to be given assistance, but to be treated as if they are the spiritual equals of their benefactors, regardless of whether they actually are. *Journals of Ayn Rand*, p. 435.

values to others solely on the basis of their need would be to abandon that end. Another person's well-being is not more important than one's own. Bill's well-being may be more important *to him* than it is to Tom; there is no reason why Tom should treat it as more important to Tom. The idea that another person's need in and of itself constitutes a morally compelling claim on a person's resources reflects the altruistic doctrine that self-sacrifice is our moral duty. This is exactly what Rand's theory rejects. Another person's need does not trump the propriety of pursuing one's own happiness. A rational dedication to achieving that end affords no basis for such an obligation to serve others.[17]

That said, egoism is not opposed to good will or to acting on good will. "The fact that a man has no claim on others (i.e., that it is not their moral duty to help him and that he cannot demand their help as his right)," Rand observes, "does not preclude or prohibit good will among men and does not make it immoral to offer or to accept voluntary, non-sacrificial assistance."[18] Helping others in need need not be a betrayal of self-interest. It is not a positive virtue, however; it is not an activity that a person should adopt as his regular, standing policy. Giving to every panhandler – or to every tenth panhandler or to every innocent victim of a natural disaster – would drain a person's resources and weaken his ability to achieve his happiness. Rand addresses the issue in an interview:

My views on charity are very simple. I do not consider it a major virtue and, above all, I do not consider it a moral duty. There is nothing wrong in helping other people, if and when they are worthy of the help and you can afford to help them. I regard charity as a marginal issue. What I am fighting is the idea that charity is a moral duty and a primary virtue.[19]

In referring to charity as a marginal issue, Rand is not denying the reality or the impact of poverty. Her point is that helping others is not what a person's life or what morality is *about*.[20] Under altruism, by contrast, charity *is* central, since some individuals' needs create other

---

[17] See Rand, "What is Capitalism?" p. 26.
[18] Rand, "The Question of Scholarships," p. 40.
[19] "*Playboy*'s Interview with Ayn Rand," 1964, p. 10. Rand asserts the same basic view in her *Journals* in 1949, p. 599. In a journal entry from 1946, she is more critical of it, but it is significant that there, Rand means "charity" to refer to aid given out of "contempt for an inferior," p. 435 ff. Given what she later said and published on the subject (which we will see more of, shortly), this rejection does not reflect her final view.
[20] More broadly, she rejects the "lifeboat ethics" that treats emergencies as the basis of moral principles. Rand, "The Ethics of Emergencies," p. 56, and *Ayn Rand Answers*, pp. 113–114.

individuals' duties, as morality revolves around serving others. (Thus the accolades for Mother Teresa.) Wrenching as others' suffering can be, however, emotions do not dictate virtue and vice. Rational self-interest is the proper measure of our actions. And by this standard, charity is not a virtue.[21]

The idea that it is inherently right to give to the needy or that charity is a policy to be practiced whenever possible contradicts Rand's conviction that an individual's own well-being should be his highest end. Not only is charity not a necessary means of furthering that end; often, it would directly undercut it by siphoning a person's means of furthering his happiness to others who do not warrant it. Treating one's own happiness as one's highest moral purpose does not entail indifference toward others, as egoism's opponents are eager to charge.[22] It does entail, however, that a person not subordinate any part of his own happiness to theirs.[23]

As Rand indicates in the passage cited, assisting a person in need can be consistent with egoism, under appropriate conditions. If one person cares about another who is in distress – as lover, friend, or fellow human being – it can be in his interest to offer help. A person can care about others without caring about all equally and without caring about another as much as about himself. Nonetheless, genuine concern is often manifested in action. Values, remember, are those things that one *acts* to gain or keep. Accordingly, "the practical implementation of friendship, affection and love," Rand writes, "consists of incorporating the welfare (the *rational* welfare) of the person involved into one's own hierarchy of values, then acting accordingly."[24] Even aid to strangers can sometimes be rational for an egoist, since strangers represent potential value, as experience abundantly teaches.[25] We have commented in previous chapters on the vast riches of knowledge and trade that a person can gain from other people. Beyond the myriad material and spiritual ways in which anonymous individuals can add such value to one's life – through their large

---

[21] In *Atlas*, Dagny, one of the heroes, observes that accusations that a person is unfeeling often actually object to the fact that the accused is just, p. 889. In effect, critics of the "unfeeling" seek to have the heart prevail over the head.

[22] See, for instance, Lomasky, p. 41.

[23] Rand, "The Ethics of Emergencies," p. 56, and *Letters of Ayn Rand*, p. 551.

[24] Rand, "The Ethics of Emergencies," p. 53, italics in original.

[25] See "The Ethics of Emergencies," pp. 53, 54. Ideally, one would know how the needy person reached his present condition and his likelihood of making constructive use of the assistance, but there is not always time to acquire such information.

and small inventions, discoveries, artistic creations, skills, inspiring traits of character, and so on – others' very existence can offer value. Knowing the endless variety of specific values that other persons make possible and their capacity to experience in all the ways that we do, we sometimes derive a welcome sense of camaraderie from the sheer awareness of similar beings' existence.

Because Rand speaks directly to the conditions under which charity is appropriate, I quote her at length:

> The proper method of judging when or whether one should help another person is by reference to one's own rational self-interest and one's own hierarchy of values: the time, money or effort one gives or the risk one takes should be proportionate to the value of the person in relation to one's own happiness.
>
> To illustrate this on the altruists' favorite example: the issue of saving a drowning person. If the person to be saved is a stranger, it is morally proper to save him only when the danger to one's own life is minimal; when the danger is great, it would be immoral to attempt it: only a lack of self-esteem could permit one to value one's life no higher than that of any random stranger. (And, conversely, if one is drowning, one cannot expect a stranger to risk his life for one's sake, remembering that one's life cannot be as valuable to him as his own.)
>
> If the person to be saved is not a stranger, then the risk one should be willing to take is greater in proportion to the greatness of that person's value to oneself. If it is the man or woman one loves, then one can be willing to give one's own life to save him or her – for the selfish reason that life without the loved person could be unbearable.[26]

The point is, egoism does not condemn helping others. When a greater value (greater to the agent's objective well-being) can be advanced by offering help, a person *should* help.[27] What egoism does reject is self-sacrifice: placing a lesser value above a greater one.[28] Because of the great value that one person can have to another and the correlative place that that person can occupy in another's hierarchy of values, however, it would be a mistake to assume that helping others will always be a sacrifice. In this vein, Rand would dispute Neera Badhwar's contention that those gentiles who rescued Jews from the Nazis were necessarily acting altruistically.[29]

---

[26] Rand, "The Ethics of Emergencies," p. 52.
[27] See more of her discussion of attempting to save a person one loves, "Ethics of Emergencies," pp. 51–52.
[28] This definition of sacrifice is from Peikoff, *Objectivism*, p. 232.
[29] Neera Kapur Badhwar, "Altruism versus Self-Interest: Sometimes a False Dichotomy," *Social Philosophy & Policy* 10 (Winter 1993), pp. 90–117. Badhwar actually claims that they were acting both altruistically and egoistically (p. 94), but this view faces obvious problems. Although a person could certainly act in ways that benefit both himself and others, he cannot act simultaneously to sacrifice his interest and to advance his interest.

Rand would readily acknowledge that some may have acted from altruistic motivations, but such actions could have also been, for other rescuers, selfish. Some rescuers might, egoistically, have been risking lesser values for greater values – great as those lesser values were in this case (namely, their own lives). An act's altruism depends on its end's *relative* status in the agent's hierarchy of values, not on the value that that end has to most people or even on the value that it normally has to the person in question. The fact that a person normally values a certain end to a particular extent does not mean that he always will or that, morally or rationally, he always should.[30]

Peikoff succinctly summarizes Rand's position:

Any action one takes to help another person . . . must be chosen within the full context of one's own goals and values. One must determine the time, the effort, the money that it is appropriate to spend, given the position of the recipient in one's evaluative hierarchy, and then act accordingly.[31]

Finally, because the term "charity" is sometimes used to mean assistance provided on the basis of need *alone*, I should underscore that when assistance to others is permissible, by Rand's code, it is not the recipient's need *per se* that warrants it. This should be plain from all the passages we have cited. Moreover, in a 1945 journal entry, Rand observes that private, voluntary, nonaltruistic help to another person

works well *only* when the recipient of help is a worthwhile person (essentially an "action" person) who is temporarily in need, purely through accident, not through his own nature. Such a person eventually gets back on his own feet and feels benevolence (or gratitude) toward the one who helped him. But when the recipient is essentially a "passive" person, chronically in need through his own nature, the help of another gets him deeper into parasitism and has vicious results: he hates the benefactor. Therefore, here's the paradox about "helping another": *one can help only those who don't actually need it.*[32]

A passage in *Atlas* echoes this perspective. Late in the novel, when Cherryl apologizes to Dagny for her previous denunciation of her, Dagny is charitable (as evidenced through several of her words and actions that

[30] Life is not an intrinsic good, on Rand's view, and valuing one's life does not require maintaining it under all conceivable circumstances. For further discussion of the relationship between one's life as the source of all values and the logic of risking or destroying that life, see *Viable Values*, chapters 4 and 5, especially pp. 136–145.
[31] Peikoff, *Objectivism*, p. 238.
[32] *Journals of Ayn Rand*, pp. 270–271, from 1945, italics in original. Also see Rand, "The Question of Scholarships," p. 41.

night) not simply because Cherryl is needy. Cherryl speaks first:

"That I happen to suffer, doesn't give me a claim on you."

"No, it doesn't. But that you value all the things I value, does."

"You mean . . . if you want to talk to me, it's not alms? Not just because you feel sorry for me?"

"I feel terribly sorry for you, Cherryl, and I'd like to help you – not because you suffer, but because you haven't deserved to suffer."[33]

The larger lesson is that a person's need may be the immediate *occasion* for assistance, but that aid will be rational only if the recipient has value to the agent and giving the aid requires no sacrifice. Lending help in response to a person's need can be appropriate, but need by itself never makes it appropriate.

GENEROSITY

A generous person gives in excess of what morality or custom requires.[34] Unlike justice, generosity is not a matter of giving others their due. As Joseph Kupfer observes, a general condition of generosity is that one provide "a benefit which is not due another because of duty, obligation, or desert."[35] Correspondingly, I am not generous when I repay a debt. Similarly, when I fail to receive what another person would have been generous in giving me, no injustice has taken place; I have not been deprived of anything that I am entitled to.[36] As Comte-Sponville somewhat loosely characterizes the difference, in a case of justice, the recipient is given what is *his*; in a case of generosity, one gives what is truly one's own.[37]

Although we primarily associate generosity with material values (evidenced in picking up the tab for dinner or offering tickets to a friend without asking him to pay for them, for instance), people can be generous in other ways, as well, such as with their time, their effort, their patience, praise, or credit. One can be generous by creating an opportunity for another person or in how one judges another person.[38] In *Atlas*, Rand refers to Hank's generosity in his reluctance to attribute the worst

[33] Rand, *Atlas Shrugged*, p. 888.

[34] Wallace, *Virtues and Vices*, pp. 131, 134.

[35] Joseph Kupfer, "Generosity of Spirit," *The Journal of Value Inquiry* 32 (1998), p. 359.

[36] Lester Hunt, *Character and Culture*, pp. 56–57.

[37] Comte-Sponville, p. 86.

[38] Wallace distinguishes three species: economic generosity, generous heartedness, and generous mindedness, p. 132. Kupfer examines these in his piece.

motives to Lillian.[39] Whatever its particular form, the distinctive mark of generosity is, according to the *Oxford English Dictionary*, "readiness or liberality in giving; munificence." Essentially, generosity consists in giving more than the recipient has reason or right to expect or demand. Indeed, this is how Rand characterizes generosity in a letter: as a "gift or favor greater than the friend involved could, in reason, expect."[40] (Notice that while an act of charity might also be generous, a generous act is not necessarily an instance of charity. Generosity hinges on what one person gives another – whether it is more than the recipient could reasonably expect. Charity, by contrast, involves assistance given for a particular reason: in response to a person's suffering or need.)

From the Greeks to the present day, generosity has been widely welcomed and encouraged, its propriety largely taken for granted.[41] The very term has become an honorific; to describe a person as generous is itself to praise him. The question for us is: Can generosity make sense for a rational egoist? And can Rand regard generosity as a virtue?[42]

Generosity is usually thought to be a reflection of altruism. (Given widespread acceptance of altruism, this no doubt explains its honored status.) Adam Smith, for instance, asserts that "we never are generous except when in some respect we prefer some other person to ourselves, and sacrifice some great and important interest of our own ..."[43] Descartes maintains that the virtue of generosity arises, in part, from a person's realization that nothing is truly his.[44] Contemporary authors follow suit. Comte-Sponville matter-of-factly writes that self-interest disqualifies an action from being generous and that to give when one loves is not a virtue.[45] Wallace's discussion of generosity takes for granted that generous people are making sacrifices.[46] Kupfer stresses that a generous person's concern is with *others'* well-being; a generous person must give up a

---

[39] *Atlas Shrugged*, p. 466.

[40] *Letters of Ayn Rand*, p. 548.

[41] Aristotle presents generosity as one of the virtues that characterizes the ideal man. Plato does not devote much direct attention to it, but his passing references to generosity are positive.

[42] I benefited from very helpful discussion of these questions with Leonard Peikoff.

[43] Adam Smith, *A Theory of Moral Sentiments*, 1759 (Indianapolis: Liberty Classics, 1976), p. 313, quoted in Tibor Machan, *Generosity – Virtue in Civil Society* (Washington, DC: Cato Institute, 1998), p. 19.

[44] *The Philosophical Writings of Descartes*, trans. J. Cottingham, R. Stoothoff, and D. Murdoch (New York: Cambridge University Press, 1985–91), vol. 1, p. 384, cited in Comte-Sponville, p. 94.

[45] Comte-Sponville, pp. 95–97.

[46] Wallace, p. 150.

real value, and "the more we value what we give, the more generous we are."[47] The generous person gives at his own expense and places others above himself.[48]

Such a conception of generosity is, clearly, anathema to Rand. She would never endorse generosity as an instrument of altruism. The standard by which to assess the propriety of any generous deed is the same as that for evaluating all action: rational self-interest. By that standard, however, it can frequently be appropriate for a person to be generous. If a person can afford to give a friend more than the friend could reasonably expect and, by so doing, contribute to the well-being of something that enhances *his* (the agent's) well-being, rationality would readily approve. As long as a generous action is consistent with rationality and with all of the virtues and as long as it is consistent with the agent's hierarchy of values such that it is not a sacrifice, generosity can be perfectly appropriate.

To be a little more concrete, suppose a woman can afford to lend college tuition to a worthy nephew who she esteems a great deal. Doing so can offer value to *her*. To the extent that she values her nephew, she wishes for his well-being. Whether she enjoys conversation with him, shared interests or hobbies, or simply the knowledge that this "good guy" is out there in the world, she benefits from the flourishing of this person who she cares about. If she is in a position to nonsacrificially contribute to that flourishing, it makes eminent sense for her to contribute.

Consider another case: a voice teacher working to prepare his most talented, most promising, and most devoted student for an important recital. We can easily imagine the teacher being generous with his time, staying beyond the scheduled sessions to work with the student, without its being a sacrifice. If he greatly values the student's development and his giving his best possible performance and if he can spare the resources on a given afternoon to go overtime, it can be in his interest to give the student more attention than the student could reasonably demand or expect.

Turn up the stakes a bit: Suppose that this is the most promising student the teacher has ever had and he has far greater hope for this student's potential than he has had for any, in over forty years of vocal instruction. Moreover, he adores this student and finds working with him immensely rewarding. In a case such as this, when, again, the teacher can nonsacrificially spare the time and effort, he *should* be generous. His own values

---

[47] Kupfer, pp. 357, 358.
[48] Kupfer, pp. 359, 361.

call for it. Generosity in such a case would be an expression of integrity. Writing in a slightly different context, Rand makes this idea plain:

The virtue involved in helping those one loves is not "selflessness" or "sacrifice," but *integrity*. Integrity is loyalty to one's convictions and values; it is the policy of acting in accordance with one's values, of expressing, upholding and translating them into practical reality.[49]

When a person is in a position to be generous with someone whose success he values more than he values alternative uses of the relevant resources, to fail to be generous would be hypocrisy. It would betray his values and abandon the rational pursuit of his happiness. Bear in mind that generosity must be consistent with a person's rational hierarchy of values. The sheer fact that I value another person a great deal does not mean that I must make sacrifices for him; sacrifices are not what is in question. When a sacrifice would not be involved, however, and when a person who truly values another person's success at some pursuit can afford to give assistance and thereby further his own values, integrity demands that he do so. On what grounds should he withhold what he can offer? On what grounds would it be rational, if he truly values that person in the way I have described? How would doing so be in his interest? A person should help another when, in the full context, his values and his life are thereby promoted.[50]

At the same time, generosity is not always appropriate. The condition that generosity be nonsacrificial is critical. One should never give to others (even others whom one sincerely values) at one's own expense.[51] A person can also be "too generous" by bestowing gifts on people who are unworthy, such as individuals who are not appreciative or who squander gifts or whose track record indicates serious vices. Giving to such people is wrong precisely because it surrenders higher values for lesser ones. The larger point is simply that, by the standards of rational egoism, generosity is not an unqualified good.[52]

---

[49] Rand, "The Ethics of Emergencies," pp. 52–53, italics in original.
[50] Peikoff, *Objectivism*, p. 239.
[51] Even some advocates of a virtue of generosity acknowledge that it is not virtuous for a person to give others so much that he jeopardizes his ability to pay his debts, for instance. Hunt, pp. 71–72.
[52] Aristotle's recognition of this is indicated by his conception of what generosity *is*, as he maintains that generosity consists in giving "to the right people, the right amounts, at the right time . . ." *Nicomachean Ethics*, trans. Irwin, 1120a25. In her journals, Rand describes Rearden as "torn by the naivete of his own generosity," implying that he was at times too generous toward Lillian and his family. *Journals of Ayn Rand*, p. 405.

Notice that when generosity is appropriate, it is so because of the *giver's* values. Also note that the propriety of generosity turns not simply on the extent of a person's resources, but on the relative values of his resources and of the person or project he contemplates assisting.[53] Even a person who has very little can, in some circumstances, rationally be generous. Consider an extreme case: prisoners in a concentration camp, given only the most meager provisions, who might share a bit of bread or soup with their companions. Clearly, such individuals could benefit from the nourishment themselves, yet their acts are not necessarily immoral, by an egoistic code. If a person deeply values the person with whom he shares his food, he may gain more than he gives from the act of generosity. The generous person might be more concerned about his friend's well-being (physical or emotional) at a given time than about what the food could do for himself. He might realize that his friend is more frail than he is or that the gesture could boost his friend's morale ever so slightly at a critical time. He might simply wish to do whatever he can to express his abiding affection because of how much he values that person. The point is, whether a given act of generosity is rationally self-interested depends on the relative value of what the giver gains and what he gives up. Generosity should never be a sacrifice, under egoism, but poverty will not necessarily make it a sacrifice.

My larger contention, then, is that on Rand's theory, generosity is neither a virtue nor a vice. While Rand would not sing unqualified praise for generosity, neither would she condemn it as always wrong. Whether it is proper to extend generosity in a given case depends entirely on what one is giving, to whom one is giving, and why one is giving. Essentially, generosity is appropriate when it reflects the rational pursuit of self-interested values. Contrary to popular assumptions, generosity need not and should not be a sacrifice.[54] If a person has enough to share with others and if doing so advances his values, self-interest will actually demand generosity. The belief that it is virtuous to adopt a standing policy of giving others more than they can reasonably expect, however, reflects the altruistic doctrine that others' well-being is more important than one's own. Such a policy finds no foundation in rational egoism and is directly antithetical to it. Like the doctrine that others' need creates an obligation of

---

[53] Aristotle similarly holds that generosity does not depend on the amount given; the person who gives less can be more generous than the person who gives more. *Nicomachean Ethics* 1120b10.

[54] *Letters of Ayn Rand*, p. 548.

charity, following it would deplete the giver's resources and sacrifice his well-being.

Some might object that this account distorts what generosity is. Doesn't generosity consist of offering a gift without seeking something in return? If Rand sanctions generosity only when the giver gets something out of it, she is converting generosity into a trade. But how could a *trade* be generous? That seems too calculated for true generosity.

Rand does endorse generosity only when it represents a rational trade. This is problematic, however, only if one assumes that generosity must be sacrificial. Offering a value to a person in exchange for another value is precluded from being generous on the presumption that generosity must result in a net loss. Yet that assumption finds no basis in our ordinary concept of generosity: "readiness or liberality in giving," as the *OED* reports. A person could give others more than they have reason to expect while still gaining value from doing so. The insistence that he cannot is baseless. Bear in mind that the return can take many forms – intellectual, emotional, the pleasure of a person's company, the deepening of a relationship. Alex might generously treat Roger to an expensive ticket to a football game because he would enjoy watching the game with the committed, knowledgeable fan that Roger is. An exchange needn't be material to be genuine (which is not to imply that material rewards are inappropriate or inferior). The possible returns are as varied as the vast range of things that are objectively valuable in individuals' lives. What Rand insists, however, is that a person committed to his happiness should treat his values *as* values and thus not be cavalier in disposing of them. It would make no sense for an egoist to spend values without thinking that he will gain something from doing so. To surrender the very things that sustain him without expectation of equal or greater value in return would be treason to his happiness, a failure to pursue his happiness as his highest goal. As Peikoff observes, in the Objectivist ethics, virtue "consists in creating values, not in giving them away."[55]

The objector might protest that he does not assume the necessity of self-sacrifice, but merely that a truly generous action is not done for the sake of the agent's gain. That is, a person need not intend to lose values, in order for his action to be generous. But he does have to act from a primary concern for the recipient's well-being rather than for his own.

This response does not rescue the objection, however. Its claim acquires superficial credibility thanks to an ambiguity in the phrase "for

---

[55] Peikoff, *Objectivism*, p. 239.

the sake of." Admittedly, a generous act is often occasioned by the desire to help another person, yet everything that a rational egoist does should be, in the grand scheme, *for the sake of* his happiness. We have no grounds for limiting the intent that motivates a generous action to the desire to benefit others rather than oneself. Even on this understanding of the objection, in other words, it begs the question. Why cannot a generous deed be done for what is ultimately the agent's well-being? That an agent gets something out of a generous action – or even that he does it because he believes that he will get something out of it – does not eradicate its generosity. It does not erase the fact that he is giving another person more than that person can reasonably expect. Why suppose that it must? That is what needs to be shown rather than merely assumed.

Bear in mind that the pursuit of individual well-being is not a zero-sum game, in Rand's view. (Recall our discussion of this in Chapter 2.) Correspondingly, self-interested generosity does not entail expense to the recipient (which *would* be at odds with the ordinary meaning of generosity). Generosity can be "win-win." In Rand's view, it should be. But the main point is, it is unfair to exclude the egoist from the ranks of the generous by fiat. If generosity is liberality in giving, then generosity is not incompatible with rationally egoistic motives.

A different objection might arise from my claim that generosity can be misdirected and that a person can be too generous. If a recipient's being unworthy can render generosity toward that person inappropriate, as I claimed, then generosity sounds like a form of justice and the gifts involved, the kind of thing that a person can deserve or not deserve. Yet I (like other authors on the topic) stressed that generosity concerns giving something other than what a person deserves.[56] Which is it? And if generosity means giving a person more than he deserves, shouldn't it be rejected as unjust?[57]

A simple distinction should dispel these confusions. A recipient should be worthy of generosity, but that is not the same thing as deserving it. Being worthy is akin to being eligible, being a qualified candidate to receive certain treatment, but it is not the equivalent of having a claim to that treatment. When a person deserves a reward or punishment, he can reasonably expect it, for it is the rational response to his conduct or character. When a person is the recipient of another person's generosity,

---

[56] Kupfer actually claims that generosity can deflect a person away from fairness, p. 359.
[57] Note that this is not the definition of generosity that I have employed.

however, that is not so. Rather, he has had good fortune. When you are generous, it has been said, you are making another person lucky.[58]

The victim of injustice – the person who is not treated as he deserves – has a valid complaint. He might have run a reputable business or achieved a solid character, for instance, and thereby earned certain opportunities. By not being evaluated objectively or treated accordingly, however, he is deprived of some of the values he has earned. Those who judge him or treat him unjustly deny him rewards that he did have reason to expect. The "victim" of the absence of others' generosity is not in a comparable position; he did not have reason to expect to be treated differently. Although, on Rand's view, generosity should be a response to *something*, then (namely, the value that the generous person finds in the recipient), it is not a response to desert. Thus, any apparent reduction of generosity to justice or tension between generosity and justice is merely that: apparent. Sometimes, acts of generosity toward a particular person will be unjust, but they are not necessarily so.

Notice that when the virtue of justice condemns treating a person better than he deserves, it is condemning treating a person better than is appropriate. When contemplating generosity, however, one is not necessarily contemplating treating a person better than is appropriate. While justice concerns desert, desert is not the salient consideration for generosity. On Rand's view, generosity can be permissible when, within the bounds of justice, while respecting individuals' deserts, a person does more for another person than can normally be expected; he gives something extra. (The other conditions on the propriety of generosity still apply.) This does not entail treating that person better than is appropriate, however, as certain forms of injustice do. (Other forms of injustice treat a person worse than he deserves.) Again, justice is measured by the barometer of desert; generosity is not.[59]

Before leaving generosity, we should briefly consider the positive aura that generosity enjoys. Generosity often seems laudable, I think, because it suggests a spirit of benevolence or a sense of life's bounty or

---

[58] Twyla Tharp, *The Creative Habit* (New York: Simon & Schuster, 2003), p. 136.

[59] Also note an ambiguity in everyday references to a person's not deserving something. Sometimes, we mean by this that his getting it is incompatible with justice; other times, merely that he neither deserves it nor does not deserve it, that it is not the sort of thing that a person can deserve, that justice does not govern the issue. It would not be wrong to give him the good in question, but justice does not demand it. Failing to distinguish these two senses can contribute to confusion about the relationship between justice and generosity.

a noncompetitive attitude toward others. A common impulse, when a person enjoys some significant success, is to share the wealth, either literally or figuratively. (In *Atlas*, Rearden, flush from the first pouring of his new metal, agrees to give his brother Philip a large check for a charity for which Philip is soliciting.)[60] Such benevolent attitudes can be completely consistent with rational egoism. A generous act does not always reflect such premises, however; it can also be motivated by less benign ends. A person might act generously to gratify an immediate urge to impress another person, for instance, and thereby betray his considered ranking of values. He might act generously to alleviate altruistic guilt. Although generosity often springs from emotions that are well-founded, because of the large role that emotions can play in prompting generosity, we must be especially on guard not to allow emotionalism to govern our exercise of generosity. On Rand's view, I should hardly need to remind us at this stage, reason must always stand at the decision-making helm.

Rand could also understand, I think, why the ungenerous person – the person who is stingy with his values, extremely reluctant ever to part with more than is absolutely necessary to meet the demands of justice – strikes most of us as deficient. Although it does not strictly entail it, such a posture suggests a failure to appreciate the true value of things. This person may be possessed by his possessions[61] or he may view money, for instance, as an intrinsic good to be hoarded rather than as a means of enhancing his experience. He apparently fails to realize that in sharing his values with others under certain conditions, he can enrich *his* life. Occasions on which a person should have been generous but failed to be typically reflect a mistaken judgment about the value of things and, correlatively, about how to serve his own happiness. When it is properly exercised, generosity manifests a healthy understanding of what the relative value of one's various possessions, material and spiritual, *is*. This is what the ungenerous person appears to lack.

Whatever genuine defects the ungenerous person suffers from, they do not warrant the conclusion that generosity is a virtue. Rather, for a rational egoist, generous action is sometimes appropriate and sometimes not. Some might object that since morality's demands are contextual, on Rand's view, this should be no obstacle to generosity's qualifying as a virtue. From the fact that a person should not tell the truth to an inquisitive Nazi, for instance, Rand does not conclude that honesty is not a

---

[60] Rand, *Atlas Shrugged*, p. 42.
[61] Comte-Sponville, p. 93.

virtue. This objection fails to appreciate the profoundly different kinds of considerations that govern the two cases, however. Barring emergencies, a person should be honest. The same applies for all of the fundamental virtues. By contrast, it is not the case that, barring emergencies, a person should be generous. The propriety of giving a person more than he could reasonably expect depends, in all cases, on more fine-grained facts about the particular individuals and relative values involved.

The principal thing to understand about generosity in relation to Rand's moral code, again, is that the propriety of generosity (like that of all kinds of action) turns on its service to a person's overall, rational interest. More specifically, it is governed by the virtue of integrity. This does not mean that integrity will dictate every act of permissible generosity or that every case of permissible generosity will turn out to be mandatory generosity. To a considerable extent, a person may exercise discretion in offering generosity. This discretion is bounded by the parameters of integrity, however. Every choice to extend or withhold generosity must be consistent with the agent's values and thus, with integrity. I will address the role of integrity further when I discuss kindness. The chief point here is that if a person values certain things, he must act like it, treating them in a way that reflects their position in his hierarchy of values. This applies to values that are optional, such as one's love of music or of a particular person, no less than to fundamental values. Accordingly, a rationally self-interested person sometimes should be generous. It is not the case, however, that he should cultivate liberal giving as a positive virtue or a default policy toward all comers. Doing so would elevate others' well-being above his own. To treat generosity as a virtue would betray the paramount value of one's own happiness.

KINDNESS

Another widely accepted virtue concerning a person's interactions with others is kindness. While kindness can sometimes be expressed through charitable or generous actions, kindness is broader in that it does not necessarily involve the provision of assistance or gifts.[62] To ensure a clear idea of what kindness refers to, I begin with a variety of examples.

It can be kind to do a favor for a person, such as offering him a ride to the airport, feeding his pets while he is away, running an errand to save

---

[62] On the interpretation of charity as love, charity and kindness are sometimes treated interchangeably.

him time. It can be kind to remember a person's birthday with cards or
calls, to send a get well note when someone is sick, to inquire about how
a person is coping with a loss not only when it first occurs, but some time
afterward (and after the customary period for polite inquiries). Sometimes, words of understanding are kind; other times, kindness is reflected
in what a person does not say, as when he is tactful in presenting a delicate topic or when he is discreet in sharing sensitive information with
others (absent any explicit pledges of confidentiality). Simply listening,
"being there" for a friend can be kind in certain circumstances,[63] as can
extending a warm welcome to a new neighbor or worker or acting to put
a person at ease (e.g., to make the lone nonfamily member at a holiday
gathering feel less the outsider or, at a party, to bring the hesitant person
on the margins into a conversation). It is kind of a host to accommodate
a weekend guest's needs or preferences by setting out the towels or night-
light or getting in the guest's preferred coffee or cream. Similarly, it is
kind of a boss to refrain from making the usual demands on a worker who
is going through a difficult divorce or to offer time off to a worker who
is celebrating a major event in his personal life. A person can be kind in
incidental interactions with strangers, such as by offering to let a person
with fewer groceries go ahead of him in the checkout line, holding the
door for a person juggling packages though he is still several yards away,
or offering his cell phone to a person having a hard time with the land
lines in an airport. Although certain such acts may seem to fall under
common courtesy, in many circumstances, they are positively kind. (I say
more on the relationship to courtesy in note 65.)

The common element that distinguishes these as cases of kindness is
one person's considerateness for another. The kind person is sensitive; he
is thoughtful about what another person's experience is like, and he acts
to enhance that person's experience. Wallace describes kindness as consisting in "a certain sort of direct concern for the happiness and well-being
of others, together with a sensitivity to the situation of other people."[64]
According to the *Oxford English Dictionary*, "kind" means "having a gentle,
sympathetic or benevolent nature; ready to assist, or show consideration
for, others." Kindness, in turn, is "a feeling of tenderness or fondness;
affection, love." I would suggest a slight modification, however, because
these do not fully capture the way we ordinarily use the term. The kind
person is not merely "ready to assist"; he does. When we describe a person

[63] Hursthouse, p. 118.
[64] Wallace, pp. 143–144.

as kind, we mean not simply that he feels a certain way toward others, but that he does something about it. Sitting around feeling affection is too passive. Kindness involves action. The action could be extremely modest; it might consist simply in saying a few encouraging words. Yet the person whose sympathetic feelings for others do not issue in correlative actions is not truly kind. He fails to deliver the very thing that makes kindness valuable. (It is also worth remembering that a person's feelings are not subject to his direct control and are thus not suitable objects of moral obligation. If kindness were simply a type of feeling, it could not be a moral virtue.)

On these grounds, then, I will take kindness to mean acting out of consideration for another person's well-being, or being considerate of another person by acting to assist or cheer him. While assisting and cheering can assume many forms, these capture the essential elements that unite all cases of kindness. When a person is kind to another, he acts, out of consideration for what it is like to be the other person, to help him or to brighten his experience in some way, however modest. The scale of the gesture is not as important as the fact that a gesture is made out of concern for the other person's well-being. Even extremely minor acts can be kind and can be greatly appreciated by the recipient.[65]

Before proceeding to assess the place of kindness within egoism, it may be useful to point out the differences between kindness and charity and generosity, since their capacity to coincide in the same action is potentially confusing. Unlike charity, kindness is not restricted to giving aid and is not necessarily a response to another person's need. Kindness can spring from love or affection or a desire simply to brighten a person's day, even when the kind person perceives no specific hardship that his act would address. And while a kind action can also be generous, neither are

---

[65] At the upper end of the spectrum of considerate acts, scale may become relevant, since it would be a misleading understatement to describe certain deeds merely as kind. Certain actions can be kind while also reflecting other traits, such as generosity or courage. At the lower end of the spectrum, one might suppose that courtesy is what is involved and that courtesy is thus a low-grade type of kindness. The fact that a person can be courteous without being kind indicates otherwise, however. Kindness and courtesy can converge in the same action, to be sure. Sometimes, it is thoughtful sensitivity to another person that inclines a person toward courteous action. Yet other times, it is the drill of a disciplined upbringing ("write thy thank you notes," "bring thy hostess gifts") rather than genuine concern for another person's well-being. Courtesy can be either thoughtful or robotic; a person can satisfy the letter of Miss Manners' laws without fulfilling their spirit, yet kindness depends on that spirit – on concern for the other person's well-being. Kindness is more personally targeted than a code of etiquette, even if the original intention behind certain rules of etiquette was respect for the value of other persons.

these two qualities identical. First, the kind person does not necessarily *give* in the sense most associated with generosity; he may simply lend an ear or express sympathy or encouragement or good wishes. Moreover, considerateness, which is key to kindness, is not essential to generosity. A person might be generous in giving time or money to a cause solely for the tax breaks or out of a misplaced sense of duty rather than from any sincere concern for the beneficiaries. His action could remain generous – a case of giving more than the recipient has right or reason to expect – without being kind.[66]

With the distinct character of kindness more sharply understood, we can now turn to the propriety of kindness, which is assumed far more often than it is argued. Given the minimal effort that is often involved and the value of human beings, this is somewhat understandable. The rationales sometimes mustered are similar to those offered on behalf of charity: what goes around comes around; there but for the grace of God go I; the Lord has commanded us to love one another as he has loved us.[67] The bumper sticker injunction to practice random acts of kindness is rarely challenged.[68] On an altruistic framework, the reasoning is clear: Since a person's paramount moral mission is to serve others, he should do whatever he can to ease others' way; kindness marks but the barest beginning of this obligation. The question for us is whether kindness can be appropriate for a rational egoist.

Interestingly, the heroes of Rand's fiction offer numerous displays of kindness. Dagny is kind to Cherryl, for instance, in the encounter referred to earlier, by having her call her Dagny and by inviting her to stay the night out of concern for her emotional state and what might happen if she goes home to Jim.[69] Dagny is kind to Jess Allen, the bum she invites to be her guest on the train and to dine with her, even before learning

---

[66] Wallace defends the idea that it is possible to be kind without being generous by citing the example of a person who, having been raised in penury, is reluctant to give of material goods yet who is nevertheless quite kind, p. 144. Note that this reflects only a lack of material generosity, however; such a person might still be generous with other resources, such as time or praise or credit.

[67] For a version of the "what goes around" argument, see Wallace, p. 146. While prominently associated with Christianity, the golden rule is "the whole of the Torah," Armstrong, pp. 72, 78, and the duty of compassion, an allied though not identical notion, is a hallmark of Buddhism, Hinduism, Confucianism, and Taoism, Armstrong, pp. 32, 44.

[68] Maimonides urged such randomness, invoking the example of "the wise men who would put money in a folded sheet, then throw it over their shoulders so poor people could pluck out coins as the wise men strolled down the street," Salamon, p. 104.

[69] Rand, *Atlas Shrugged*, pp. 887–892.

that he possesses valuable information.[70] Rearden is kind to Mr. Ward, the earnest businessman for whom he goes to some trouble to sell a large quantity of scarce steel, as well as to the "wet nurse" at his factory.[71] Roark, in *The Fountainhead*, is kind to Keating and to Wynand at various stages.[72] This should not surprise us.

By the standard of rational self-interest, kindness offers positive value of at least three distinct types. First of all, kindness is a means of furthering the agent's values. To the extent that a person cares about the people to whom he is kind, he is helping those individuals by making their path, if ever so slightly, smoother. Actions need not be extravagant in order to bring real benefits to their recipient. Any saving of time, any effort of inclusion, any soothing word is typically welcomed as a definite gain for the recipient. We all know how agreeable it is to be on the receiving end of kindness – whether a door is held, a welcome is extended, or one simply feels nurtured by the other person's solicitousness. Kindness cushions the coarser edges of a day. Much of what kindness offers is the knowledge that another person cares. It is not only the card on the mantle or the minutes saved by a friend's favor, but the concern that the kind act expresses that is valuable. In fact, the emotional impact of kindness can

---

[70] Rand, *Atlas Shrugged*, pp. 656 ff.

[71] Rand, *Atlas Shrugged*, pp. 209–213 and 989–994.

[72] Roark refrains from harsh criticisms and "I told you so's" of Keating's art work and ulti-mately self-destructive decisions. With Wynand after the trial, he is as coolly professional as Wynand seems to desire, so as not to exacerbate Wynand's pain by reminding him of their previous relationship and its loss. For a portrait of the abuse of kindness, see Rand's play "Think Twice," in Leonard Peikoff, ed., *The Early Ayn Rand – A Selection from her Unpublished Fiction* (New York: Signet, 1984), pp. 293–377. For statements of what Rand regards as a vicious view of kindness, see the pleas for kindness made by two of the villains in *Atlas*, Jim Taggart and Rearden's mother, pp. 388–389 and 209. At one stage, when his mother implores him to be kind, Rearden replies, "I'm not." I take this to mean not that Rand opposes all kindness, but that Rearden rejects the form of kindness that his mother demands. It is useful to note an explanation that Rand gives a young fan, in a letter, of how literally to take the words and actions of characters in a novel:

do not read any statement out of context, particularly when you read fiction. In analyzing the philosophical ideas presented in fiction, you must identify the total meaning of the story, of its plot, its main events and its characters. You must never judge any incident out of context, and this applies particularly to the dialogue. In real life and in fiction, people do not speak in terms of precise, legalistic philosophical definitions. This does not mean that people contradict philosophical principles, but it means that one must learn to distinguish when a particular statement does represent a precise definition and when it is a verbal part of a wider whole. In reading literature, one must learn how to analyze its parts, but one must never forget to put them together again, that is, one must know how to analyze and how to integrate. (*Letters of Ayn Rand*, pp. 631–632.)

be strikingly disproportionate to the substance of the act, as even minute gestures can buoy a person's spirits. The point is, receiving kindness can genuinely benefit a person, often more for its spiritual boost than for any material assistance. Thus if one person values another, kindness is a way of nurturing that value.

Second, kindness can strengthen the relationship between two people. I mean not that it necessarily will, but simply that it can play such a role. By indicating the sincerity and some of the depth of one person's regard for another, kind acts can lead to increased understanding of mutual attitudes, which might encourage a greater investment on each person's part and foster a gradual strengthening of their bonds, over time.

Yet another benefit of kindness lies in its contribution to a warmer social climate. To some extent, kindness breeds kindness, as many people are more inclined to be considerate of others the more they find others being considerate of them. The more frequently other drivers allow a person to fold into a lane of traffic, for instance, the more inclined he may be to do the same for others. In the era of road rage, I will venture no hard and fast claims about the reasoning of motorists. Here again, I am not claiming necessary connections, but simply observing that the experience of others' kindness often does have the effect of putting people in a more hospitable mode. Thus, if a person finds a kinder environment congenial, his own kindness can help to bring that about. When a person is kind, he makes the world more to his liking and may subtly incline others to be more disposed to kindness, as well.[73]

The larger lesson is that kindness can offer definite value to an egoist and therefore will often be appropriate. Its chief value is the first: Kindness is a means of tending the values one finds in specific other people. Nonetheless, kindness is not a virtue for the simple reason that kindness is not always appropriate. It is not always in one's interest. Like charity and generosity, kindness must never involve self-sacrifice. Whether kindness is appropriate depends on the prospective recipient's value to the agent.

[73] This should not be mistaken for the "what goes around, comes around" argument, as it is not a calculation that others will do things for a kind person when he would benefit from kindness, but a matter of contributing to a certain atmosphere that a person finds desirable. Through acts of kindness, a person is enhancing that atmosphere now, regardless of what the future holds; the gesture is not a wager, as it is in the typical "goes around" rationale. (Wallace likens helping others to taking out insurance against catastrophe, p. 146.) A kind action is simply a step toward achieving the hospitable atmosphere in which one prefers to exist.

On the moral theory that Rand has defended, human beings do not possess intrinsic value. Other people do not exert a freestanding claim on a person's energy that he is duty-bound to respect through acts of kindness. Indeed, certain individuals are unworthy of kindness. No kindness is owed to the cheater or ingrate or malicious manipulator, for instance, let alone to Stalin, Pol Pot, or Osama bin Laden. Such people are unworthy because kindness toward them would be self-destructive; it would work against the agent's happiness. Others' vices make a person's life, at best, more difficult. Others' dishonesty or injustice or lack of productiveness, for instance, create burdens and erect obstacles that hinder a person's ability to flourish. (The greater a person's vices, the greater their destructiveness.) It would be perverse for anyone committed to his own flourishing to reward such individuals with kindness. The contention that kindness *per se* is virtuous and is thus appropriate toward all comers completely contradicts the egoistic thesis that a person's own life is properly his highest value and is the source of anything else's value to him. Individuals who do not merit feelings of "tenderness, fondness, affection or love" (recall the *OED*) should not be treated as if they did.

Lest the rejection of kindness from the ranks of moral virtues seem harsh, bear in mind that on Rand's moral code, respect for individual rights and the virtue of justice demand that a person always respect others' freedom and treat others as they deserve. Thus, in denying that kindness is a virtue, Rand is hardly sanctioning the abuse of other people. Beyond respect for rights and justice, however, no policy of assisting or cheering others is essential to a person's survival.

It may also be helpful to recognize that failing to be kind leaves two alternatives: being positively *un*kind or being neither particularly kind nor unkind. The rejection of kindness as a virtue does not entail endorsement of the former. While Rand's account of justice makes plain that one should sometimes treat others in ways that they are unlikely to welcome (punishing them, when that is what they deserve), nothing in her writings suggests that a person should ever be cruel, malicious, or callous. Indeed, such actions would usually violate justice. A person's default attitude toward his fellow men, Rand observes in her *Journals*, should be "a benevolent neutrality."[74]

What, then, of kindness toward strangers? I have alluded to the fact that being the recipient of kindness tends to feel good. Moreover, observing an act of kindness, even when the observer is not the beneficiary, can

[74] *Journals of Ayn Rand,* p. 246.

be heartwarming (e.g., witnessing a waiter's good-natured patience with a slow-witted elderly patron or a young man's cheerfully giving a seat on a bus to a clearly weary woman). Considering the reasons for these common reactions can help us understand the stakes of interactions with strangers.

Gestures of kindness – holding a door a few moments more than minimal courtesy would require, pausing to inquire whether a solitary walker on a country road needs assistance – signal respect for the value of a person's life. A person need not seek his self-esteem from such encounters to welcome them. When a stranger extends kindness, precisely because he does not know the recipient or the distinct values that that person brings to the world, his action is a way of saying: "We – human beings – are special. Whatever else is going on, it is individual human beings who are the greatest values in the world, it is we who create values; therefore, I will exert this small effort on your behalf." Kindness, in short, is an affirmation of value – of a particular recipient's distinctive value, when the agent knows the recipient, or of the value of human life as such, when he does not. Accordingly, if a person values his fellow human beings and has no reason to think a particular individual unworthy of kindness, it is fine to perform acts of kindness on suitable occasions. Given the tremendous value that individuals can have to one another, it is sensible to extend the benefit of the doubt to people one knows nothing about. Kindness will be appropriate far more often than not. Indeed, the reason that it can seem odd to argue for kindness is that the value of other people is so plain and the actions in question are so inexpensive. Resistance to kindness suggests a stunted appreciation of human beings' value.

Can it make sense, then, for an egoist to aspire to kindness? Although kindness is not a virtue, on Rand's view, and although the alternative to kindness is not necessarily unkindness, I do not think it a mistake for the egoist to aspire to kindness – *toward appropriate people.* Let me explain.

Indiscriminate kindness – a person's bestowing kindness on all others regardless of their value to him – *would* be a mistake insofar as it would squander the person's values and thereby sabotage his own well-being. Rand would definitely condemn the recklessness with the substance of one's own happiness that is reflected in random acts of kindness. For a person to cultivate kindness toward persons whom he values, however, is a means of advancing his values. Given that rationality is the cardinal virtue and that rationality consists in governing one's thoughts and actions by reality, we should hardly expect obliviousness or insensitivity to the people one values to win approval. Being considerate of another person means tuning in to the actual concretes of his context. This is a requirement of objectivity. If one values another person, then such considerateness and corollary action are the logical way of *valuing* him.

When a person is insensitive – not considerate of the experience of those people he values – he fails to realize opportunities to promote his values. When, alternatively, a person is sufficiently sensitive to recognize salient features of a valued person's situation but then does not do anything to help or cheer him (assuming that the relevant conditions concerning sacrifice and respect for other virtues are met), he fails to live by his professed values. If a person's good friend achieves some significant success or suffers a serious loss, for example, the person should, at minimum, acknowledge this by expressing his congratulations or condolences. As with generosity, in other words, integrity sometimes demands kind actions.

One might suspect that this is too strong a claim. For it appears to eliminate the discretion that seems crucial to what kindness is and to why we appreciate it. "That was so nice of him," the recipient of kindness typically thinks, "he didn't have to do that." I am not proposing that all permissible acts of kindness are required by integrity, however. Nor am I claiming that if a person values human beings, then every time he can do something nice for someone, he should. That would be sacrificial; a person has his own life to lead, his own happiness to pursue as his primary end. What I am proposing is precisely what I wrote: Sometimes, integrity demands kind actions.

Some acts of kindness are optional. An action could be compatible with a person's values without being required by them. Attending a particular concert is not required by my love of music; buying a particular rare coin is not required by my being a collector. Similarly, many acts of kindness will be compatible with a person's values without being required by them. Nonetheless, in certain circumstances, a person's values (and thus his integrity) will require that he take kind actions.

It may be helpful to highlight the distinction between kindness and kind acts. On the interpretation of Rand's view that I am advocating, particular acts of kindness will sometimes be optional and sometimes be required by a person's integrity. Yet aspiring to be a kind person, to kindness as a characteristic, is not optional (again and throughout this discussion, I am speaking of kindness toward appropriate people). If a person values human beings and values particular individuals, then kindness on certain occasions is required by his values.

A person does not fail to be a kind person if he does not seize every opportunity to be kind, any more than he would cease to be an opera lover by failing to seize every opportunity to attend an opera performance. While many specific acts of kindness are optional, what is salient to my claim about integrity is that all optional actions and optional values must be rational and self-interested. They must be consistent with a person's broader values. Any suspicion that this cancels their being optional indicates a misunderstanding of what optional values are. Optional values are not a free pass from rational values or virtues; they are not an island, off on their own and exempt from morality's authority. All optional values are subject to the fundamentals of a rational moral code, on Rand's view. Accordingly, integrity can never be side-stepped. Integrity will not dictate every action that a person should take, but it must give permission to every action that a person takes. This is the way in which integrity governs kindness.

Thus, again, particular acts of kindness are often optional (not always), but being a person who will be kind *when his values call for it* is not optional. That is required by integrity (and by rational self-interest). Notice that these observations do not elevate kindness to the status of a virtue. They simply recognize the fact that kindness toward appropriate persons is a way of valuing what one values – in action, rather than in mere lip service – and as such, should be encouraged. Barring serious psychological problems, I would not expect a rational egoist to need to battle fierce internal resistance to kindness or to need to mount an arduous, deliberate campaign to be kind. Kindness toward many people will come naturally and many ways of being kind are extremely inexpensive. Nonetheless, although the scale of kind deeds can be quite modest, it is not the size of an action's stakes that determines its propriety. Rational self-interest does. And by that standard, kindness is not a virtue because it is not in all cases in one's interest. Extended toward certain individuals, being kind would work against the agent's happiness. Thus, a rational egoist should be kind selectively and nonsacrificially.

TEMPERANCE

Finally, let us consider a different kind of quality that is often praised as a virtue, temperance. While charity, generosity, and kindness concern a person's relations with others, temperance concerns a person's management of his self-regarding desires.[75] Because its effects can be quite beneficial, temperance seems a natural fit for an egoistic code.

[75] Temperate actions could affect other people, but the term is used primarily to refer to self-regarding actions.

To determine the status of temperance in Rand's ethics, we must first untangle confusions concerning precisely what temperance is. Often, when people speak of temperance, they have in mind moderation. Aristotle's doctrine that virtue lies in a mean has filtered down into a widespread belief that temperance is a policy of pursuing "all things in moderation" and avoiding extremes, not having or doing "too much" of anything.[76] According to the *Oxford English Dictionary*, temperance is "the practice or habit of restraining oneself in provocation, passion, desire, etc.; rational self-restraint. Self-restraint in the indulgence of any natural affection or appetance; moderation in the pursuit of a gratification, in the exercise of a feeling, or in the use of anything." (The dictionary also gives the more specialized senses of the term, which refer to avoidance of excess in eating and drinking or to total abstinence from drink, as advocated by temperance movements.) Aristotle understands temperance as specifically governing the "slavish" bodily pleasures of touch and taste that we share with other animals.[77] Although temperance is often associated with physical appetites, people also speak of temperance in regard to other activities, as well, such as TV-watching, Web-surfing, shopping, collecting, even working. Accordingly, I will use temperance in this broader sense rather than as referring to the governance of exclusively physical desires.[78]

Notice that "moderation" is used in the definition of temperance. Similarly, "temperance" appears in the *OED*'s definition of moderation: "The action or an act of moderating; the quality of being moderate, in various senses; now only with reference to conduct, opinions, demands, desires or their indulgence; avoidance of extremes, self-control, temperance; occasionally, avoidance of severity or rigor, lenity, clemency."[79] Despite the close relationship between temperance and moderation, I do not think that we can simply use the two interchangeably. Essentially, temperance means self-restraint. Note, however, that self-restraint could be exercised either through complete self-denial (refusing to satisfy a particular desire

---

[76] I do not mean that this is an accurate depiction of Aristotle's view (see *Nicomachean Ethics*, 1107a10 ff) or that most people have ever heard of Aristotle, let alone attribute this doctrine to him.

[77] *Nicomachean Ethics*, 1118a25.

[78] Note that although I will sometimes speak of moderating or muting one's desires, strictly, temperance concerns a person's reactions in the face of his desires rather than manipulation of the desires themselves. I will nonetheless occasionally use such expressions as a convenient shorthand and they should be read only as such.

[79] To "moderate," in turn, is "to abate the excessiveness of; to render less violent, intense, rigorous, or burdensome; to reduce the amount of (a fine, charge, financial burden); to exercise a controlling influence over; to regulate, restrain, control, rule."

at all) or through a measured or partial satisfaction (gratifying the desire to some extent, though not fully). The latter is what we usually mean by moderation. This suggests that moderation is one form of self-restraint rather than its equivalent; self-restraint is the wider concept. Henceforth, then, when I refer to temperance, one should bear in mind that it can take either form. Because moderation often seems the more reasonable form of temperance and because, in order to determine the morality of temperance for egoism, we must consider it in its most tenable incarnations, I will also sometimes specifically discuss moderation.[80]

The most prominent rationales traditionally given for the propriety of temperance can be broadly divided into three schools: the ascetic, the altruistic, and the *eudaimonistic*.[81] In the ascetic school, one finds thinkers such as Augustine, who holds that "the flesh is at war with the spirit" and that "temperance must bridle our fleshly lusts if they are not to drag our will to consent to abominations of every sort."[82] The life of virtue is one of unending war against evil inclinations, Augustine believes, and temperance is a vital tool for waging this ongoing struggle to defeat our lower, beastly nature. On this line of thinking, restraint of bodily pleasures is good because the body is bad, or at best, inferior, as it lures us away from our duties to God and others.

On the altruistic model, temperance is deemed appropriate as a means to serving the welfare of others. By limiting the indulgence of his own desires, a person leaves more for others to enjoy. If service to others' well-being is more important than advancement of one's own, then temperance can facilitate a person's fulfilling his altruistic obligations. Certain environmentalists employ reasoning of this sort, arguing that your self-restraint today will enhance the well-being of others tomorrow by preserving resources for future generations. Although the ascetic and altruistic rationales for temperance are sometimes teamed, the ascetic

---

[80] The Greek term that has been traditionally translated as temperance or as moderation (and sometimes, though more problematically, as self-control) is *sophrosune*. Literally, *sophrosune* means "soundness of mind" and is linked with temperance and moderation insofar as it connotes practical sensibility or keeping one's good sense, in action. Thanks to Allan Gotthelf, Robert Mayhew, Greg Salmieri, and Paul Woodruff for sharing their knowledge of ancient Greek.

[81] John Elia and Warren von Eschenbach helpfully prodded me to distinguish these. Note that some advocates of these schools conceive of temperance in the narrow sense as pertaining to physical desires.

[82] The first is a quotation from Saint Paul that Augustine approvingly invokes. Augustine, *City of God*, ed. Vernon J. Bourke, translation Gerald G. Walsh, Demetrius B. Zerna, Grace Monahan, Daniel J. Honan (New York: Doubleday, 1958), pp. 438–439.

need not be defended for its altruistic payoffs. The more strict advocates of asceticism would view self-denial or self-restraint as good in its own right – for example, as an act intended to please God, but not to help him.

On the third, *eudaimonistic* rationale, temperance is urged as a means to the agent's own well-being. Plato and Aristotle are exemplars of this perspective. Plato tenders somewhat differing accounts of what temperance is in different dialogues, but its value to a person's happiness is never in serious question. At the conclusion of the *Charmides*, he goes so far as to insist that temperance insures happiness.[83] Aristotle describes the temperate person as desiring "moderately and in the right way" those things that are "conducive to health or fitness."[84] The temperate person's appetites agree with reason, in Aristotle's view, and by following the direction of such appetites, he will avoid various ills that would result from indulgence of irrational appetites. If a person's own *eudaimonia* is enhanced by the exercise of temperance, then it seems obvious to these thinkers that temperance should be encouraged.[85]

Our question, of course, is how temperance fares under rational egoism. To answer, we must further refine our basic conception of temperance, for at root, the answer depends on whether we understand temperance to mean rational self-restraint, as part of the *OED*'s account has it, or as simply self-restraint, as another part does. Although everyday references to temperance usually imply its propriety, they do not always imply the grounds for this propriety, let alone that these grounds are its rationality. One might compliment a companion's restraint at a buffet table as temperate, for instance, when in fact, that person needs to gain a few pounds and his self-denial is not truly advisable. Self-restraint on behalf of an ill-conceived end remains self-restraint, however. For this reason, the neutral interpretation of temperance (i.e., as not necessarily rational) seems to more accurately reflect ordinary usage. Moreover,

---

[83] Terence Irwin, *Plato's Ethics* (New York: Oxford University Press, 1995), p. 42. Also see discussions of temperance (of varying depth) in Plato's *Gorgias, Republic, Statesman, Laws, Philebus,* and *Protagoras.*

[84] *Nicomachean Ethics,* 1119a17, trans. Irwin.

[85] The Epicureans valued temperance as a means of leading a life of pleasure. Aquinas sounds Aristotelian when he writes that temperance observes the mean in all things and curbs passions when they incite against reason, though he also contends that humility is a part of temperance and that moderation is the same as humility, which sounds more Augustinian. *Basic Writings of St. Thomas Aquinas,* ed. Anton C. Pegis (New York: Random House, 1945), vol. 2, pp. 472, 468 and *Summa Theologica* (London: Burn, Oates and Washbourne, 1932), p. 223.

taking temperance to mean *rational* self-restraint would skirt the substantive question. Because Rand's theory recognizes rationality as the paramount virtue, the rational exercise of a quality will naturally win its approval. The meaty question is whether temperance or moderation will always *be* rational. Thus, understanding temperance in this broader sense to mean simply self-restraint, let us proceed to consider that.[86]

Once the question is so distilled, the answer, I think, is clearly negative. Restraint in and of itself is of no value. Life requires the satisfaction of many desires, including desires for certain physical pleasures. The desires for food, drink, and sex are natural and play an important role in human beings' survival. Desires for these things often reflect genuine needs and the desires' satisfaction, genuine goods for the person's life. Consequently, far from its being wrong to pursue such desires or to enjoy their gratification, doing so can vitally advance a person's flourishing. Beyond the realm of purely physical desires, bear in mind that living consists of goal-directed action. The maintenance of a person's life requires the achievement of countless subordinate and constitutive ends. It is healthy for a person to desire rational values, whether small or large in scale, and to reap pleasure when he achieves them. Indeed, enjoying the generation and satisfaction of desires is much of what enjoying life consists of.

By itself, this might seem an argument against self-denial rather than against moderation or all self-restraint. For overindulgence can carry self-destructive effects, such as headache, nausea, disease, debt. The sheer prescription of restraint or moderation leaves unanswered a crucial question, however: What constitutes overindulgence? We cannot answer that – we cannot determine the proper degree of satisfaction of any desires – without reference to the substance of a particular individual's desires and circumstances. What would be too much for one individual might be too little for another, given their different (yet perfectly rational) ends and priorities. Too much food for Bill, who needs to lose weight to alleviate heart problems, may be too little for Tom, the professional linebacker who needs to maintain considerable strength and stamina.[87] Whether it

---

[86] Aristotle's conception of the temperate person's appetites as "for the right things, in the right ways, at the right times, which is just what reason also prescribes" (*Nicomachean Ethics* 1119b16 ff, trans. Irwin) clearly makes rationality a condition of temperance. By contrast, Plato's distinction between "popular temperance" and temperance that involves wisdom implies that temperance does not necessarily involve rational restraint. See Irwin, *Plato's Ethics*, pp. 347–348, and *Laws* 710a–b.

[87] Aristotle uses similar examples when presenting his doctrine of the mean.

is proper to satisfy a desire to *any* extent depends on the object of the desire and the effect that its satisfaction would have on the person's overall well-being. We cannot simply declare that self-denial is always wrong and that the weaker form of self-restraint, moderation, is always right. With some desires, self-denial is right and mere moderation would be wrong. The folk wisdom "all things in moderation" is too shallow to offer sound guidance. One immediately wonders: *All* things? Gin? Cocaine? Unprotected sex? And "moderation" between what boundaries? The borders that locate moderation are obviously all-important to the sense of following any allegedly moderate course. This fact alone reveals the inadequacy of "moderation" as a criterion of moral virtue. Further, consider the person who experiences conflicting desires. Does moderation advise him to indulge each of them to some degree? If a man is torn between desires for fidelity and for adultery, should he see his wife three nights a week and his mistress another three? Or suppose that a recovering alcoholic longs to be sober. He also longs for that bottle of bourbon. The moderate course might be to have a couple of shots, but the most likely result of that would be continued alcoholism.

Although moderation might make sense in certain circumstances (e.g., as a policy for eating prudently while also enjoying the lavish party that marks a special occasion), in others, it would be self-defeating. It would deprive a person of values that enrich his life. This is because moderation *per se* is too superficial an aspect of actions to reliably indicate the rationally self-interested course. When the satisfaction of desires should be tempered by something else, we need a compelling account of what that is and of why that is. In short, a blanket endorsement of even the more moderate form of self-restraint, moderation, cannot withstand logical scrutiny.

Even if a reader accepts the reasoning thus far, he may experience the lingering sense that *something* is right about the ideal of temperance. This is understandable. For the prevalent image of a temperate person as in command of himself, master of his desires, sober in his decisions, is, quite reasonably, attractive. The exercise of temperance often reflects a person's resisting an urge to act on impulse and, correspondingly, a rejection of emotionalism. This is implicit in many descriptions of temperance. N. J. H. Dent, for instance, describes temperance as a desire for sense pleasures that is moderated by a person's judgment of its appropriateness.[88]

---

[88] N. J. H. Dent, *The Moral Psychology of the Virtues* (New York: Cambridge University Press, 1984), p. 147.

Comte-Sponville writes that "temperance is . . . an affirmation especially of the power of the mind over the irrational impulses of our affects and appetites."[89] What such portraits of temperance indicate, however, is the fact that what enables an admirably temperate person to gratify his desires wisely is not the raw exertion of restraint, but reason. Temperance does frequently make sense, in other words, but only when and because it is rational. Often, temperance is proper, and it is so because it is an exercise of reason; it is never a good in itself.

Correspondingly, the proper ideal for a rational egoist is not to mute or moderate his desires, but, when determining whether to act on them, to recognize the full context. The proper management of desires does not consist in fighting them as if they posed a mortal menace that must always be resisted. Rather, rational egoism counsels identifying all of the values that stand to be affected by a given course. A person should think through the long-range repercussions of whether and how he indulges a specific desire, weighing the different effects' relative significance for his values. He must then determine the best means of serving his values in the circumstances, which will sometimes permit satisfying the desire and sometimes not. (Obviously, intermediate alternatives might also be available, such as postponing gratification or modifying the desires' demands. "I don't have to have the *whole* pint of hazelnut gelato.") In her elaboration of the practical meaning of the virtue of rationality, Rand writes that "one must never make any decisions . . . or seek any values out of context, i.e., apart from or against the total, integrated sum of one's knowledge."[90] Intemperance, frequently, is precisely that. And when it is, it is wrong, on Rand's view. What is truly called for in order to respond to one's desires constructively and to achieve one's interest is, again, reason.

It is crucial to appreciate that to starve or to moderate one's desires is not always good. To be rational, is. A person should pursue his values and respond to his desires as reason, in light of his hierarchy of values and present circumstances, dictates. Accordingly, however, the rational course will sometimes be immoderate. Deep commitment to a particular value will sometimes require a disproportionate amount of time or thought or money extended on its behalf. A person whose work in a demanding field is by far his highest value might reasonably devote the overwhelming bulk of his energy to that work. This can be immoderate yet entirely rational. A person committed to having a wrongly convicted loved one exonerated

---

[89] Comte-Sponville, p. 43.
[90] Rand, "The Objectivist Ethics," p. 28.

or to a particular political cause or athletic ambition or romantic partner might similarly be rationally immoderate in the pursuit of this value. The point is not that we can discover a list of ends "approved" for intemperate pursuit. Any end can be, in appropriate circumstances. Normally, this is restricted only by the fundamental moral virtues. A person should not pursue his love affair with however worthy a partner at the expense of the virtue of productiveness, for instance. Yet under abnormal circumstances, such as when a person is diagnosed with a fatal disease, it makes perfect sense to set aside the usual demands of productiveness to mount an all-out (immoderate) effort to beat his illness.

The larger point is that, whether in ordinary or extraordinary circumstances, passionate immoderation is not incompatible with reason. Acting purely from passion, without examining the basis of the passion or the likely consequences of indulging it, would be. But the moderate course is not always preferable to the immoderate course. Pursuing a desire passionately or to an extreme degree need not thwart greater values or harm a person's overall interest. Under certain conditions, it can actually be the best way to achieve one's happiness.

If the proper exercise of temperance is an application of rationality, we should also recognize that it particularly reflects the more specific virtues of honesty and integrity. In order to "never make any decisions . . . or seek any values out of context,"[91] a person must be honest with himself about the relative merits of various desires and the full effects of satisfying them. He must be honest about what his true values and rankings of values are. Misrepresenting one's priorities often provides the green light to irrationally intemperate indulgence. Other times, inappropriate intemperance is facilitated by self-deceptive rationalizations. By kidding himself about what constitutes adequate justification for taking an action, a person can manufacture permission to indulge irrationally. ("I can have the whole bottle because I didn't have a drink last week.") More generally, inappropriate indulgence of appetites often results from evasion. The person fakes reality by ignoring relevant facts or misgivings. He simply avoids thinking through the consequences of his course – the impact on his cholesterol or diabetes, for instance, or how he will feel afterward, physically or emotionally, or how he is weakening his ability to make difficult decisions in the future or to achieve other ends that he values more highly. He shoves aside any inklings that these issues ought to be squarely confronted and focuses solely on the appeal of his immediate desire.

---

[91] Rand, "The Objectivist Ethics," p. 28.

The proper exercise of temperance also reflects integrity: fidelity to one's values.[92] The rationally temperate person does not act as if a fleeting pleasure is more important to him than his higher values, such as the marathon he is training for, the business he is saving for, or the marriage that he treasures. If he recognizes that satisfaction of a particular desire would jeopardize things of greater value to him, he will not satisfy that desire. Rational temperance demands the discipline to adhere to one's considered priorities. Note that the passionate person whose rationality I defended above is also exhibiting integrity. Because he values certain ends far more than others, he pursues those ends in proportion to that significance. While the distribution of his activities might look very unbalanced to an outside observer, to maintain some abstract notion of balance that is detached from a person's values would require compromising his integrity, that is, betraying the true value that different ends hold for him. The larger point, again, is simply that temperance, when it is appropriate, involves honesty concerning the value that various things hold for a person as well as integrity in acting accordingly.

In sum, *rational* self-restraint is an important tool in the pursuit of a person's objective well-being. Irrational indulgence of desires for pleasures (such as pursuing keenly desired ends disproportionately to their objective value) ultimately hurts the agent himself. Although such cases arise far less often, under-indulgence has the same effect, since it also reflects a gap between values and actions. Deficient gratification forfeits opportunities to achieve values that would enhance a person's life and thus impedes the flourishing that is possible to him.

While the rational exercise of temperance is vital to egoism, however, temperance *per se* (understood simply as self-restraint and taken to refer to either self-denial or moderation) is not a virtue. Denial or restraint of desires offers no inherent value; a "moderate" indulgence of appetites is not necessarily superior to the immoderate alternatives. Egoism allows passion – in action as well as in feeling. When temperance *is* called for, it is so not out of respect for a duty to refrain from taking "more than one's share" or as a means of combating inherently base desires, nor for any other reason that is independent of the agent's self-interest. The proper exercise of temperance requires acting with a clear vision of the full context, deliberately identifying the implications of one's alternatives for all the values at stake. On Rand's view, temperance is appropriate when and to the extent that it serves the individual's happiness.

---

[92] Gabriele Taylor also links weakness of will to failures of integrity. "Integrity," p. 146.

CONCLUSION

Our explorations in this chapter have shown that neither charity, generosity, kindness, nor temperance qualifies as a virtue, on Rand's theory. To deny that these are virtues is not to condemn them as vices. Each is compatible with rational egoism, under the right conditions. Not only can the egoist be charitable, generous, kind, or temperate; sometimes, he should be. Insofar as giving to the needy, giving others more than they can reasonably expect, acting considerately to help or cheer a person, or restraining satisfaction of one's desires can often be contrary to a person's interest, however, these types of actions cannot be blessed as proper moral principles to guide the rational egoist. In order for egoism to approve of such actions, they must be consistent with rationality, with all the other fundamental moral virtues (honesty, justice, etc.), and with the agent's hierarchy of values. It is by satisfying these conditions that a person can ensure that he is not making sacrifices. For the standard that governs the proper exercise of these traits is the same that governs all action, on Rand's theory: rational self-interest. And continual reference to that should help a person to determine the status of other purported virtues, as well.

Conclusion

While several of the virtues that Ayn Rand advocates are familiar in name, the moral code that she defends is a bold departure. Ethics is not essentially social, in her view; it does not revolve around a person's relationship to others. Even more at odds with prevailing orthodoxy, Rand rejects altruism, which, however diluted its actual practice, is still widely assumed to be the ultimate moral ideal. Less recognized and equally important, however, Rand's ethics is a departure from conventional conceptions of egoism. Although recent discussions of virtue ethics, *eudaimonism*, and ethical naturalism logically raise questions about the moral status of egoism, ethicists have been slow to confront these. This is largely, I think, because of the images of egoism that have historically been presented as altruism's alternative. As long as egoism is portrayed as materialistic, hedonistic, emotion-driven, or predatory, we can readily sympathize with those looking elsewhere for guidance.

The essence of egoism, in Rand's view, is "concern with one's own interests."[1] What is mistaken about most of the attitudes and practices commonly labeled "selfish" is not the pursuit of what is good for oneself, but warped ideas of what a person's self-interest is and of how he can truly serve it. Rand's ethics is animated by the recognition that human life can be sustained only by specific types of actions. This unshakeable fact gives rise to the need for a moral code to guide individuals' actions. The code that Rand prescribes does not call for the conquest of others. Nor is it hedonistic, materialistic, or emotionalistic. Any such course would work against the agent's interest. Rand contends that a human

[1] Rand, "Introduction," *The Virtue of Selfishness*, p. vii.

284

being's flourishing requires his adherence to rational principles. Rationality reflects the respect for reality that is a prerequisite of human survival. No living being can expect to exist by defying its nature and circumstances. Principles, in turn, are the form in which a conceptual being can grasp rational instruction so that it can guide him in making an endless array of specific decisions. The moral virtues that we have discussed are simply another way of speaking of principles and designate the fundamental types of actions that human life requires.

The egoist who emerges from Rand's theory is a person of principle who exercises the virtues of rationality, honesty, independence, justice, integrity, productiveness, and pride. If this profile rattles entrenched assumptions about egoism, so much the worse for those assumptions and all the more reason to investigate the egoism that Rand proposes. It is only the virtuous egoist described here who truly serves his interest, in Rand's view, and who can live the life of a human being.

Appendix

Egoistic Friendship

In the course of presenting the virtues of the rational egoist, I have addressed several aspects of an egoist's relations with others, most prominently in my discussions of independence, justice (which included forgiveness, mercy, and sanction), and the conventional virtues of charity, generosity, and kindness. A particular misapprehension concerning friendship and love also warrants some attention, however. Many people suppose that even if the egoist can be kind, charitable, or generous on certain occasions, his egoism undermines his capacity to enjoy deeper, more rewarding personal relationships. After all, isn't the egoist committed to always putting himself first? And as a consequence, won't he be too wrapped up in himself to care about others – or at least, to care in the way that a true friend would? Without a less calculated commitment to another person's well-being, the soul of love and friendship seems unavailable to him. Egoists cannot be authentic friends or lovers, the suspicion is, since, qua egoists, they can value others only instrumentally.[1]

---

[1] Laurence Thomas, "Ethical Egoism and Psychological Dispositions," *American Philosophical Quarterly* 17 (1980), pp. 73–78. In a later book, Thomas contends that self-interest militates against trust and thus impedes friendship. Friendship, moreover, is what allows altruism, which Thomas takes to be the proper morality. *Living Morally*, pp. 68, 183, 132; see related comments on love as central to morality on pp. x, 153, 232, 243. One finds similar skepticism about the possibility of egoistic love and friendship in John van Ingen, *Why be Moral? The Egoistic Challenge* (New York: Peter Lang, 1994), pp. 167–174; Lawrence Blum, "Friendship as a Moral Phenomenon," in Neera Badhwar, ed., *Friendship: A Philosophical Reader* (Ithaca, NY: Cornell University Press, 1993), pp. 192–210; Michael J. Meyer, "Rights Between Friends," *Journal of Philosophy* 89 (September 1992), pp. 467–483; and Robert Nozick, *The Examined Life* (New York: Simon & Schuster, 1989), p. 80 ff.

While the nature and basis of friendship and love is a huge subject which presents intricate and heavily psychological questions that extend far beyond the scope of this project, in order to round out my portrait of the life of a rational egoist, I will offer a few comments simply to indicate how this is, indeed, a misapprehension of the egoism that Rand endorses. Necessarily, I must delimit even this. Because romantic love represents more than simply a difference of degree from even the most loving forms of friendship and introduces still further complexities such as sexual attraction, I will confine my remarks to love as it occurs in the strongest forms of friendship. By friendship, I mean a relationship between two people marked by mutual esteem and affection, concern for the other's well-being, pleasure in the other's company, and comparatively intimate levels of communication.[2] Participation in shared activities is often a significant dimension of friendship, though this is not always logistically feasible. A long-distance friendship can be as authentic as one in which the friends are next-door neighbors, though the opportunity for shared activities will obviously be diminished. Although some of my observations may also apply to romantic love, I am not seeking to explain that phenomenon. (Accordingly, I will use the term "lover" to refer to a person who loves another rather than to the narrower category of romantic lover.) "Friends" is the English language's catch-all for a range of associations that vary greatly in degrees of contact, affection, and intimacy, not all of which involve love. The friendships I consider here, however, will be those that do. I am concerned with what Aristotle considers the best and truest type of friendship, sometimes called friendship of character.[3]

We should also note at the outset that in ordinary conversation, we use the term "love" equivocally, sometimes to refer to the feeling of love and other times, to the judgment that is responsible for the feeling. Although we might primarily think of love as a feeling, people often say things such as "I really admire him" or "I really respect what he's doing" as explanations of what they mean in claiming to love a person. Used in this sense, "love" designates an evaluation of another person. Rand herself, in different places, speaks of love as "an emotion," an "expression of values," a "response to values," and a form of valuing, writing that "to love is to

---

[2] Peikoff, *Objectivism*, p. 134.

[3] Thus I am not speaking of what Aristotle dubs friendships of utility or pleasure, which are based on narrow ends. *Nicomachean Ethics*, Book VIII, chapter 3. I am also leaving aside parental and other forms of familial love.

value."[4] This equivocal usage need not be problematic, as long as we understand that both a feeling and a judgment are typically involved. That is, the feeling of love is stimulated, at least in part, by a (possibly subconscious) judgment about the object of love; different uses of the word "love" simply call attention to one or the other of these. References to love as an emotion focus on the lover and on how the other person makes him feel. References to love as a judgment, by contrast, focus on the beloved, on the external basis for the lover's emotional response. Reference to the judgment emphasizes the cause, we might say, whereas reference to the feeling emphasizes the effect.

A final preliminary: I will be speaking of love as ideally experienced, as a feeling of a psychologically healthy person whose feelings are in sync with his judgments and whose judgments are themselves rationally justified. This is not to deny the existence of less rational or less healthy feelings of love, but to consider whether love can be an objective value for a rational egoist. Ill-founded love would not be a suitable testing ground. The salient question, after all, is whether egoism is compatible with love at its best.

LOVE IS SELFISH

In order to understand that rational egoism is not incompatible with genuine, worthwhile friendship, the main thing to grasp is that love is selfish. When Rand writes that "to love is to value," she means that a person loves because he sees value in another person. To love another person is to value him highly. It is not simply to feel good will toward him or to recognize the potential value that he carries in virtue of being human. Love is discriminating; the emotional response of love is a result of finding especially prized traits in a particular individual. One person loves another for specific qualities that he possesses, such as his inquisitiveness or playfulness or idealism or ambition. Bill might love Alex because Alex values some of the same things that Bill does or because Alex exemplifies some of the qualities that Bill most esteems. They might share an interest in the same arts or sports or books or share the same moral or aesthetic or political ideals. A person might also love another because of the kinds

---

[4] Rand, "Of Living Death," *The Objectivist* 7 (October 1968), p. 2; *Atlas Shrugged*, p. 1034; "Philosophy and Sense of Life," in *The Romantic Manifesto*, p. 32; "The Ethics of Emergencies," p. 51; "The Objectivist Ethics," p. 35. In some of these cases, Rand's subject is romantic love, but nowhere does she suggest that any of these descriptions do not apply to nonromantic love.

of experiences he has when with that person. In the company of Alex, Bill might find that normally dormant parts of himself come to life, for instance. It can be *through* their interactions that certain values are realized, and love takes root not simply because each encounters another person who independently possesses prized qualities. The chemistry of the dynamic – of how the two individuals think and feel and act when together – can create new value that forms part of the basis of the friendship. The depth and resonance of the love will depend on the number and significance of such features. What is crucial, however, is that those features of the other person and of his experience with the other person that the lover values are valuable to *him*, the lover; they enhance his life. For a rational egoist, to value something is to recognize it as in one's interest, as personally beneficial in some way. Loving another person, insofar as it reflects valuing, is a thoroughly self-interested proposition.[5]

Accordingly, Rand observes, "Concern for the welfare of those one loves is a rational part of one's selfish interests. If a man who is passionately in love with his wife spends a fortune to cure her of a dangerous illness, it would be absurd to claim that he does it as a 'sacrifice' for *her* sake, not his own, and that it makes no difference to *him*, personally and selfishly, whether she lives or dies."[6] When one person loves another, the well-being of his friend becomes folded into his own; the scope of the lover's interest expands to encompass the other's, as well. In the deep forms of friendship that I am focusing on, a lover will respond to his friend's good and bad fortunes as spontaneously, as naturally, and as effortlessly as to his own. He will identify with his friend's struggles, triumphs, and failures because

5 Obviously, a person might be mistaken in his judgment of another person's value, so more strictly, love is a response to perceived values, on Rand's view. A person might also *discover* values through his relationship with another person, for example, by learning to appreciate certain things that he previously had not. In the case of romantic love, Rand believes that one falls in love with another person's sense of life, which is "an emotional, subconsciously integrated appraisal of man and of existence" that "sets the nature of a man's emotional responses and the essence of his character." For her explanation of this phenomenon and its role in aesthetic as well as romantic responses, see "Philosophy and Sense of Life" and "Art and Sense of Life," in *The Romantic Manifesto*, pp. 25–33 and pp. 34–44. On its role in love in particular, see pp. 32–33. The quotation is from p. 25. Rand also believes that love can provide a unique type of self-awareness or visibility. This idea has affinities with Aristotle's contention that a friend is another self. *Nicomachean Ethics*, 1166a 10; 1166a 30–32. Allan Gotthelf discusses some of the similarities and differences between Rand's and Aristotle's conceptions of love in his unpublished lecture, "Love and Philosophy – Aristotelian versus Platonic."

6 Rand, "The Ethics of Emergencies," p. 51, emphasis in original.

his friend's well-being has become one of his significant values, among the things that contribute to his own well-being. I am better off when a person I love enjoys some significant success (a major achievement in his career, for instance) because the flourishing of someone who is of value to me strengthens my own capacity to flourish. Everything that supports my (objective) values nourishes my life, expanding and enriching my potential to flourish. Threats or injuries to those I love (those I rationally love and who are objectively valuable to me), by contrast, are threats or injuries to my well-being. When things that are good for me suffer, I suffer, for the foundation of my own flourishing is thereby weakened. As Aristotle writes of those in the best form of friendship, "in loving their friend they love what is good for themselves; for when a good person becomes a friend he becomes a good *for* his friend."[7]

Elizabeth Telfer, in a defense of friendship that is not particularly egoistic, recognizes several specific benefits that a person typically gains from friendship. Friendship increases our stake in the world and thus our capacity for emotions; it makes us *feel* more, she writes, and enables us to have life "more abundantly." Friendship enhances many of our activities by intensifying our absorption in them and hence the quality of our performance. This is partly a product of the pleasure of joint activity and partly of our increased emotional commitment. Moreover, by encouraging us to sympathetically adopt the viewpoint of another, friendship enlarges our knowledge, as we acquire a greater understanding of the gamut of human experience.[8]

Skeptics of egoistic friendship sometimes make the mistake of regarding isolated aspects or incidents within a friendship as decisive indicators of the overall character of the friendship itself. Their thinking suffers from the fallacy of composition, in other words, insofar as they assume that whatever is true of some part of a whole must also be true of the whole. In fact, a friendship is an ongoing, multi-faceted relationship

---

[7] *Nicomachean Ethics*, 1157b33, emphasis added, trans. Irwin. Steven Wall has pointed out to me that the identity of interests will be less than complete, if two friends' interests diverge (e.g., when one is hiring and his friend applies for the job, though the friend would not be the best person to hire). Bear in mind Rand's rejection of the possibility of conflicts between rational interests, however (explained in Chapter 2). When the full context is taken into account, we find that friends' objective interests (as opposed to their desires) are not at odds.

[8] Elizabeth Telfer, "Friendship," in Michael Pakaluk, ed., *Other Selves – Philosophers on Friendship* (Indianapolis: Hackett, 1991), pp. 266–267.

whose essential character cannot be judged by a snapshot of any single aspect. The egoistic character of a friendship does not require that each friend experience no inconveniences, for instance, or that he always get his way. The self-interested character of a relationship is compatible with periods of more "giving" than "getting." What is important is the overall benefit of the friendship – which can only be measured from a long-range, all-things-considered perspective.

Other skeptics might stress the risks involved in friendship.[9] Particularly during the early stages of acquaintance, when a relationship's relative rewards and demands are not yet clear, a person might consider himself better off devoting his time and energies to other, more assuredly self-interested ends, such as major projects expected to advance his career. Why should an egoist risk wasting his time on a relationship that might not pan out?

While the cultivation of certain potential friendships will not be worthwhile for a rational egoist, it does not follow that no such friendships will be worthwhile. Rand maintains that an egoist should always evaluate his options (regarding friendship or any other pursuit) from a comprehensive, principled perspective. Given that human beings are not omniscient about the future or able to control other people's actions, the rational pursuit of one's interest demands that a person make investments of various sorts. It is in the nature of investments that their ultimate fruit is not known in advance. Friendship is one such investment. Not every possible friendship is worth pursuing. Because of the tremendous value that good friendships can offer, however, some of them are. Thus an egoist must be careful not to hastily dismiss the potential of certain relationships on the basis of shortsighted calculations of where his interest rests or of how much he can reasonably expect to know, at present. The rational egoist will realize that some risks are worth taking – because they are in his interest.

My larger point is that love – in its ideal, rational form – is a value that advances the lover's life. Both the value of another person that gives rise to the love and the experience of love, that unique and intensely pleasurable feeling, can provide inestimable enrichment of a person's existence. Because rational egoism is a value-driven ethics and because friendships can bring enormous value to one's life, Rand advocates the active pursuit of such relationships. The egoist should identify those qualities in others that are objectively valuable to him; he should be on the lookout

9 Neil Tennant, in an e-mail exchange, has urged me to consider this.

for these qualities, striving to recognize them when he encounters them; and when he does, he should seek to develop the forms and degrees of friendship that are appropriate to the degrees of value-affinity he finds with the relevant individuals.[10]

Rand rejects any conception of love as an exercise of altruism, such as Laurence Thomas advocates.[11] Properly, love is not some sort of handout or alms.[12] "Love, friendship, respect, admiration are the emotional responses of one man to the virtues of another, the spiritual *payment* given in exchange for the personal, selfish pleasure which one man derives from the virtues of another man's character."[13] A selfless or disinterested love, she observes, is a contradiction in terms. Since loving is a type of valuing, it would mean "that one is indifferent to that which one values."[14] In fact, she holds, "Love and friendship are profoundly personal, selfish values: love is an expression and assertion of self-esteem, a response to one's own values in the person of another. One gains a profoundly personal, selfish joy from the mere existence of the person one loves."[15]

In order to be valuable, in other words – to offer objective benefit to the lover – love must be selfish both in its source and in its aim.[16] It must emanate from a self and it must be for the self, i.e., rooted in the conviction that the object of love offers genuine enrichment of the lover's life. To understand the first condition, recall a line from *The Fountainhead* that I quoted in our discussion of the virtue of independence: "To say 'I love you' one must know first how to say the 'I.' "[17] Rand later elaborates on this thought:

To love is to value. Only a rationally selfish man, a man of *self-esteem*, is capable of love – because he is the only man capable of holding firm, consistent, uncompromising, unbetrayed values. The man who does not value himself, cannot value anything or anyone.[18]

[10] Peikoff, *Objectivism*, p. 237.
[11] Thomas, *Living Morally*, pp. 64, 132.
[12] *Journals of Ayn Rand*, p. 278.
[13] "The Objectivist Ethics," p. 35, emphasis in original.
[14] "The Ethics of Emergencies," p. 51.
[15] "The Ethics of Emergencies," p. 51. Also see *"Playboy*'s Interview with Ayn Rand," p. 7.
[16] Peikoff, *Objectivism*, pp. 237–238. Lest I appear to be shifting between describing what love is and the value of love, remember that I am examining Rand's idea of the ideal of love – of love, properly experienced. It is only proper love that will be objectively valuable. Thus in looking into what (proper) love is, I am simultaneously looking for the value of love.
[17] *The Fountainhead*, p. 400. Obviously, not every profession of love reflects genuine independence.
[18] Rand, "The Objectivist Ethics," p. 35, emphasis in original.

To appreciate what she means, consider the alternative. What kind of value would nonegoistic love offer? If love did not emanate from a true self – from an independent person who was "his own man," with a rationally established identity and correlative self-esteem – its recipient could reap no satisfaction. For such love would be transient; its underpinnings, fickle. When a person whose identity fluctuates week-to-week or audience-to-audience professes to love someone, this reflects a fleeting impulse rather than a stable, firmly grounded set of judgments and values. By the same token, such vacant expressions of love reflect no objective value for the lover, since the "values" it is premised on are not truly his. A selfish source of love is a prerequisite of love's filling a genuinely *self*-interested (and thus valuable) role. A person has got to *have* a self in order for anything to truly serve his self.

Furthermore, to return to the second condition, that love be *for* the self, notice that even the independent person who chose to pursue friendships unselfishly could gain no objective value from doing so. If the "love" in question does not reflect his honest conclusion of the recipient's value to him, what does it represent? The decision that he will make sacrifices for the sake of a recipient about whom he is indifferent? The conclusion that the recipient is of no particular value to him, but he will pretend that he is? Indifference to all concern with values? Sacrifices represent the surrender of values. Indifference to values is not the path to gaining values. And pretending that someone has qualities that he does not or that he stands in a positive relationship to one's life does not inject him with those qualities or place him in that relationship. Faking one's judgment does not alter the facts judged, and faking one's feelings does not make "make believe" feelings suddenly warranted. Recognition of value in another person typically causes a positive emotional response. Faking that response, however, cannot create the cause.

The larger point is, selfless love is a charade that offers objective value to neither lover nor recipient. All of this explanation, of course, rests on Rand's account of values as those things that objectively advance an individual's life. Lingering reservations about that do not weaken the force of my explanation, however, as my task in addressing the question of the compatibility of egoism with friendship is simply to indicate why, *on the rational egoist's terms,* friendship of the deepest sort, infused with authentic concern for the friend's well-being, can be an objective value. Questions about those terms themselves are a separate matter.

LOVING A PERSON FOR HIMSELF

At the same time that love is selfish, on Rand's view, she also believes that to love a person is to value him for himself, as those who question the feasibility of egoistic love maintain.[19] In her *Journals*, Rand attributes this attitude to Roark: "When he likes a man, he likes him for that man's own sake; not for what he, Roark, can get from that man."[20] This is the way that healthy love is portrayed in all of her novels. To love a person is to value *him*. Yet this may seem the nub of the problem. Van Ingen maintains that "All of [the egoist's] so-called friends, whether they know it or not, will be friends incidentally because of the utility or pleasure that [the egoist] accrues from the relationship."[21] How can one selfishly love a person for his own sake? Aren't those ideas in conflict?

The tension is only superficial, in fact, and the confusion arises from the ambiguity of loving another person "for himself" or "for his own sake." (I will use the two phrases interchangeably. Whatever their differing nuances, both phrases carry the same basic ambiguity.) To love a person for himself could mean different things, depending on what "for himself" is contrasted with. If one takes Rand to mean loving a person for his sake as opposed to loving him for his value to oneself – i.e., loving him altruistically, so as to advance his benefit rather than one's own – then this would be incompatible with egoism. Love offered on such grounds is clearly at odds with the pursuit of self-interest. That is not the only possible interpretation of this claim, however. In holding that an egoist loves another person for himself, Rand means primarily to contrast this with two other possibilities: causeless or indiscriminate love and love that is based on a person's nonessential characteristics.

Many people (religious and nonreligious) endorse the Sermon on the Mount's pronouncement that one should love one's neighbors regardless of their desert or character.[22] Our model should be the Judeo-Christian god, conceived as a loving father "whose perfection empowers [him] to love the imperfect" and "who cares for each of his children as they are," refusing to "apportion affection to merit."[23] Thomas' claim that morality requires a significant quotient of unconditional love seems a truism, to

---

[19] See, for instance, Blum, p. 200.

[20] *Journals of Ayn Rand*, p. 224.

[21] Van Ingen, p. 171; also see Blum, p. 197.

[22] Matthew 5; also see Matthew 22:39. Peikoff discusses this briefly, *Objectivism*, p. 288.

[23] Gregory Vlastos, "The Individual as an Object of Love in Plato," *Platonic Studies* (Princeton: Princeton University Press, 1973), p. 33.

many.[24] This ideal is usually premised on the view that all human beings possess an inherent value which renders them equally worthy objects of love. In several places, including her discussion of justice, Rand makes plain her rejection of this idea.[25] As she explains in Galt's speech, "To love is to *value*. The man who tells you that it is possible to value without values, to love those whom you appraise as worthless, is the man who tells you that it is possible to grow rich by consuming without producing . . ."[26] The ideal of unconditional love, in other words, is fraudulent. Love rests on reasons. Only certain causes will generate love.

In Rand's mind, accordingly, loving a person for his own sake does not mean loving him for no reason, without grounds. Rather, it means loving him for who he is as an individual, for his thoughts, actions, and character. Some would object that if one person loves another for specific qualities that he possesses, then it is those qualities that he loves and not truly the person. Robert Nozick, for instance, argues along these lines, perhaps in overreaction to Plato's "placeholder" view, on which what a person loves is actually abstractions or Forms that are reflected in a particular individual.[27] As I have argued elsewhere, however, it would be bizarre to think that reasons for loving preclude love.[28] On the contrary, it is specific reasons that make love possible. They are the foundation of genuine valuing – and of genuine value. As Peikoff observes, "love as a response to a person's value is an acknowledgment of facts."[29] To explain those facts that are responsible for love is not to invalidate the love. The belief that it is rests on an artificial division of a person from his characteristics. What would loving a person apart from his characteristics come to? *What* would one love, in such a case? A character in *Atlas*, Cherryl, essentially poses this question in an exchange with the husband who she has gradually realized is not the man she thought he was:

"Jim, what is it that you want to be loved for?"

    . . .

---

[24] Thomas, p. 64.
[25] Also see *Letters of Ayn Rand*, p. 345; *Atlas Shrugged*, pp. 209, 305, 972, in the words of some of the novel's villains.
[26] Rand, *Atlas Shrugged*, p. 1033.
[27] Vlastos critiques Plato's view and, to my knowledge, is responsible for the apt "place-holder" label for it. Nozick's discussion is in *The Examined Life*, pp. 68–86.
[28] Tara Smith, "Why Do I Love Thee? A Response to Nozick's Account of Romantic Love," *Southwest Philosophy Review* 7 (January 1991), pp. 47–57. For a more limited discussion of egoism in friendship, see my "Rights, Friends and Egoism," *Journal of Philosophy* XC (March 1993), pp. 144–148.
[29] Peikoff, *Objectivism*, p. 288.

"To be loved *for!*" he said, his voice grating with mockery and righteousness. "So you think that love is a matter of mathematics, of exchange, of weighing and measuring, like a pound of butter on a grocery counter? I don't want to be loved *for* anything. I want to be loved for myself – not for anything I do or have or say or think. For myself – not for my body or mind or words or works or actions."

"But then . . . what *is* yourself?"[30]

Lest this seem literary exaggeration, we should note that Nozick's position essentially echoes that of Jim. Nozick writes: "You can fall in love with someone because of certain characteristics and you can continue to delight in these; but eventually you must love the person himself, and not *for* the characteristics, not, at any rate, for any delimited list of them." Nozick proceeds to liken human love to "imprinting in ducks, where a duckling will attach itself to the first sizable moving object it sees in a certain time period and follow that as its mother. With people, perhaps characteristics set off the imprint of love, but then the person is loved in a way that is no longer based upon retaining those characteristics."[31]

On Rand's view, what is actually true is thus the reverse of what the objection claims. It is loving a person in the absence of his possessing valued characteristics that would not truly be love. If a person loved indiscriminately, his feeling would not be love. Love is a distinctive response to values, felt only in reaction to certain individuals. As a matter of observable fact, we do not feel equally positively toward all other persons.[32] Pretending that we do cannot make such mock love valuable. "I love you, but not for a blessed thing about you" signifies no recognition of value and offers the recipient no tribute.[33]

---

[30] *Atlas Shrugged*, p. 883, emphasis in original.

[31] Nozick, p. 75, emphasis in original.

[32] Cf. Aristotle, who observes that "we do not feel affection for everything," *Nicomachean Ethics*, 1155b 18, trans. Ostwald. Irwin translates: "it seems, not everything is loved, but [only] the loveable."

[33] See Rand, "*Playboy's* Interview," p. 7. I am not denying that innocently misplaced love is love. A response to what a person sincerely believes to be values in another still qualifies as love even if the person loved does not actually possess the qualities that one thinks he does. My point, rather, is that to deliberately feign love – to pretend to see value in others when one does not and to pretend to feel positively toward others when one does not – is not to experience love and does not reflect an objective value that the egoist (or anyone else) has reason to seek. In light of this, my claim at the opening that, while discussing love in its ideal, rational, and psychologically healthy form, I did not mean to deny the existence of less rational or less healthy feelings of love, still holds. Strictly, I am denying only that "loving" a person *while knowing* that he lacks valued characteristics actually constitutes love.

By emphasizing love as a response to a person's specific qualities, I do
not mean that a person loves those qualities in a vacuum, as if they were
detached from their bearers. Plato's view (that what we love are pure
abstractions) is not the only alternative to Nozick's (that what we love are
persons apart from their characteristics). Rather, a person loves certain
qualities *as embodied* by a particular individual. Speaking of romantic love,
Rand writes that "One falls in love with the embodiment of the values
that formed a person's character, which are reflected in his widest goals
or smallest gestures, which create the *style* of his soul – the individual
style of a unique, unrepeatable, irreplaceable consciousness."[34] The basic
idea applicable to friendship is that when one person loves another, he
loves that individual for specific qualities that he possesses. The affection
is grounded on those qualities, though the lover is also responding to
this individual's combination of qualities and his distinctive manner of
manifesting them. This helps to explain why a person does not feel love
for everyone he knows who exhibits traits that he prizes. Bill will not love
every individual he meets who likes the same works of art or shares his
political convictions, for instance.[35]

This also sheds light on the second feature of love that Rand means to
highlight by claiming that an egoist loves another person for himself. In
the journal passage on Roark that I quoted earlier, Rand contrasts valuing
a person for his own sake with valuing him for what one can get out of
him, which a reader might take to mean that this ideal of love is opposed
to the pursuit of self-interest. Yet the meaning that makes sense, in light
of all of Rand's writing, is that the lover values the other person not simply
for a particular useful attribute or set of attributes, such as his wealth or
professional connections, but for his overall character. Loving a person is
different from simply valuing a person's service toward some utilitarian
end, such as free meals or a job. Although a person might value certain
individuals for such limited purposes – Paul as a terrific source of hard-
to-get theater tickets, for example, or Tom as a knowledgeable consultant
for computer problems – that kind of valuing is not love. Love of another
person responds to the integrated sum of that person's qualities. An egoist
loves a friend for who he is – for himself – as opposed to: for a nonessential characteristic, for some isolated features that are incidental to his
identity, or for certain traits which might be essential to his identity, but

---

[34] Rand, "Philosophy and Sense of Life," in *The Romantic Manifesto*, p. 32, emphasis in
original.
[35] Nozick also recognizes this, pp. 81–82.

that one loves for their own sake, apart from what they tell about *him*. It is possible to love traits that a person possesses without loving the bearer of those traits. To love a person, however, is to love the bearer.

(Aristotle often suggests a similar view of the meaning of loving a person for his own sake. "Those who wish for their friends' good for their friends' sake," he writes, "are friends in the truest sense, since their attitude is determined by what their friends are and not by incidental considerations."[36] Terence Irwin observes that Aristotle assumes that "A would not find B worth loving for B's own sake if he did not love B for himself, for what B essentially is . . ."[37] Aristotle also points out that lesser friendships of utility are dissolved much more quickly than the fullest kind of friendship precisely because "Those whose friendship is based on the useful . . . were friends not of one another but of what was profitable for them."[38] More broadly, Aristotle does not seem to conceive of loving a person for his own sake as a possibility that excludes loving him for one's own. Gregory Vlastos writes that for Aristotle, "In friendships with good and noble men one who is himself good and noble will find both profit and delight; he will love his friends for his own sake as well as for theirs."[39])

Even if one concedes that love must be grounded in reasons and must respond to specific facts about the person loved, one might still contend that the nature of those reasons causes problems for egoistic friendship. Given that what the egoist ultimately seeks is his own happiness, the only features of other persons that he will value will be those that serve his interest. But won't this prevent genuine love for another person?

By this stage, it should not be difficult to see through this objection.[40] Why should an egoist value another person, if not for qualities that are of value to him, the lover? To insist that a person's reasons for loving must be of no value to him (or of less value than what he gives, in loving) is to assume that love must be sacrificial, an expenditure of energy without compensating rewards. Such an assumption begs the question, however, insofar as it decrees love to be selfless without providing reasons that show that it is. And ordinary usage lends no support to this assumption. According to the *Oxford English Dictionary*, love is "that disposition

---

[36] *Nicomachean Ethics*, 1156b 9–14, trans. Ostwald.

[37] Irwin, p. 276. For a contrary implication, however, see *Nicomachean Ethics*, 1168a 34–35.

[38] *Nicomachean Ethics*, 1157a 15, trans. Ostwald.

[39] Vlastos, pp. 5–6.

[40] For extended consideration of an apparent counterexample along these lines, see my "Egoistic Friendship," forthcoming, *American Philosophical Quarterly*.

or state of feeling with regard to a person which (arising from recognition of attractive qualities, from instincts of natural relationship, or from
sympathy) manifests itself in solicitude for the welfare of the object, and
usually also in delight in his presence and desire for his approval; warm
affection, attachment." To love (the verb), in turn, means "to entertain a
great affection or regard for; to hold dear." Nothing in either definition
requires self-sacrifice or the absence of value to the lover.[41] A feeling for
another person that arises from "instincts of natural relationship" or from
"sympathy" might be altruistic, in a given case, but what is important here
is that it does not need to be. Thus egoism's opponents cannot proceed
as if love simply is selfless.

Suspicion that the egoist cannot truly love another person may be
prompted in part by a confusion over the role of pleasure in friendship.
Human beings typically enjoy the experience of things that are good for
us, be they material or spiritual values. Biology explains the basic reasons
for this, as the prospect of pleasure can encourage organisms to take
life-furthering actions. We need not explore the details here.[42] What is
salient is that an egoist (like any lover) will tend to take pleasure in his
friend. A person might even come to value another person, in part, as a
source of pleasure. Some might infer from this that the egoist's greatest
concern is therefore with his own pleasure. That would be a mistake,
however. The friend would not be a source of pleasure unless he had (or
was believed to have) a particular character. This is what the egoist loves.
(Bear in mind that I am still speaking of the strongest and fullest forms
of friendship, rather than of friendships of pleasure or utility.)

The psychology of pleasure and its exact relations with love are far
more complex than we can do justice to here. The essential thing to
understand in order to appreciate Rand's view on this is that while an
egoist will take pleasure in a loved one's well-being, that pleasure is not
the object of his love.[43] Nor is it the reason for which one person loves
another. We should not mistake egoism for hedonism. Selfish love is

---

[41] Nor is such a requirement found in any of the subsequent definitions provided in the
OED. The closest is in that designated the religious sense of love, according to which a
person's affection for another is "prompted by the sense of their common relationship
to God."

[42] I discuss this briefly in *Viable Values*, pp. 89–90, and "A Response to Julia Driver's Com-
ments on *Viable Values*," paper delivered at the Ayn Rand Society, Author Meets Critics
Panel on *Viable Values*, American Philosophical Association, December 2000, New York.
For further discussion, see Harry Binswanger, *The Biological Basis of Teleological Concepts*
(Marina del Rey, CA: Ayn Rand Institute Press, 1990), pp. 66–67, 129–137.

[43] Blum acknowledges this, p. 200.

not love of pleasure. Bishop Butler's insight about the dependence of satisfaction on the independent value of the sources of satisfaction is instructive in this context. A person would not derive pleasure of the relevant sort from his experience of a friend if he did not truly value that friend. The egoist does not love *so that* he can have pleasure. He does not decide, "I'd enjoy some pleasure, so let me love this person, to get some." Rather, he loves a person because of who that person is; the person's character is such that it gives the egoist pleasure. As he gets to know the other person's character, he finds that it brings him pleasure, whether or not he sought or anticipated that.

Moreover, the fact that the egoist primarily values his own well-being does not entail that he can value *nothing but* his own well-being, such that he cannot truly value other persons. As Peikoff observes, "The Objectivist does not say 'I value only myself.' He says: 'If you are a certain kind of person, you become thereby a value to me, in the furtherance of my own life and happiness.' "[44] That self-interest is the egoist's overriding concern does not entail that it is his exclusive concern. Indeed, to treat it as if it were would not serve his happiness, as should become clear in the final segment of our discussion.

AREN'T AN EGOIST'S VALUES INSTRUMENTAL?

All of this notwithstanding, a final doubt about an egoist's capacity for friendship might persist, stemming from the question: But doesn't egoism render all values instrumental? All, that is, other than an agent's own happiness, since that is his single, overarching objective? And if so, doesn't that prevent the egoist from valuing other persons in the ways that make genuine love possible?

This reasoning depends on an equivocation over "instrumental." For the sense of "instrumental" that would preclude authentic love is not the sense in which values are instrumental, on Rand's account. Speaking precisely, values are relational, according to Rand. As we saw in Chapter 2, things can be valuable only in relation to some person and for some end.[45] And the ultimate end by reference to which we can determine things' value is an individual's life. Nothing can be objectively valuable that does not contribute to this end in some way. "Instrumental" value,

---

[44] Peikoff, *Objectivism*, p. 238.
[45] Rand, "The Objectivist Ethics," p. 16. See my fuller explanation in *Viable Values*, pp. 83–101.

however, typically denotes a circumscribed, often short-term, means-end relationship. References to "instrumental" values frequently carry the connotation of disposable tools, items to be used and then discarded with little further thought. To call some things instrumentally valuable suggests indifference to the things themselves, as if they are valued solely for their consequences and are completely interchangeable with other things that could serve their utilitarian function equally well. This is not an accurate portrait of all those things that Rand recognizes as values, however.

First, it fails to take account of the many different ways in which things can be valuable to a person. Although certain things might be valuable to a person in a direct means-end manner as the causes of other values in his life, things can also be valuable as enhancements of other values, as preconditions of other values, as equipment that allows the enjoyment of other values, or as components of multi-faceted values, for instance.[46] One person might provide considerable value to another through his understanding or outlook or constructive example. A strong marriage can enrich a person's life profoundly, without being the cause of that person's happiness. Another person might be valuable by becoming a vital ingredient of what a person's happiness consists of rather than as a causal means to that happiness, which remains a distinct, detachable end. The broader point is, the fact that a person benefits from the values he reaps from his associations with other people does not mean that he does not value those individuals or that he values them only with a cavalier, throwaway attitude. Certain values are not easily replaceable. Certain values are not replaceable at all (as Gershwin, for one, realized, lyricizing about "you irreplaceable you.")[47] Accordingly, to suggest that an egoist can value other persons "merely" instrumentally is, at best, extremely misleading. It unduly constricts the range of ways that other persons can be objectively valuable to him.

Second and perhaps even more significantly, the denial that an egoist can value things in anything beyond this narrowly instrumental way rests on a serious confusion about the way in which values function in a person's life. Remember that values are those things that a person pursues, on Rand's view, those things that he acts to gain and protect

---

[46] For further discussion of this, see my "Intrinsic Value: Look-Say Ethics," *Journal of Value Inquiry* 32 (December 1998), pp. 539–553, especially p. 548.

[47] Ira Gershwin, lyrics, "Embraceable You." He was speaking of romantic love, though certain friends can fall into this category.

and preserve. Values run the gamut from ends that can be secured relatively easily and quickly to those that are more difficult to attain and that require a sustained effort over an extended period. Values can carry limited consequences or far-reaching repercussions for a person's life. Values encompass such disparate ends as a reliable dry cleaners, a reliable bridge partner, a driver's license, a particular business contract, a career in pharmacy, a fulfilling marriage. My point is, values are the content of life. It is these that a person seeks when he seeks his happiness. Happiness is not a goal that is independent of values, as if values existed in one sphere and a person's happiness, in another. Values are not stepping stones to a happiness that is a distinct and separate product from the use and enjoyment of those values. Happiness and values are not two alternatives between which a person must choose, at any given time ("today, I'll attend to values; tomorrow, I'll attend to happiness"). Happiness is a happy life. And the happy life that a person seeks to enjoy is a value-stocked life. This is not simply a matter of subjective preferences. Life depends on the achievement of values. Life consists of the achievement of values (since that is, literally, what keeps one going). What a person must do, in the process of living, in order to maintain that process, is to achieve those ends that objectively advance his life (i.e., values). Correlatively, when a person embraces his life as his principal objective, values are what he seeks.

The contention that the egoist, because he is primarily committed to his own well-being, cannot value anything other than that (or cannot value anything other than in a narrowly instrumental way), is completely blind to this. It fails to understand Rand's view of the relationship between values and life. The numerous values that sustain a person's life could seem "merely" instrumental only if one accepted an artificial separation between life and values. In fact, in seeking to promote his own life, what the egoist seeks is a world of values.[48]

* * *

While friendship and love are, again, large subjects unto themselves, I hope to have indicated how it makes sense for Rand's egoist to seek and enjoy friendship of the most objectively worthwhile sort. The rational egoist can love another person for himself in the sense that is crucial for such friendship. Loving a person for himself does not mean offering love as a sacrifice, which obviously would contradict the prescriptions of

[48] Thanks to Tom Miles for suggesting this formulation.

egoism. It means, rather, loving a person for his specific character – not for no reasons, as some urge, and not for incidental reasons that are inessential to his character. The egoist will love another person because that person is valuable to him *and* because of who that person is. The latter explains the former: It explains why the egoist values him, in particular. The fact that a person has self-interested reasons for loving does not mean that what he feels is not genuine love, as critics contend. On the contrary, it is these reasons that allow the love to be rational.

Select List of Works Consulted

Anagostopoulos, Georgios. "Ancient Perfectionism and its Modern Critics." *Social Philosophy and Policy* 16, no. 1 (Winter 1999): 197–232.

Annas, Julia. *The Morality of Happiness.* New York: Oxford University Press, 1993.

Annas, Julia. "Wickedness as Psychological Breakdown." *The Southern Journal of Philosophy.* Spindel supplement XLIII (2005): 1–19.

Aquinas, Thomas. *Basic Writings of St. Thomas Aquinas.* Edited by Anton C. Pegis. New York: Random House, 1945.

Aquinas, Thomas. *Summa Theologica.* London: Burn, Oates and Washbourne, 1932.

Aristotle. *Nicomachean Ethics.*

Armstrong, Karen. *A History of God.* New York: Ballantine, 1993.

Badhwar, Neera K. "Self-Interest and Virtue." *Social Philosophy and Policy* 14, no. 1 (Winter 1997): 226–263.

Badhwar, Neera Kapur. "Altruism versus Self-Interest: Sometimes a False Dichotomy." *Social Philosophy and Policy* 10, no. 1 (Winter 1993): 90–117.

Baron, Marcia. "On de-Kantianizing the Perfectly Moral Person." *Journal of Value Inquiry* 17 (1983): 281–294.

Berliner, Michael S., ed. *Letters of Ayn Rand.* New York: Penguin, 1995.

Biddle, Craig. *Loving Life.* Richmond, VA: Glen Allen Press, 2002.

Binswanger, Harry, ed. *The Ayn Rand Lexicon.* New York: New American Library, 1986.

Binswanger, Harry. *The Biological Basis of Teleological Concepts.* Marina del Rey, CA: Ayn Rand Institute Press, 1990.

Binswanger, Harry. "The Possible Dream," Part 1. *The Objectivist Forum* 2, no. 1 (Feb. 1981): 1–5.

Blum, Lawrence. "Altruism." *Encyclopedia of Ethics.* Edited by Lawrence C. Becker. New York: Garland, 1992. Vol. 1. 50–54.

Blum, Lawrence. "Friendship as a Moral Phenomenon." *Friendship: A Philosophical Reader.* Edited by Neera Badhwar. Ithaca, NY: Cornell University Press, 1993. 192–210.

Bok, Sissela. *Lying: Moral Choice in Public and Private Life.* New York: Random House. 3rd edition, 1999.

Bond, E. J. "Theories of the Good." *Encyclopedia of Ethics.* Edited by Lawrence C. Becker. New York: Garland, 1992. Vol. 1. 620–624.

Brink, David. "Self-Love and Altruism." *Social Philosophy and Policy* 14, no. 1 (1997): 122–157.

Butler, Joseph. *Fifteen Sermons Preached at the Rolls Chapel.* In *The British Moralists – 1650–1800,* Vol. I. Edited by D. D. Raphael. Oxford: Clarendon Press, 1969.

Cabot, Richard C. *Honesty.* New York: MacMillan, 1938.

Calhoun, Cheshire. "Standing for Something." *The Journal of Philosophy* XCII, no. 5 (May 1995): 256–260.

Chazan, Pauline. "Self-Esteem, Self-Respect, and Love of Self: Ways of Valuing the Self." *Philosophia* 26 (1998): 41–63.

Comte-Sponville, Andre. *A Small Treatise on the Great Virtues.* Translated by Catherine Temerson. New York: Henry Holt, 2001.

Cooper, John. *Reason and Human Good in Aristotle.* Indianapolis: Hackett, 1986.

Cox, Damian, Marguerite Lacaze, and Michael P. Levine. "Should We Strive for Integrity?" *Journal of Value Inquiry* 33 (1999): 519–530.

Dalai Lama. "On Pride, Courage, and Self." *Virtuous Persons, Vicious Deeds.* Edited by Alexander E. Hooke. Mountain View, CA: Mayfield, 1999. 423–437.

Darwall, Stephen L. *Impartial Reason.* Ithaca, NY: Cornell University Press, 1983.

Dent, N. J. H. *The Moral Psychology of the Virtues.* New York: Cambridge University Press, 1984.

Den Uyl, Douglas. "The Right to Welfare and the Virtue of Charity." *Social Philosophy and Policy* 10 (Winter 1993): 192–224.

Douglass, Frederick. "Self-Made Men." *The Frederick Douglass Papers,* Series One, vol. 5. Edited by John W. Blassingame and John R. McKivigan. New Haven, CT: Yale University Press, 1992. 545–575.

Driver, Julia. *Uneasy Virtue.* New York: Cambridge University Press, 2001.

Foot, Philippa. *Natural Goodness.* Oxford: Clarendon Press, 2001.

French, Peter A. *The Virtues of Vengeance.* Lawrence: University Press of Kansas, 2001.

Fried, Charles. "The Evil of Lying." *Vice and Virtue in Everyday Life.* Edited by Christina Sommers and Fred Sommers. New York: Harcourt Brace Jovanovich, 2nd edition, 1989. 346–356.

Garnett, A. Campbell. "Charity and Natural Law." *Ethics* 66, no. 2 (Jan. 1956): 117–122.

Gaut, Berys. "The Structure of Practical Reason." *Ethics and Practical Reason.* Edited by Garrett Cullity and Berys Gaut. Oxford: Clarendon Press, 1997. 161–188.

Gewirth, Alan. *Self-Fulfillment.* Princeton: Princeton University Press, 1998.

Gotthelf, Allan. *On Ayn Rand.* Belmont, CA: Wadsworth, 2000.

Graham, Jody. "Does Integrity Require Moral Goodness?" *Ratio* XIV, no. 3 (Sept 2001): 234–251.

Greenspan, Patricia. *Emotions and Reasons.* New York: Routledge, 1988.

Griffiths, Paul E. *What Emotions Really Are.* Chicago: University of Chicago Press, 1997.

Haber, Joram Graf. *Forgiveness.* Lanham, MD: Rowman & Littlefield, 1991.

Hampton, Jean. "Selflessness and the Loss of Self." *Social Philosophy and Policy* 10, no. 1 (Winter 1993): 135–165.

Hampton, Jean. "The Wisdom of the Egoist: The Moral and Political Implications of Valuing the Self." *Social Philosophy and Policy* 14, no. 1 (Winter 1997): 21–51.

Harman, Gilbert. "Moral Psychology Meets Social Psychology." *Proceedings of the Aristotelian Society* 93 (1999): 315–331.

Harriman, David, ed. *Journals of Ayn Rand.* New York: Penguin, 1997.

Hart, H. L. A. "Are There Any Natural Rights?" *Rights.* Edited by David Lyons. Belmont, CA: Wadsworth, 1979. 14–25.

Hull, Gary, and Leonard Peikoff, eds. *The Ayn Rand Reader.* New York: Penguin, 1999.

Hunt, Lester H. *Character and Culture.* Lanham, MD: Rowman & Littlefield, 1997.

Hursthouse, Rosalind. *On Virtue Ethics.* New York: Oxford University Press, 1999.

Irwin, Terence. *Plato's Ethics.* New York: Oxford University Press, 1995.

Khawaja, Irfan. "Tara Smith's *Viable Values: A Study of Life as the Root and Reward of Morality.*" *Reason Papers* 26 (Summer 2003): 63–88.

Korsgaard, Christine. *The Sources of Normativity.* New York: Cambridge University Press, 1996.

Kraut, Richard. *Aristotle on the Human Good.* Princeton: Princeton University Press, 1989.

Kristjansn, Kristjan. "Pridefulness." *The Journal of Value Inquiry* 35 (2001): 165–178.

Kupfer, Joseph. "Generosity of Spirit." *The Journal of Value Inquiry* 32 (1998): 357–368.

Lennox, James G. "Health as an Objective Value." *Journal of Medicine and Philosophy* 20 (1995): 499–511.

Lewis, C. S. *Mere Christianity.* New York: MacMillan, 1952.

Lomasky, Loren. "Justice to Charity." *Social Philosophy and Policy* 12, no 2 (Summer 1995): 32–53.

Machan, Tibor. *Generosity – Virtue in Civil Society.* Washington, DC: Cato Institute, 1998.

MacIntyre, Alasdair. "The Nature of the Virtues." *Virtue Ethics.* Edited by Roger Crisp and Michael Slote. Oxford: Oxford University Press, 1997. 118–140.

Mayhew, Robert, ed. *Ayn Rand Answers.* New York: Penguin, 2005.

McFall, Lynne. "Integrity." *Ethics* 98 (October 1987): 5–20.

Murphy, Jeffrie G. and Jean Hampton. *Forgiveness and Mercy.* New York: Cambridge University Press, 1988.

Murphy, Jeffrie G. *Getting Even – Forgiveness and its Limits.* New York: Oxford University Press, 2003.

Nagel, Thomas. *The Possibility of Altruism.* Oxford: Clarendon Press, 1970.

Nagel, Thomas. *The View from Nowhere.* Oxford: Oxford University Press, 1986.

Newberry, Paul. "Joseph Butler on Forgiveness: A Presupposed Theory of Emotion." *Journal of the History of Ideas* 62 (April 2001): 233–244.

Nozick, Robert. *The Examined Life.* New York: Simon & Schuster, 1989.

Osterberg, Jan. *Self and Others – A Study of Ethical Egoism.* Boston: Kluwer, 1988.

Passmore, John. *The Perfectibility of Man.* New York: Charles Scribner's Sons, 1970.

Peikoff, Leonard. *Objectivism: The Philosophy of Ayn Rand.* New York: Penguin, 1991.

Peikoff, Leonard. *The Ominous Parallels.* New York: Stein & Day, 1982.

Pope, Stephen. "Aquinas on Almsgiving, Justice and Charity: An Interpretation and Reassessment." *The Heythrop Journal* 32, no. 2 (April 1991): 167–191.

Railton, Peter. "Facts and Values." *Philosophical Topics* 14 (Fall 1986): 5–31.

Rand, Ayn. *Atlas Shrugged.* 1957. New York: Dutton, 1992 edition.

Rand, Ayn. *Capitalism: The Unknown Ideal.* New York: Signet, 1967.

Rand, Ayn. *For the New Intellectual.* New York: Random House, 1961.

Rand, Ayn. *The Fountainhead.* New York: Bobbs-Merrill, 1943.

Rand, Ayn. *Introduction to Objectivist Epistemology.* Edited by Leonard Peikoff and Harry Binswanger. New York: Penguin, 2nd edition, 1990.

Rand, Ayn. "The Money-Making Personality." *Why Businessmen Need Philosophy.* Edited by Richard E. Ralston. Marina Del Rey, CA: Ayn Rand Institute Press, 1999.

Rand, Ayn. *Philosophy: Who Needs It.* New York: Bobbs-Merrill, 1982.

Rand, Ayn. "*Playboy*'s Interview with Ayn Rand." (March 1964). Reprint pamphlet published by *The Intellectual Activist.*

Rand, Ayn. *Return of the Primitive – The Anti-Industrial Revolution.* Edited by Peter Schwartz. New York: Meridian, 1999.

Rand, Ayn. *The Romantic Manifesto.* New York: Penguin, 1975.

Rand, Ayn. *The Virtue of Selfishness.* New York: Signet/Penguin, 1964.

Rand, Ayn. *The Voice of Reason – Essays in Objectivist Thought.* Edited by Leonard Peikoff. New York: New American Library, 1988.

Rand, Ayn. Ayn Rand Papers. Ayn Rand Audio Collection. The Ayn Rand Program, Series #A3, WKCR, New York: NY, 1962; and Interviews by Barbara and Nathaniel Branden, tape recording, New York, New York, December 1960–May 1961, The Ayn Rand Archives, A Collection of the Ayn Rand Institute.

Richards, Norvin. *Humility.* Philadelphia: Temple University Press, 1992.

Roberts, Robert C. "What is Wrong with Wicked Feelings?" *American Philosophical Quarterly* 28 (Jan. 1991): 13–24.

Roberts, Robert C. "Will Power and the Virtues." *Vice and Virtue in Everyday Life.* Edited by Christina Sommers and Fred Sommers. New York: Harcourt Brace Jovanovich, 2nd edition, 1989. 232–253.

Rogers, Kelly. "Beyond Self and Other." *Social Philosophy and Policy* 14, no. 1 (Winter 1997): 1–20.

Sachs, David. "How to Distinguish Self-Respect from Self-Esteem." *Philosophy and Public Affairs* 10, no. 4 (1981): 346–360.

Salamon, Julie. *Rambam's Ladder – A Meditation on Generosity and Why It Is Necessary to Give.* New York: Workman Publishing, 2003.

Schmidtz, David. "Reasons for Altruism." *Social Philosophy and Policy* 10, no. 1 (Winter 1993): 52–68.

Schmidtz, David. "Self-Interest: What's in It for Me?" *Social Philosophy and Policy* 14, no. 1 (Winter 1997): 107–121.

Shaver, Robert. *Rational Egoism.* New York: Cambridge University Press, 1998.

Sitwell, Edith. "Pride." *Virtuous Persons, Vicious Deeds.* Edited by Alexander E. Hooke. Mountain View, CA: Mayfield, 1999. 437–442.

Smith, Tara. "Egoistic Friendship." *American Philosophical Quarterly.* Forthcoming.

Smith, Tara. "Intrinsic Value: Look-Say Ethics." *Journal of Value Inquiry* 32 (December 1998): 539–553.

Smith, Tara. "Justice as a Personal Virtue." *Social Theory and Practice* 25, no. 3 (Fall 1999): pp. 361–384.

Smith, Tara. "The Metaphysical Case for Honesty." *Journal of Value Inquiry* 37 (2003): 517–531.

Smith, Tara. "Morality Without the Wink: A Defense of Moral Perfection." *Journal of Philosophical Research* 29 (2004): 315–331.

Smith, Tara. *Moral Rights and Political Freedom.* Lanham, MD: Rowman & Littlefield, 1995.

Smith, Tara. "The Practice of Pride." *Virtue and Vice.* Edited by Ellen Frankel Paul, Fred D. Miller, Jr., and Jeffrey Paul. New York: Cambridge University Press, 1988. 71–90.

Smith, Tara. "Rights, Friends and Egoism." *Journal of Philosophy* XC (March 1993): 144–148.

Smith, Tara. "Tolerance and Forgiveness: Virtues or Vices?" *Journal of Applied Philosophy* 14, no. 1 (1997): 31–41.

Smith, Tara. *Viable Values: A Study of Life as the Root and Reward of Morality.* Lanham, MD: Rowman & Littlefield, 2000.

Smith, Tara. "Why do I Love Thee? A Response to Nozick's Account of Romantic Love." *Southwest Philosophy Review* 7 (January 1991): 47–57.

Snow, Nancy. "Humility." *Journal of Value Inquiry* 29 (1995): 203–216.

Solomon, Robert C., ed. *Wicked Pleasures – Meditations on the Seven "Deadly" Sins.* New York: Rowman & Littlefield, 1999.

de Sousa, Ronald. *The Rationality of Emotion.* Cambridge, MA: MIT Press, 1987.

Spinoza, Baruch. *The Ethics and Selected Letters.* Edited by Seymour Feldman. Indianapolis: Hackett, 1982.

Taylor, Gabriele. "Deadly Vices?" *How Should One Live?* Edited by Roger Crisp. Oxford: Clarendon, 1996. 157–172.

Taylor, Gabriele. "Integrity." *Proceedings of the Aristotelian Society* supp. vol. (1981): 143–159.

Telfer, Elizabeth. "Friendship." *Other Selves – Philosophers on Friendship.* Edited by Michael Pakaluk. Indianapolis: Hackett, 1991. 248–267.

Thomas, Laurence. "Ethical Egoism and Psychological Dispositions." *American Philosophical Quarterly* 17 (1980): 73–78.

Thomas, Laurence. *Living Morally – A Psychology of Moral Character.* Philadelphia: Temple University Press, 1989.

Twambley, P. "Mercy and Forgiveness." *Analysis* 36, no. 2 (January 1976): 84–90.

van Ingen, John. *Why Be Moral? The Egoistic Challenge.* New York: Peter Lang, 1994.

Vlastos, Gregory. "The Individual as an Object of Love in Plato." *Platonic Studies.* Princeton: Princeton University Press, 1973. 3–34.

Wallace, James D. *Virtues and Vices.* Ithaca, NY: Cornell University Press, 1978.

Wellman, Carl. *A Theory of Rights.* Totowa, NJ: Rowman & Allanheld, 1985.

Woodruff, Paul. *Reverence – Renewing a Forgotten Virtue.* Oxford: Oxford University Press, 2001.

Zagzebski, Linda. *Virtues of the Mind.* New York: Cambridge University Press, 1996.

Index

active mind, 64, 91, 92

Akston, Hugh, 124, 129, 130

alternative of life or death as basis for value, 20, 21, 24

altruism, 1, 112
  as causing confusion about human relationships, 247
  as explantion for impossibility of moral perfection, 238
  as second-handed, 110
  criterion of altruistic action, 255
  egalitarianism as, 159
  nature of, 38, 39
  relation to friendship, 245, 287
  relation to love, 293
  relation to virtues, 102, 148, 149, 194, 205, 245, 252, 257

ambition, 217, 219, 222, 223, 225, 235, 289, *See also* moral ambitiousness

Ambrose, St., 250

animals, 2, 20, 22, 44, 54, 57, 201, 206, 239, 275

Annas, Julia, 55

Anselm, St., 106, 168, 243

Aquinas, St. Thomas, 205, 243, 249, 250, 277

Aristotle, 33, 49–51, 61, 66, 221, 223, 257, 259, 275, 277, 278, 288, 290, 291, 299

art, 32, 45, 80, 199, 215, 298

Atlas Shrugged, 5, 8, 48, 57, 68, 107, 114, 115, 124, 127, 129, 137, 150, 159, 169, 184, 187, 195, 199, 200, 219, 224, 227, 228, 253, 255, 256, 264, 268, 269, 296

Augustine, St., 250, 276

autonomy, 108

Badhwar, Neera, 1, 254

Basil, St., 250

Biddle, Craig, 142

Binswanger, Harry, 45, 71, 155, 184

Blum, Lawrence, 39

Bond, E. J., 38

Bonevac, Dan, 40

Butler, Bishop Joseph, 165, 215, 301

Cabot, Richard, 87

Calhoun, Cheshire, 182

career, 30, 32, 80, 82, 90, 111, 112, 213, 215, 291, 292

primacy of existence, 58–60, 63, 68,
  74, 79, 93, 105, 108, 112, 147,
  209
principles, 3, 7, 11, 12, 14, 22, 28,
  33–38, 41, 43, 44, 47, 49–52, 54,
  69, 73, 94–100, 102, 104, 110,
  116, 118, 131, 137, 141–143, 157,
  160, 161, 163, 171, 176–197, 215,
  224, 225, 227, 230–235, 237,
  238, 240–242, 252, 269, 283,
  285
  authority of, 7, 36, 38, 60, 69, 74,
    87, 95, 96, 99, 188, 191, 232,
    251, 274
productiveness, 8, 9, 12, 13, 44, 45, 63,
  111, 127, 145, 170, 198–221,
  233, 239, 271, 281, 285
psychological egoism, 24
psychologizing, 153
punishment, 11, 136, 138, 143, 144,
  155, 162, 163, 168, 169, 174,
  175, 206, 262
purpose, 8, 13, 17, 19, 23, 30–32, 51,
  55, 56, 62–64, 94, 104, 108, 114,
  126, 139, 140, 149, 151, 153,
  155, 165, 172, 173, 188, 190,
  197–200, 202, 204, 207,
  209–212, 216, 227, 228, 230,
  253

Railton, Peter, 23, 27
rational egoism, *See* egoism
rationality, 3, 4, 7–12, 14, 17, 37, 42,
  44, 48, 52–61, 63–71, 73–75, 77,
  78, 84, 91, 95, 96, 107, 110,
  113–115, 118, 120, 122–125,
  128, 129, 134, 135, 137, 141,
  142, 149, 151–153, 169, 171,
  176, 177, 179, 182–185, 187,
  193, 197, 201, 203, 206, 207,

  215, 220, 222, 227, 233, 234,
  236, 237, 240, 241, 258, 264,
  272, 277, 278, 280–283, 285
Rawls, John, 156
Rearden, Hank, 169, 219, 259, 264, 269
Rearden, Lillian, 257, 259
responsibility, 9, 67, 83, 107, 109, 114,
  123, 127, 153, 158, 162, 203,
  205, 220
Richards, Norvin, 244
rights, 11, 98, 157, 170–175, 219, 227,
  251, 271
Roark, Howard, 52, 107, 110, 112, 113,
  130, 131, 195, 269, 295, 298
Roberts, Robert C., 194

sacrifice, 10, 12, 15, 23, 37–39, 44, 110,
  120, 127, 135, 148, 149, 162,
  163, 176, 178, 186, 191, 194,
  238, 252, 254, 256–261, 270,
  273, 283, 290, 294, 300, 303
Salmieri, Greg, 69, 276
Schmidtz, David, 1
second-handedness, 109–112,
  117–123, 125, 126, 131, 134,
  142, 153, 161, 180, 246
self-confidence, *See* confidence
self-deception, 9, 77, 89–91
self-denial, 16, 238, 275, 277, 278,
  282, *See also* sacrifice
self-esteem, 1, 8, 12, 13, 21, 32, 85, 86,
  125, 204, 205, 223, 226–231, 233,
  234, 236, 244–246, 254, 272,
  293, 294, *See also* confidence
selfishness, *See* egoism
Sidgwick, Henry, 243
Singer, Peter, 249
Sitwell, Edith, 222
Skinner, B. F., 129
sloth, 198, 205

CPSIA information can be obtained at www.ICGtesting.com
Printed in the USA
LVOW040325060612

284805LV00001B/63/P